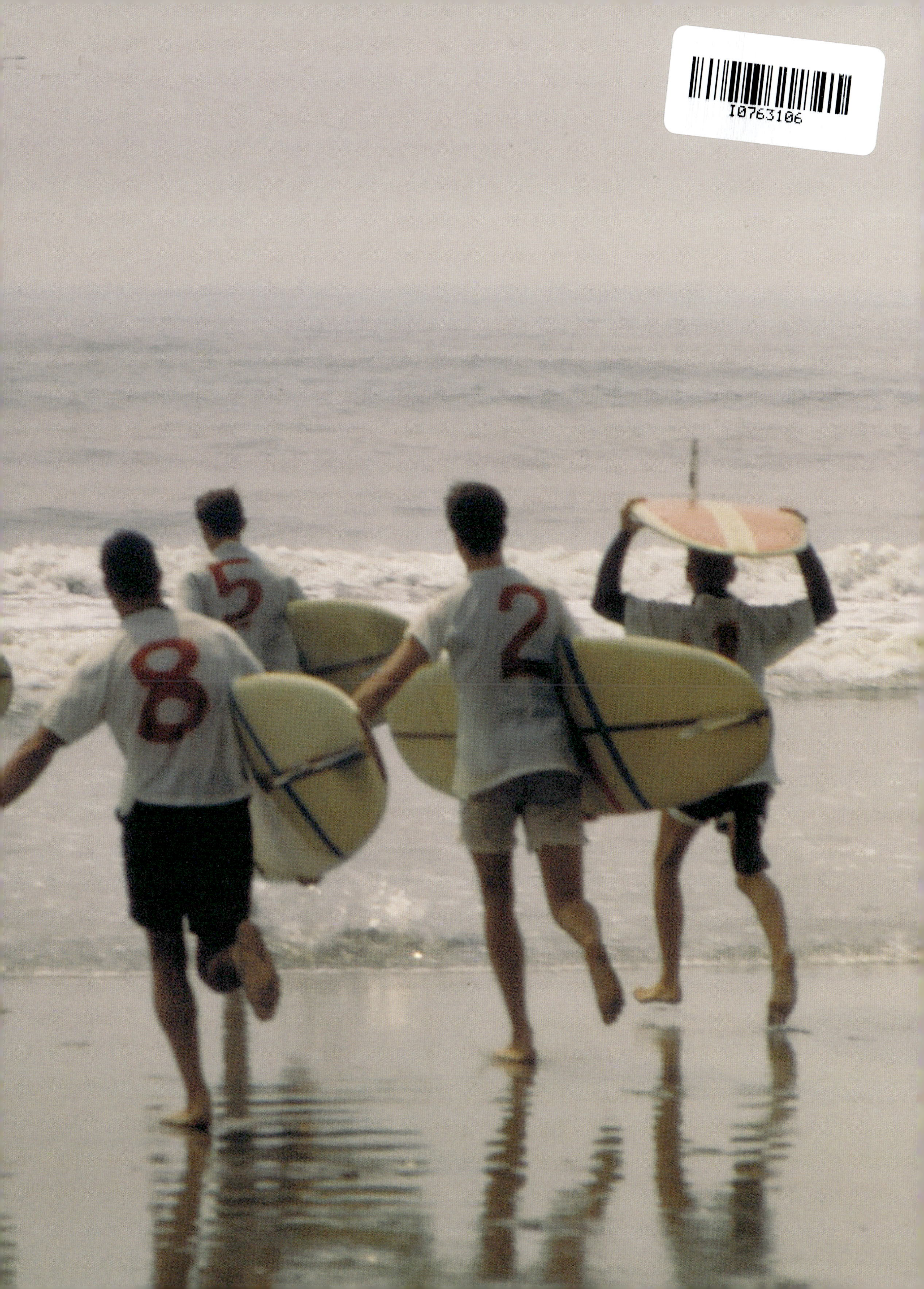

I0763106

I HEARD THERE WERE
NO WAVES IN NEW JERSEY

I HEARD THERE WERE NO WAVES IN NEW JERSEY

SURFING ON THE JERSEY SHORE
1888–1984

EDITED BY

DANNY DIMAURO

JOHAN KUGELBERG

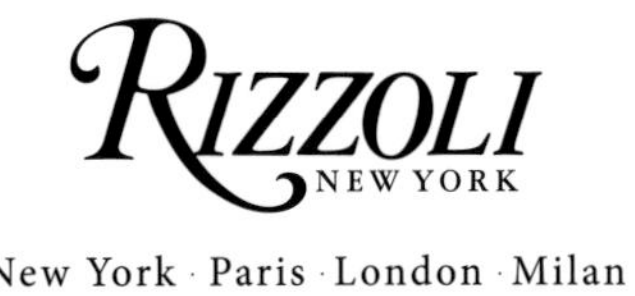

New York · Paris · London · Milan

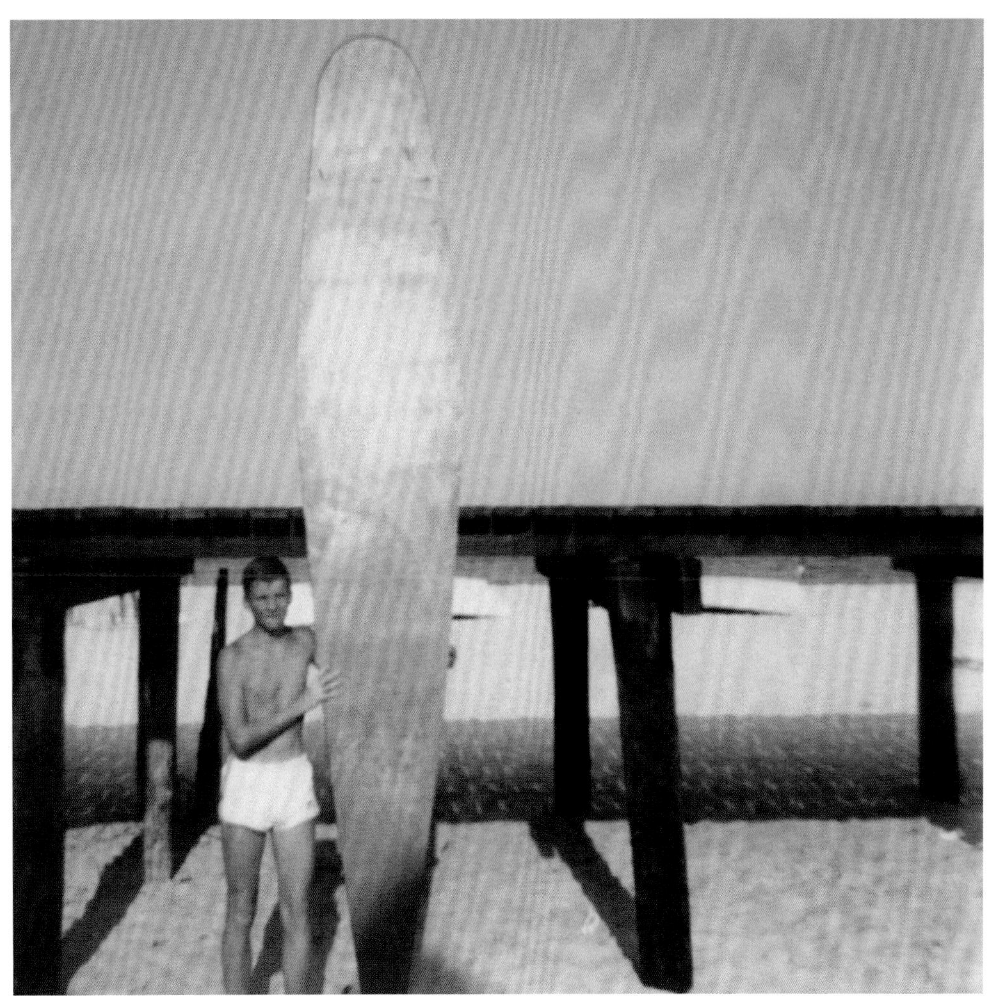

DEDICATED TO THE NEW JERSEY SURFING HALL OF FAME AND NEW JERSEY SURF MUSEUM

"Balsa Bill" Yerkes, circa 1950s

TABLE OF CONTENTS

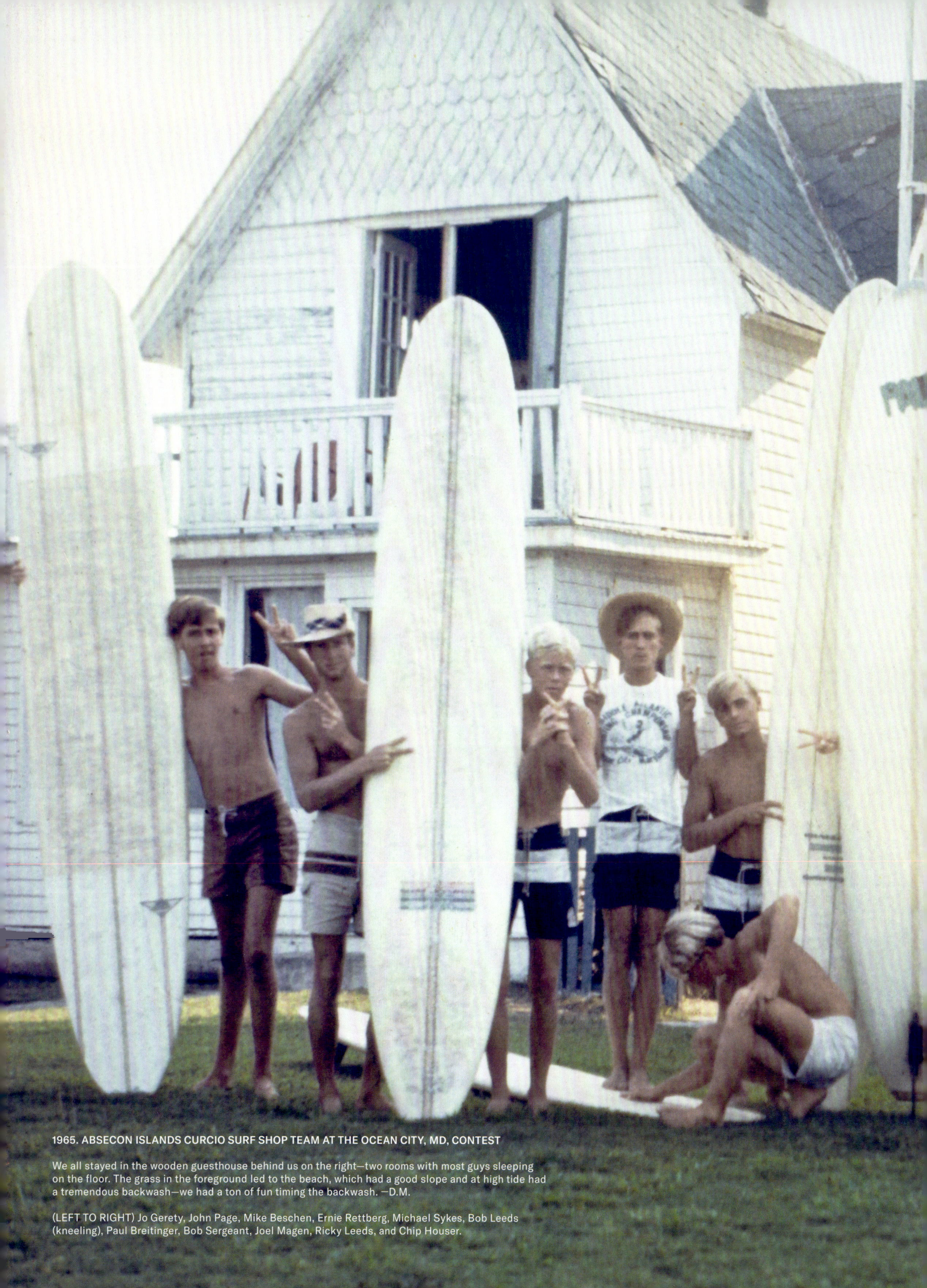

1965. ABSECON ISLANDS CURCIO SURF SHOP TEAM AT THE OCEAN CITY, MD, CONTEST

We all stayed in the wooden guesthouse behind us on the right—two rooms with most guys sleeping on the floor. The grass in the foreground led to the beach, which had a good slope and at high tide had a tremendous backwash—we had a ton of fun timing the backwash. —D.M.

(LEFT TO RIGHT) Jo Gerety, John Page, Mike Beschen, Ernie Rettberg, Michael Sykes, Bob Leeds (kneeling), Paul Breitinger, Bob Sergeant, Joel Magen, Ricky Leeds, and Chip Houser.

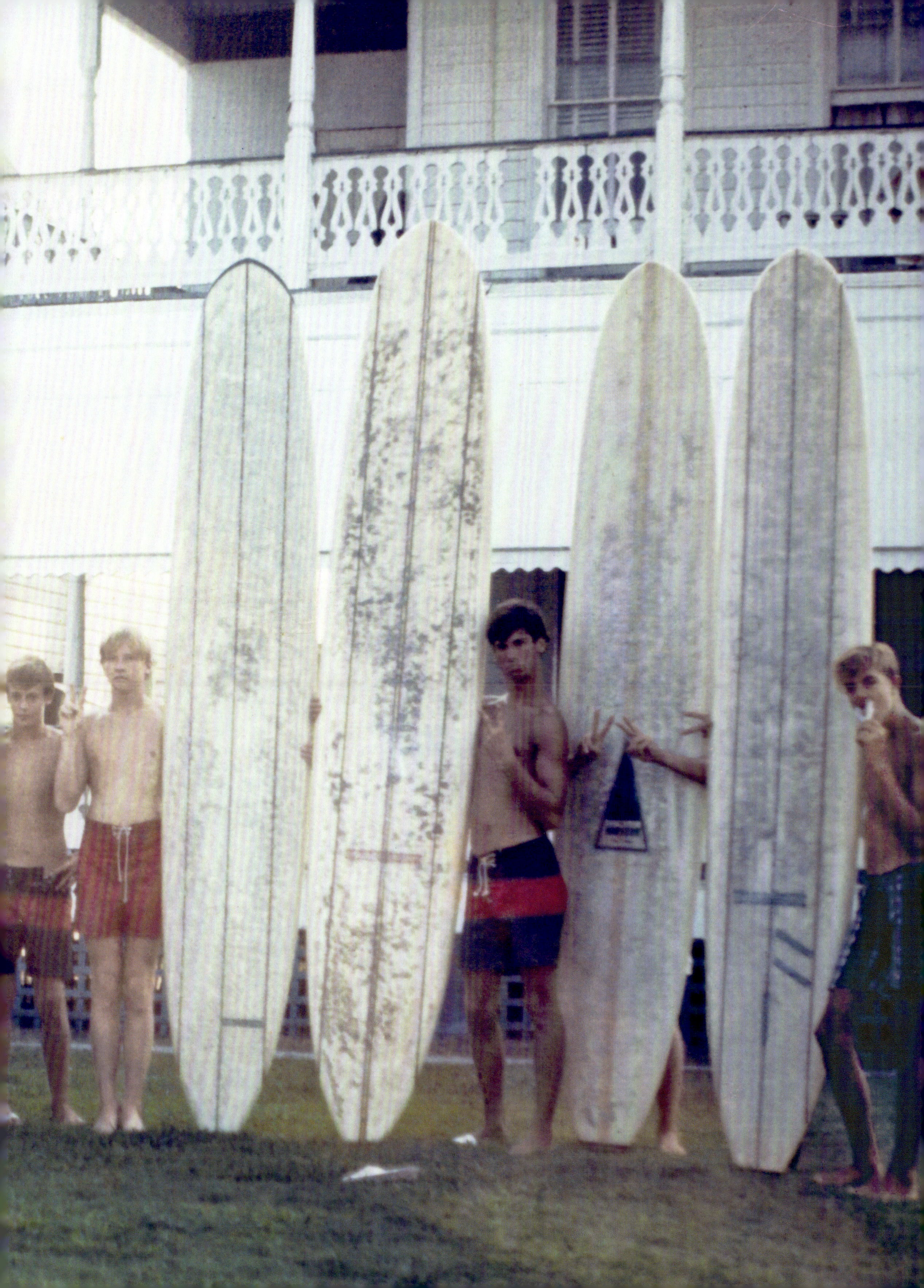

A GAY QUEEN OF THE WAVES

"**A GROUP OF SUMMER LOUNGERS** on the beach at Asbury Park, N.J., were watching the extraordinary antics of a dark eyed, bronze-faced girl in the sea a few mornings ago. The object of all this interest and solicitude was beyond the line of breakers and standing on a plank that rose and fell with the swelling waves. Her bathing dress was of some dark material, fitting close to the figure, the skirts reaching scarce to her knee. Her stockings were of amber hue, adorned with what from the shore seemed to be vines and roses in colored embroidery. She wore no hat or cap. Her hair, bound across the forehead and above the ears by a silver fillet, tumbled down upon her shoulders or streamed out upon the wind in black and shining profusion. Her tunic was quite sleeveless, and one could scarcely fail to observe the perfect development and grace of her arms. As a wave larger than those which had gone before slowly lifted the plank upon its swelling surface, she poised herself daintily upon the support, her round arms stretched out and her body swaying to and fro in harmony with the motion of the waters. As the wave reached its fullest volume she suddenly, quick as thought, and with a laugh that rang full into shore, drew herself together, sprang into the air, and, her hands clasped together and clearing her a way, plunged into the rolling sea. There was a little cry from timid feminine watchers on the sand, but the smiling face was above water again while they cried, and the daring Triton was up on the plank again in another moment and waiting for a second high roller. So she has been amusing herself and interesting the mob for three mornings. She is as completely at ease in the sea as you or I on land, and the broad plank obeys her slightest touch."

THE NATIONAL POLICE GAZETTE,
Saturday, August 18, 1888

HAVLIN-MURPHY INTERNATIONAL BATTLE

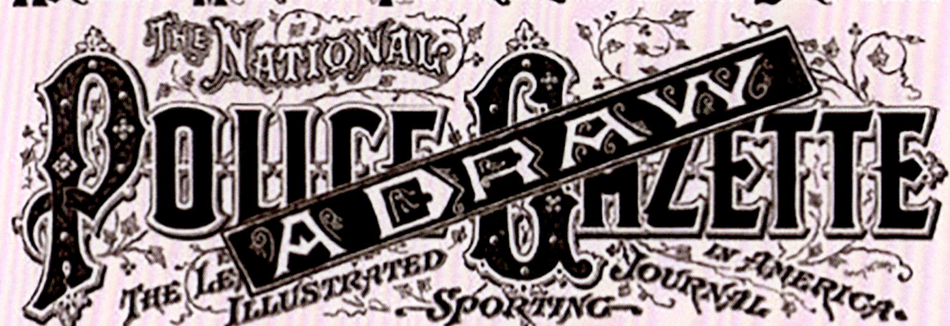

NEW YORK, SATURDAY, AUGUST 18, 1888.

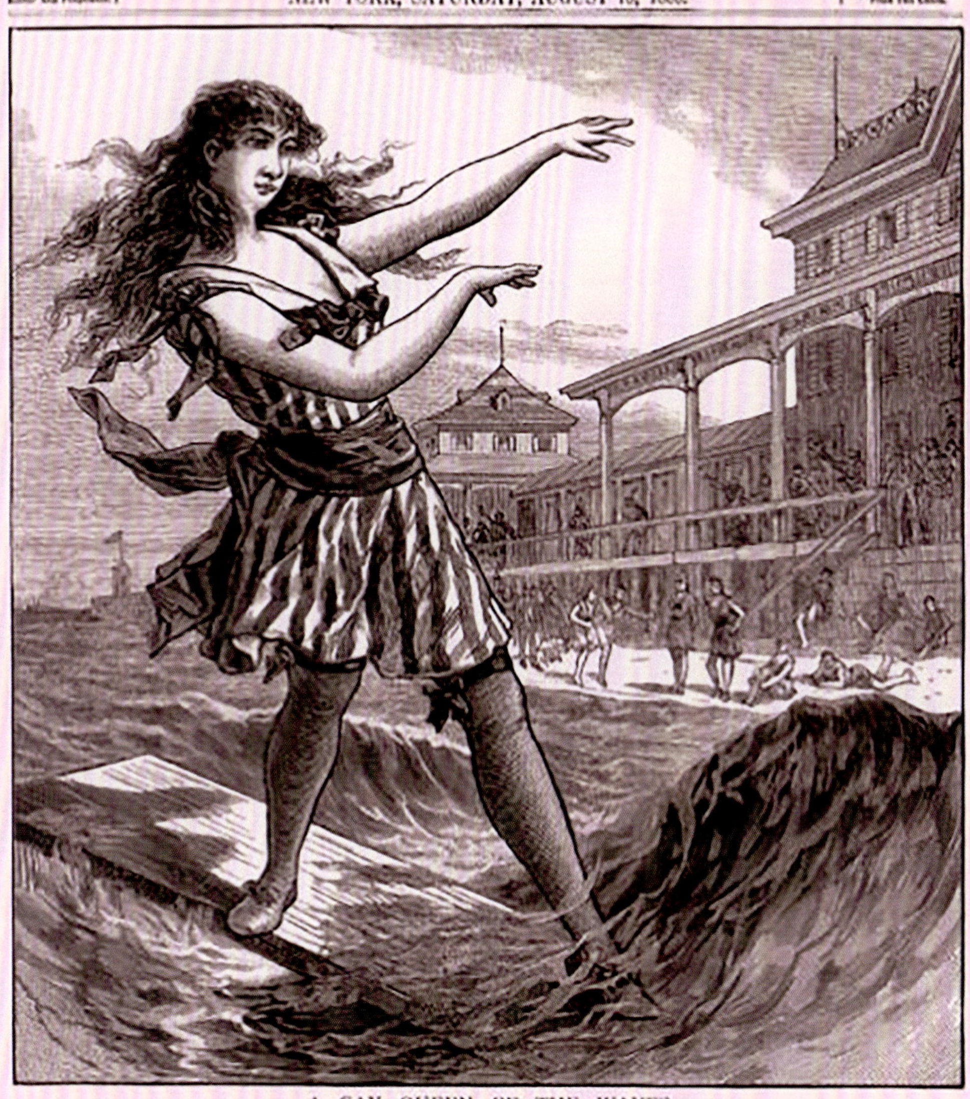

A GAY QUEEN OF THE WAVES.

ASBURY PARK, NEW JERSEY, SURPRISED BY THE DARING OF A SANDWICH ISLAND GIRL.

THE SANDWICH ISLAND GIRL

EMMA SPRECKELS, WHO SURFED ASBURY PARK IN AUGUST 1888

SURF HISTORIANS CAN ALL AGREE ON ONE THING about who first brought surfing to the continental United States: a well-documented visit by young Hawaiian princes to Santa Cruz, California, in 1885, and their riding of the local waves on surfboards shaped from wood provided by the Redwood trees in the area is not disputed. California subsequently credits Hawaiian George Freeth, who moved to Los Angeles around 1907, and who brought not only his skills as a lifeguard but also his skills as a surfer, learned at Waikiki.

The East Coast has historically credited Duke Kahanamoku as being the first to bring surf riding to the Atlantic shores with demonstrations in the waves of Atlantic City in 1912 next to the Million Dollar Pier. Duke Kahanamoku is certainly the true catalyst for the interest in surfboarding on both coasts of the United States, and will always be considered the father of modern surfing, but it has turned out that a few others rode those waves before him. There are documented stories of surfers riding waves in Wrightsville Beach, North Carolina, in 1909, and recently a treasure trove of articles describing how a young Hawaiian by the name of Alvin D. Keech gave surfing demonstrations during the summer of 1910 in Atlantic City and Asbury Park, New Jersey. Alvin Keech was going to school outside Philadelphia and was a replacement for the great George Freeth, who had been booked to instruct but who remained in California where he was spreading surf stoke.

In the past year or so, a mysterious story about a young girl from the Sandwich Islands (Hawaii) who surfed a board on the waves in Asbury Park in 1888 has become more than just a historic novelty. It is actually the true story of the first person to ride a surfboard on the East Coast of the USA. I recently finished an article on Sam Reid who as a young boy in Atlantic City saw Duke Kahanamoku give a surfing demonstration in 1912. Reid was so excited he took his mother's ironing board and jumped right into the ocean the next day to surf the waves like his newfound hero. Reid would go on to move to California in 1919, and in 1926 he and the legendary Tom Blake would be the first to surf the fabled point in Malibu. So, the first two people to surf Malibu were from Wisconsin and New Jersey.

During my research I again came across the story of the "Sandwich Island Girl," who surfed in Asbury Park. The issue of *National Police Gazette* dated August 18, 1888, published a short article with a picture of a young girl standing on a wood plank riding a wave, the first depiction of a person surfing on either coast of the USA. Until now this was brushed off as just a silly story made up by a writer from the *National Police Gazette*, a publication considered the *National Enquirer* of its day. While reading *Surf and Rescue*, Patrick Moser's book on George Freeth, I came across a footnote referencing a New Jersey historian by the name of Vinnie Dick who believed the Sandwich Island Girl was actually Emma Spreckels, the

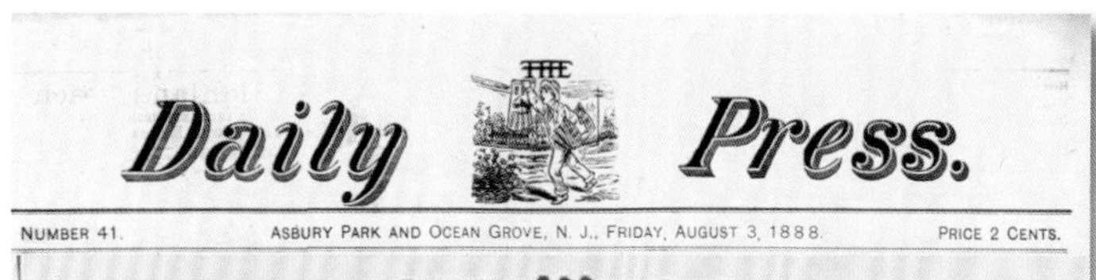

Daily Press.

NUMBER 41. ASBURY PARK AND OCEAN GROVE, N. J., FRIDAY, AUGUST 3, 1888. PRICE 2 CENTS.

Will the Search be Successful.

Yesterday a gentleman called at THE DAILY PRESS office and said that he had seen in one of the New York papers a personal notice of the arrival in Asbury Park of a young lady from the Sandwich Islands. His home was located there—he knew the young lady and desired to find her, and accordingly placed an advertisement in this paper asking for her whereabouts.

only daughter of Claus Spreckels, the famed sugar baron of Hawaii. Before I could get in touch with Vinnie Dick, who was in turn finishing up a book on Emma and the Spreckels family, I began my own investigation into the possibility that the Sandwich Island Girl was a real person.

The first confirmation I found was from the actual article itself. The story was published in various newspapers: the *Pittsburgh News* published a lengthier version of the *National Police Gazette* piece, and in a part the *Gazette* did not publish it stated that the young girl from the Sandwich Islands was visiting Asbury Park for a few days and that her father was an enormously rich planter. The only rich planter that was in any close proximity during that time was Claus Spreckels, who had moved to Philadelphia that year with his entire family to open a sugar refinery. My research brought me to numerous articles about Claus Spreckels and his sons, who at the time were working on moving their business from Hawaii. A short blurb in the *Philadelphia Times* from early August 1888 describes the Spreckels brothers as "sons of the Sugar Baron staying at the Brighton Hotel in Atlantic City." In the *Philadelphia Times* from July 1888, Emma Spreckels is described as the "Belle of the Wissahickon who was born in the Sandwich islands who rides her white horse." Soon after the articles about the Sandwich Island Girl made it to the newspapers, an advertisement was taken out in the local Asbury Park classifieds by J. L. Graham, a friend of the Spreckels family from Sea Girt, New Jersey, asking for information on her, stating that he knew her and that he owned a home in the Sandwich Islands.

I was convinced and after speaking with Vinnie Dick, who had done extensive research for his recently published novel, *Forgotten Kings: Emma Spreckels the Asbury Park Surfer*, I reached out to Matt Warshaw, the publisher of the *Encyclopedia of Surfing*. I filled him in on my findings. Matt Warshaw is never one to just accept a story: he soon was going down the rabbit hole of the Spreckel family history, and specifically Emma. Warshaw, after doing his due diligence to confirm all of what I told him, dedicated his weekly blog post to this story, letting the surfing world know that we had found the Sandwich Island Girl and she is Emma Spreckels. Emma now has an honored place in the *Encyclopedia of Surfing* as the first wave rider on the East Coast. Special thanks to Vinnie Dick for finding Emma. Articles about Emma as the Sandwich Island Girl have now run in *USA Today*, in the *Asbury Park Press*, and now here!

As a footnote, another fascinating part of this story is that Emma Spreckels was the great aunt of Bunker Spreckels, a legendary bad boy surfer of the 1970s, whose life has been documented both in print and on film.

—MIKE MAY

I HEARD THERE WERE NO WAVES IN NEW JERSEY

I CAN'T REMEMBER A TIME when I wasn't surfing. There is a photo of me in a diaper around 16 months old in 1971, being held up by my mother on a transition-era single fin that belonged to my dad. My father was a terrible surfer, but nonetheless he was out there all the time, struggling to paddle correctly and get to his feet. He really seemed to enjoy the challenge. I remember watching my dad out there with some of the other surfers, thinking that it was all I wanted to do. It bordered on obsession. My surfing evolution was simple, at 7 years old, riding blue and white Styrofoam belly boards from the five-and-dime, first to one knee then to my feet and spinning out onto the shoreline. Over and over again in front of the lifeguard stand imitating the older kids surfing at the nearby pier in a state of delirious intoxication.

In 1982, at the age of 12 years old, after working all summer bussing tables at a Jewish delicatessen, I had saved enough money to buy my first surfboard. Surfing in those days was still considered a pretty lowbrow activity, and my parents, in an attempt to instill in me some work ethic, insisted if I wanted a surfboard I would have to buy it myself. I believe my parents thought this tactic would somehow dissuade me from surfing, as they didn't think it was going to get me anywhere in life.

My first surfboard I purchased was a Caster Channel Hull Twinfin with rainbow channels. Unfortunately the board was confiscated before I could use it by Tony Tubs, who at the age of 15 had a pack-a-day Marlboro Red habit, a vicious temper, and a clear disdain for new people.

I watched one wave after another from the bulkhead in a state of total humiliation, wondering if anyone had seen him take the board from me. A couple hours later Tubs came back with my board, threw it in the sand, spit on me, and told me to "beat it."

You really didn't just "turn up" and start surfing in those days, at least in my neighborhood. It was a rough-and-tumble neighborhood made up of mostly Jews, Italians, and Irish, and abuse of younger kids was dished out generously and frequently. Tony Tubs was in a surf gang called "The Dudes," and I still remember their names; there was Monster, Cheeks, and Joe "Dazer" Randazzo, who would surf through the pilings of the pier from way outside the long way, nearly missing every piling. His younger brother Dean Randazzo is arguably the greatest surfer to come out of New Jersey ever competitively. He was known on the then ASP tour as the "Jersey Devil," only rivaled by Linda Davoli, a surfer from neighboring Brigantine, New Jersey, who was ranked number three in the world in 1980.

In 1986, when I was 16 years old, I ran away from home. I had a one-way ticket to California, with a very clear idea in my mind's eye of what to expect when I landed. Awaiting me were perfect waves, burnt orange sunsets, and real blond hair on the gorgeous beach babes, like I'd seen in *Surfer* magazine. Growing up in the 1980s in southern New Jersey, I had a very polarized view of the surfing world, which was mostly relegated to my neighborhood and some of the neighboring towns' beaches. An early morning dawn patrol to somewhat more exotic Atlantic City consisted of counting how many sex workers were still walking the streets on the way up to "Gas Chambers," a surfing spot at States Avenue. Atlantic City, once known as the world's playground, was a depraved and dilapidated shell of its former grandeur in the early

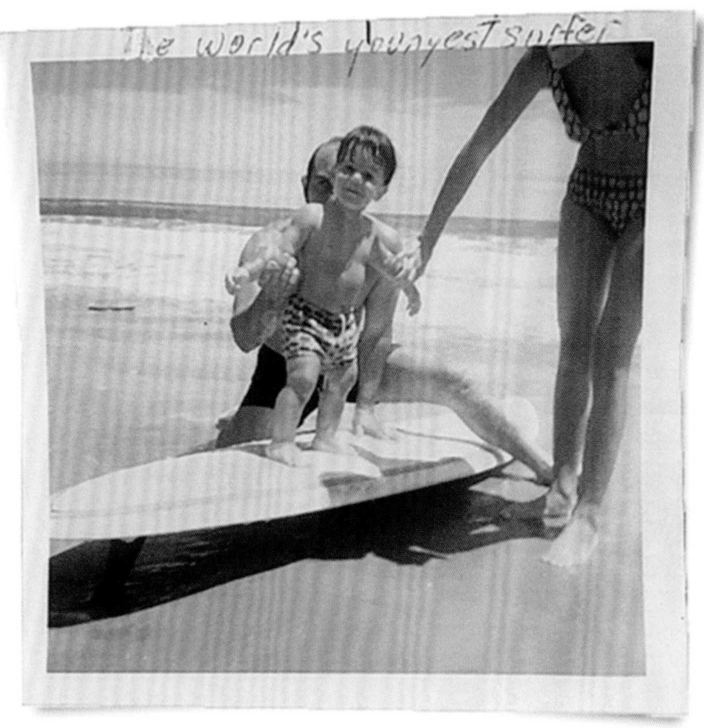

to mid-1980s. As the city's newly approved casino gaming referendum took hold, the disorganized crime syndicate known as the Philly Mob was ironing out its differences, and bodies were turning up in cars fairly regularly as warring factions fought for control over the city's illegal rackets. The casinos and the empty promises of the politicians did very little to improve the rest of Atlantic City or its infrastructure outside of their own interests. The opulence and grandeur of Trump's newly built Taj Mahal sat and loomed directly over the most disenfranchised population of the city's inhabitants. Pacific Avenue was peppered with monstrous glamorous hotels that sat right beside fleabags, tenements, pawn shops, and strip joints.

The West Coast's version of the surfing life, peppered with palm trees, bikinis, and warm weather, seemed like a proposition preferable to the moody, frigid, unseasonable Northeast's. There simply had to be something better than what I was experiencing in New Jersey, and in my mind it was California.

The surfing magazines had portrayed this somewhat mythical place called Echo Beach as the cultural axis of all that was relevant in surfing, and surfing was all that was relevant. It was surfing's neon dayglow era, succinct and fortified with an accompanying soundtrack of music called New Wave. A post-punk menagerie of checkerboards and polka dots, accompanied with an irreverence that was intoxicating. The burgeoning surf industry was quick to capitalize, 'cause everyone wanted in. I was no exception, and though it was strange to see a Guido with gold chains in a rash guard at a nightclub in New Jersey, it was apparent to the world at large there was nothing cooler than being a surfer in the 1980s. I knew that California was the place to be if you were a "real surfer," and I had to experience what that might feel like if even for a brief moment. I'll never forget when someone asked me "what brought you to California," and I said, "I'm a surfer from New Jersey." The guy laughed and said, "I heard there are no waves in New Jersey," and it was pointless to argue because comparatively I had zero frame of reference. This was the first time I'd been anywhere; I was just a pimply faced teenager searching for the promised land. I felt ashamed because I knew what he meant—he was letting me know that we were irrelevant in the surfing world.

I am not a professional surfer, nor am I a passive observer. I am a fan of surfing and a participant, and to see it performed well still commands my attention to this day. I am not one for flowery prose or poetic metaphors alluding to its spiritual nature or meditative qualities. I consider romanticizing something, speaking from my own personal experience, a very hedonistic pursuit. As the Black Knight of Surfing, Miklos Dora, once said, "Chasing after such fleeting mirages is a total waste of time." I'm a partaker in an activity that has held a grip over my life and my imagination for more than 40 years. Nothing else I can think of comparatively has consumed that much time or space in my head; it has at different times in my life bordered on an obsession or pathology. Appointments canceled, events unattended, excuses made, obligations less than squarely met, I'm somewhat ashamed to divulge. I may even venture to say in my case that surfing is an addiction, with such potent euphoric recall, only rivaled by some of the more, shall I say, recreational drugs I've consumed.

—**DANNY DIMAURO**

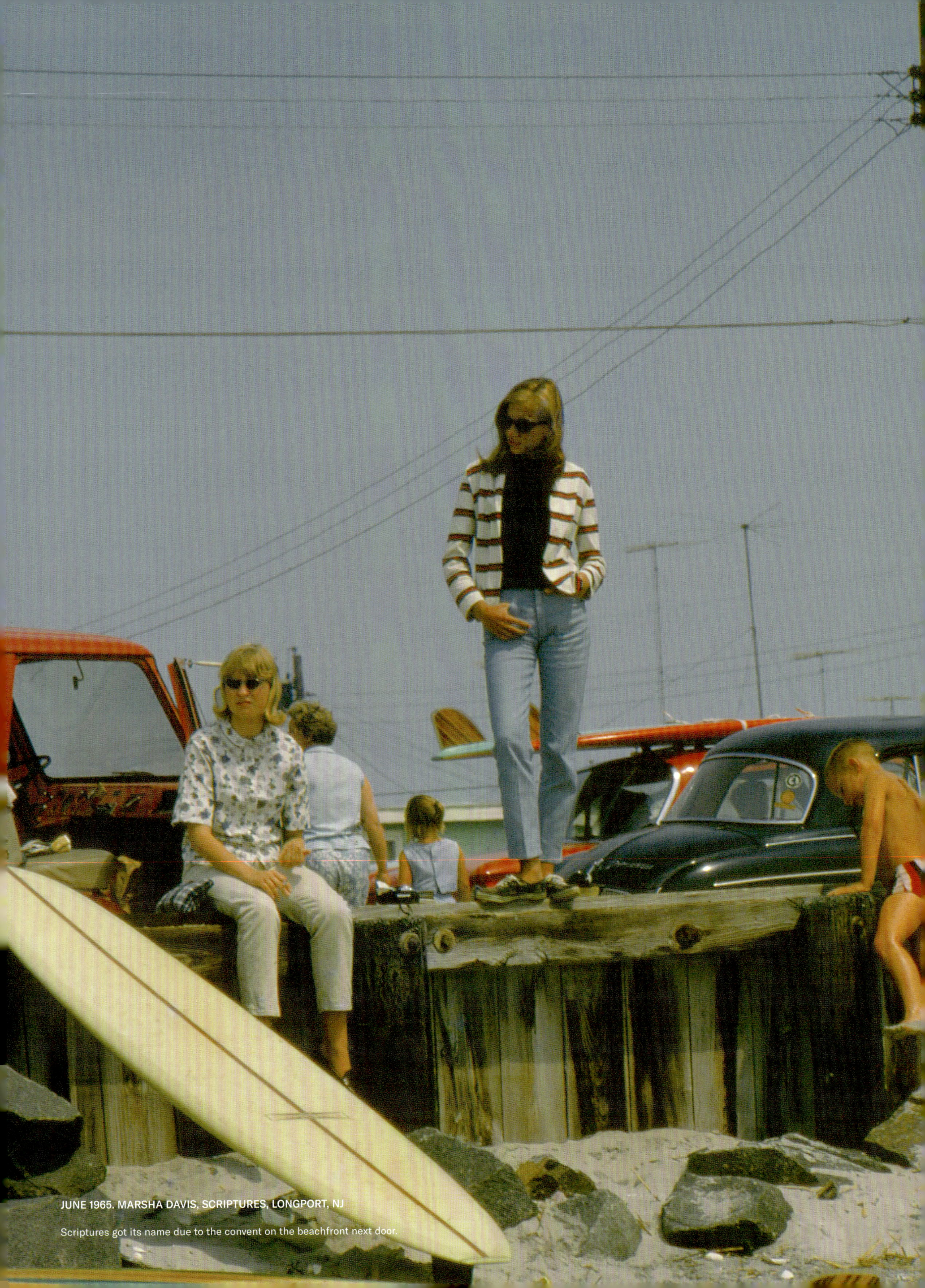

JUNE 1965. MARSHA DAVIS, SCRIPTURES, LONGPORT, NJ

Scriptures got its name due to the convent on the beachfront next door.

DAN MITTELMAN

I WAS BORN IN 1950. MY YOUTH WAS SPENT ON MARGATE, AN ISLAND A FEW MILES SOUTH OF ATLANTIC CITY. BY AGE 10, I WAS THE KID WHO FIXED BICYCLES FOR MY CLASSMATES AND NEIGHBORS. I WAS RAISED BY TWO JEWISH PARENTS AND REACHED BAR MITZVAH THE SAME YEAR I HAD TWO OTHER DEFINING MOMENTS—LEARNING THE CONCEPT OF INFINITY AND SURFING.

I GOT MY FIRST SURFBOARD in the summer of 1964. That winter with no wetsuit I took some photos of the guys who had wetsuits. By 1965 I was traveling up and down the East Coast, surfing and taking photos. That year, my photos appeared in *Atlantic Surfing* and *Competition Surf* magazines. School was not a priority; girls, cars, photography, and surfing were pretty much it. In 1967, a $50 Dodge from 1951 was an expanded freedom. Weather forecasting and shoreline geography mapped my way. Judging surf contests from Rhode Island to Florida in the summer of 1968 ended with my enrollment at the University of Miami. In November of 1968 I shot the World Surfing Championships in Puerto Rico; my eye through a lens was my lab work.

Moving on to Newport Beach, California, and naming my new puppy an appropriate name, Sunshine, says a lot about the world at that time. Carpentry work financed the regular road trips between the Pacific Ocean and the Atlantic Ocean with Sunshine in my van. Sometimes spending weeks at National Parks and other times trying for the cross-country land speed record. Taking a "real job" with US Homes, cutting my hair and beard—it didn't last long. Regular trips to Hawaii, Florida, Barbados, and California followed over the next few years. Eventually I started a building business. My marriage produced a son and a daughter. The kids, raised Jewish, asked for a trip to Hawaii instead of a party for their mitzvahs. Guess the love of the ocean got passed on.

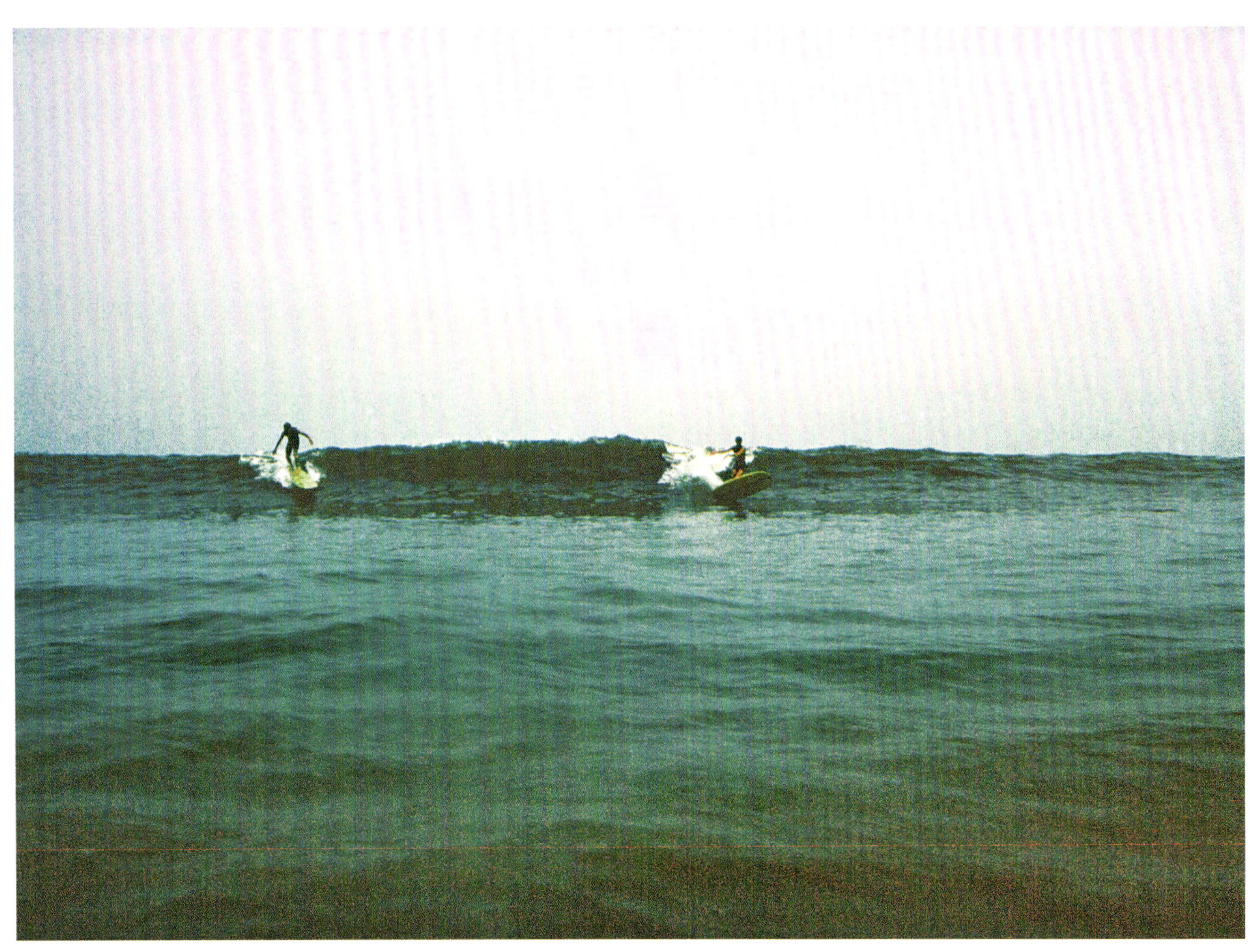

JULY 1966. JACKSON AVENUE, ATLANTIC CITY, NJ

Bob Sergeant turning backside with Randy Whited about to go frontside.

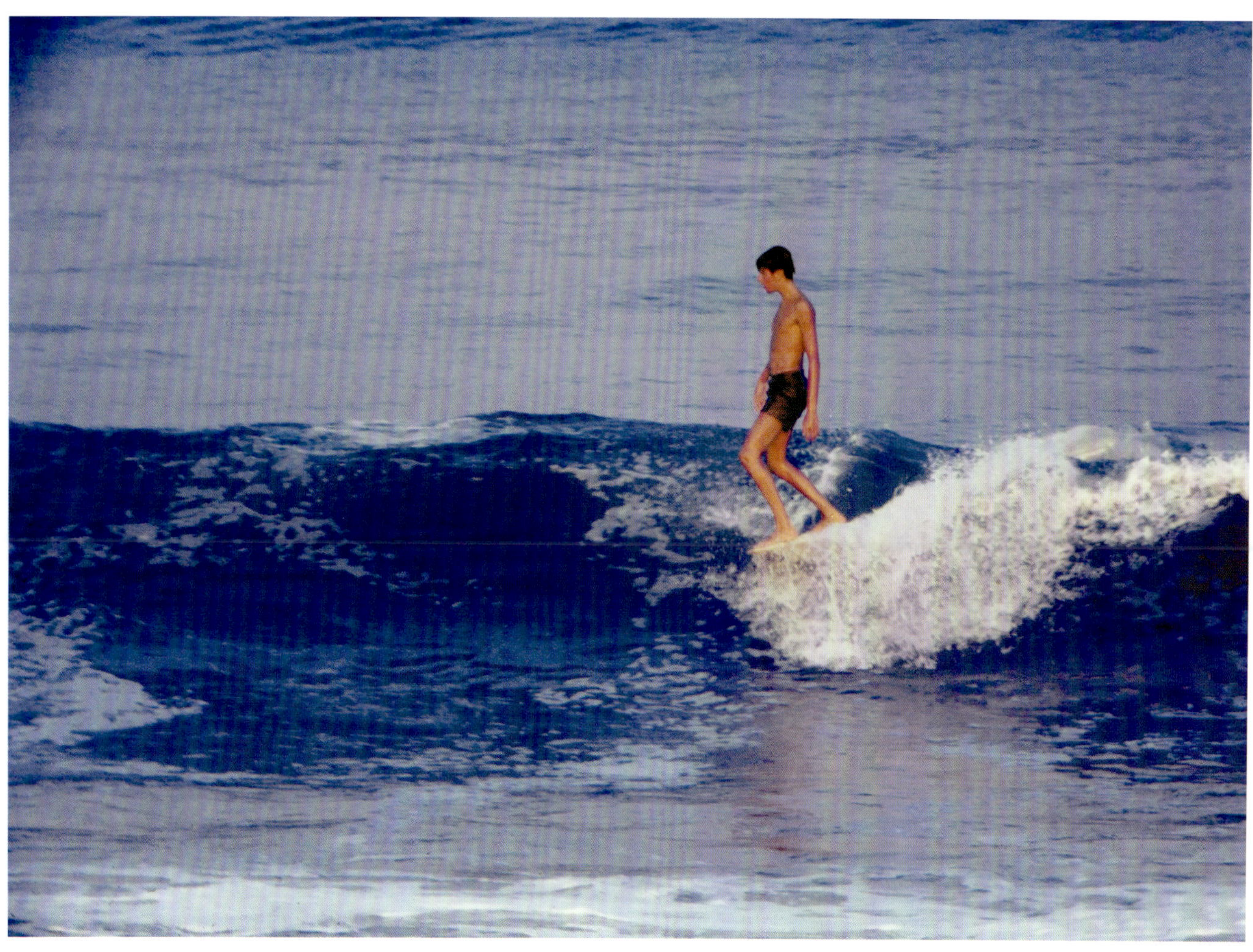

SUMMER 1966. OCEAN CITY, MD

Absecon Islands Curcio surf team rider Jo Gerety, summer '66 surf trip to OC, Maryland—you can see the backwash at the base of the wave about to clobber him.

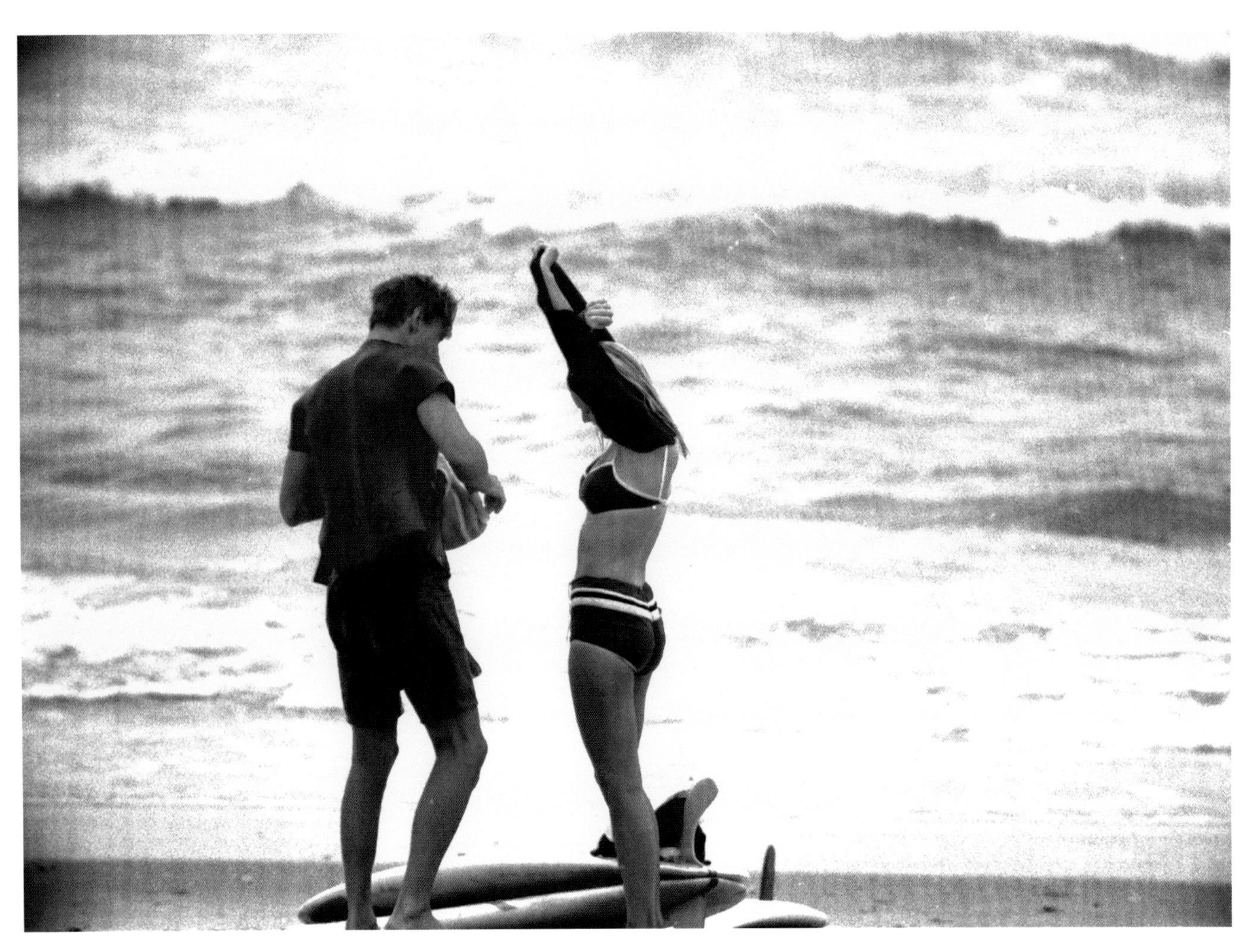

SUMMER 1965. VENTNOR PIER, NJ

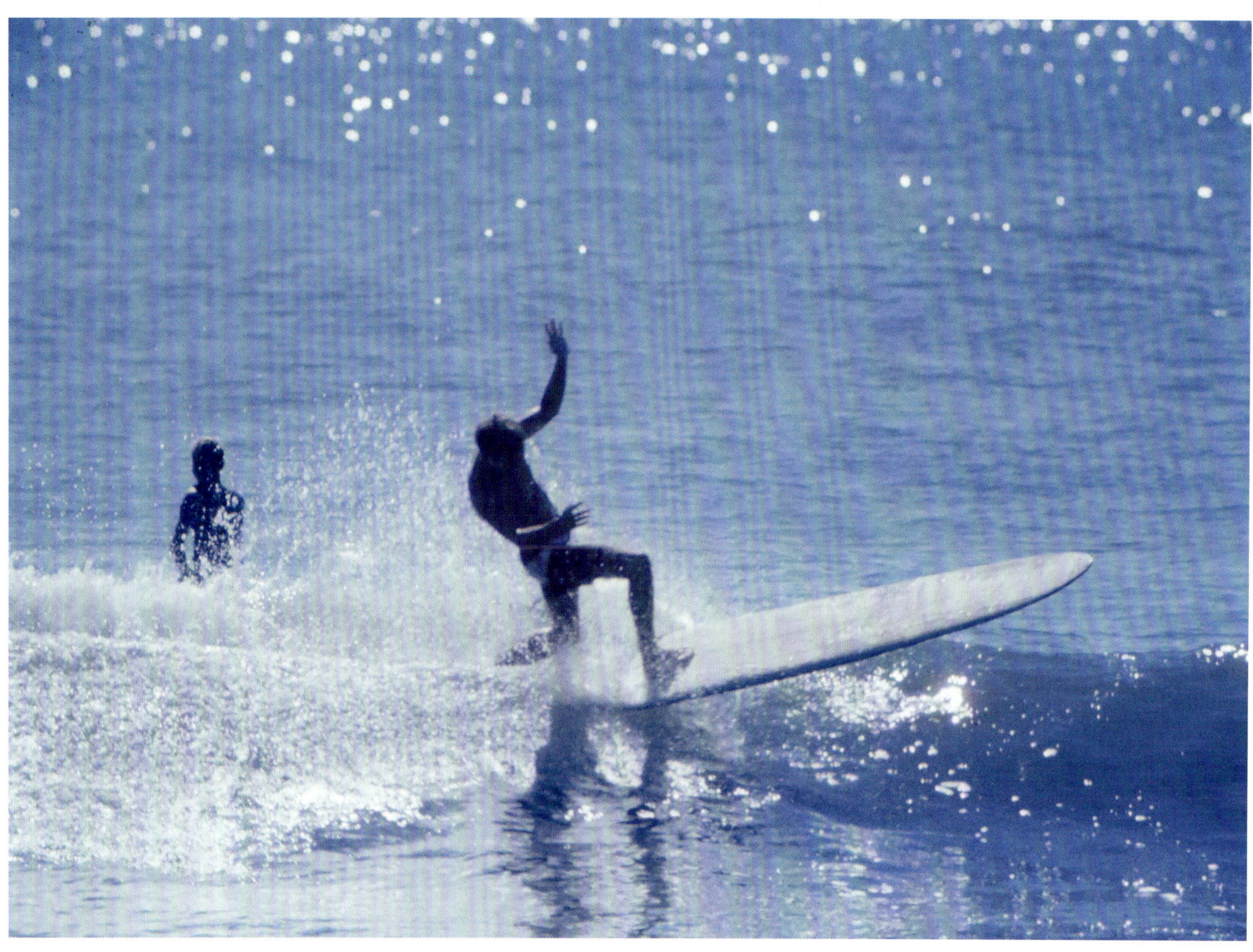

AUGUST 1966. BOB LEEDS, GAS CHAMBER, ATLANTIC CITY, NJ

Shot with Ektachrome film and a developing process that emphasized the natural elements of sun angle and water conditions.

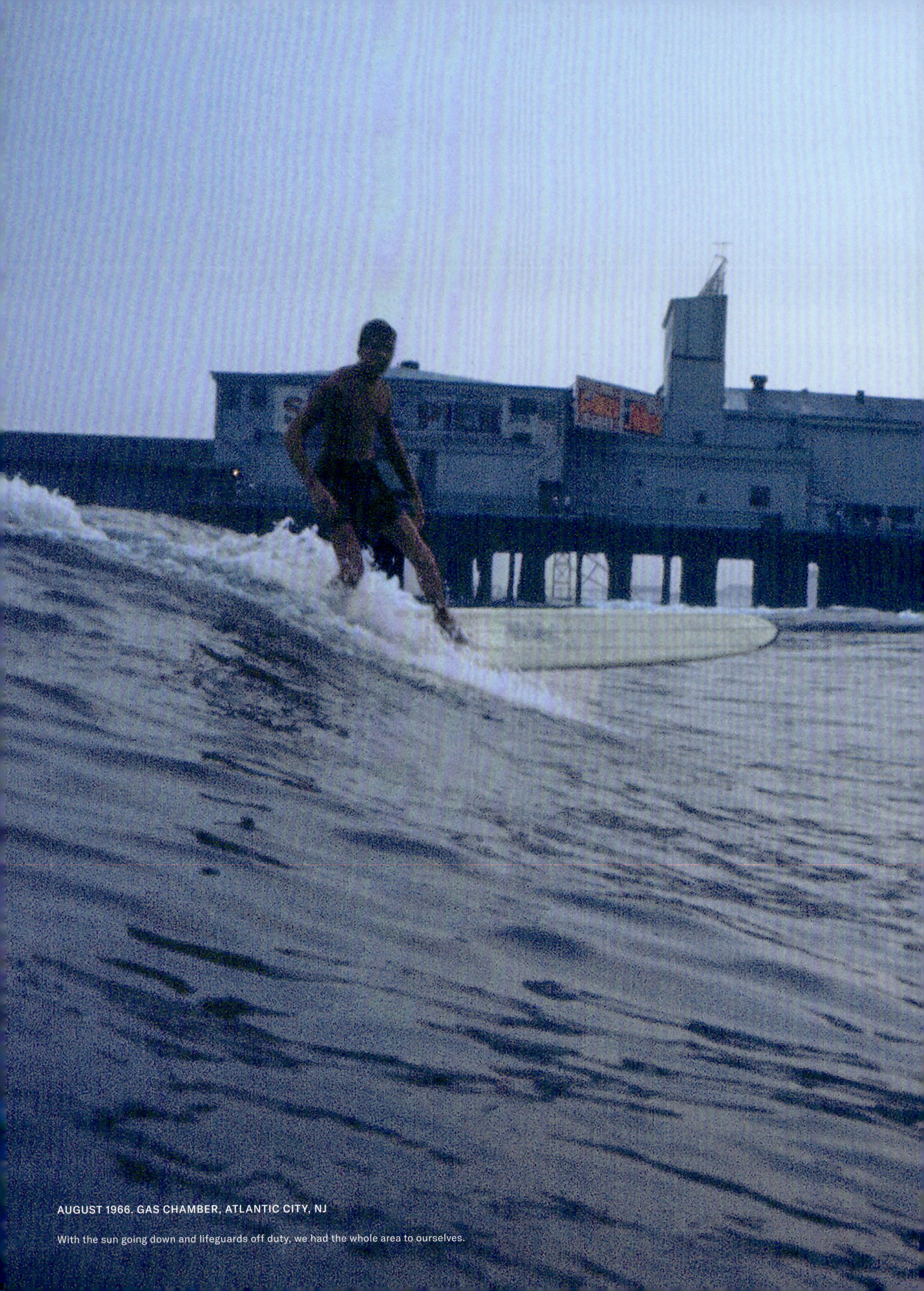

AUGUST 1966. GAS CHAMBER, ATLANTIC CITY, NJ

With the sun going down and lifeguards off duty, we had the whole area to ourselves.

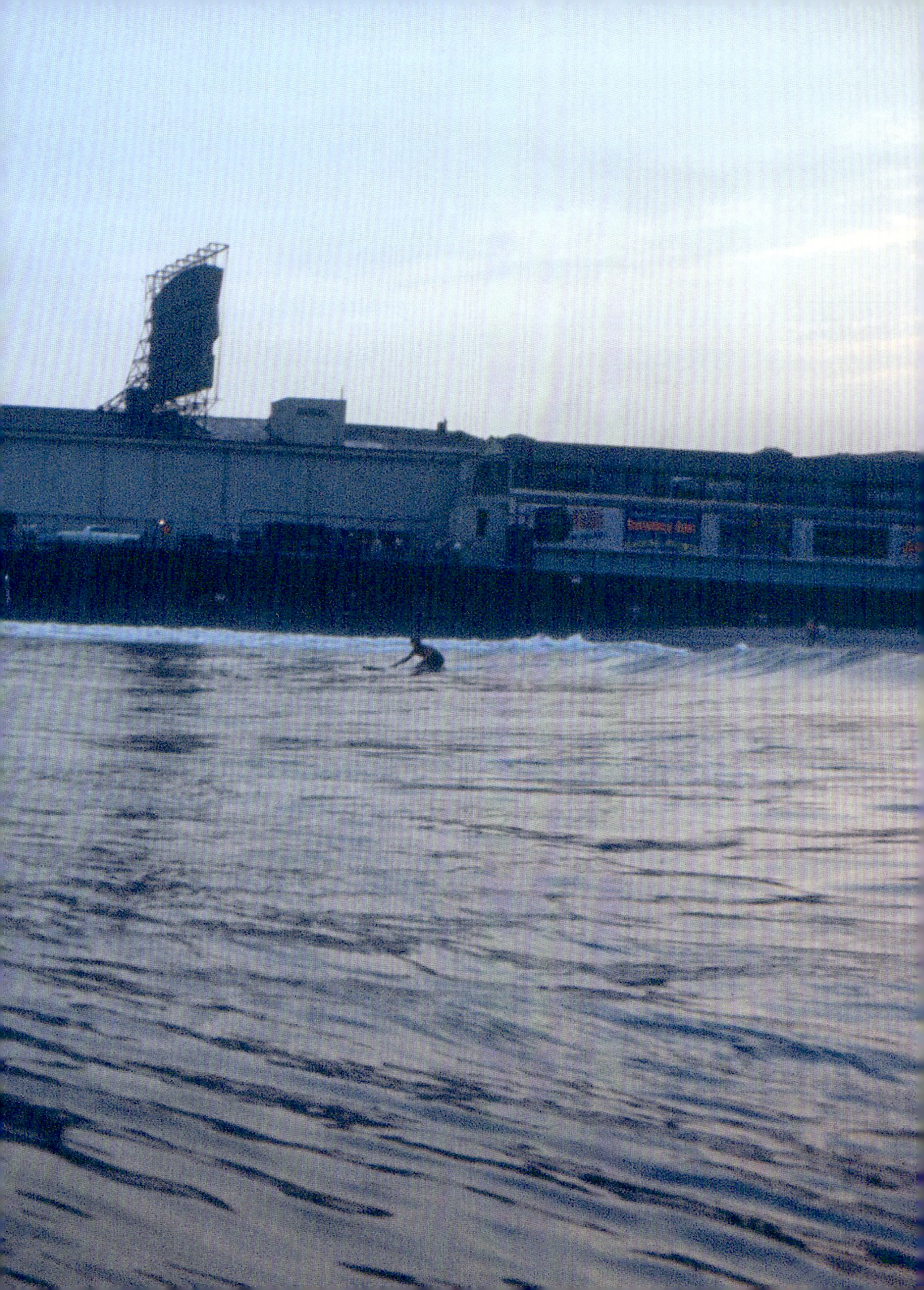

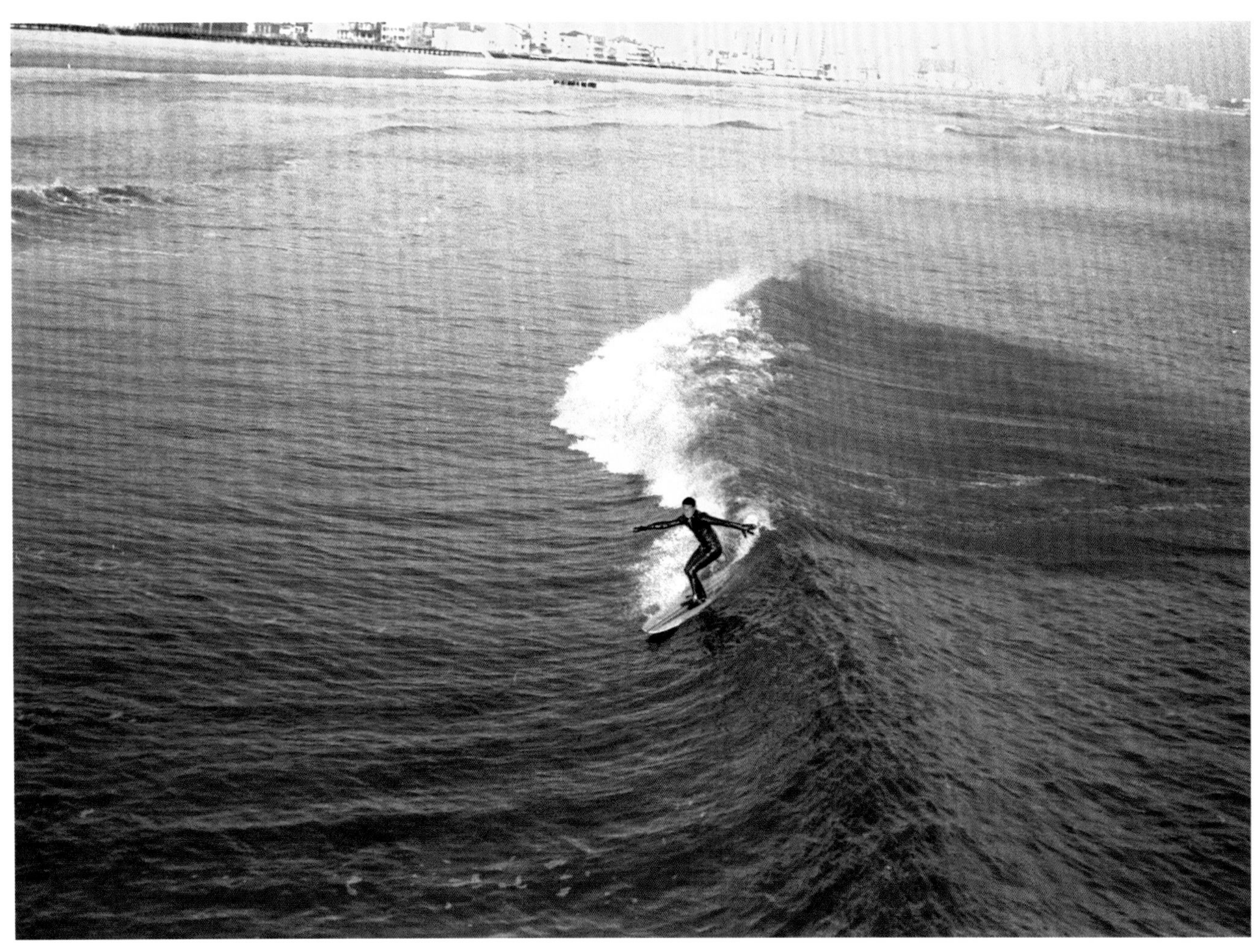

NOVEMBER 1964. VENTNOR PIER, NJ

Glenn Klotz, taken from Ventnor Pier. A beautiful winter day—the three fingers of the wetsuit gloves stand out.

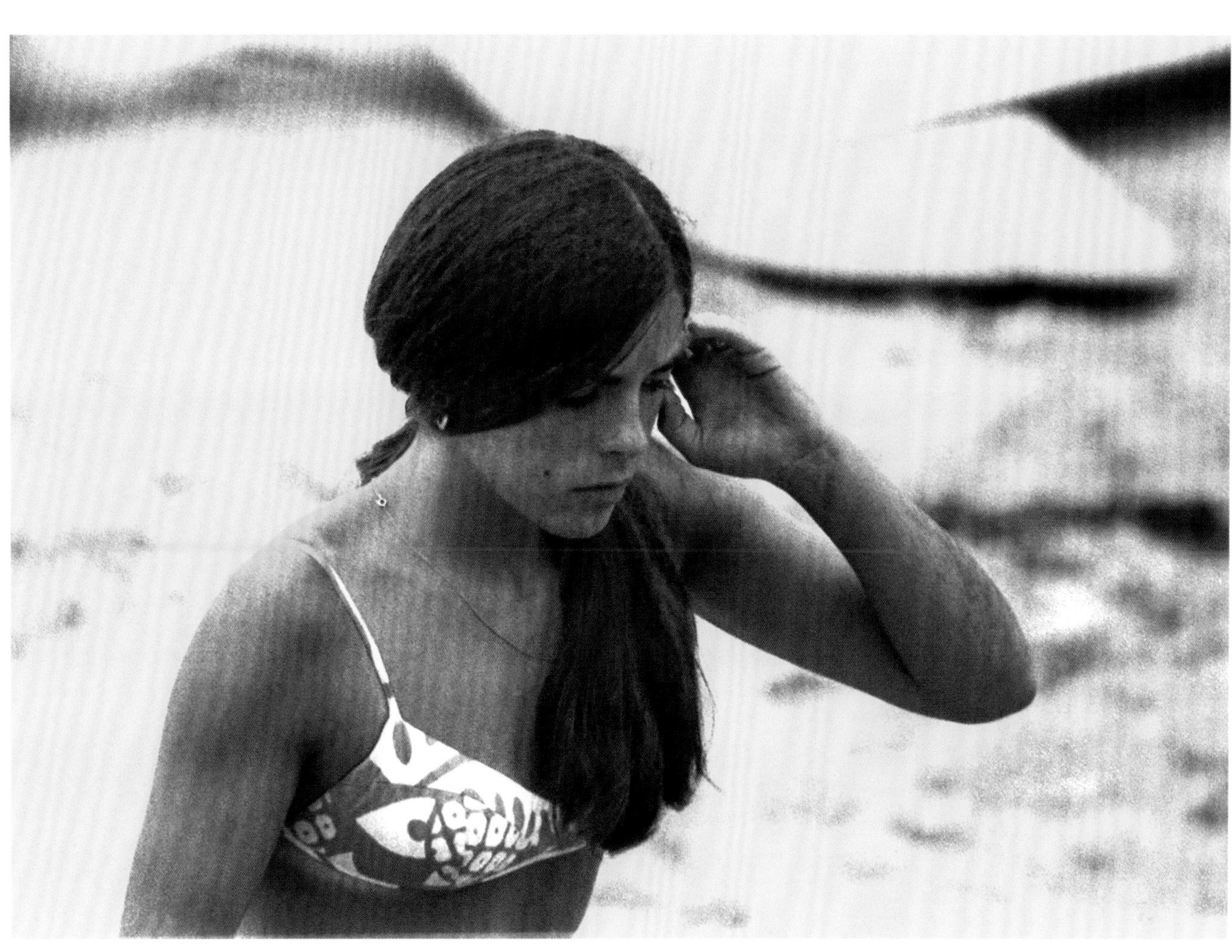

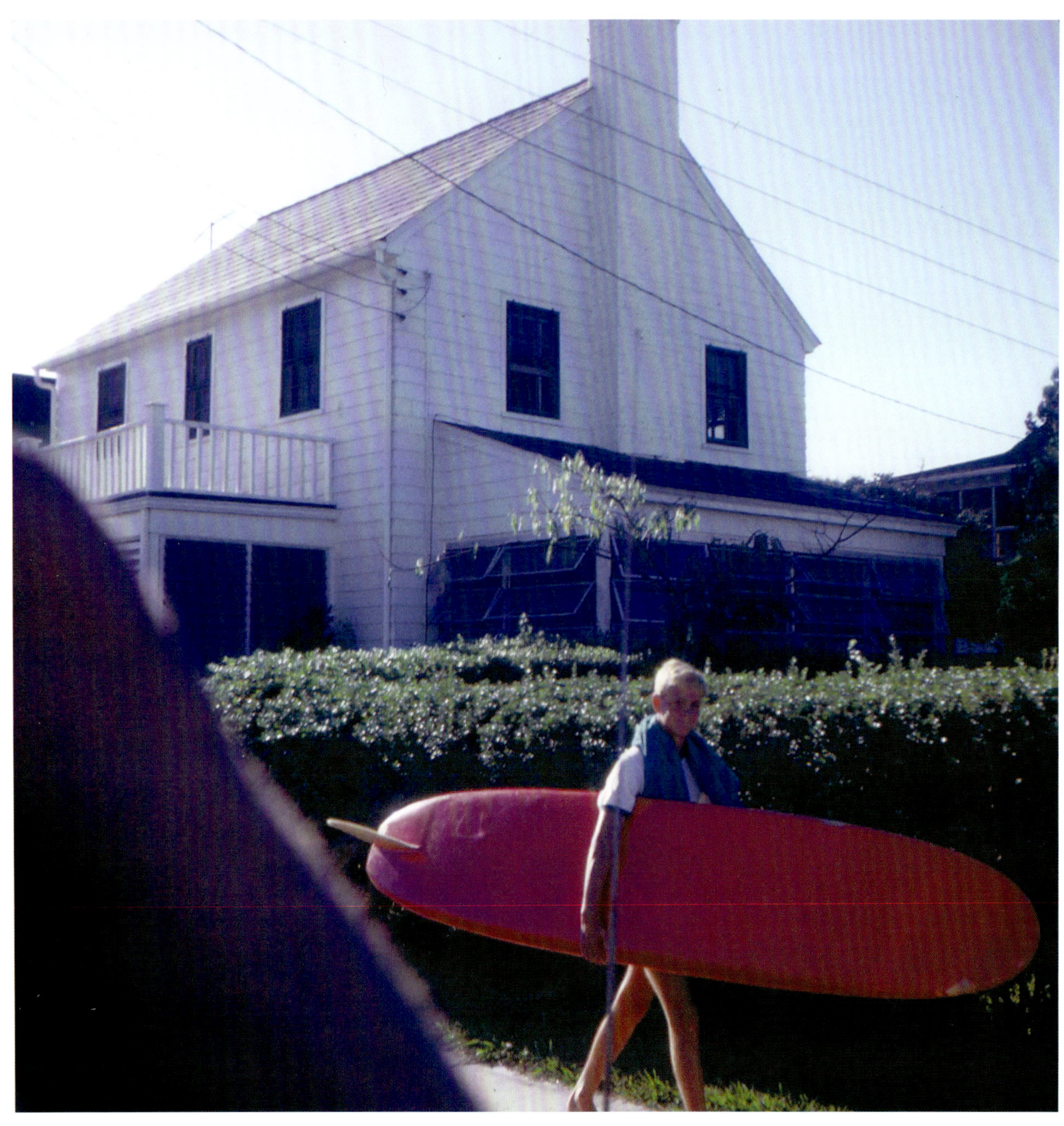

AUGUST 1965. OCEAN CITY, MD

While waiting in a car I shot this photo because it was unusual to see someone walking down the street with a surfboard, even though it was summer in Ocean City.

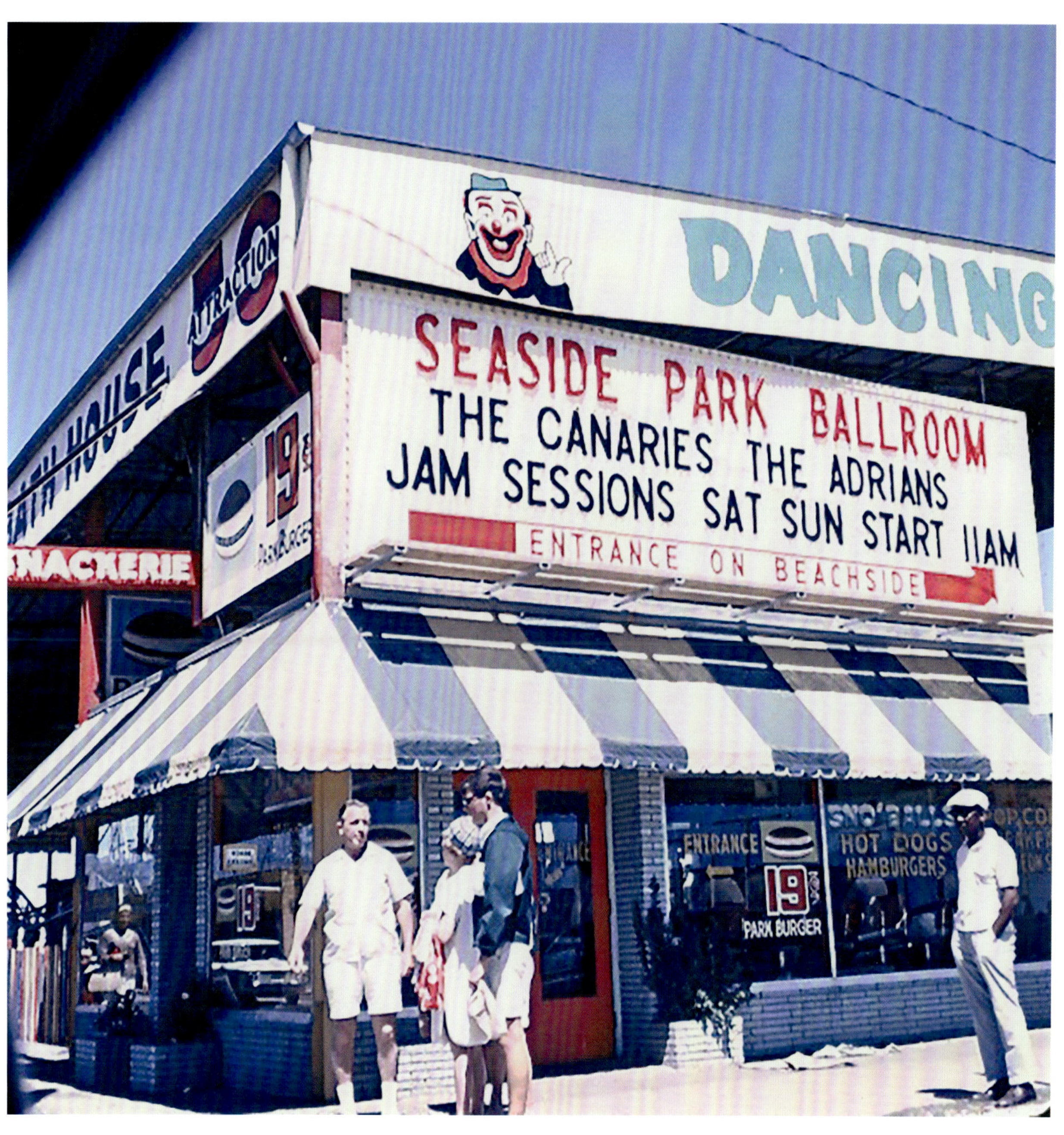

SUMMER 1965. SEASIDE PARK, NJ

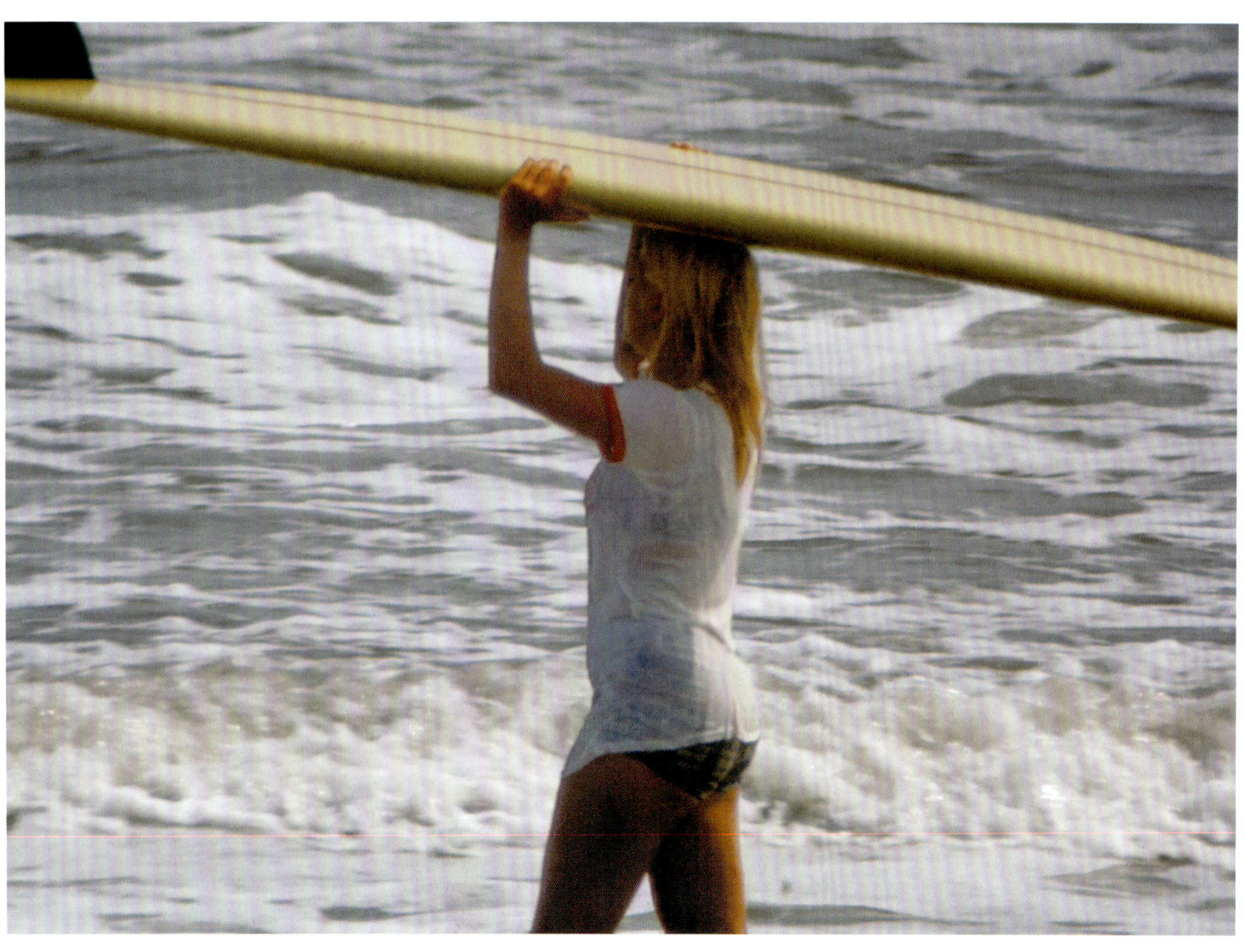

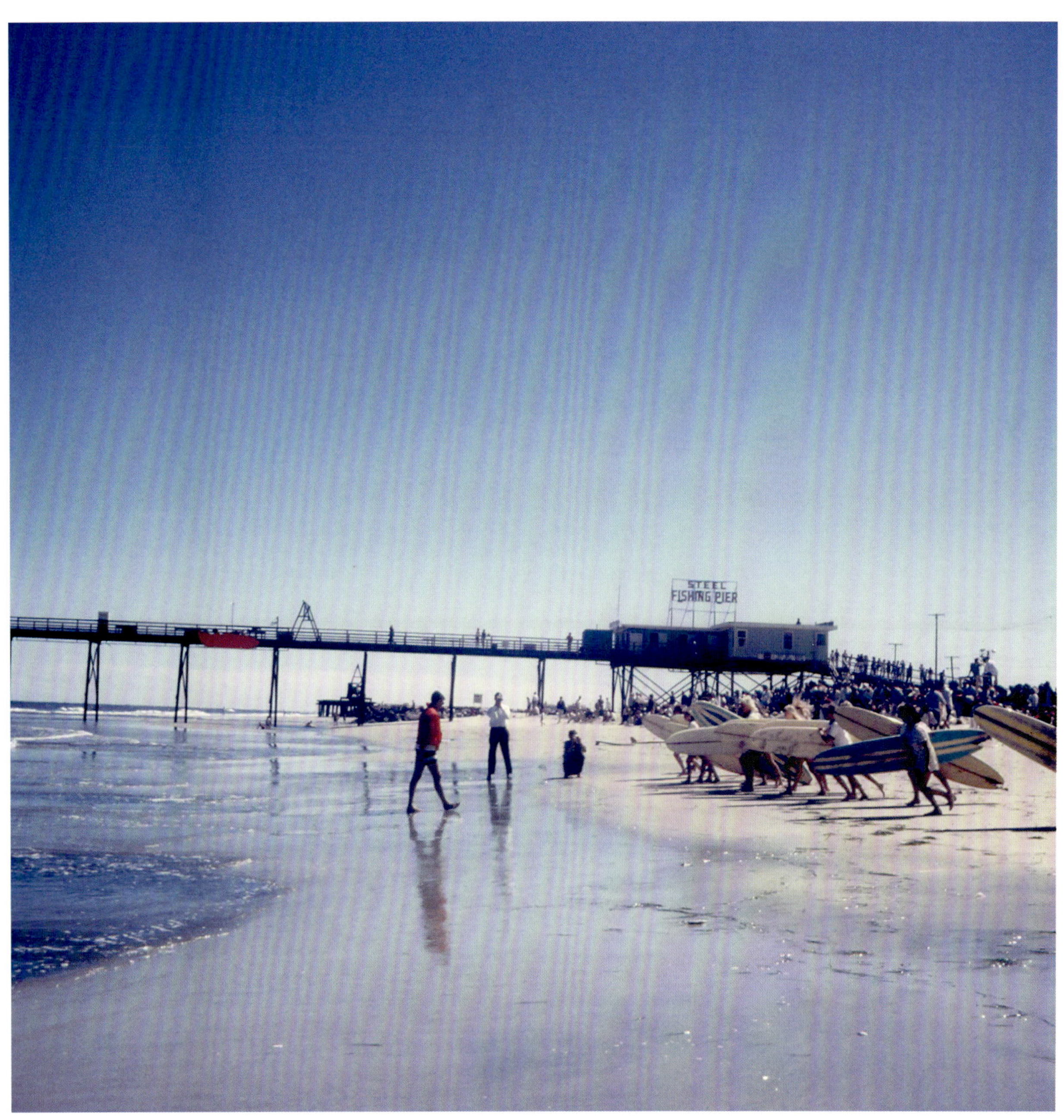

AUGUST 1965. STEEL PIER VIRGINIA BEACH CONTEST, VA

Curcio's Surf Shop team vs. Dick Catri's team from Florida, competing in Virginia Beach.

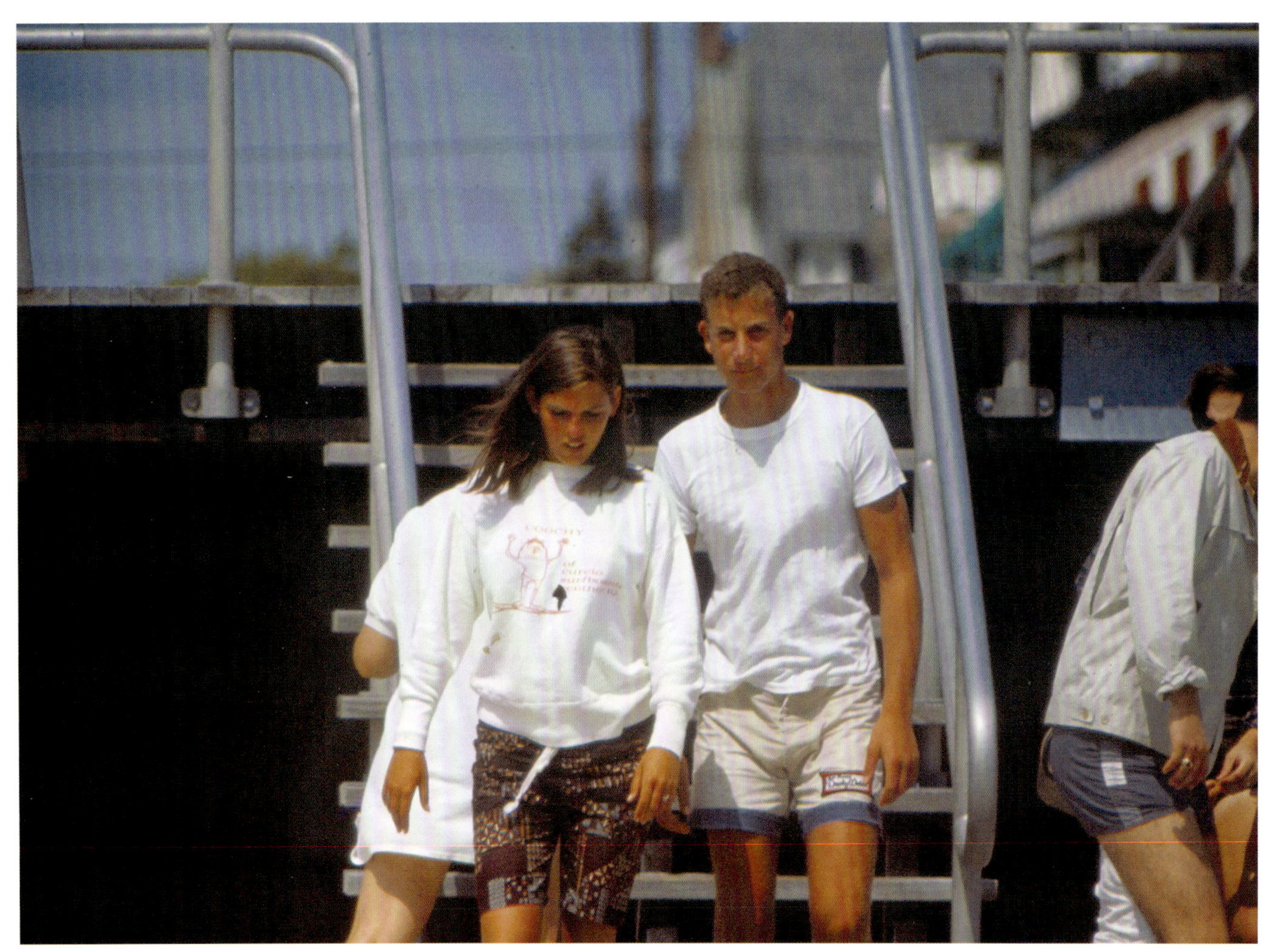

AUGUST 1965. MARK LEVINE AND BONNIE WRIGHT, VENTNOR PIER, NJ

Mark Levine sold Dewey Weber Surfboards out of his garage at age 15. The following year Curcio Surf Shop was selling Greg Noll Surfboards. Bonnie is wearing a Curcio sweatshirt and was the only girl regularly in the water at Ventnor Pier. —D.M.

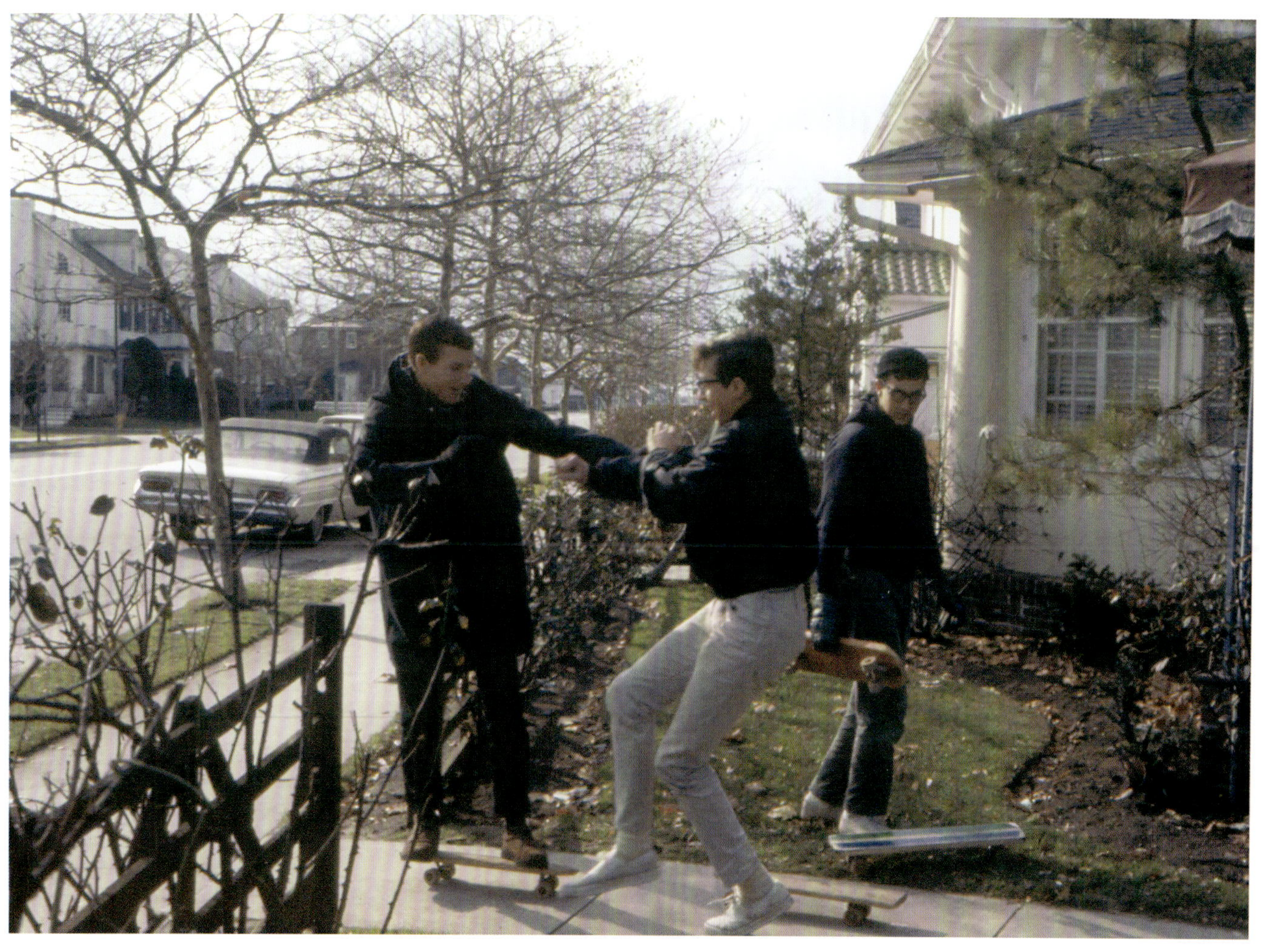

DECEMBER 1964. GLENN KLOTZ'S HOUSE, MARVEN GARDENS, MARGATE, NJ
(LEFT TO RIGHT) JOHN PAGE, MARK VINIKOOR, AND LENNY LEBONA

We made those early skateboards of wood with trucks removed from roller skates. The wheels from the indoor skates wore down very fast. Some guys used the metal outdoor skates, but their trucks had the wheels closer together. They were noisy and slid out easier.

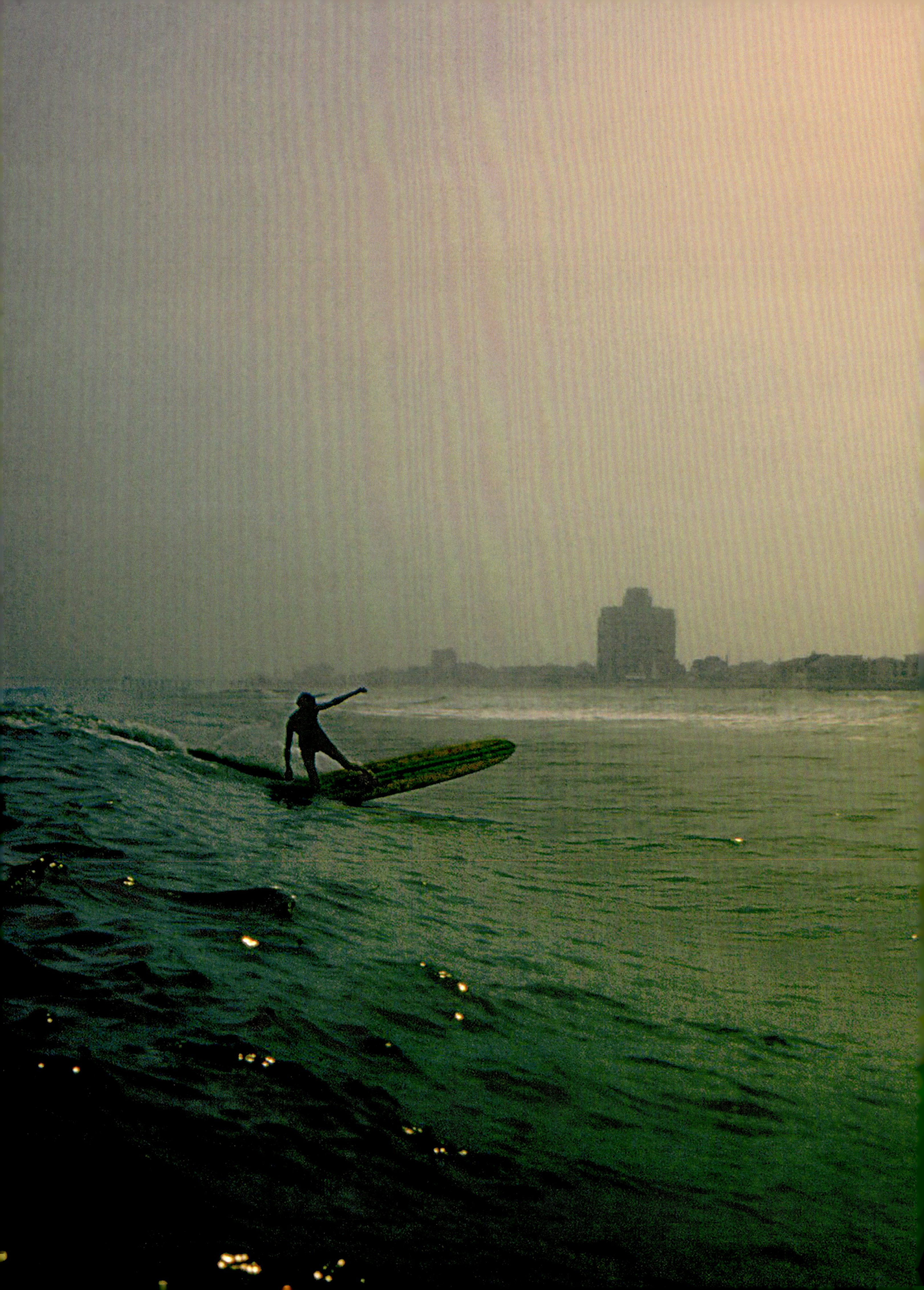

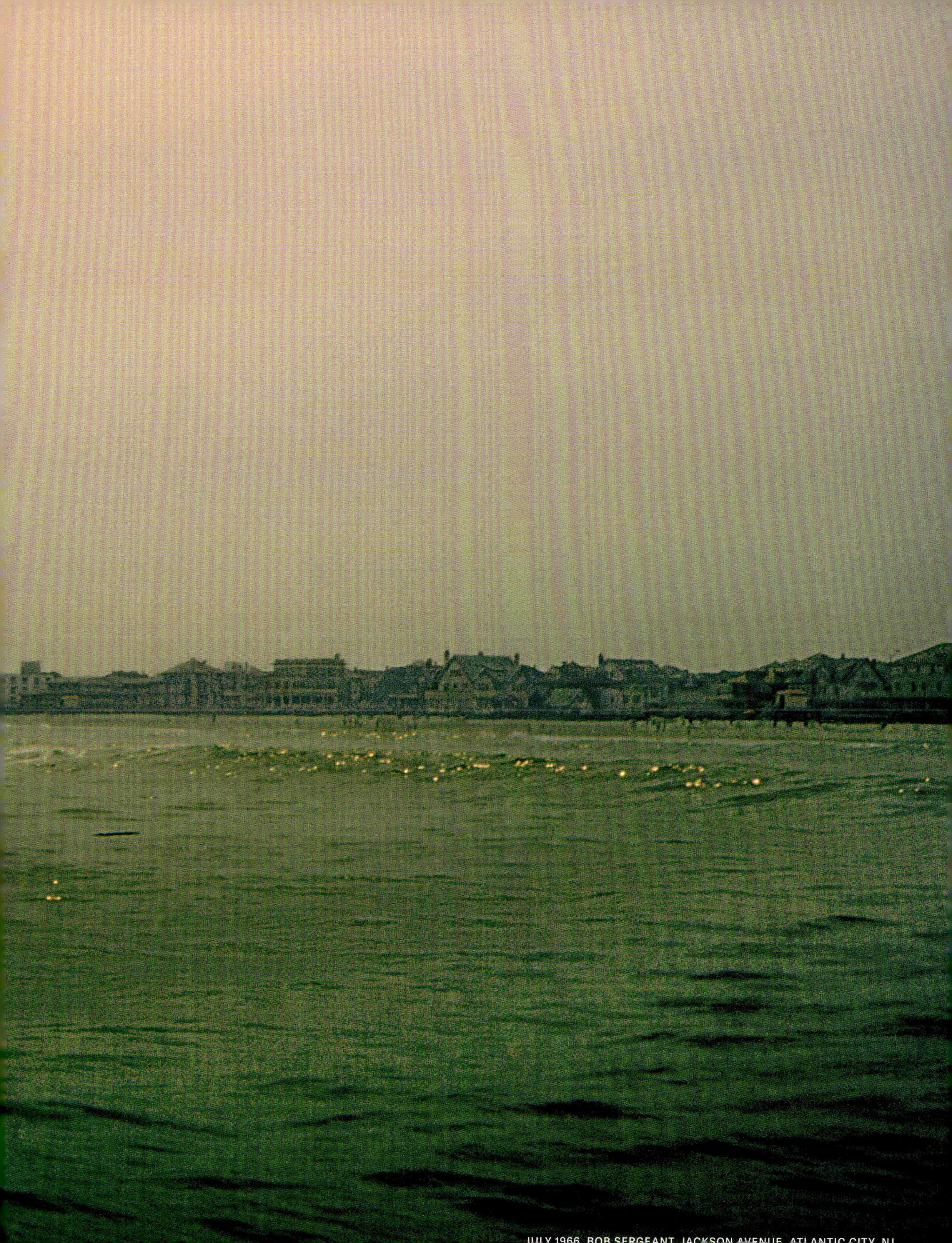

JULY 1966, BOB SERGEANT, JACKSON AVENUE, ATLANTIC CITY, NJ

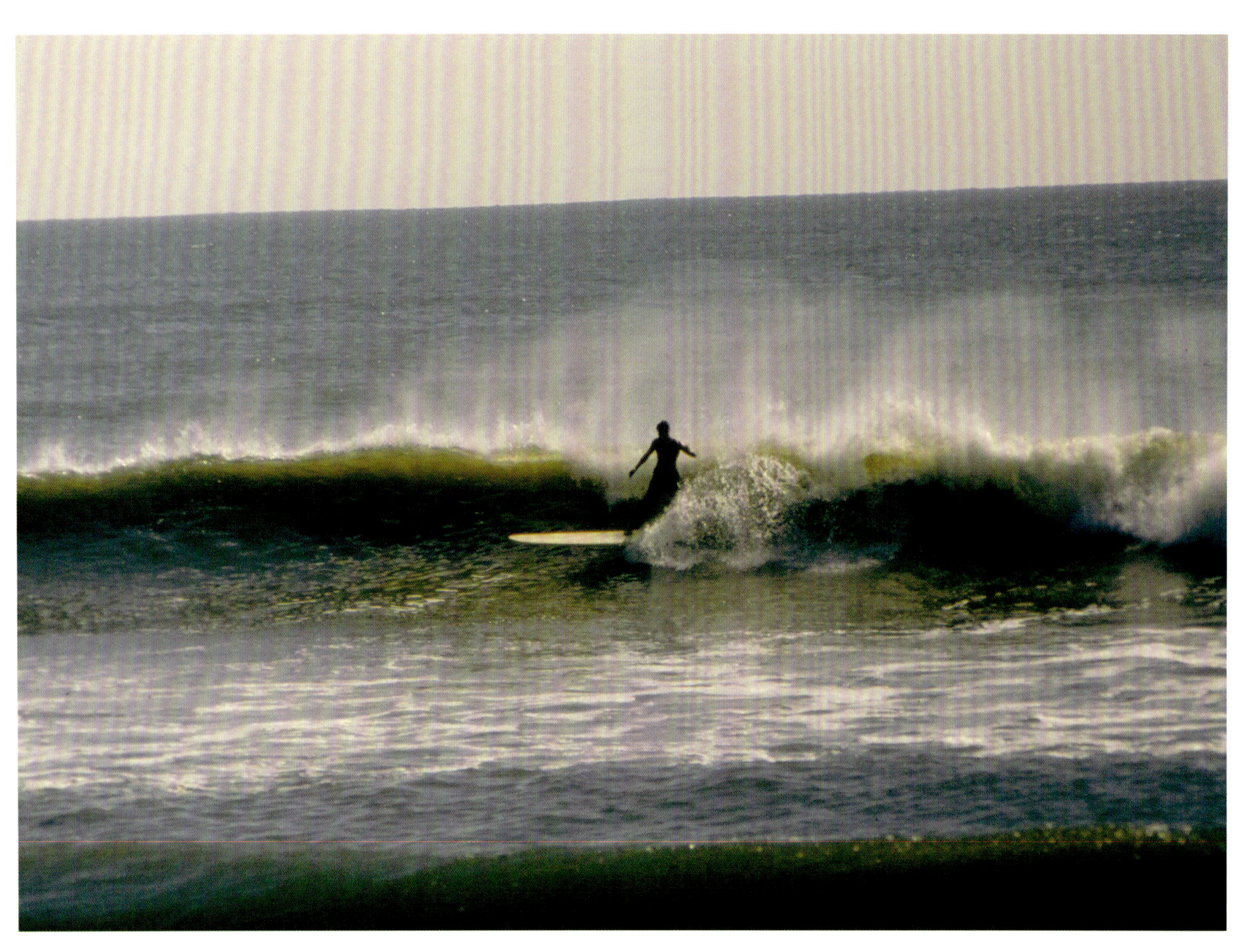

OCTOBER 1965

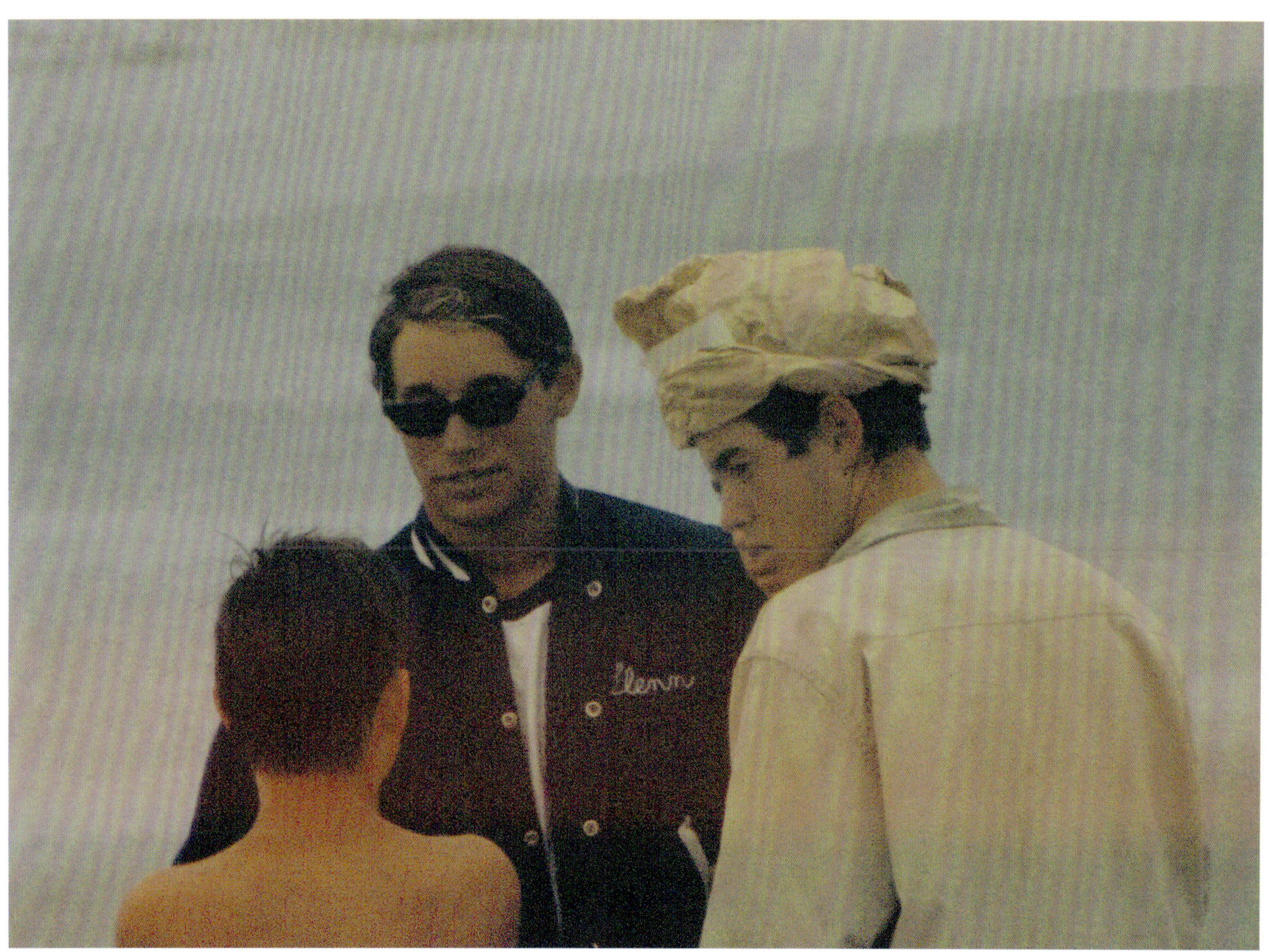

JUNE 1966. ATLANTIC CITY, NJ

Glenn Klotz in the sunglasses and Kelly Leonard with the paper bag hat. Glenn moved to Atlantic City from Palm Desert, California, in 1966. A guy moving to New Jersey from California was an instant rock star.

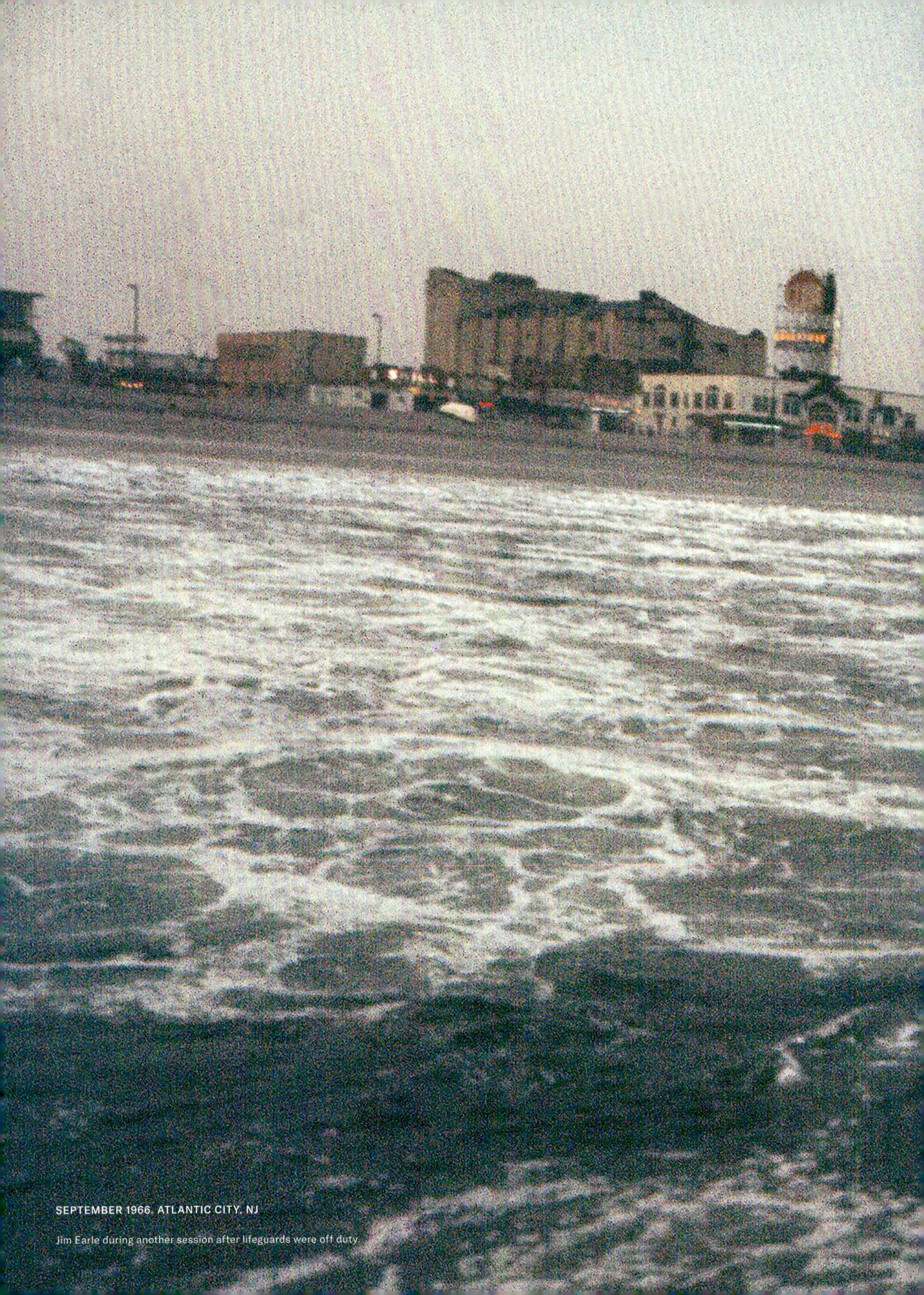

SEPTEMBER 1966. ATLANTIC CITY, NJ

Jim Earle during another session after lifeguards were off duty.

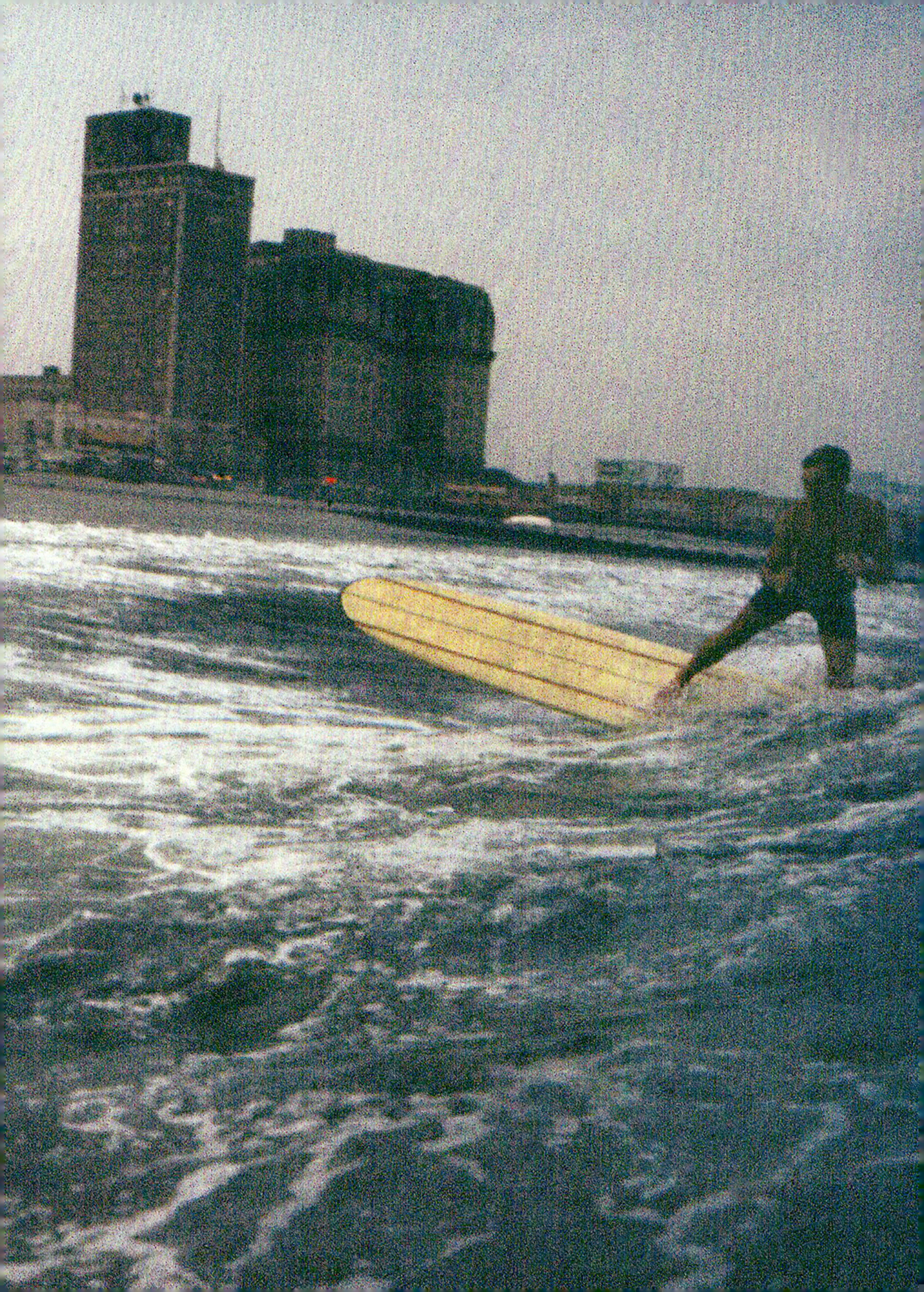

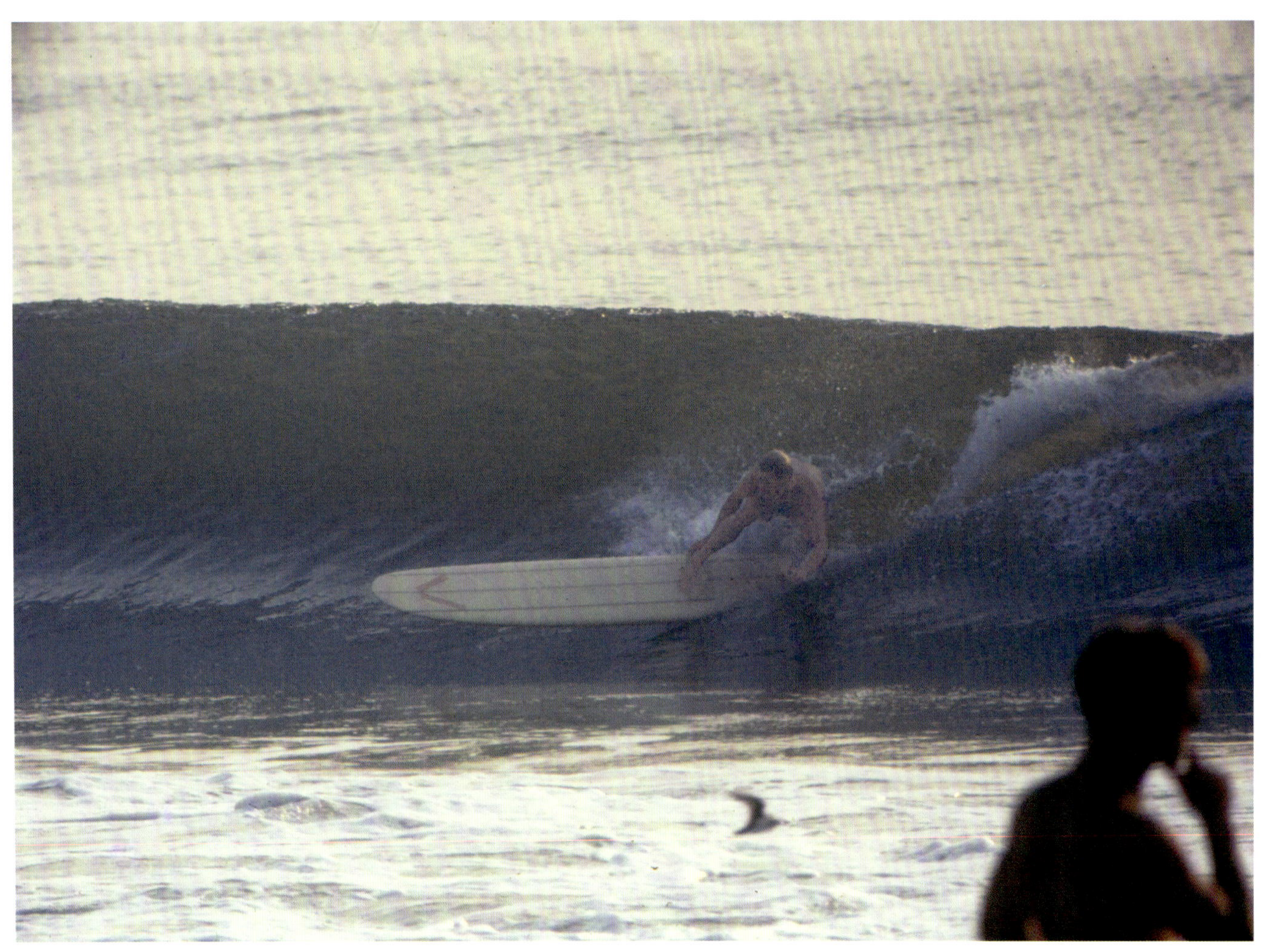

AUGUST 1966. OCEAN CITY, MD, CONTEST

Bob Leeds on a classic Challenger Surfboard with John Page in the foreground. Absecon Islands Curcio Surf Shop Team at the Ocean City, Maryland, Contest.

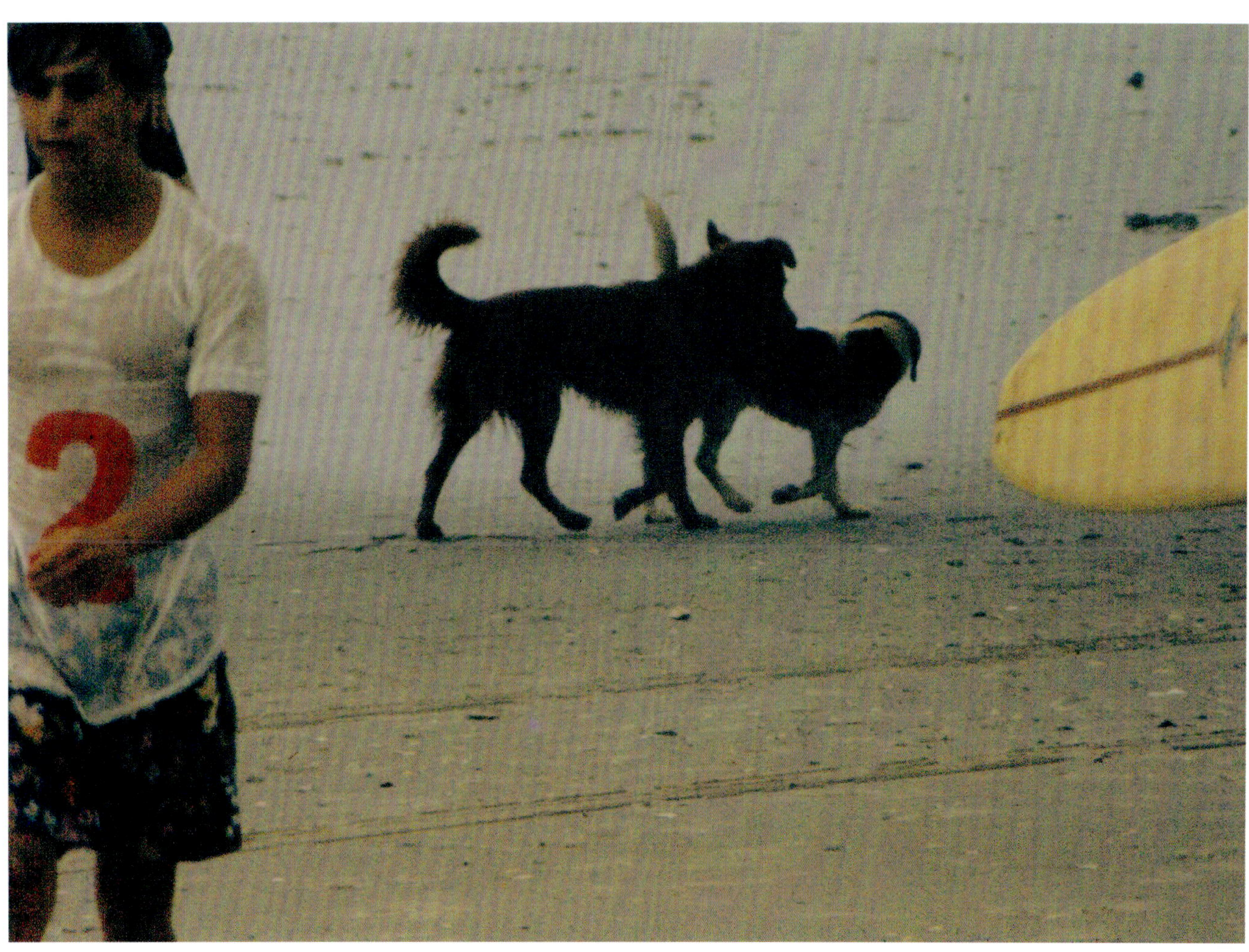

AUGUST 1966. STATES AVENUE, ATLANTIC CITY, NJ

Dogs roaming freely on the beach during a surf contest is fitting of the attitude of surfers. A regular fixture on States Avenue in Atlantic City was Kim Fioriglio's dog, Duchess.

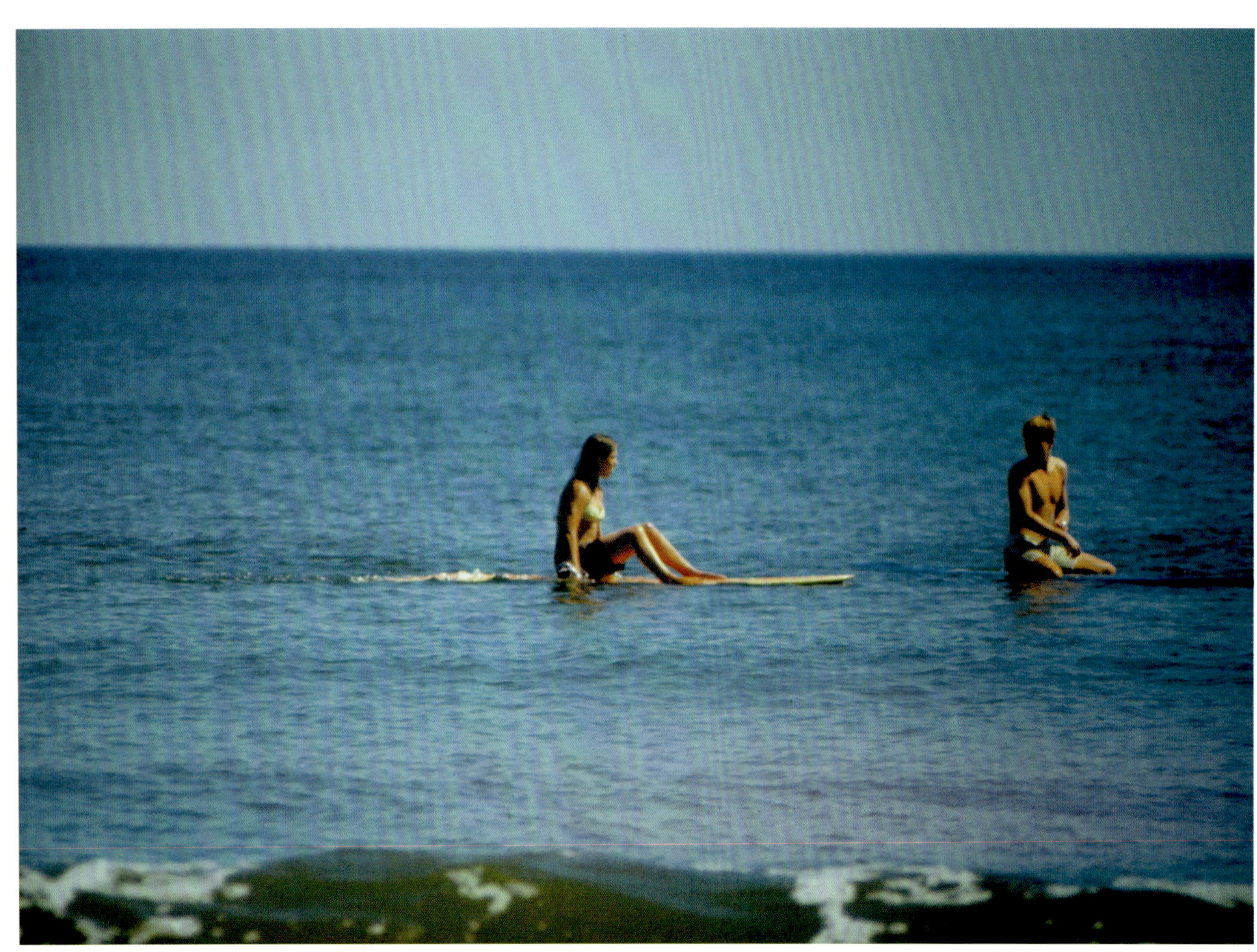

SUMMER 1967. VENTNOR PIER, NJ

Bonnie Wright at Ventnor Pier. When there were few or no waves on the hot days of summer, hanging out in the water was a good place to be. Ventnor Pier was designated a surfing beach around 1967 in large part due to the efforts of Alan Wolf, one of the older surfers of the day. There are many unsung heroes like him, who spent much time and effort to get us a designated place to surf.

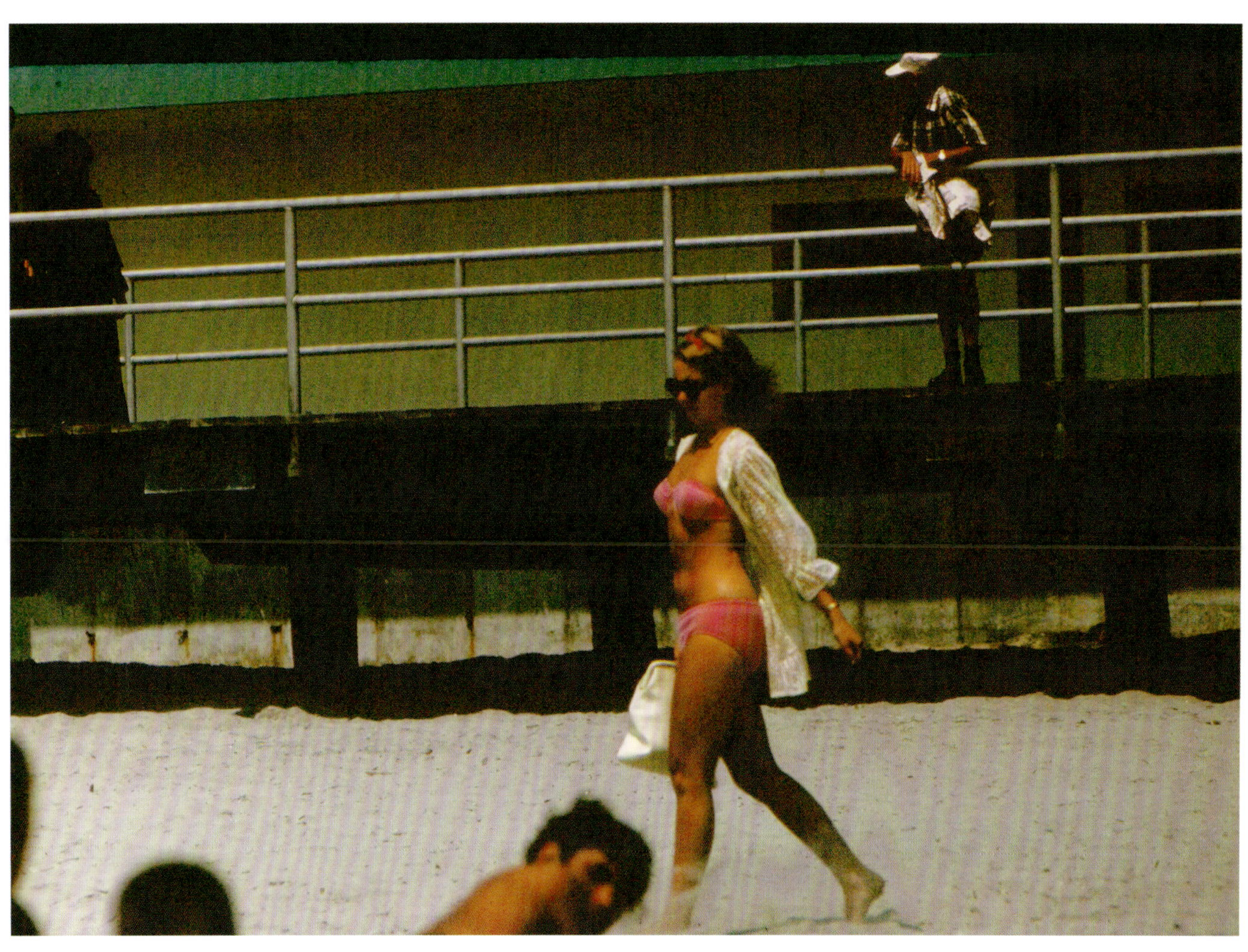

AUGUST 1965. VENTNOR PIER, NJ

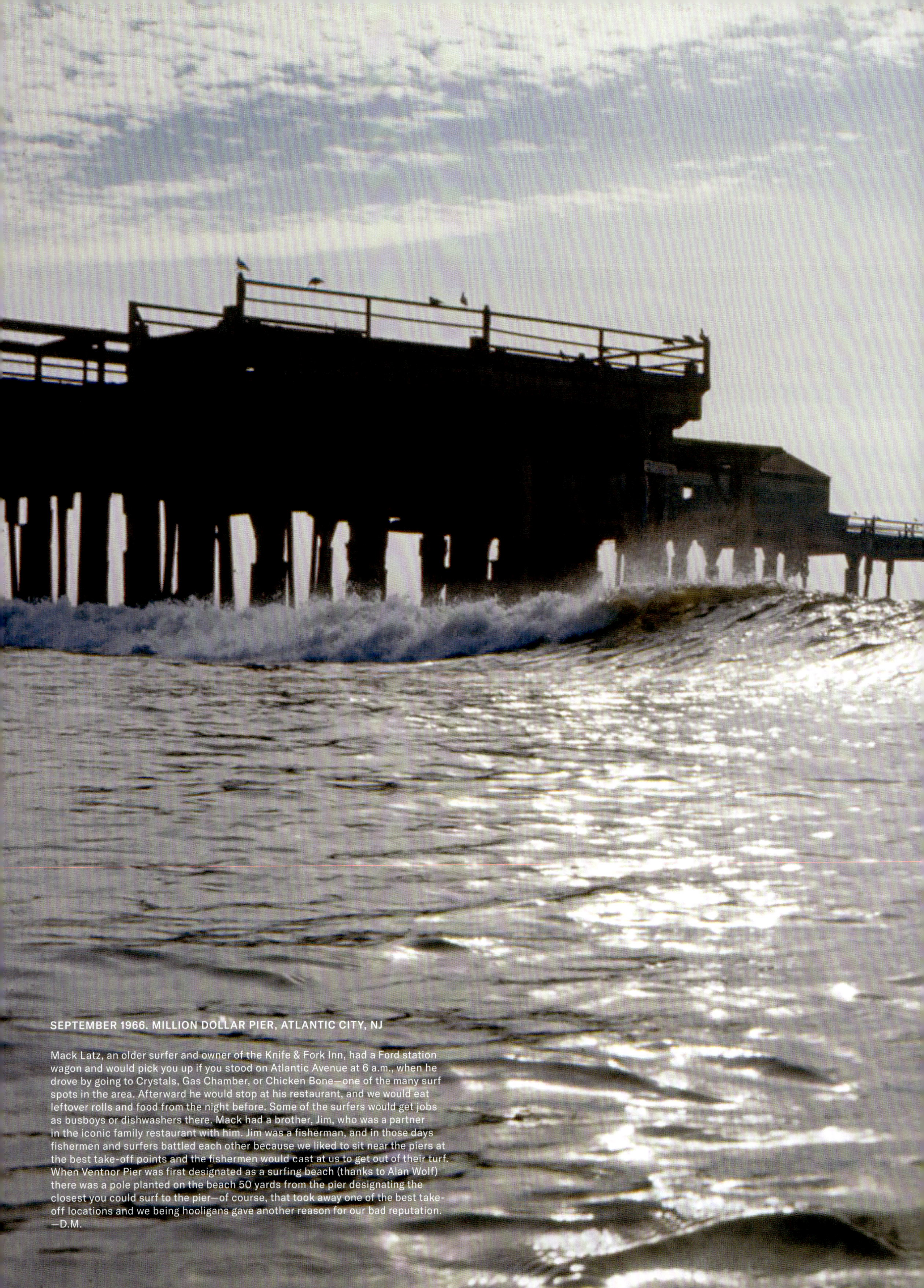

SEPTEMBER 1966. MILLION DOLLAR PIER, ATLANTIC CITY, NJ

Mack Latz, an older surfer and owner of the Knife & Fork Inn, had a Ford station wagon and would pick you up if you stood on Atlantic Avenue at 6 a.m., when he drove by going to Crystals, Gas Chamber, or Chicken Bone—one of the many surf spots in the area. Afterward he would stop at his restaurant, and we would eat leftover rolls and food from the night before. Some of the surfers would get jobs as busboys or dishwashers there. Mack had a brother, Jim, who was a partner in the iconic family restaurant with him. Jim was a fisherman, and in those days fishermen and surfers battled each other because we liked to sit near the piers at the best take-off points and the fishermen would cast at us to get out of their turf. When Ventnor Pier was first designated as a surfing beach (thanks to Alan Wolf) there was a pole planted on the beach 50 yards from the pier designating the closest you could surf to the pier—of course, that took away one of the best take-off locations and we being hooligans gave another reason for our bad reputation. —D.M.

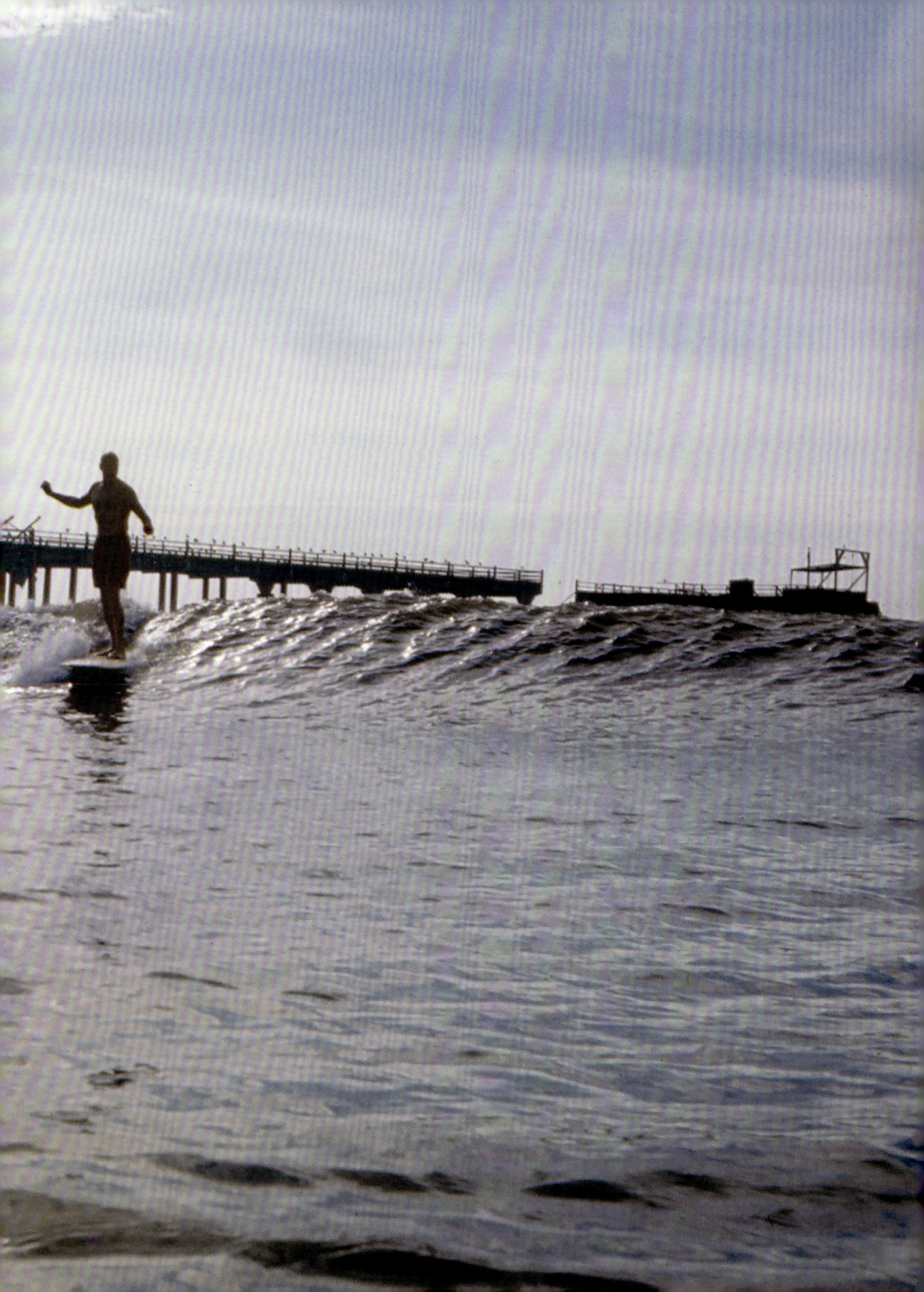

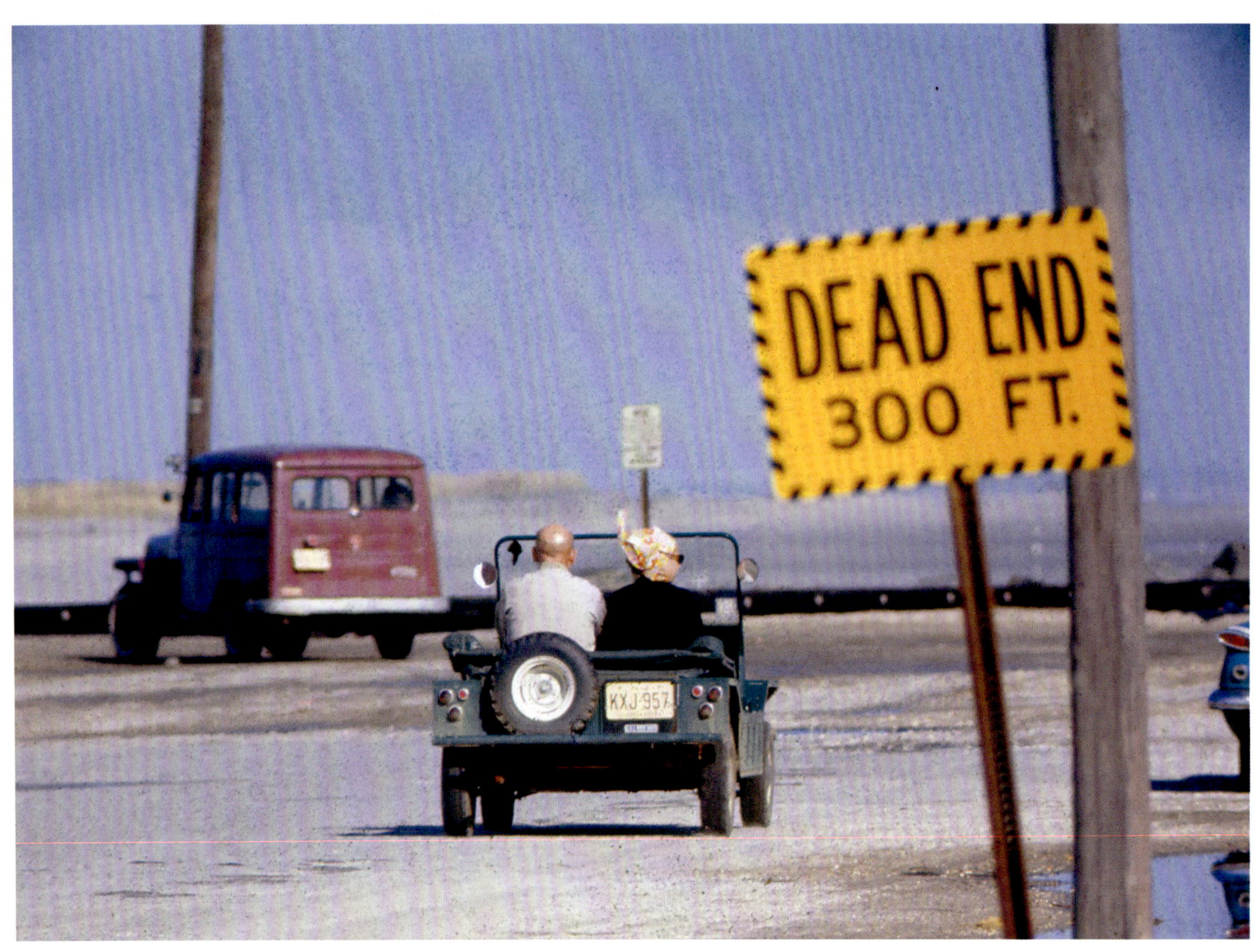

OCTOBER 1966. NORTH END BRIGANTINE, NJ

This little vehicle was ahead of its time—many or most beach towns are so overbuilt and full of big vehicles nowadays. Note: it has a legit tag showing it was registered.

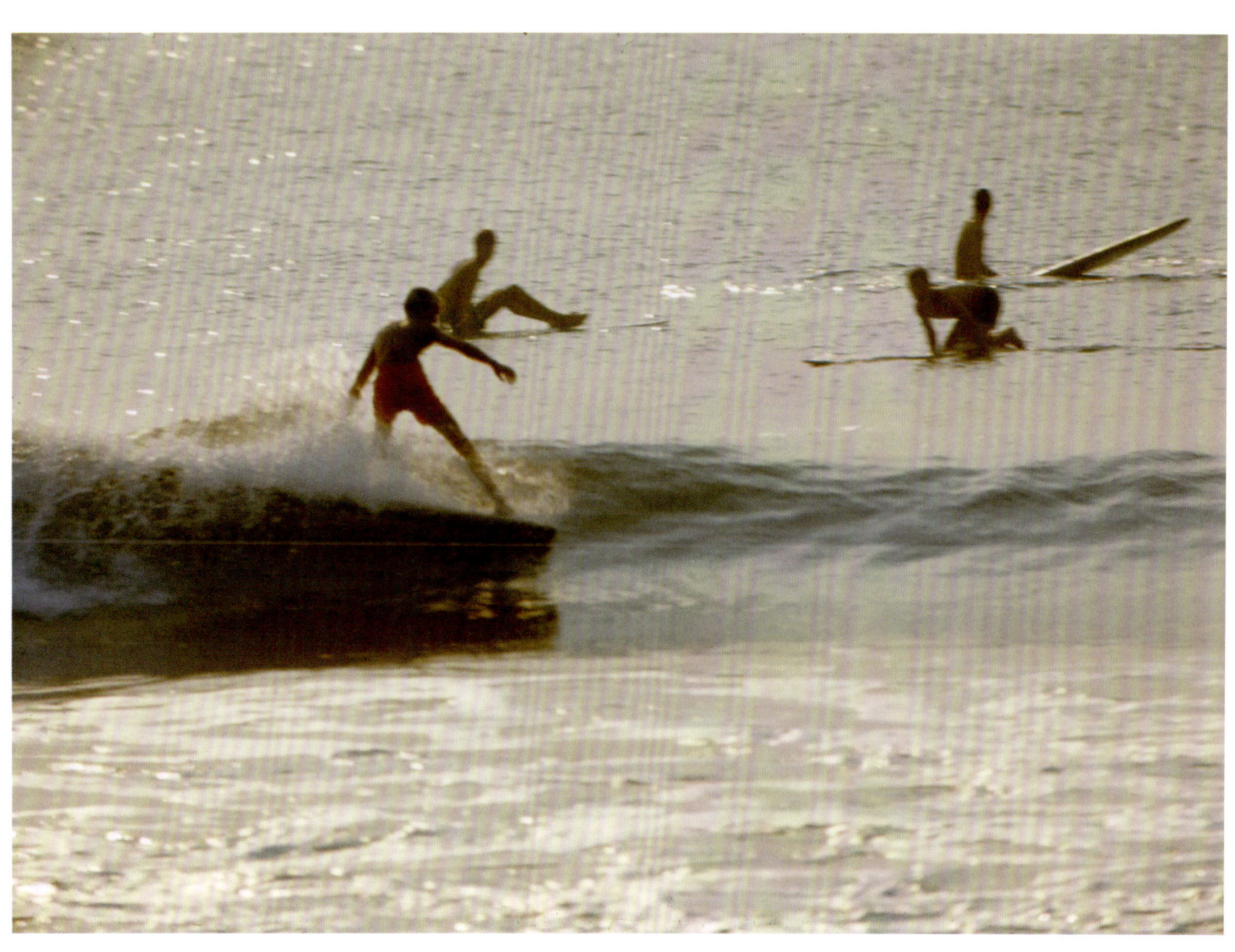

SEPTEMBER 1966. 15TH STREET, OCEAN CITY, NJ

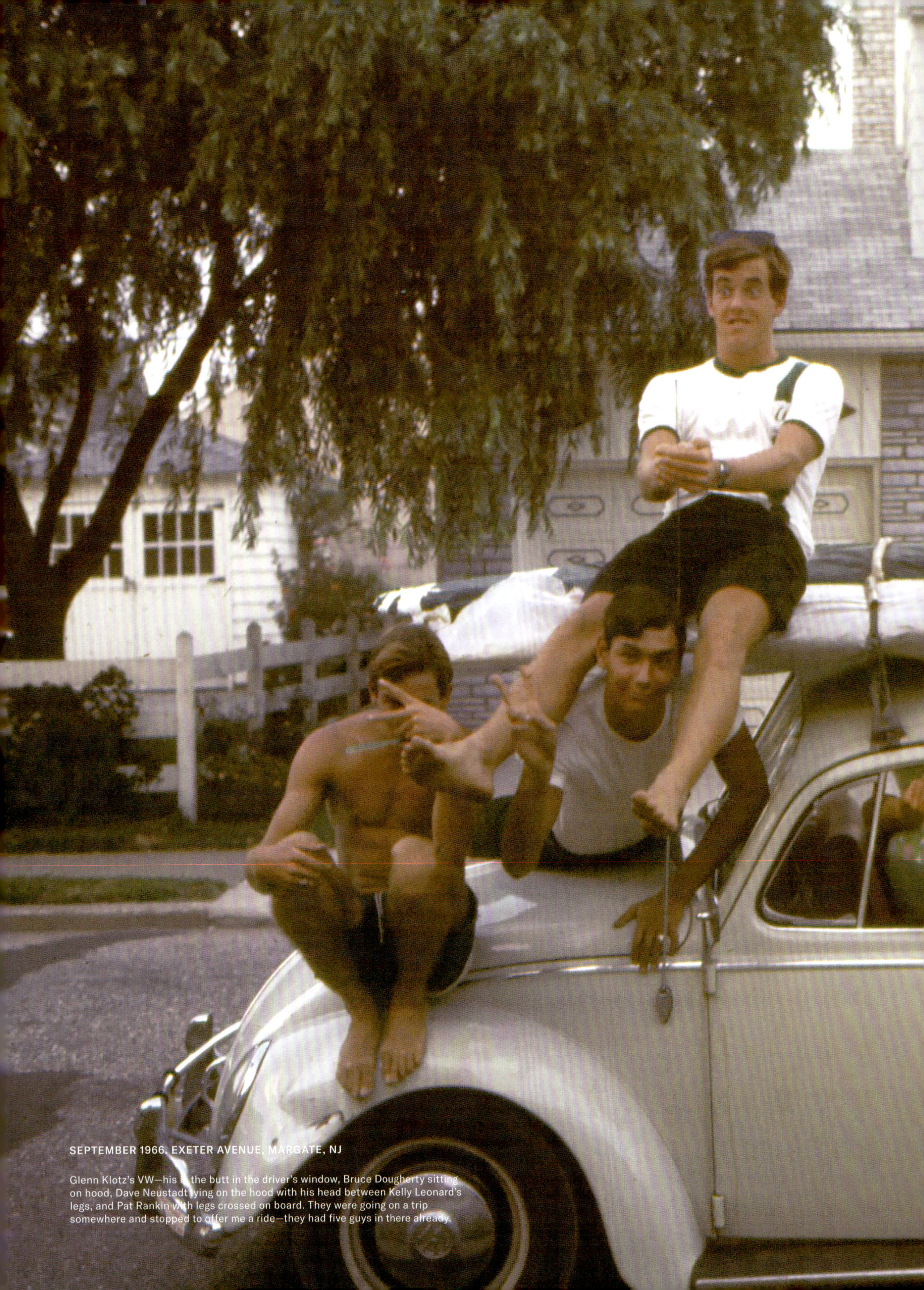

SEPTEMBER 1966, EXETER AVENUE, MARGATE, NJ

Glenn Klotz's VW—his is the butt in the driver's window, Bruce Dougherty sitting on hood, Dave Neustadt lying on the hood with his head between Kelly Leonard's legs, and Pat Rankin with legs crossed on board. They were going on a trip somewhere and stopped to offer me a ride—they had five guys in there already.

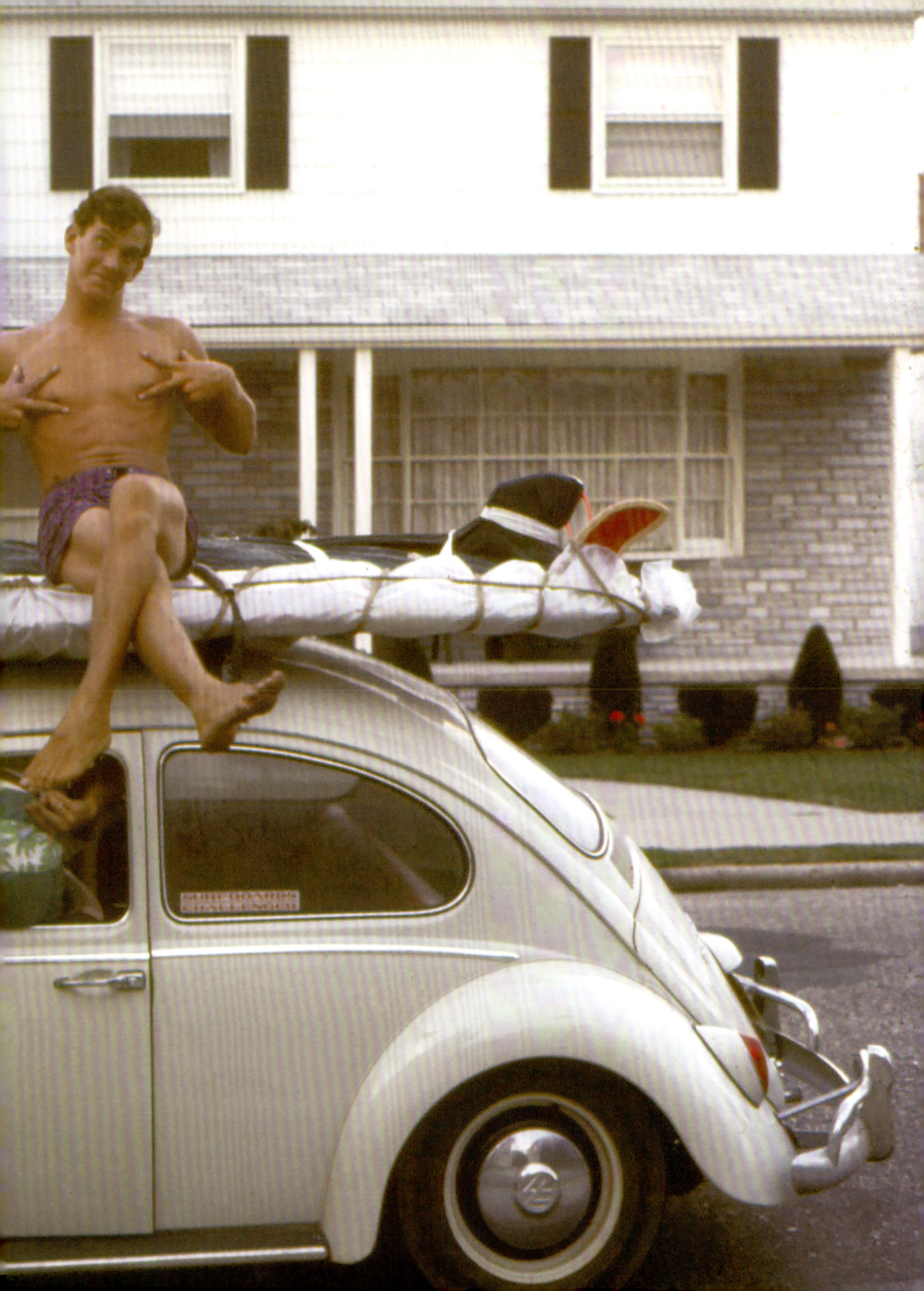

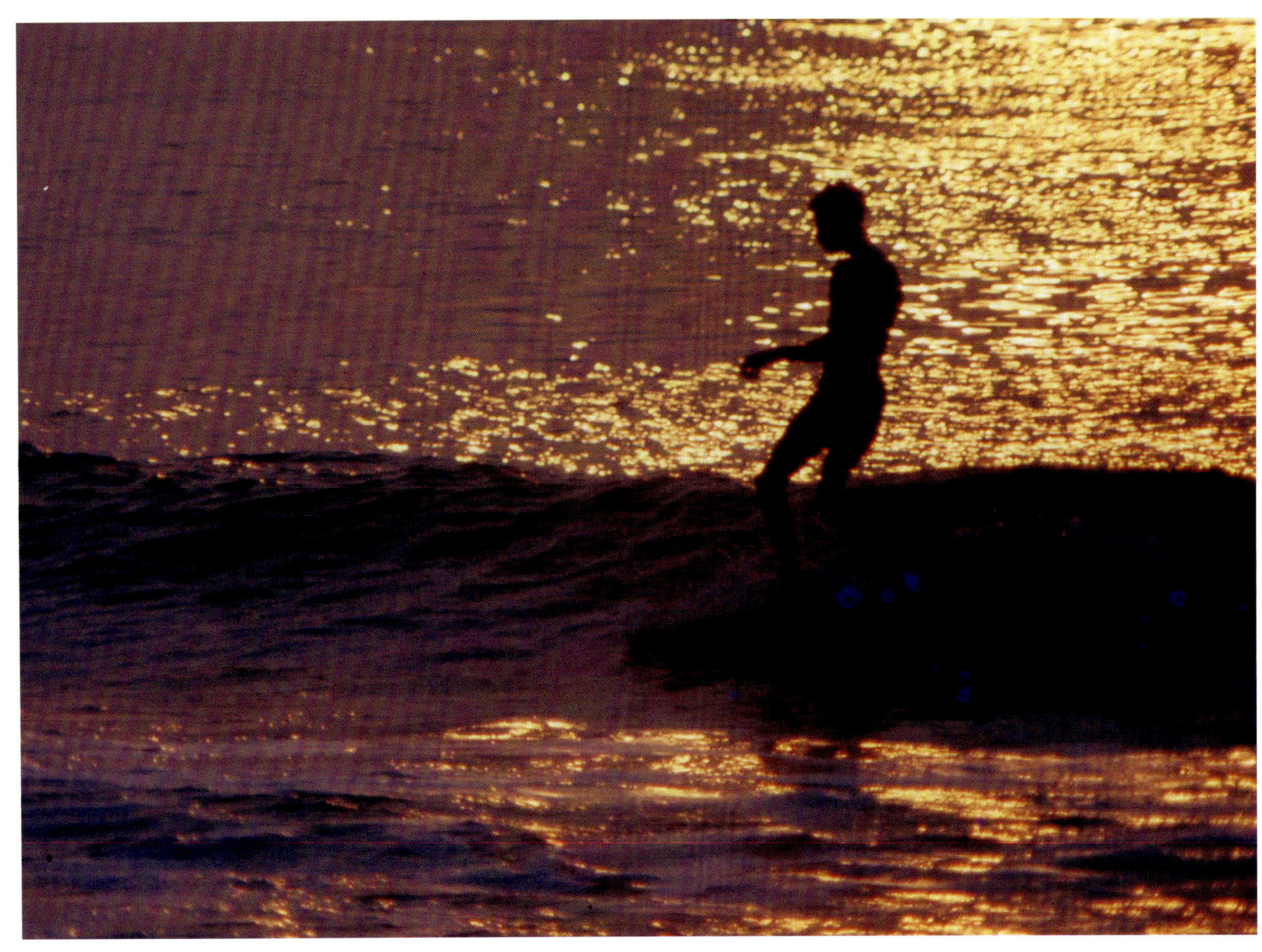

JULY 1966

Sunrise on the East Coast can create wonderful colors.

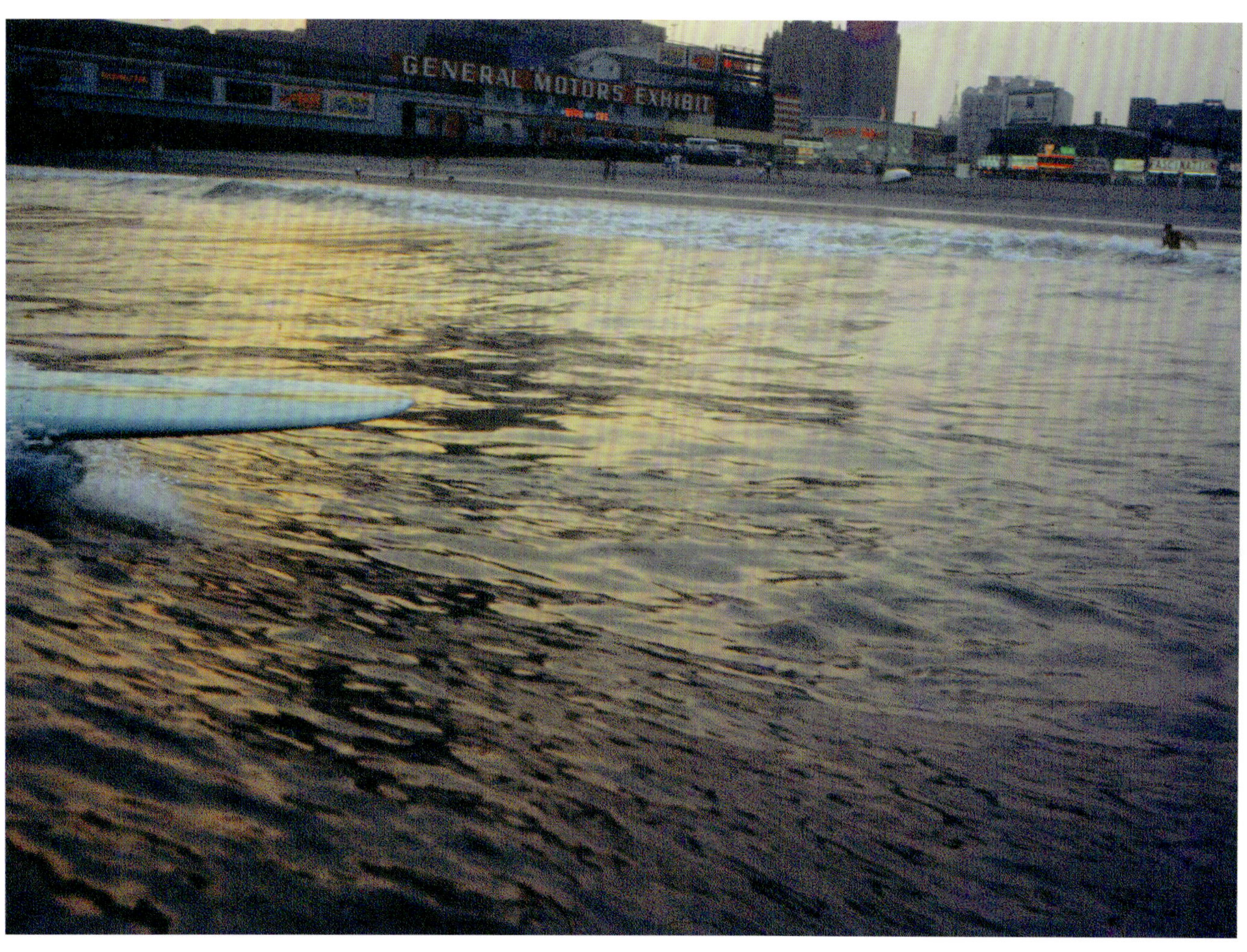

STEEL PIER, STATES AVENUE, ATLANTIC CITY, NJ

Warm water, sun going down, getting every last wave.

AUGUST 1967. VENTNOR PIER, NJ

Looking toward Atlantic City—take note of the green slipcheck on the front of the surfboard of the surfer on the far right.

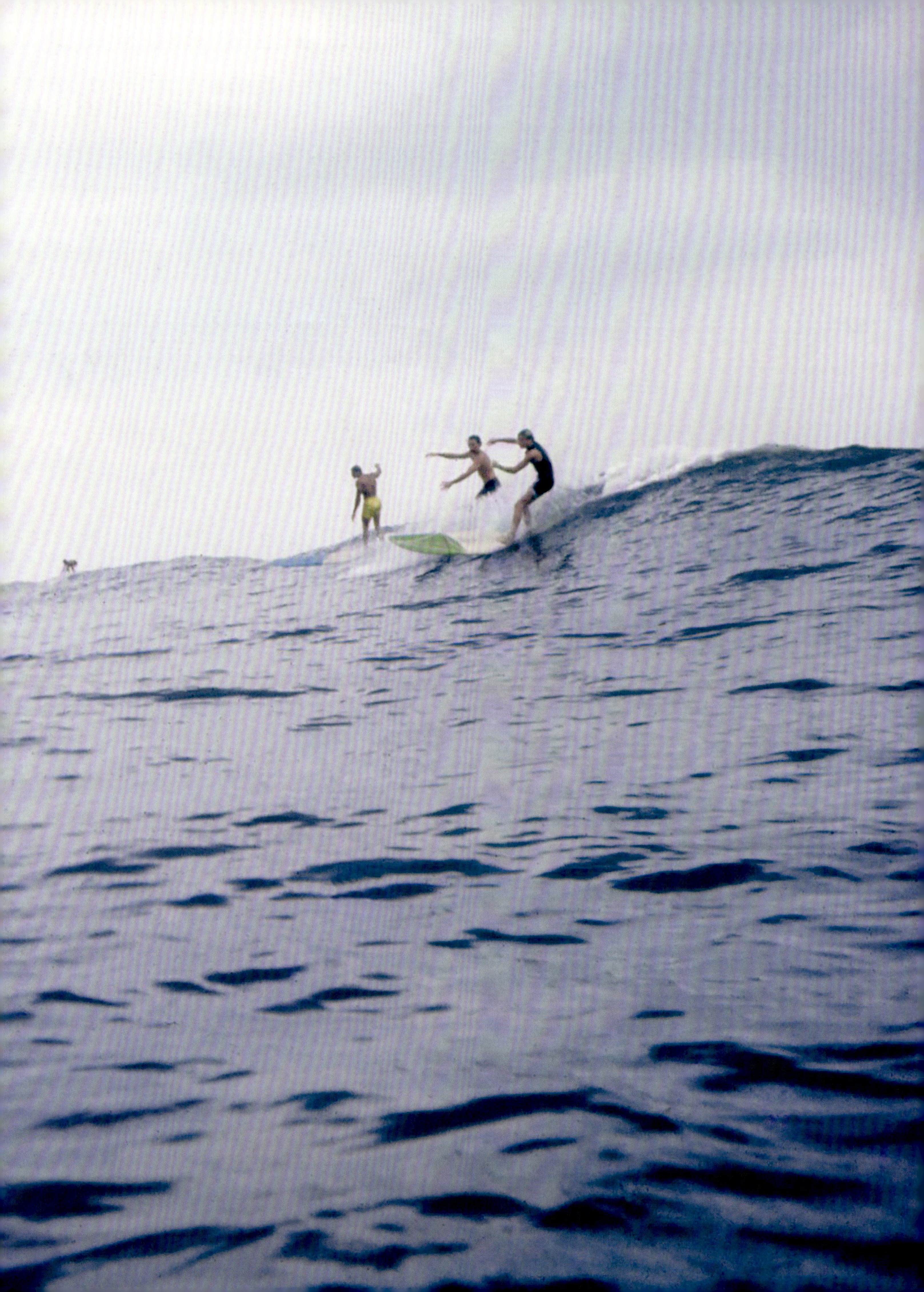

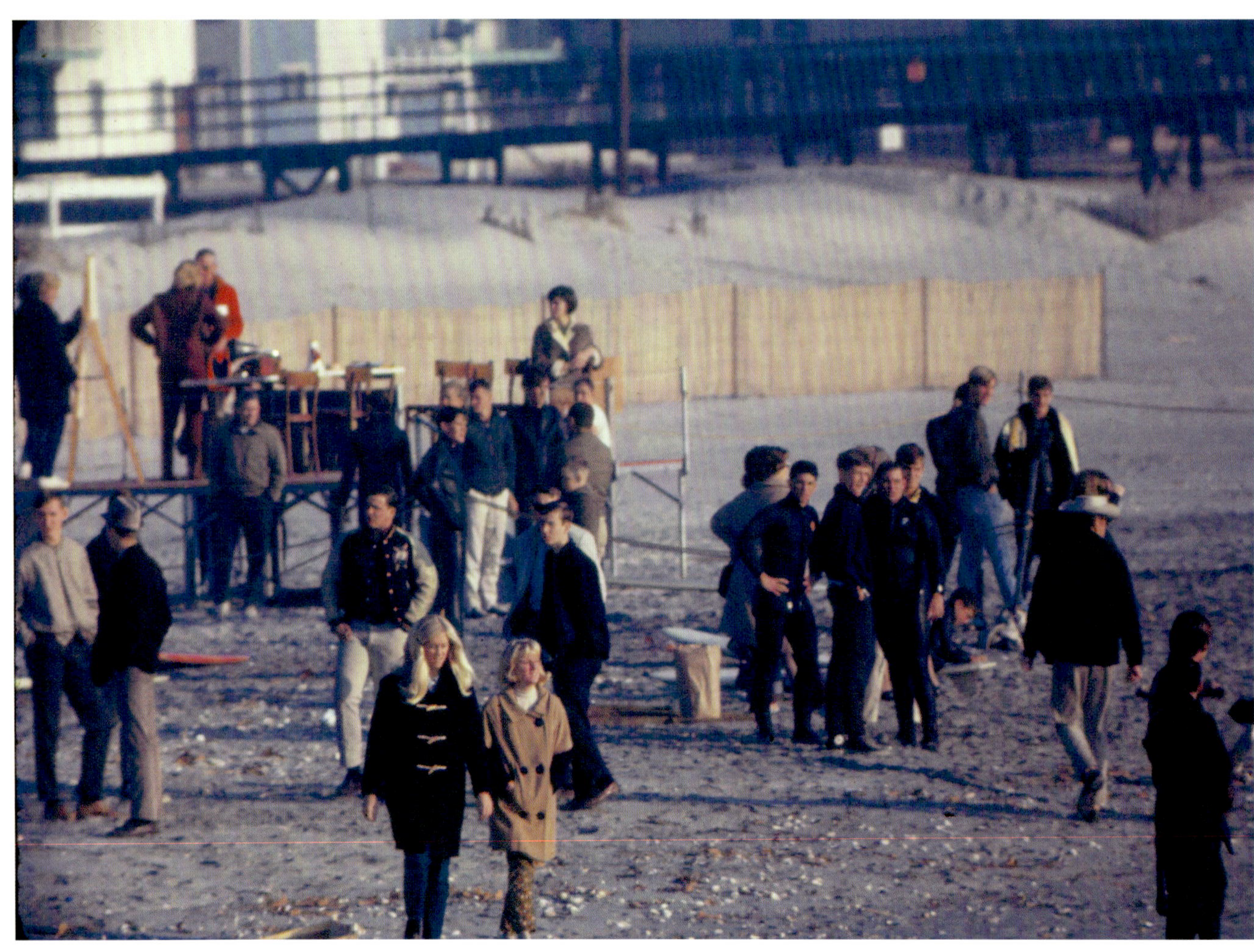

NOVEMBER 1966. TURKEY TROT CONTEST, OCEAN CITY, NJ

Ocean City, New Jersey, had George Gerlach, the owner of Surfers Supplies, who helped get the city involved with surfing activities—they held regular contests and would rent you a space to show the early surfing movies. Doug Fiske was one of the early film presenters.

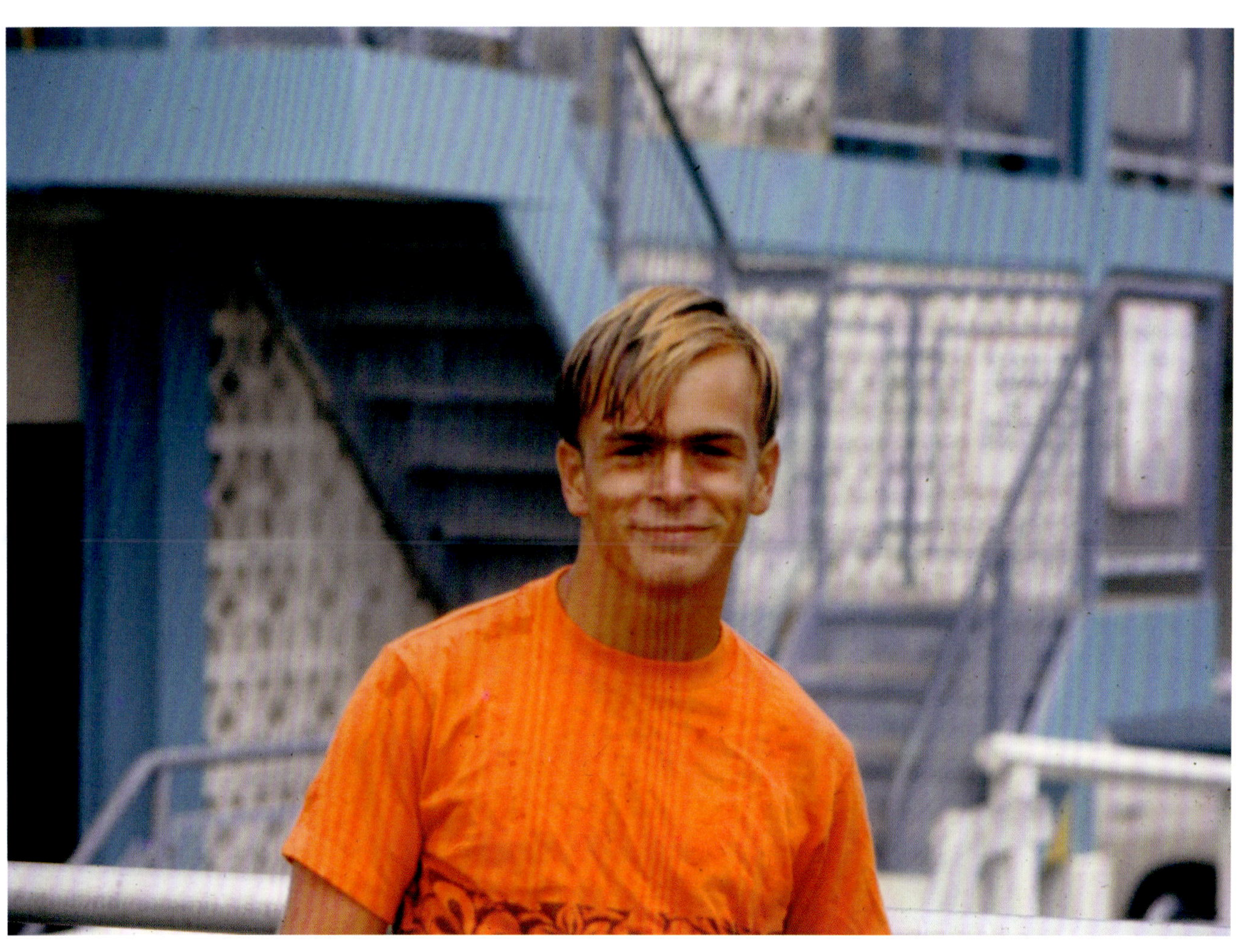

SUMMER 1967. MICHAEL SYKES, VENTNOR PIER, NJ

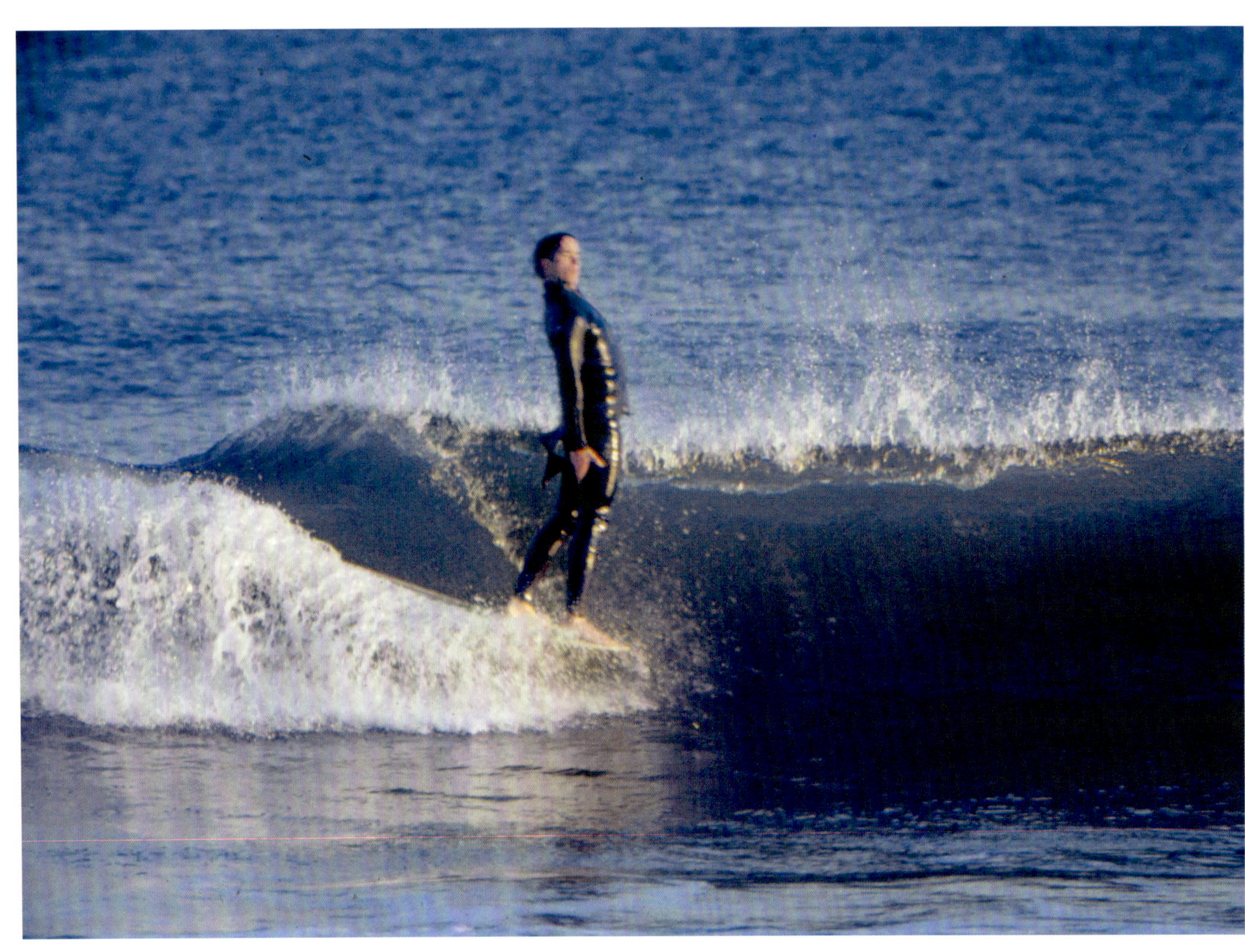

NOVEMBER 1967. DENNIS “GATOR” GALLAGHER, STATES AVENUE, ATLANTIC CITY, NJ

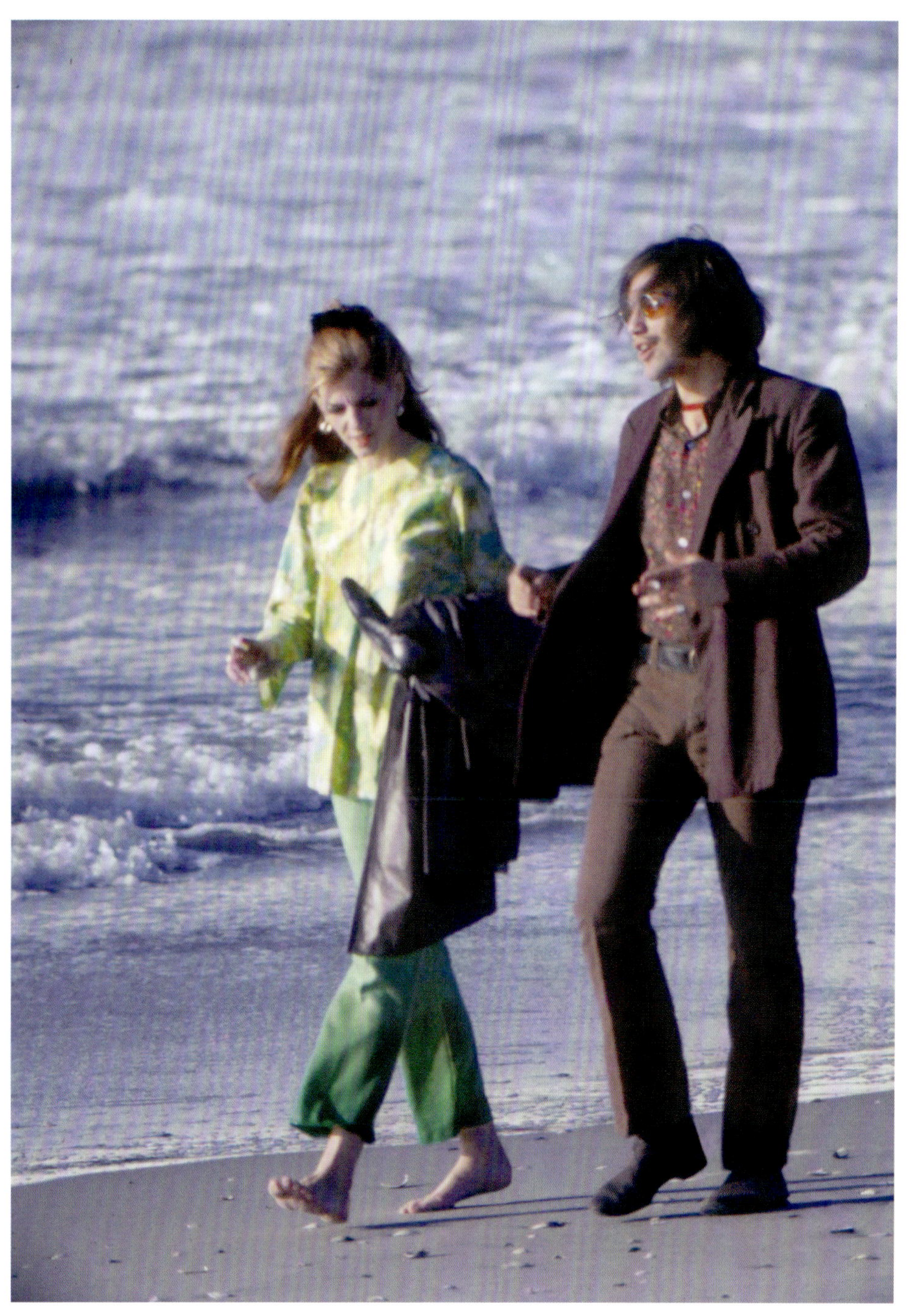

AUGUST 1967. STATES AVENUE, ATLANTIC CITY, NJ

East Coast hippies or leftover beatniks, shortly after I learned what all-nighters were. I recall in the early summer of '69 driving with Mike Beschen and Bob Sergeant from Newport Beach, California, to Atlantic City, New Jersey, arriving at 5 a.m., waiting for the sun to come up, and going directly in the water at States Avenue.

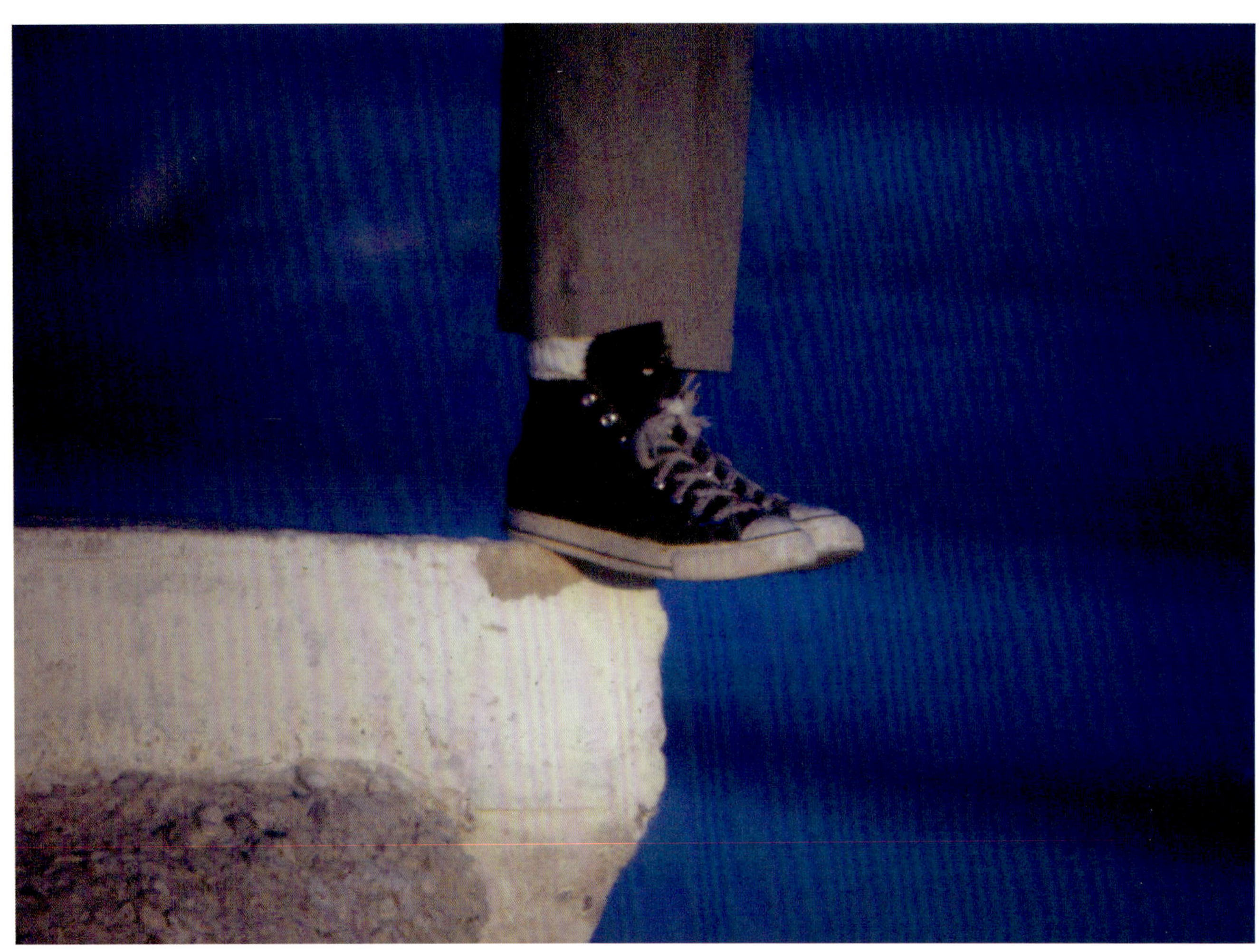

FEBRUARY 1968. JOEY SYKES, KENYON AVENUE, MARGATE, NJ

Bulkhead in front of Fred Webber's house.

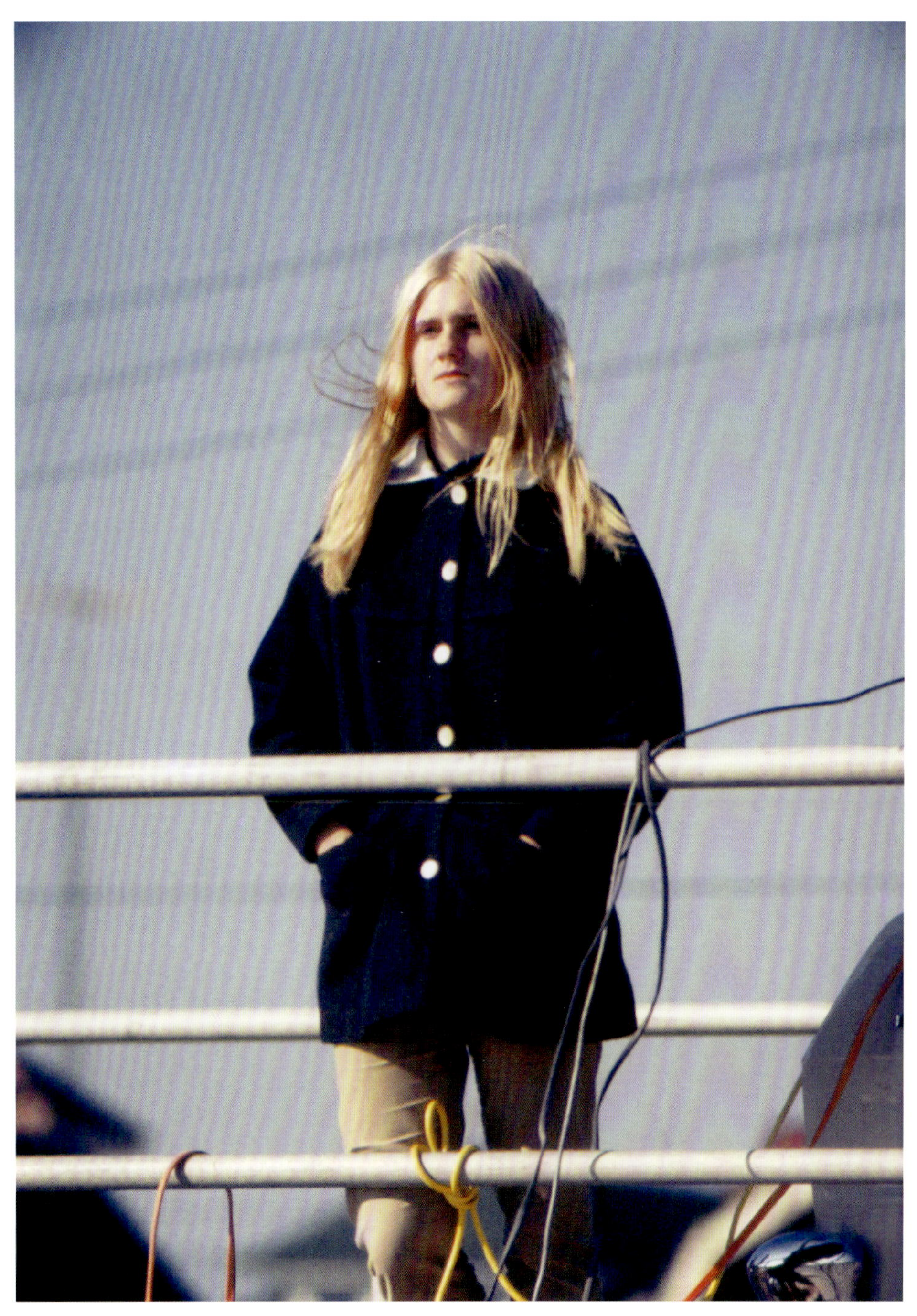

NOVEMBER 1967. 15TH STREET, OCEAN CITY, NJ

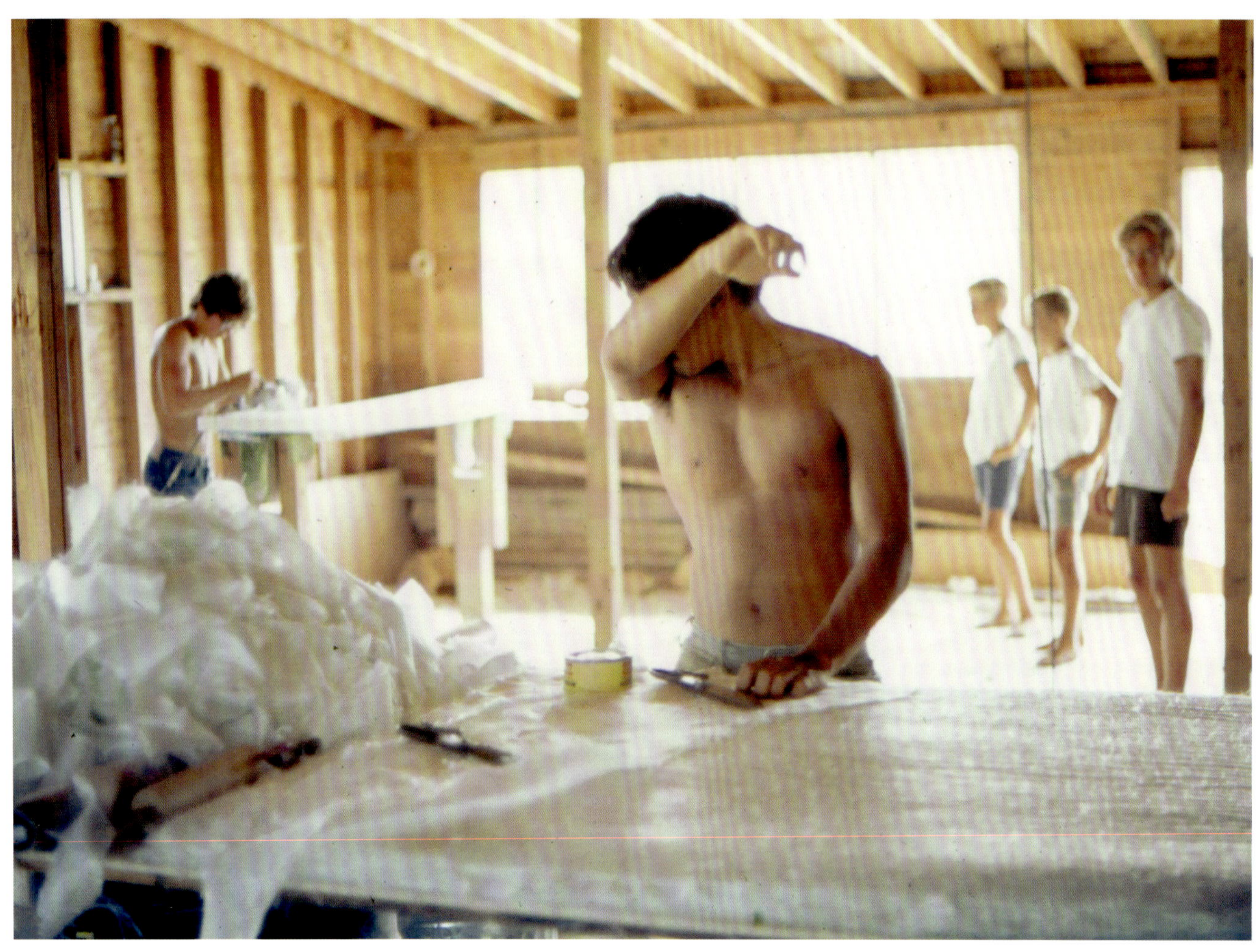

AUGUST 1968. CHALLENGER EAST SURFBOARD FACTORY, ASBURY PARK, NJ

An 18-year-old Michel Junod shaping boards at the Challenger East Factory.
Jack Snider, Enos Magill, Bob Sergeant, and Mike Beschen standing by post.

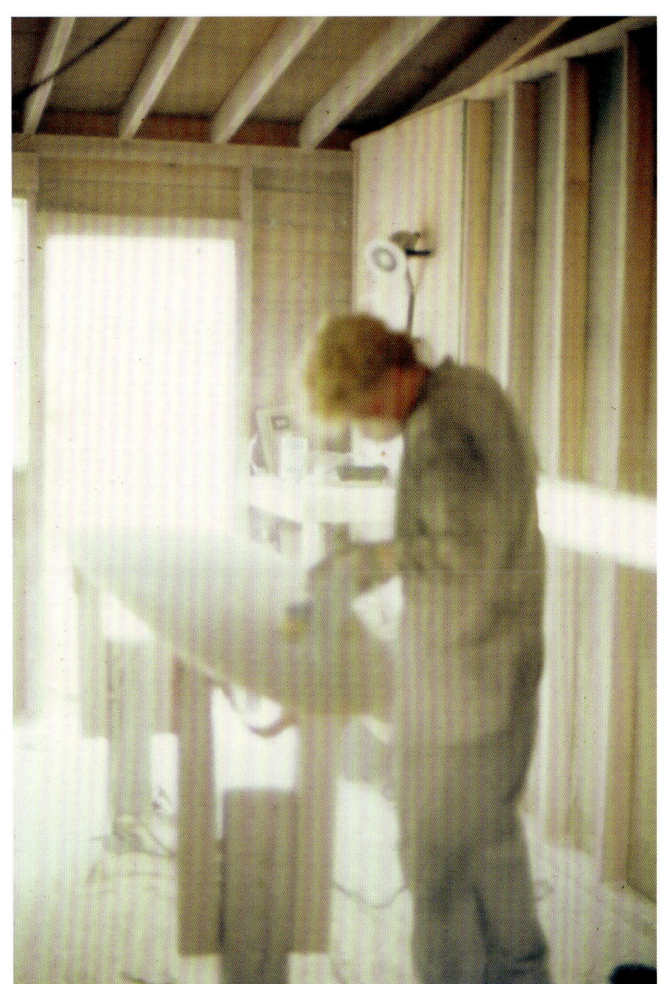
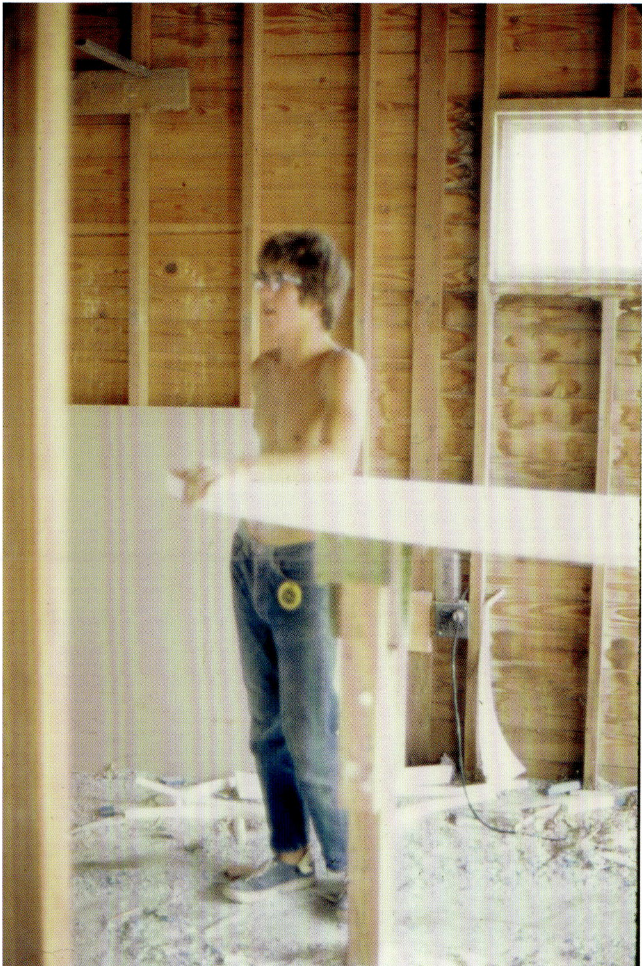

AUGUST 1968. CHALLENGER EAST SURFBOARD FACTORY, ASBURY PARK, NJ

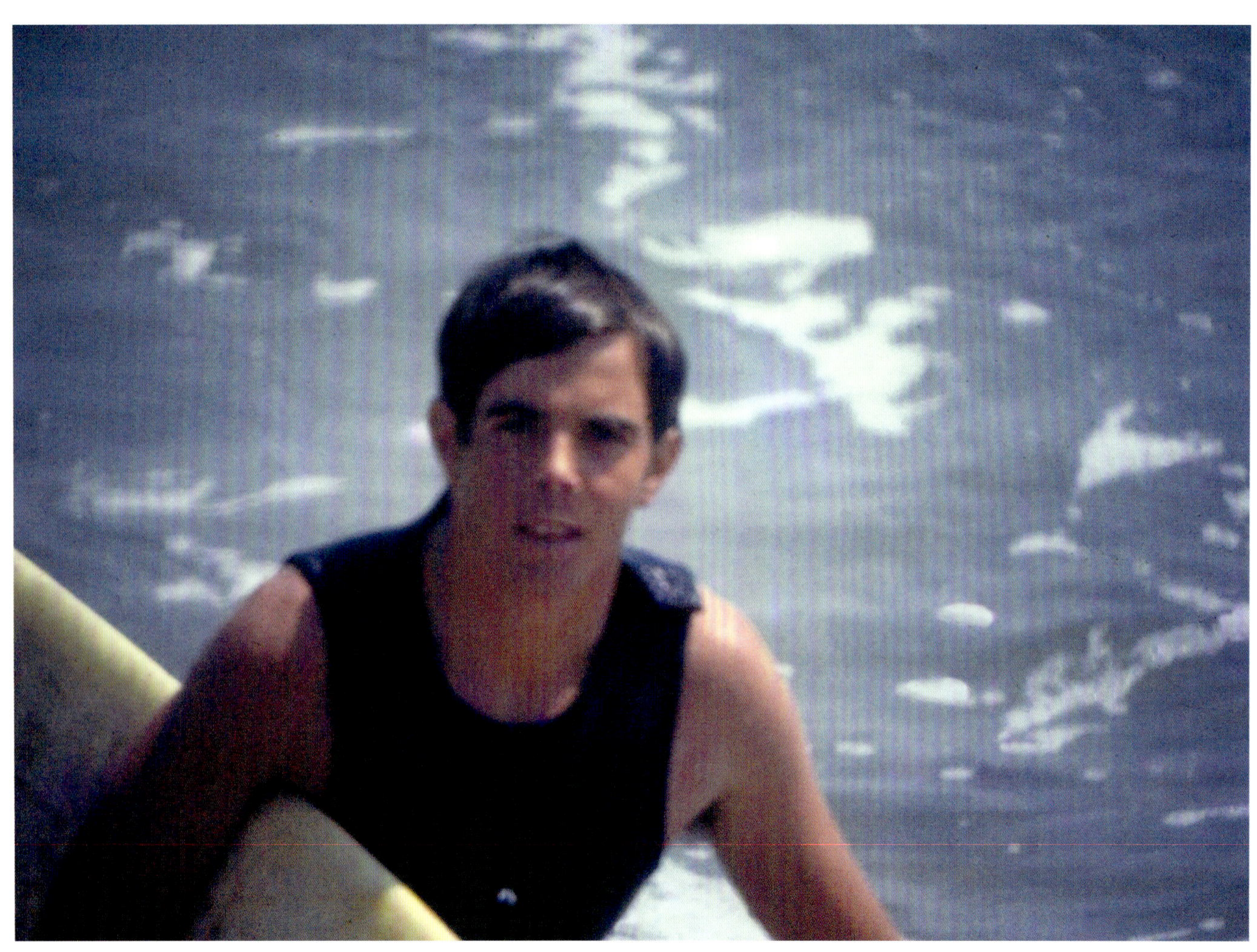

MAY 1968. JOEY SYKES

An Atlantic City lifeguard who ran the rookie school for many years.

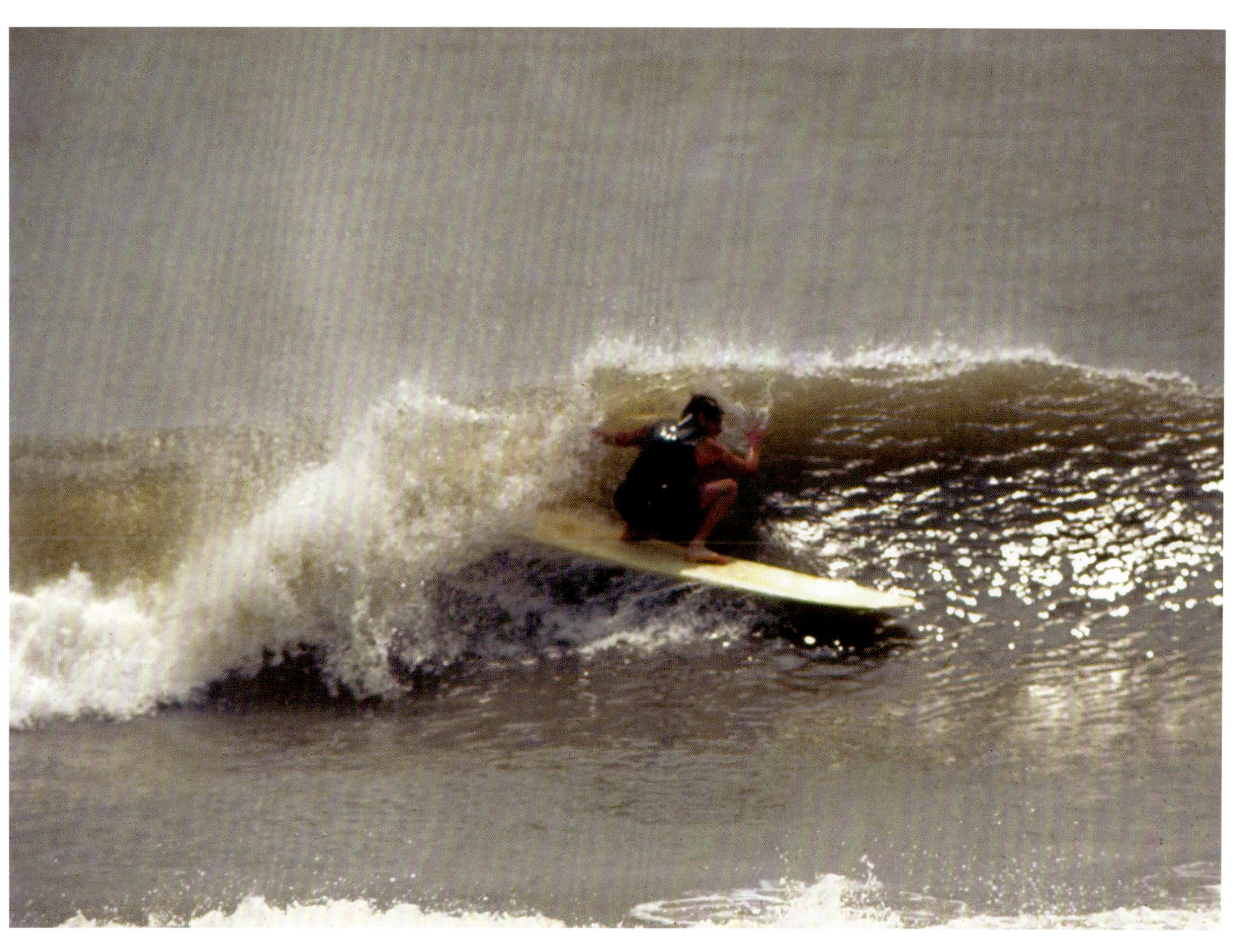

MAY 1968. JOEY SYKES, STATES AVENUE, ATLANTIC CITY, NJ

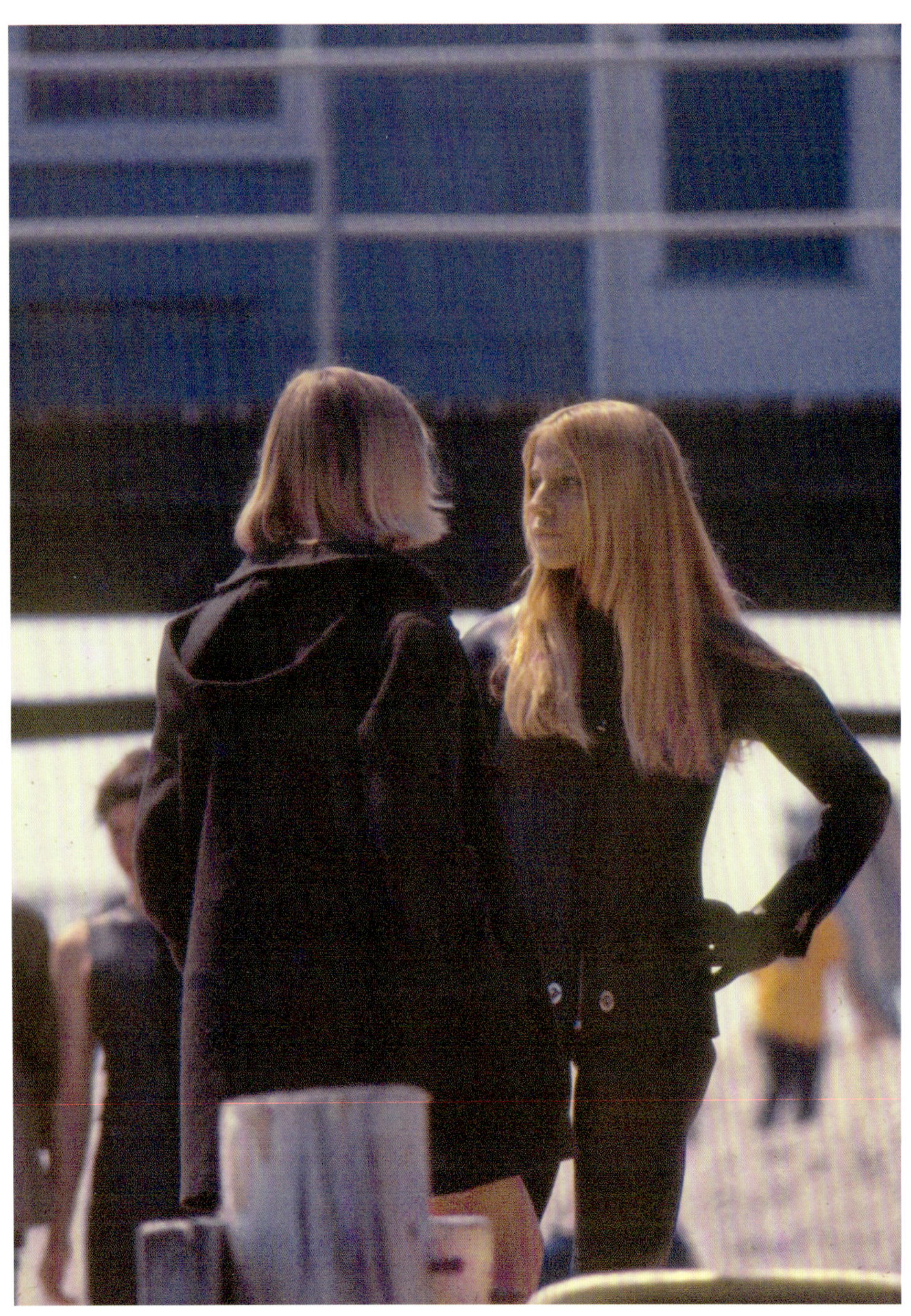

1968. POLLY WILKINSON, OCEAN CITY SPRING FLING CONTEST, OCEAN CITY, NJ

Polly Wilkinson is wearing a deep-sea diver suit. Note the flap from the top went under, and the metal twist pins went through a metal grommet and turned to lock. It was very uncomfortable to lay down and paddle. Good thing the boards were big enough to knee paddle.

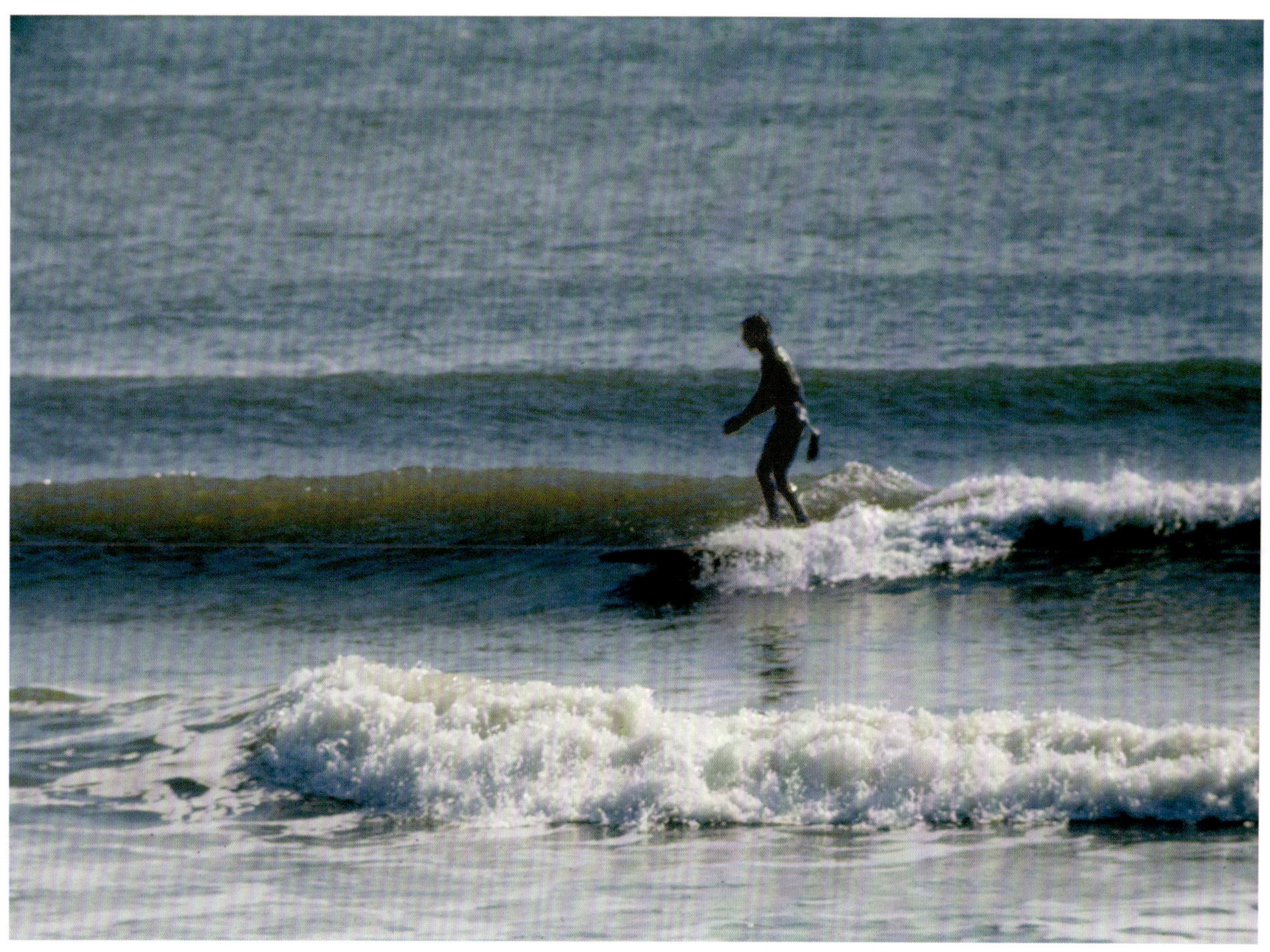

JANUARY 1967. OCEAN CITY, NJ

Glenn Klotz in full winter gear—we bought our wetsuits from Captain Ira's in the Atlantic City back bay commercial fishing and barge section—it was divers' gear. We bought glue there too and made a lot of repairs as needed.

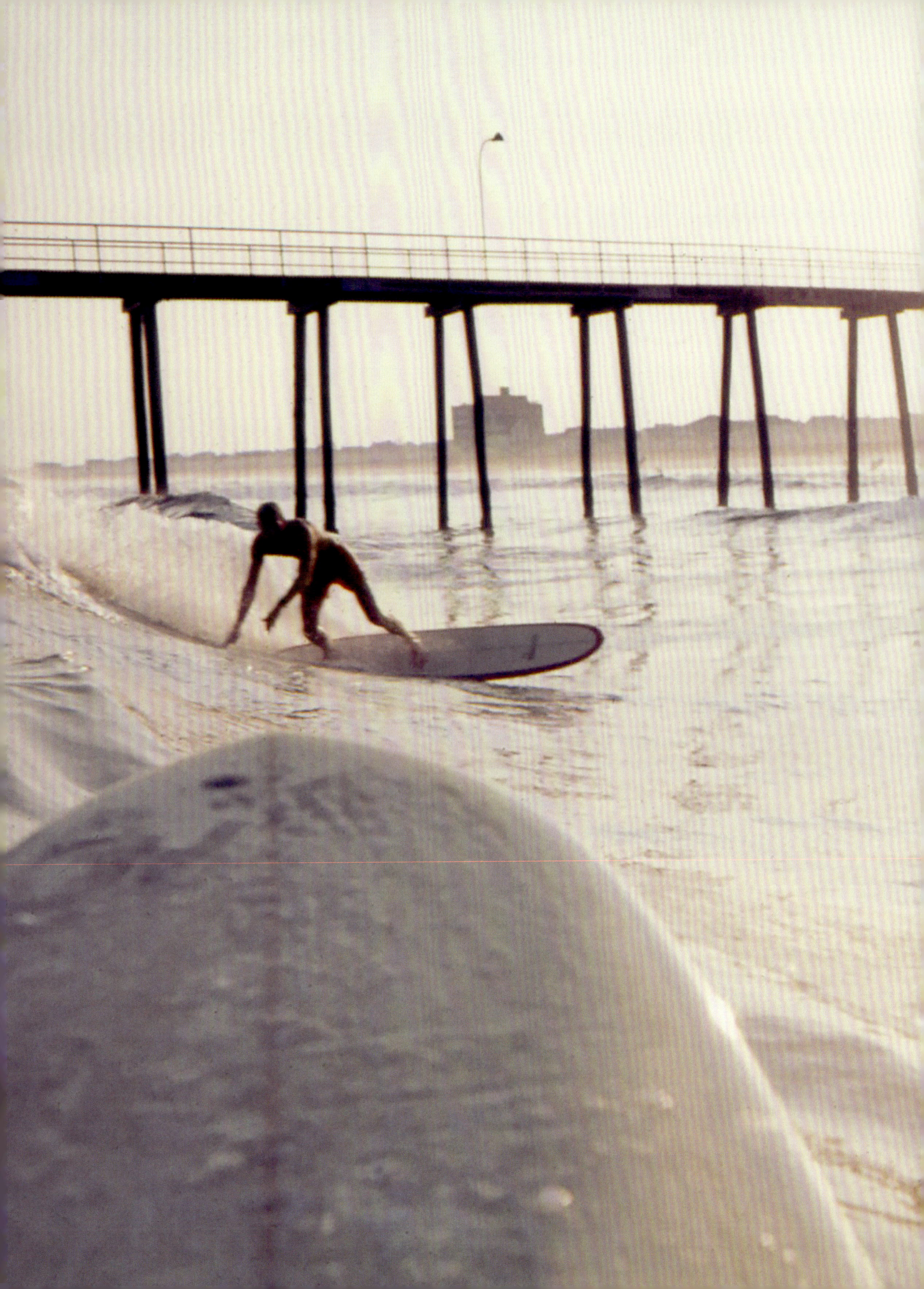

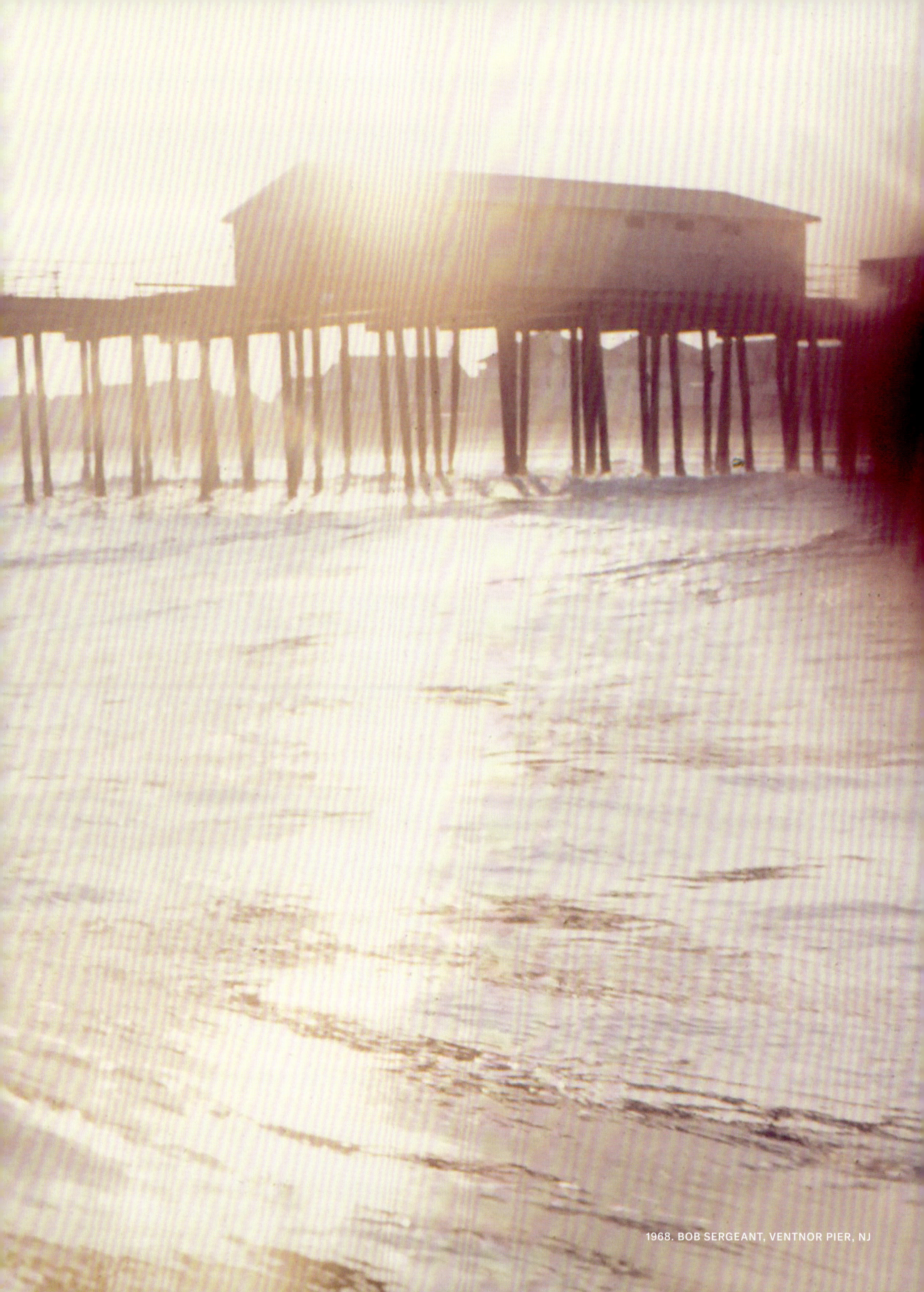

1968. BOB SERGEANT, VENTNOR PIER, NJ

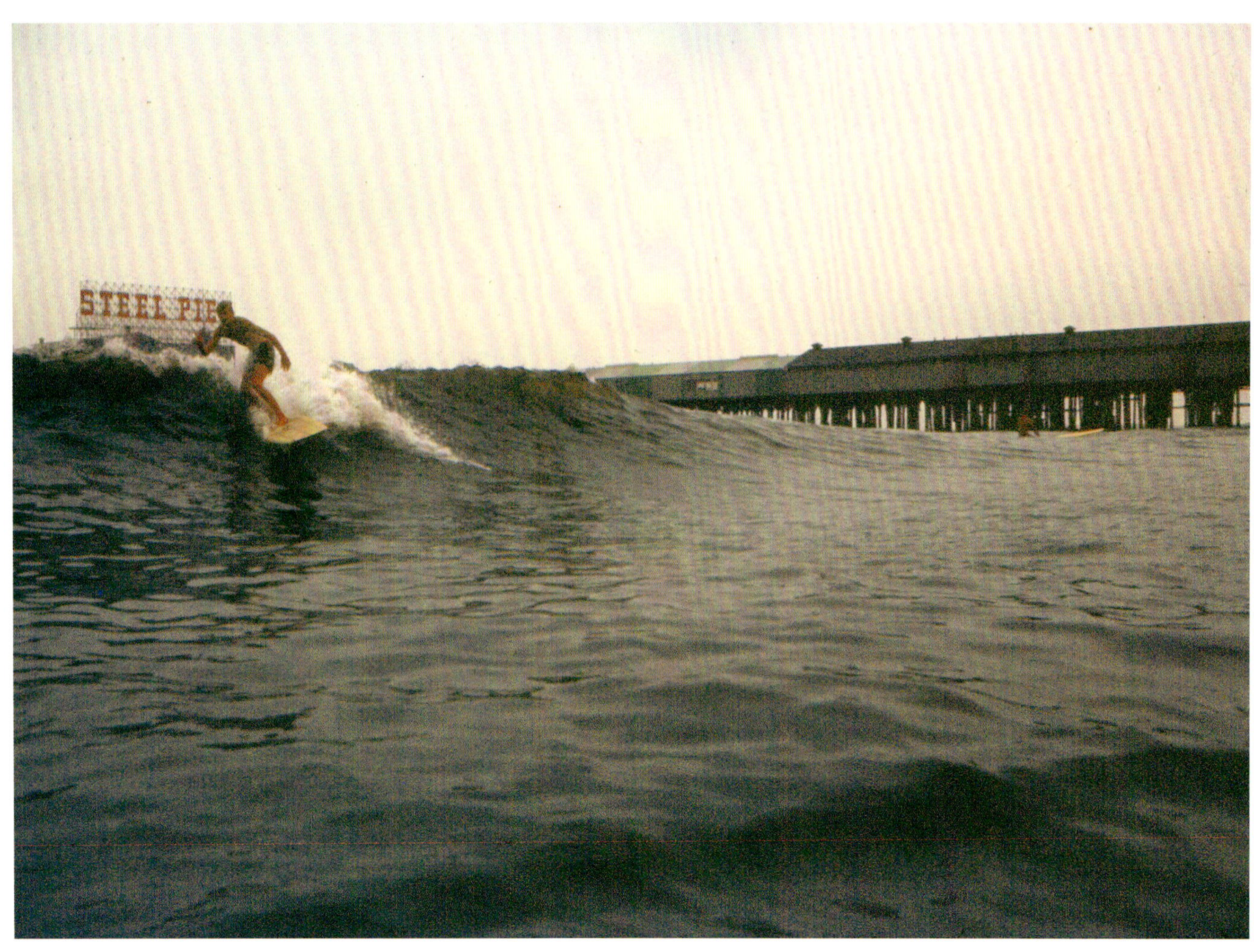

STEEL PIER, ATLANTIC CITY, NJ

Atlantic City Steel Pier with the General Motors car display: the diving horse show and American Bandstand were broadcast from there.

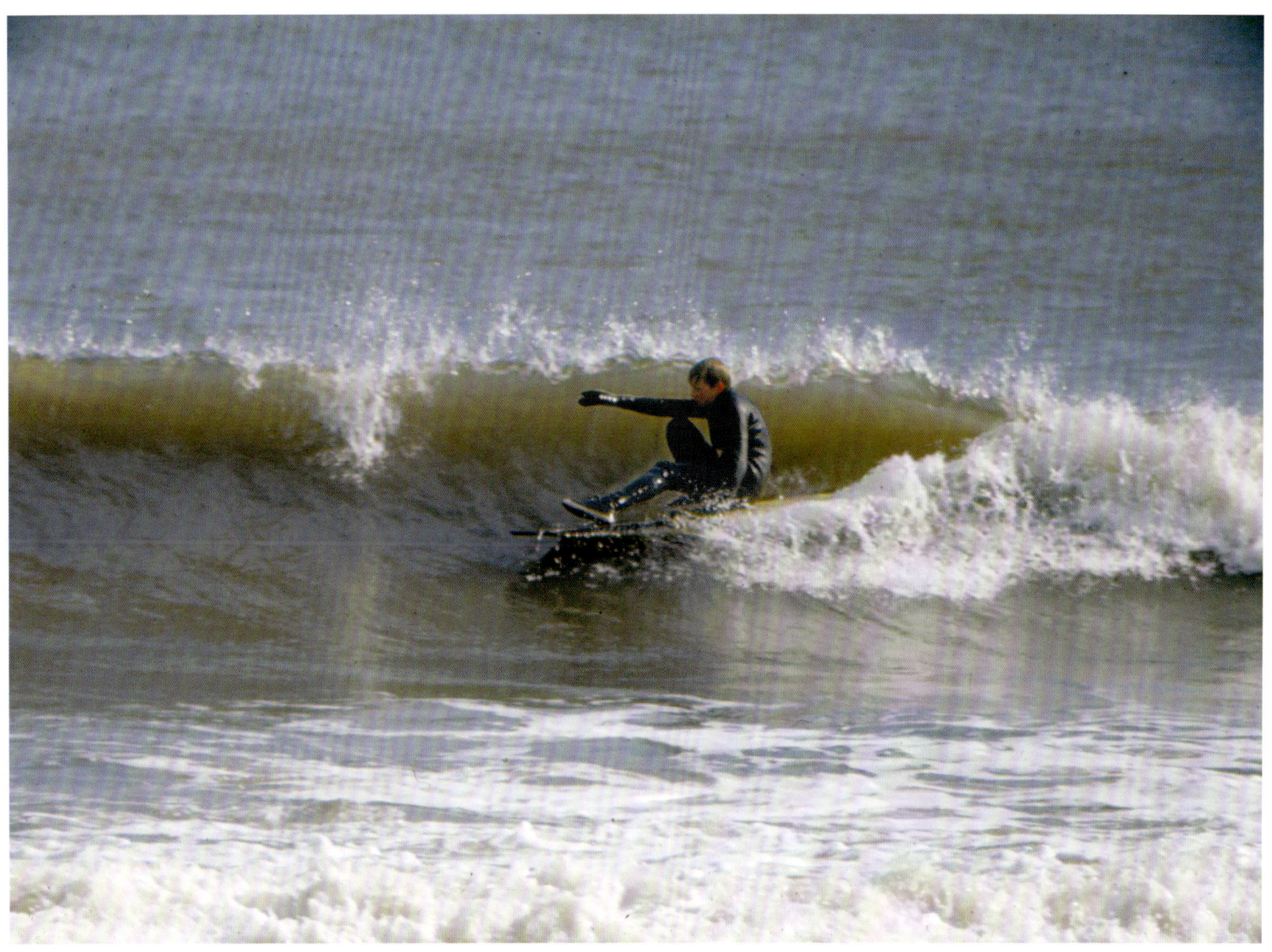

APRIL 1966. ATLANTIC CITY, NJ

Bob Sergeant with rubberized Converse over his diving socks. There were the Purcell people like Klotz and the Converse people like Sergeant. These were the two basic sneakers of the day.

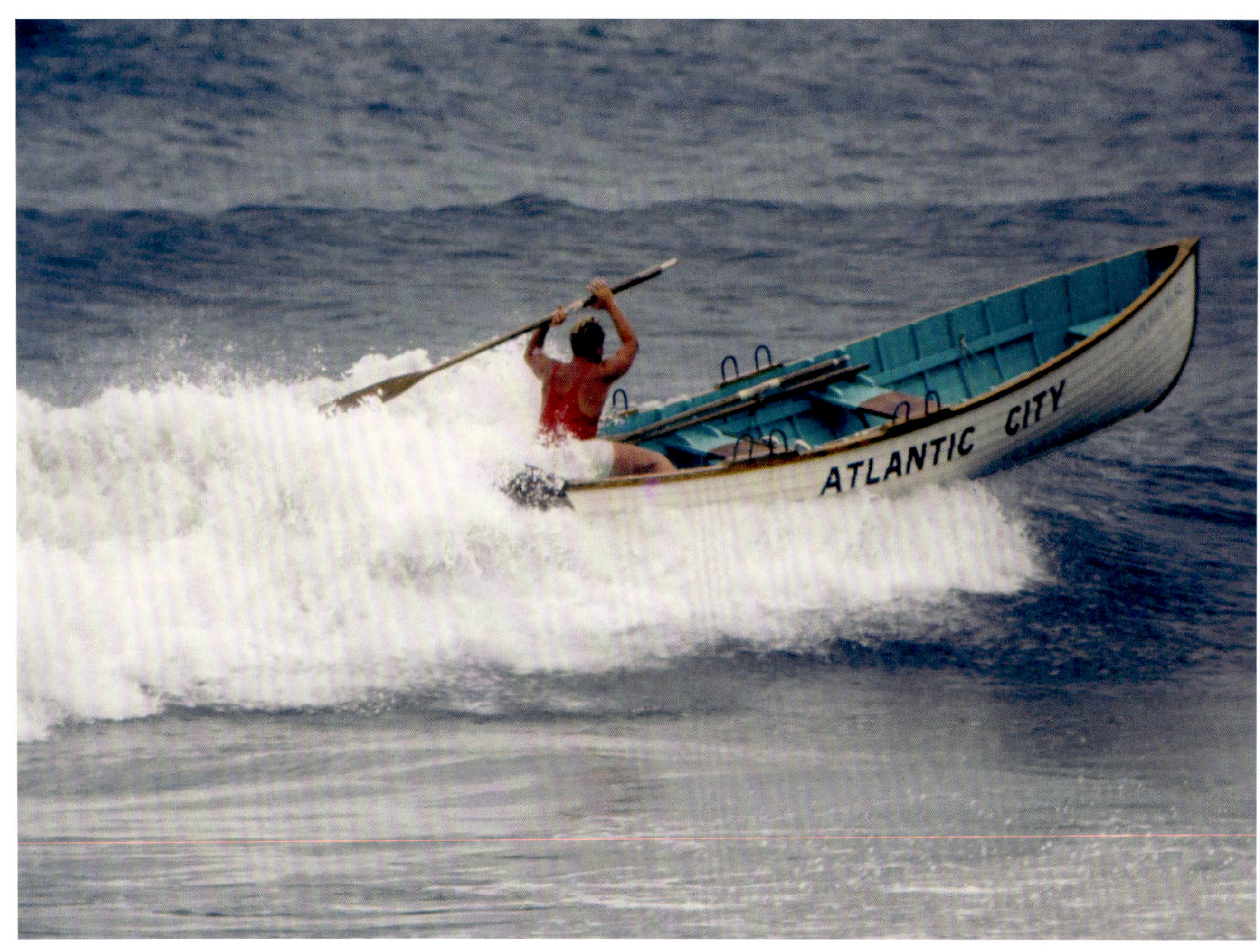

BOBBY YATES, STATES AVENUE, ATLANTIC CITY, NJ

Bobby Yates, lifeguard at States Avenue, one of the greatest guards at shooting seas. That is a wooden boat that could get out through big seas if you had power like he did.

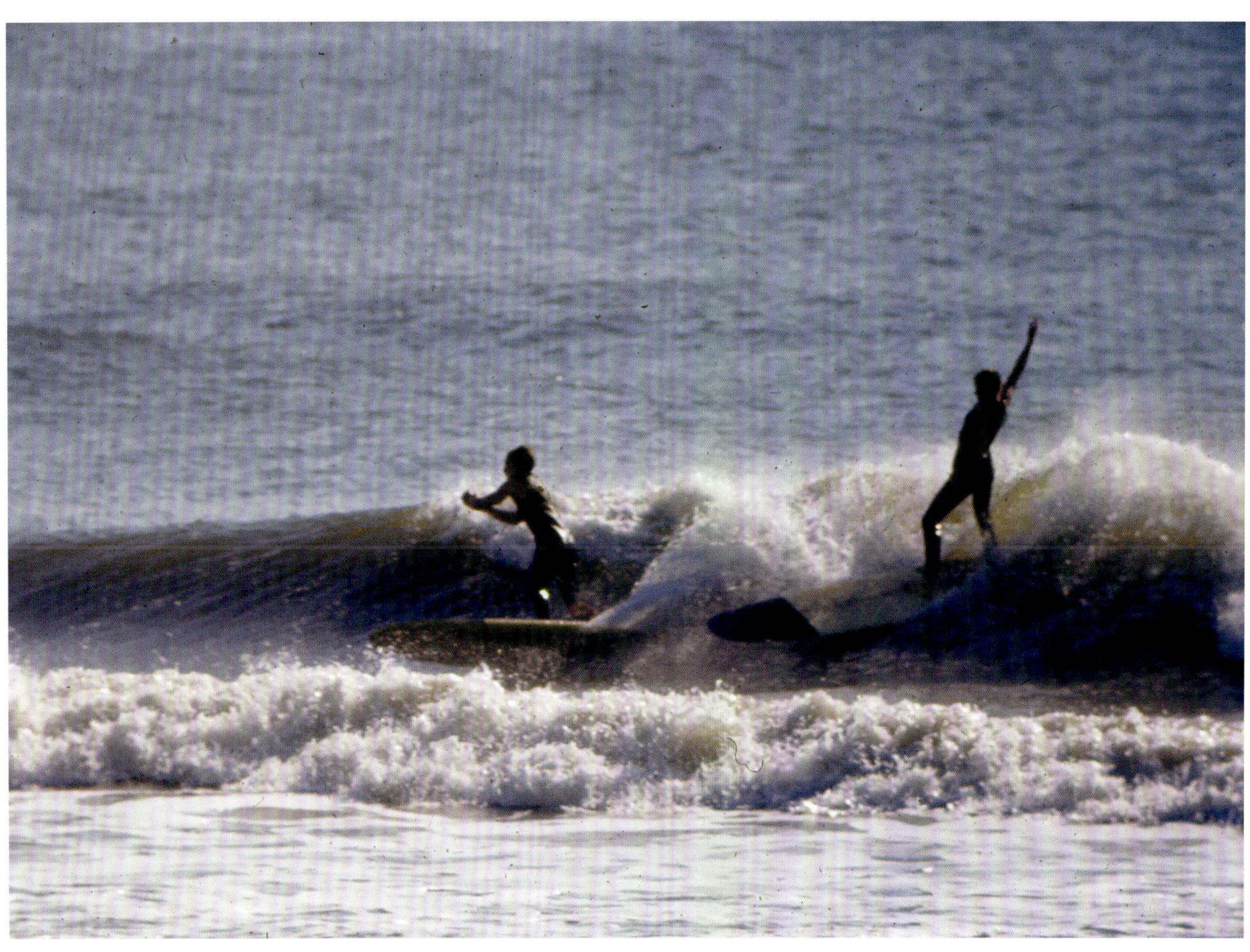

BRUCE DOUGHERTY, BRIGANTINE, NJ

Bruce Dougherty dropping in on Mike Beschen.
Check out the slipcheck on the nose of the surfboard; everyone was using it.

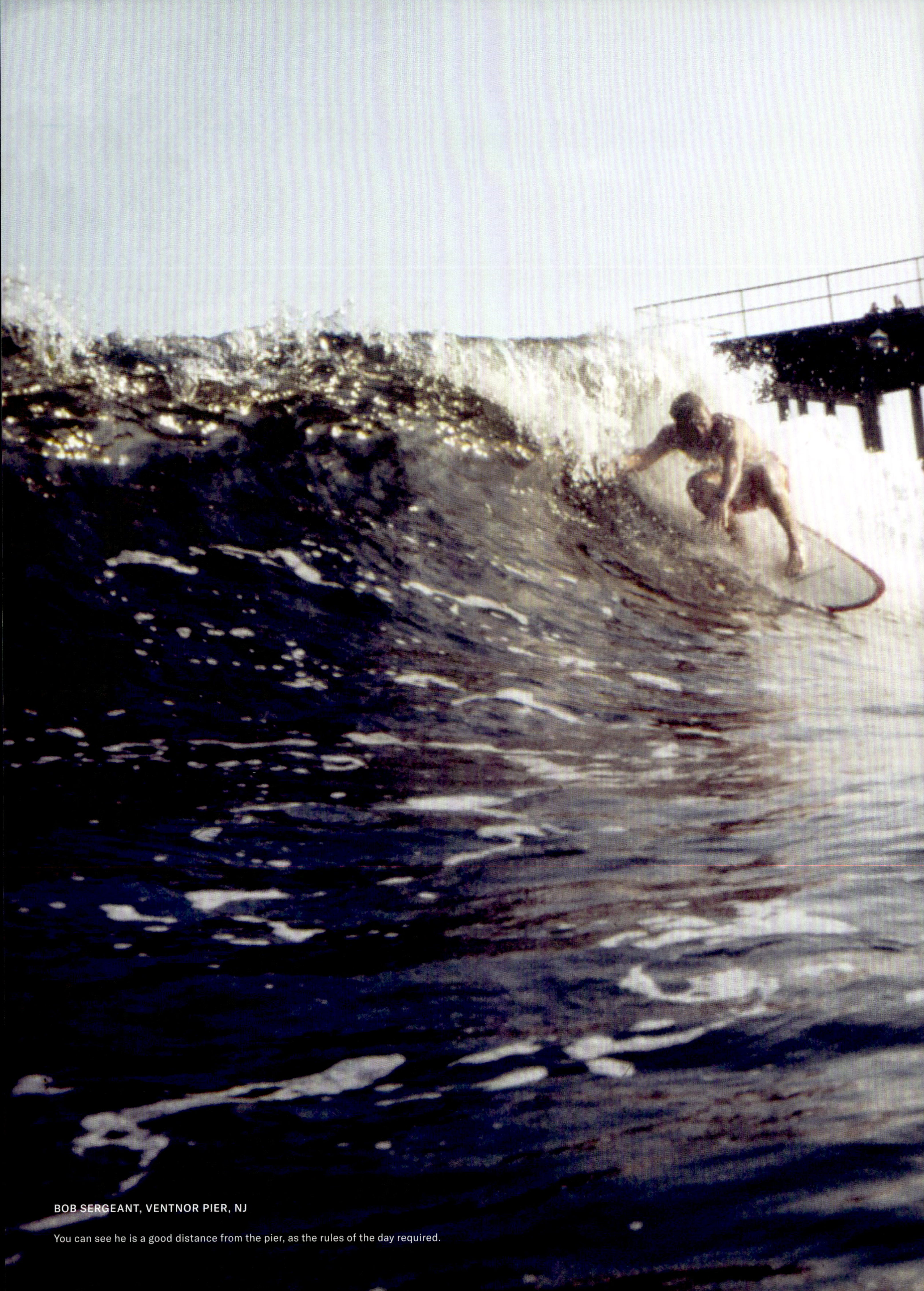

BOB SERGEANT, VENTNOR PIER, NJ

You can see he is a good distance from the pier, as the rules of the day required.

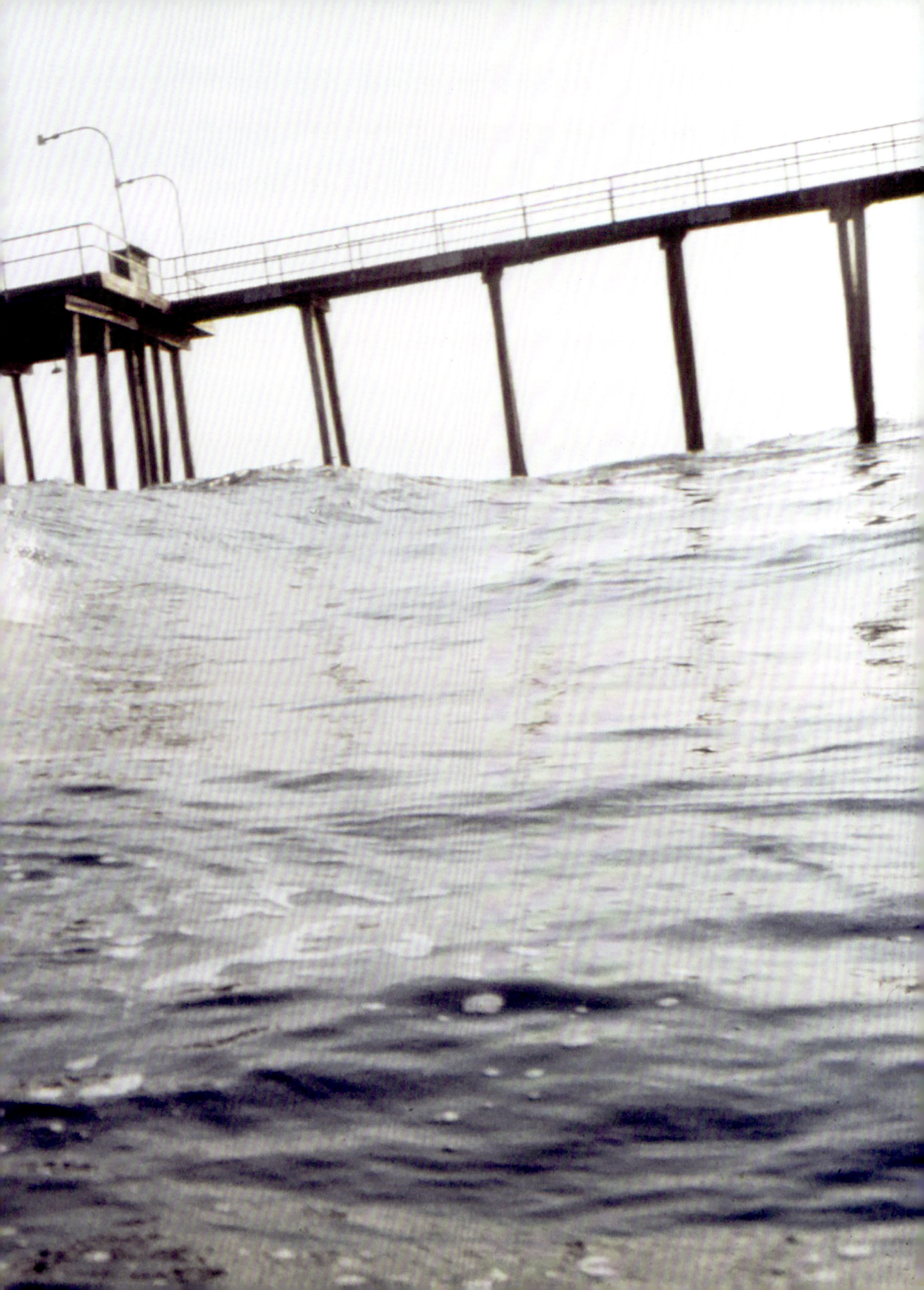

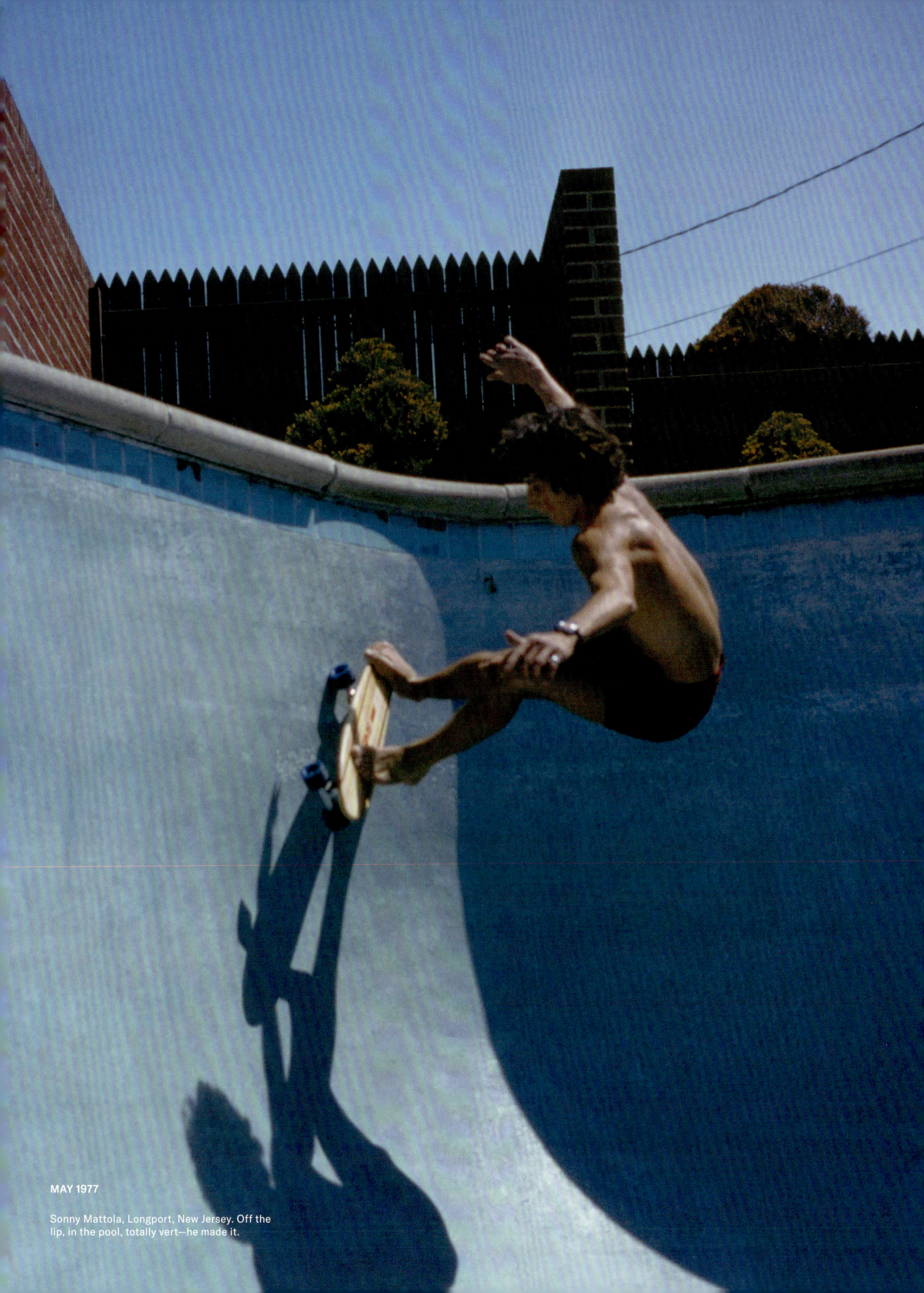

MAY 1977

Sonny Mattola, Longport, New Jersey. Off the lip, in the pool, totally vert—he made it.

MARK NEUSTADTER

MY PARENTS MOVED TO A BEACHFRONT HOME IN MARGATE, A SLEEPY TOWN WITH GORGEOUS BEACHES AND GOOD WAVES, WHEN I WAS EIGHT YEARS OLD. I BEGAN SURFING ON A BOARD GIFTED BY MY PARENTS FOR MY BAR MITZVAH. AROUND THE SAME TIME, I WAS GIFTED MY FIRST CAMERA, A SUPER 8, AND BEGAN FILMING MY FRIENDS RIDING WAVES.

I BECAME A LIFEGUARD at my local beach during high school. I began to compete in local surfing contests up and down the Jersey coast, and eventually in the Eastern Surfing Association championships. I was hired by Australia's wetsuit manufacturer Rip Curl in the late 1970s to help establish the business in the USA. Through these years, I photographed surfing action and everyday surfing life. I had access to Rip Curl's world-class surfers, including Wayne Lynch and World Champions Nat Young, Tom Carroll, Rabbit Bartholomew, and Tom Curren. This access gave me the opportunity to take many of my favorite candid photographs. I also dabbled in commercial photography through Rip Curl's global print advertising campaigns as well as contributing to *Surfer*.

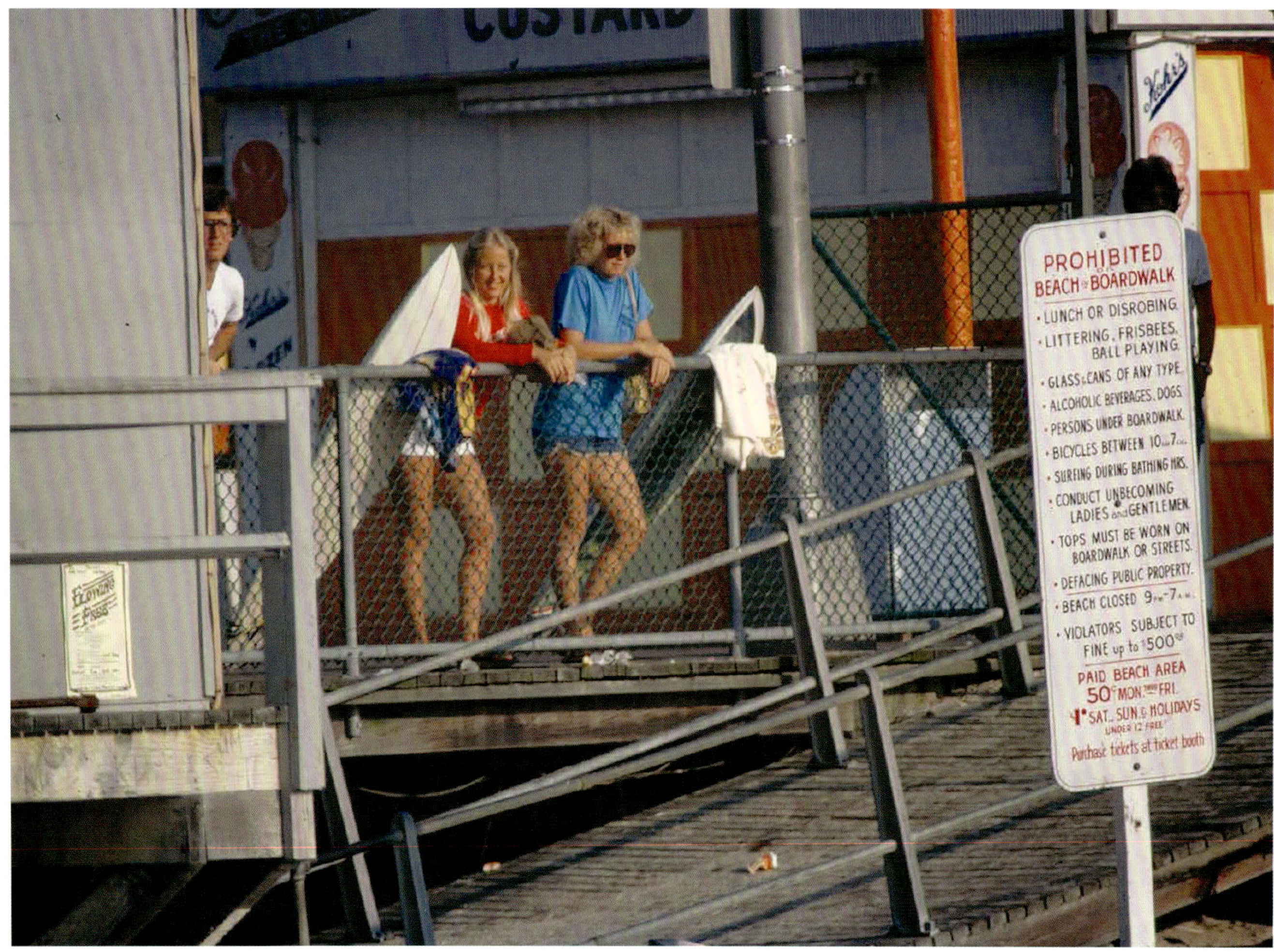

1978. GROG'S SEASIDE PRO CONTEST, SEASIDE HEIGHTS, NJ

Elaine Davis from St. Augustine, Florida, on the left standing next to Linda Davoli, the top women's surfer from New Jersey and world runner-up, late '70s.

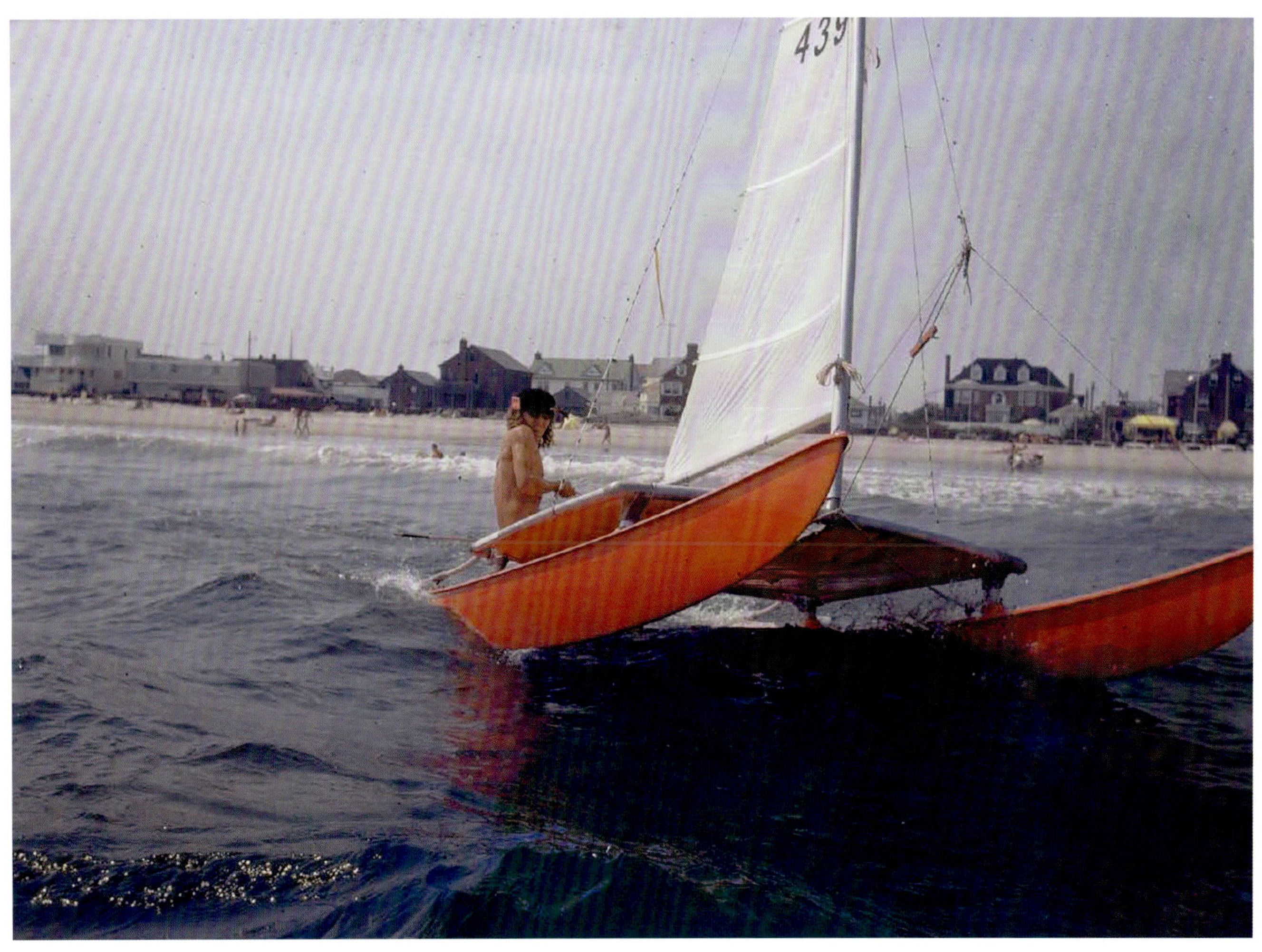

JULY 1975. MARGATE, NJ

Christopher Cook Gilmore of Margate, New Jersey, world traveler and American writer.

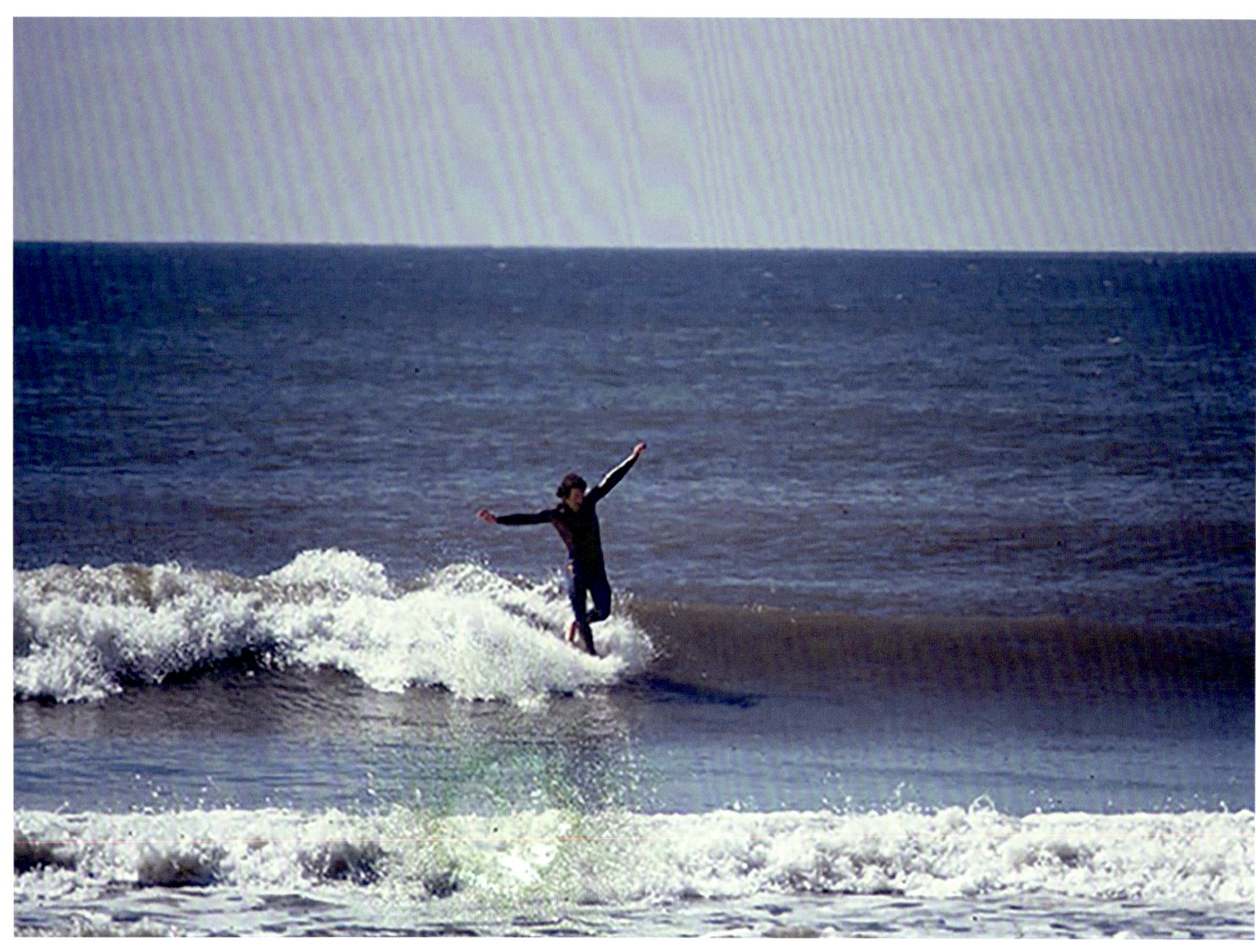

JULY 1977. MARGATE, NJ

Walking the board in front of my parents' house in Margate, New Jersey. I started getting back into longboards in the late '80s and early '90s when I competed on the world professional longboard tour, with surfing greats Nat Young, Joel Tudor, Randy Rarick, and a whole lot more. Photographed by Steve Alper.

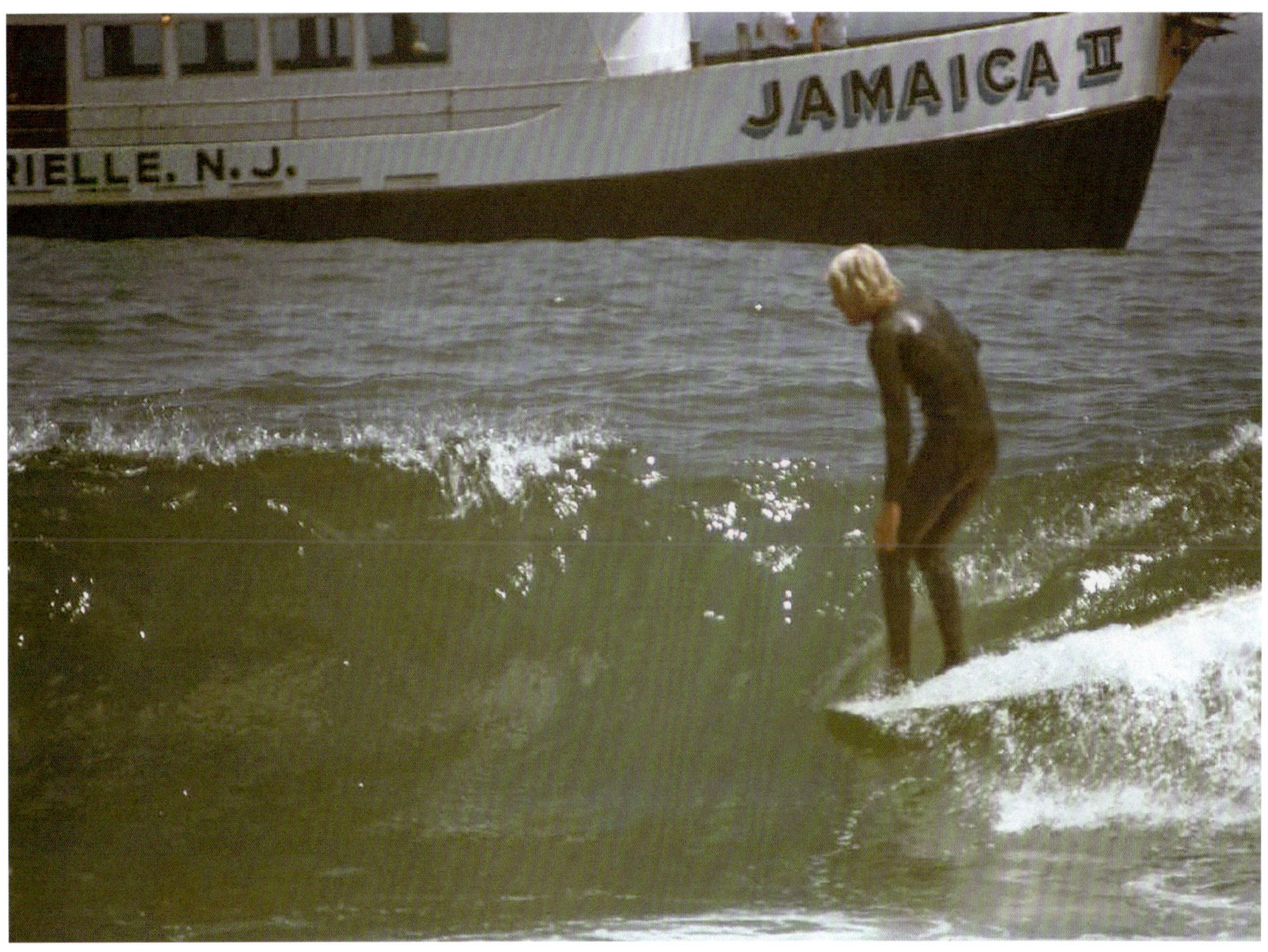

AUGUST 1978. SEASIDE HEIGHTS, NJ

David "DCB" Balzerack warming up for the Grog's Seaside Pro in Seaside Heights, New Jersey.

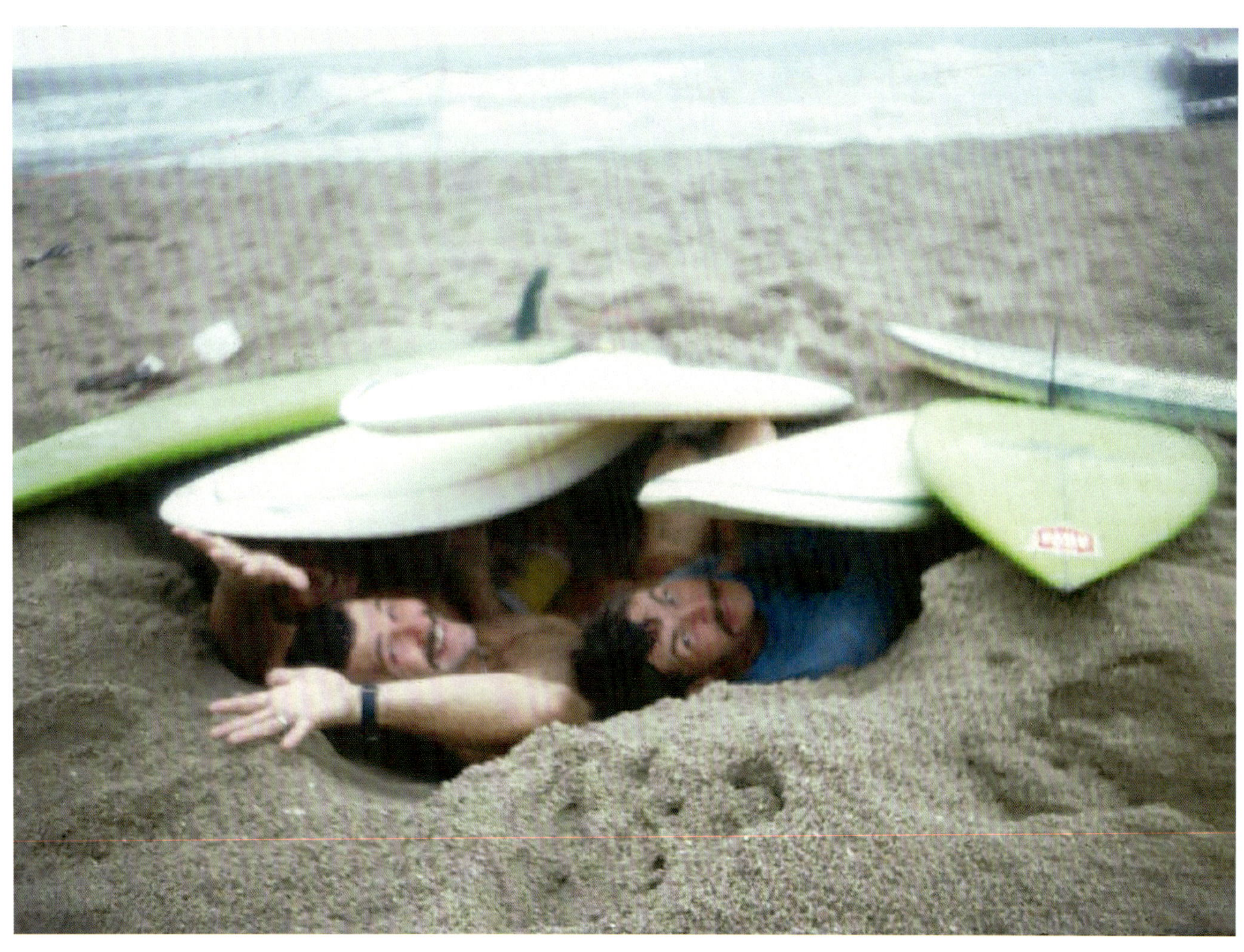

SUMMER 1978. SEASIDE HEIGHTS, NJ

Taking cover from a huge front that moved in.

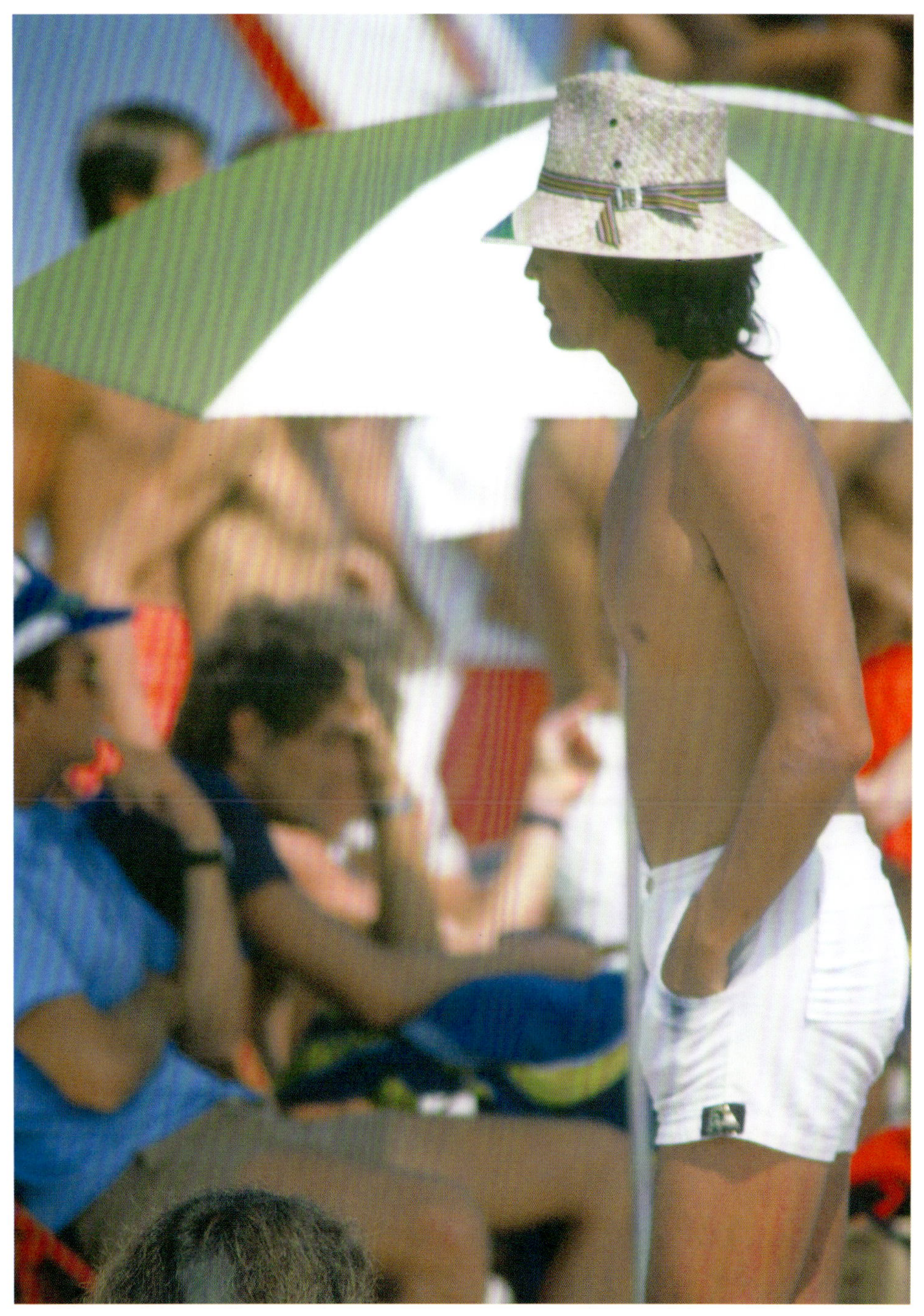

SUMMER 1978. SEASIDE HEIGHTS, NJ

David Nuuhiwa cruising the contest area at the Grog's Seaside Pro, August 1978. Lots of style and swagger.

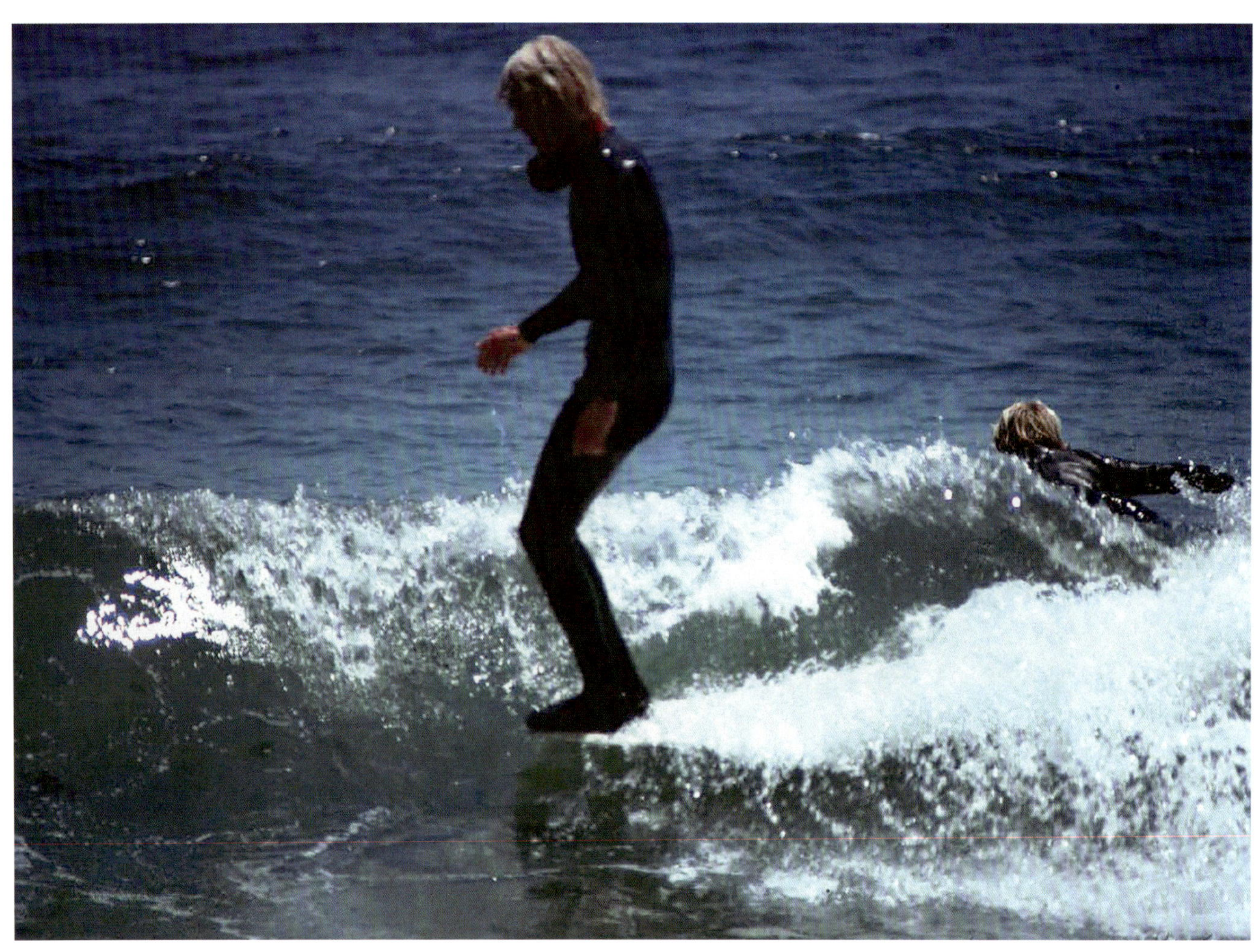

SUMMER 1977. SEASIDE HEIGHTS, NJ

David “DCB” Balzerack from Florida “hanging ten” in Seaside Heights.
David was a force and a seriously great surfer.

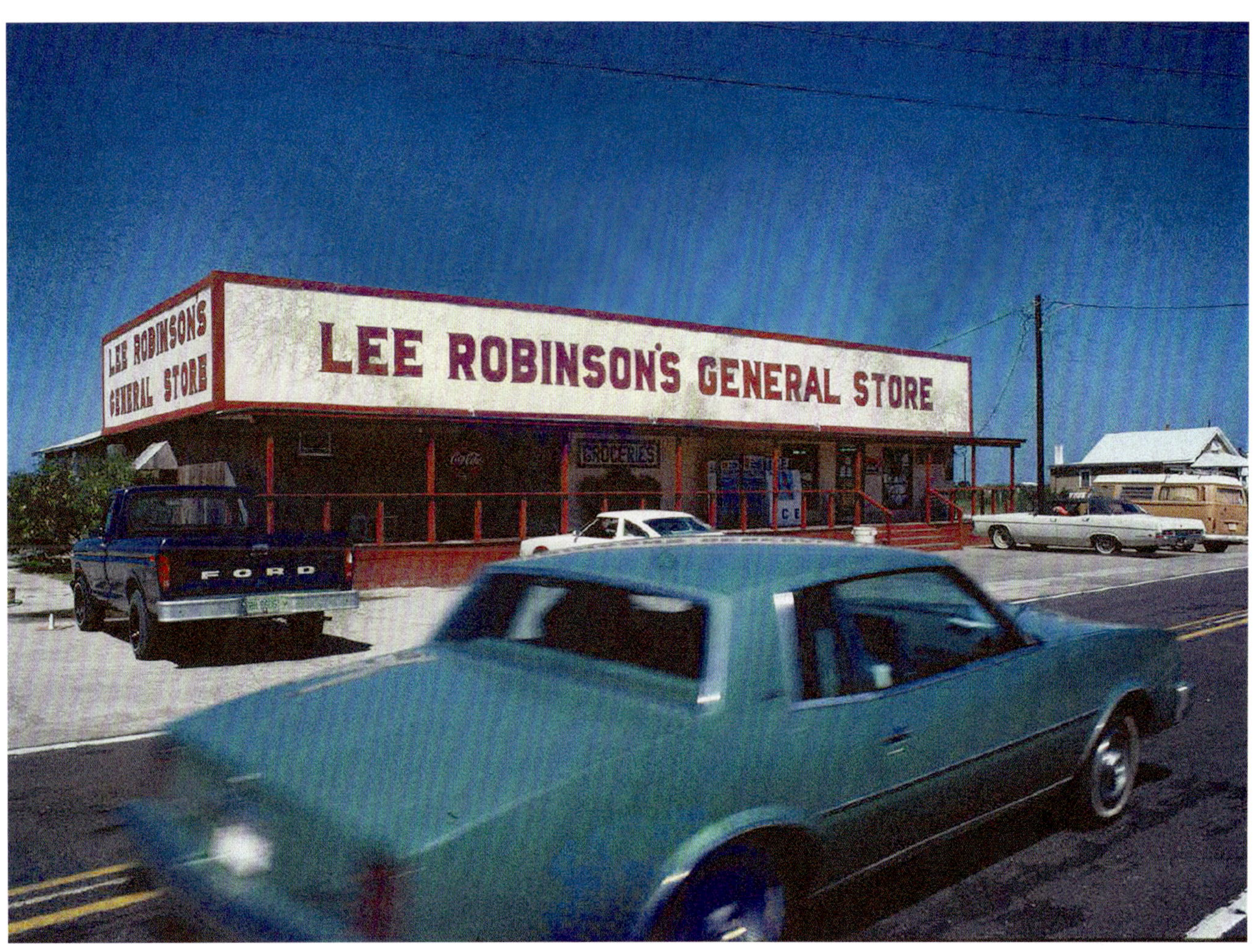

AUGUST 1974. CAPE HATTERAS, NC

Many of the Jersey crew would often travel to Cape Hatteras, North Carolina, for surf and great fishing. For almost 50 years, it has also been the home of the East Coast Surfing Championships. In the '70s, there weren't many stores to shop for essentials—they didn't even sell beer, wine, or any alcohol. Cape Hatteras is part of the National Seashore, which is considered a protected area in some parts, so you had to go to Nags Head, 50 miles away, to get what you needed. That's my yellow VW bus in the parking lot, on the right.

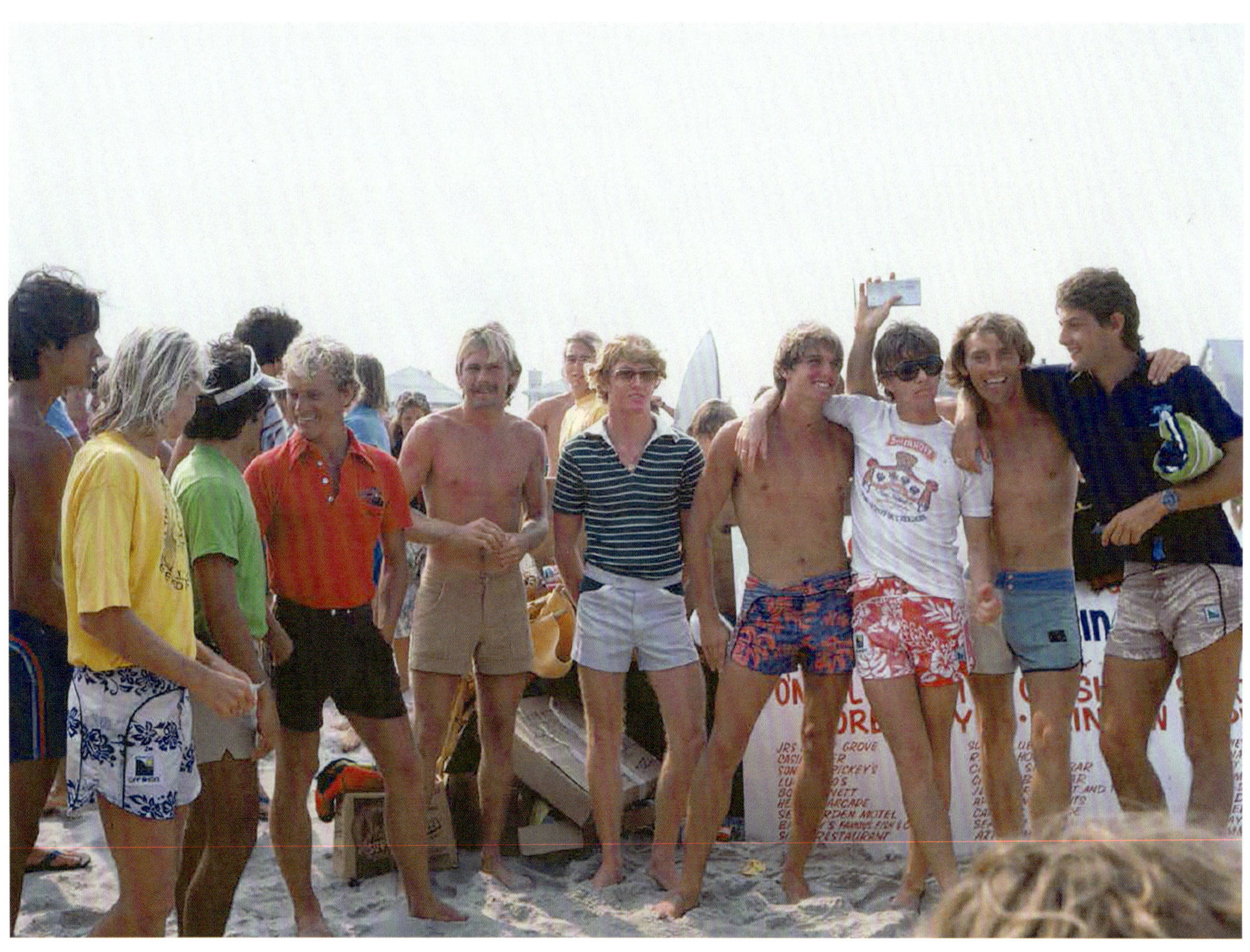

AUGUST 1978. GROG'S SEASIDE PRO, SEASIDE HEIGHTS, NJ

(RIGHT TO LEFT) Shaun Tomson, Greg Mesanko, Rabbit Bartholomew, Buzzy Kerbox, Bobby Owens, Jeff Crawford, Peter "PT" Townend, Michael Ho, and Pat Mulhern.

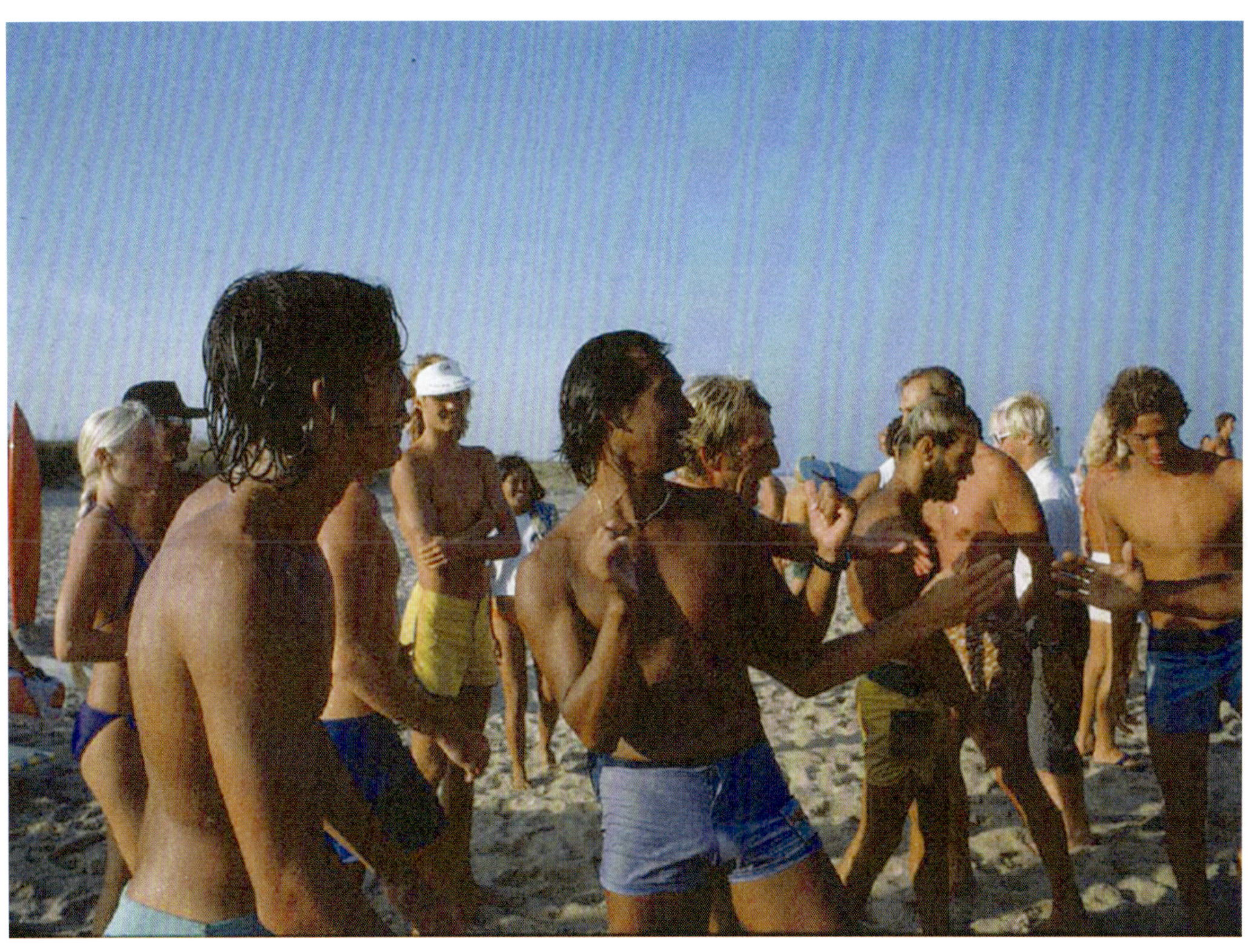

SUMMER 1974. CAPE HATTERAS, NC

Paddleboard race finish.

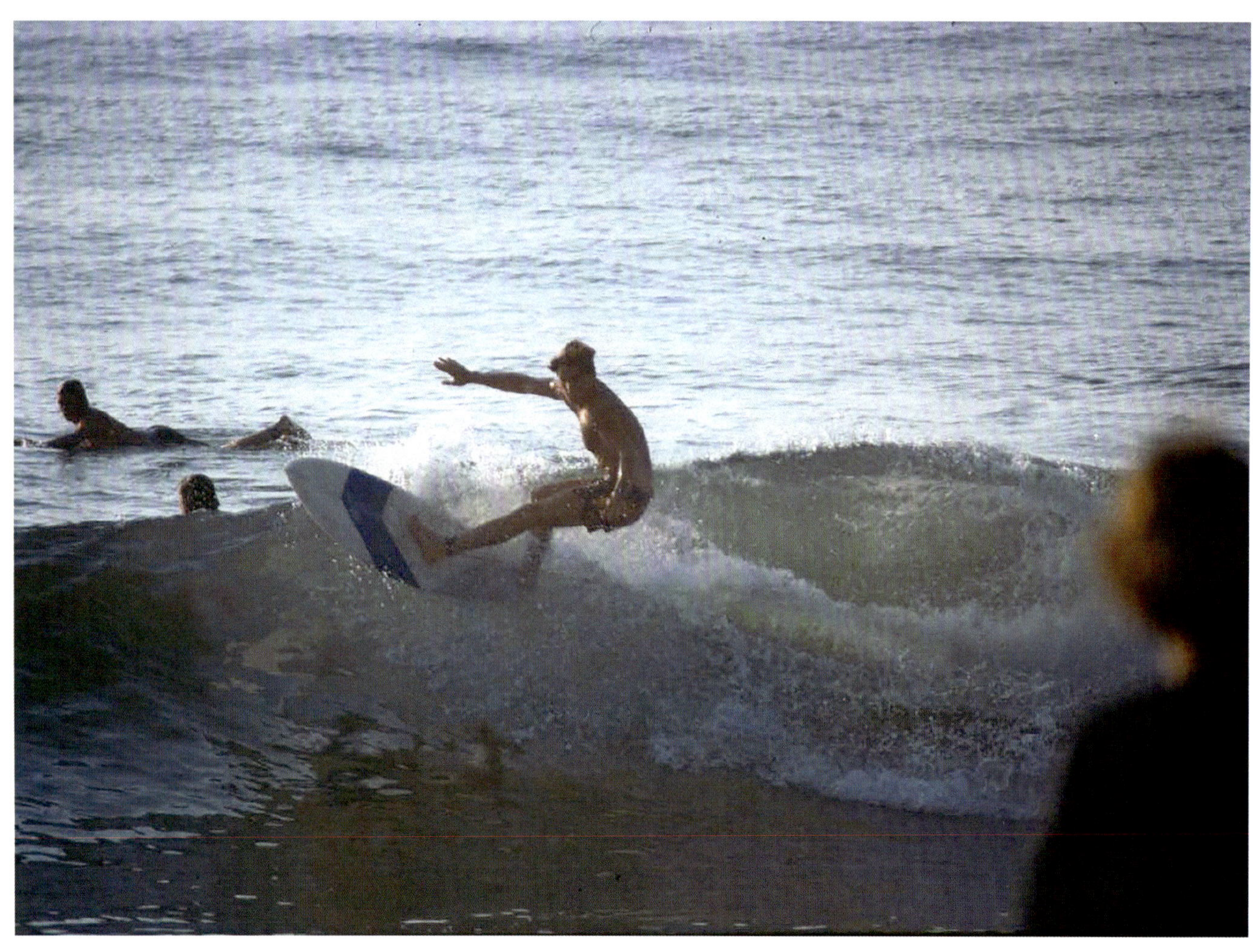

AUGUST 1978. SEASIDE HEIGHTS, NJ

Buzzy Kerbox warming up for Grog's Seaside Pro.

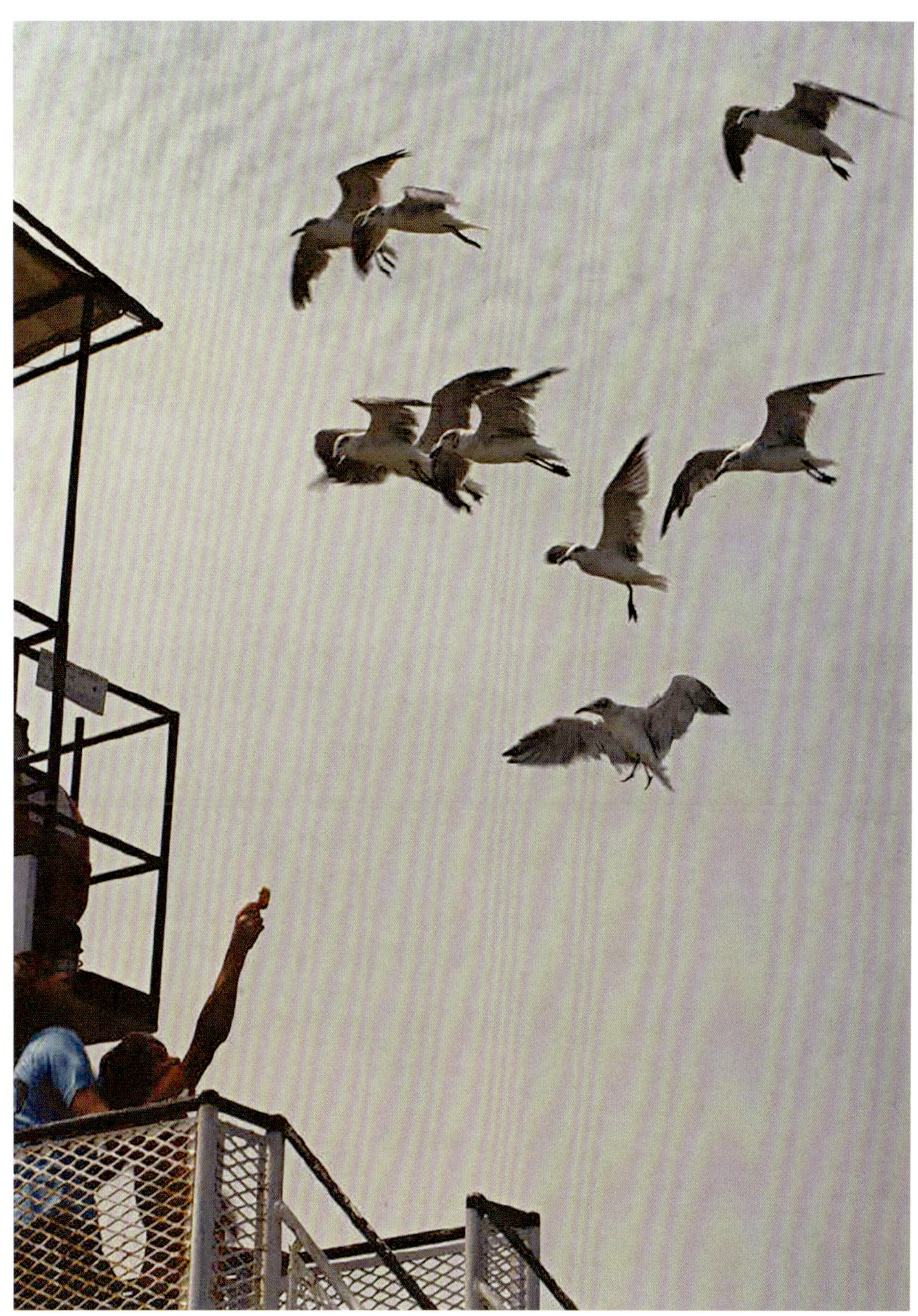

SEPTEMBER 1978. CAPE HATTERAS, NC

New Jersey has a famous ferry ride across the Delaware Bay. The Cape May-Lewes Ferry started in the '60s. This shot is from another famous ferry ride, south of New Jersey, to Ocracoke Island from Hatteras, North Carolina.

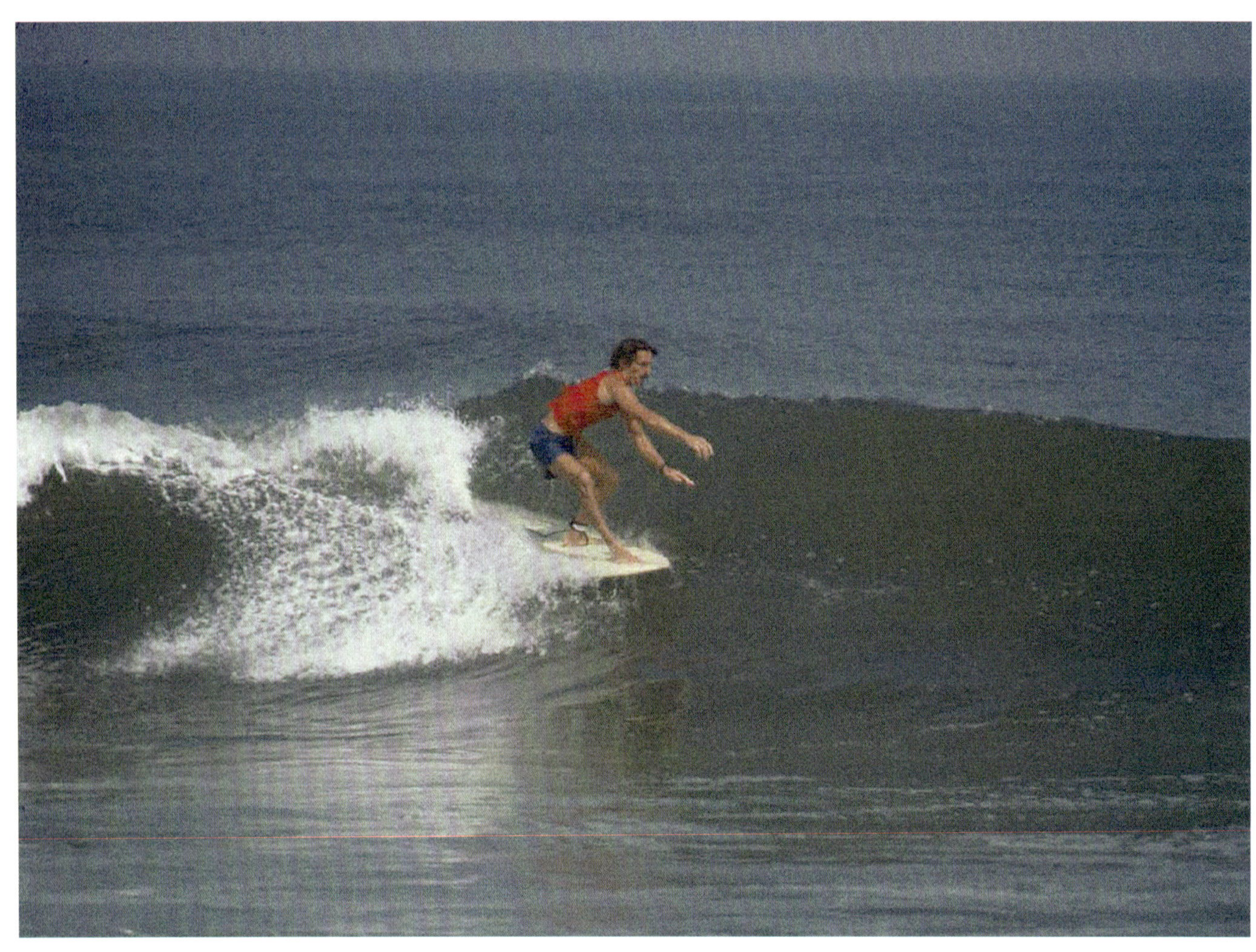

SUMMER 1978. SEASIDE HEIGHTS, NJ

Tim Gilly, Florida shredder traveling north to escape the Florida summertime flat spells.

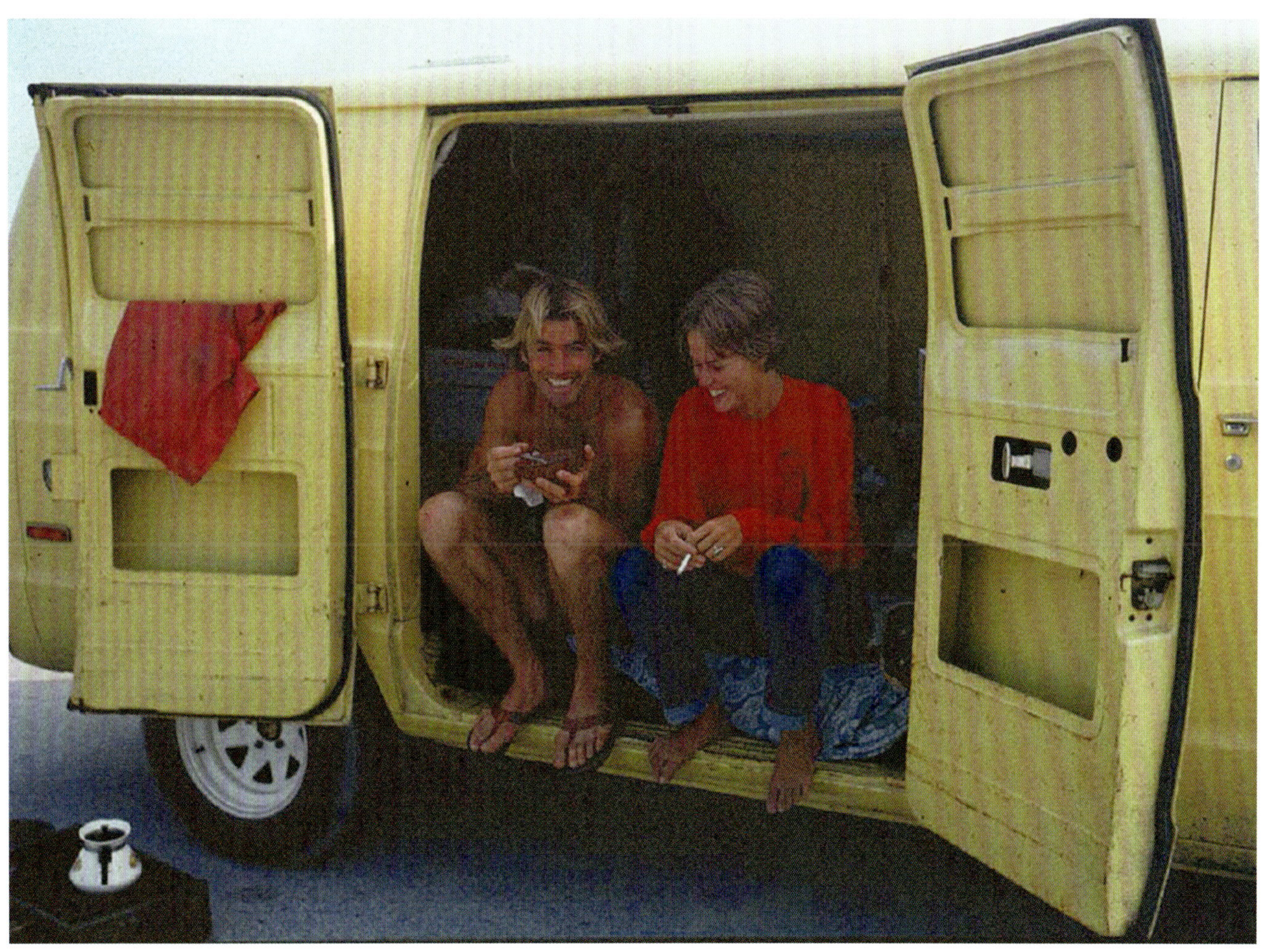

SUMMER 1978

Early days of van life on the road, camping out and surfing all day. Grab your girl and throw a mattress in your van and hit the road. Simple days of a young traveling surfer.

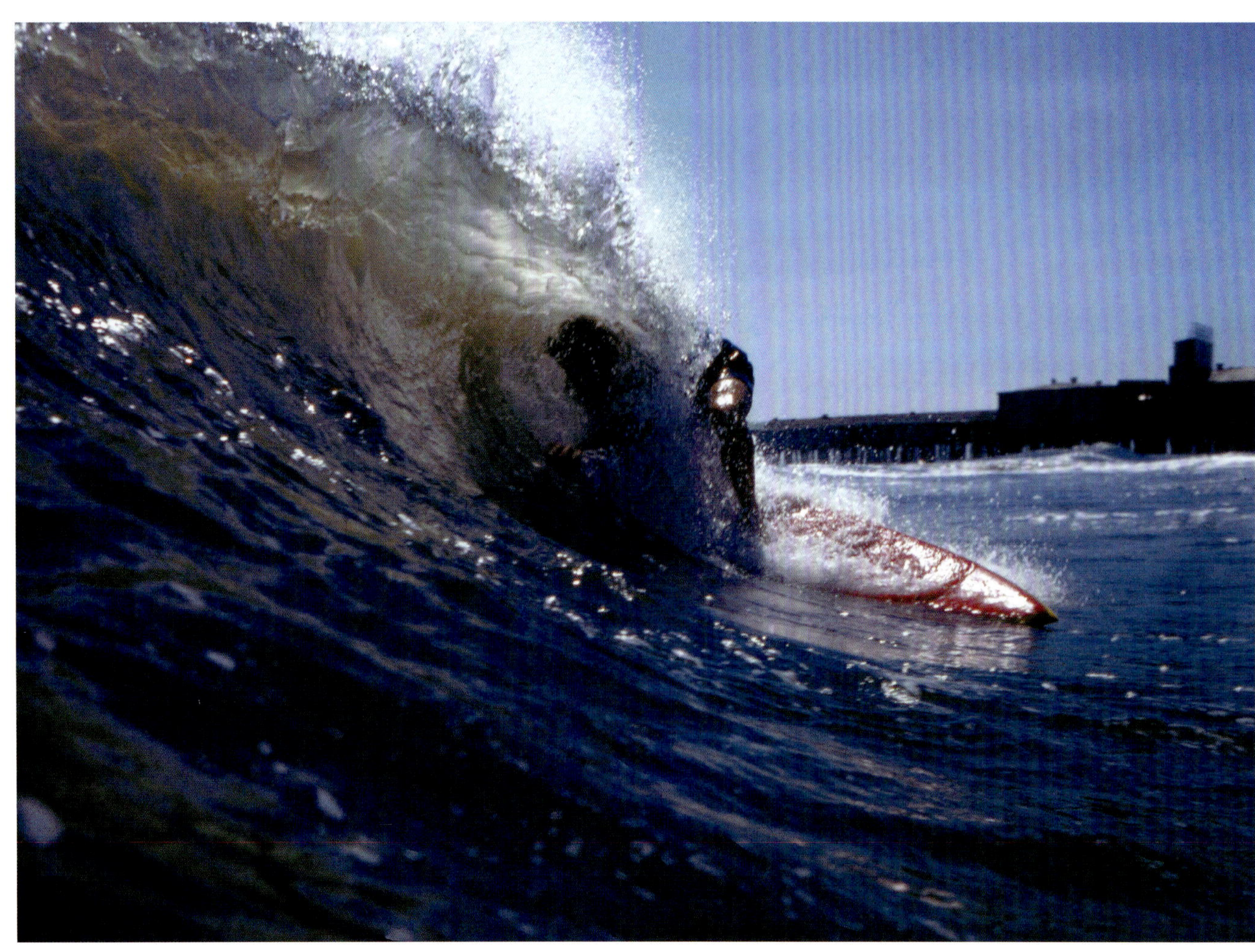

SEPTEMBER 1976. ATLANTIC CITY, NJ

Phil Van Wickle trying to squeeze into the right bowl off the groin, with Steel Pier in the background. Phil was an inspiration to a lot of young surfers and was our version of "The Bert" (Larry Bertlemann) on Absecon Island.

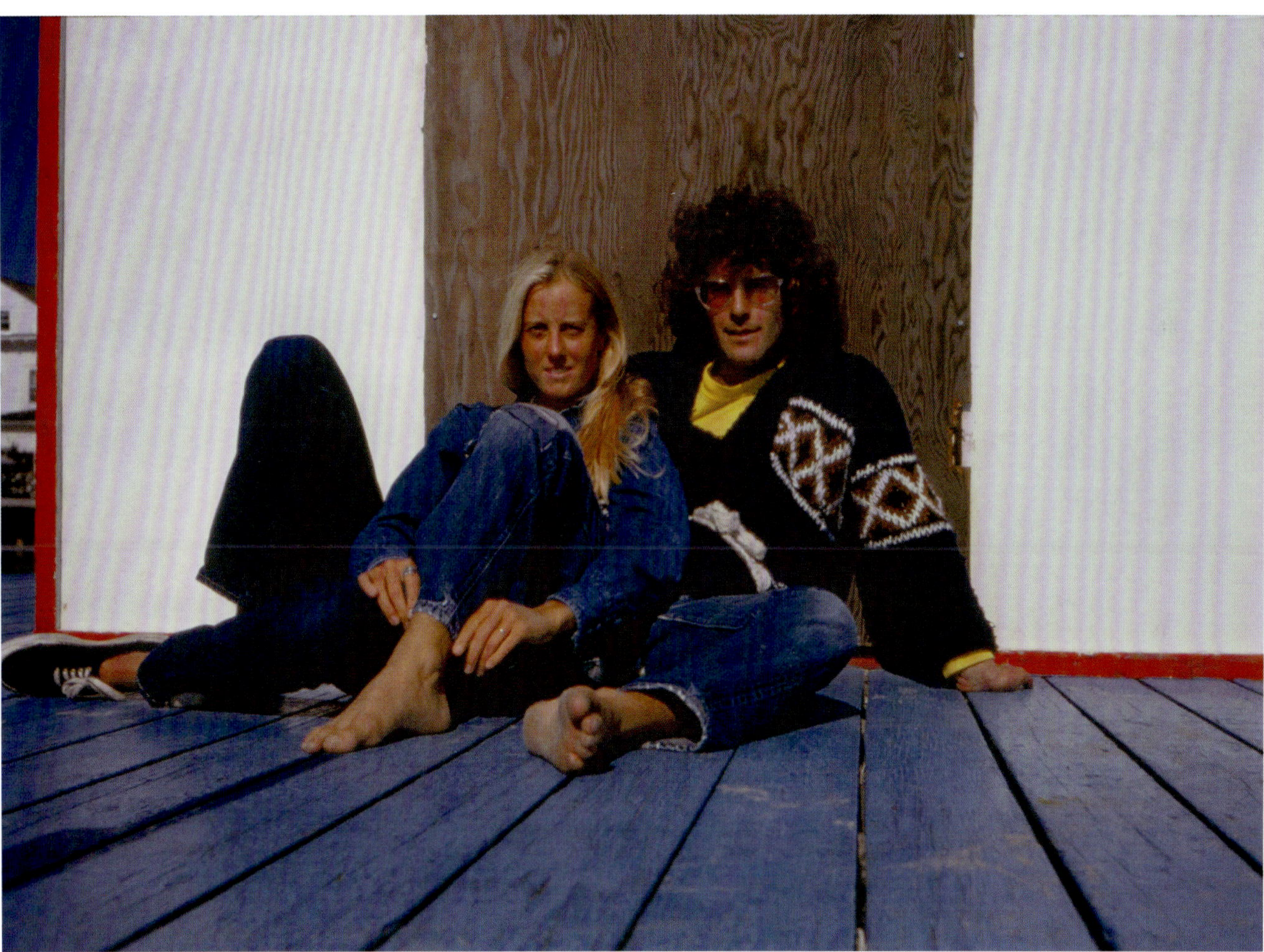

OCTOBER 1975. VENTNOR, NJ

With Nancy Hyde Gudauskas, an early version of a selfie. Many fall days were spent on the boardwalk hanging and watching the surf. Nancy would later move to California, marry, and raise three sons, who are now all amazing, well-known surfers.

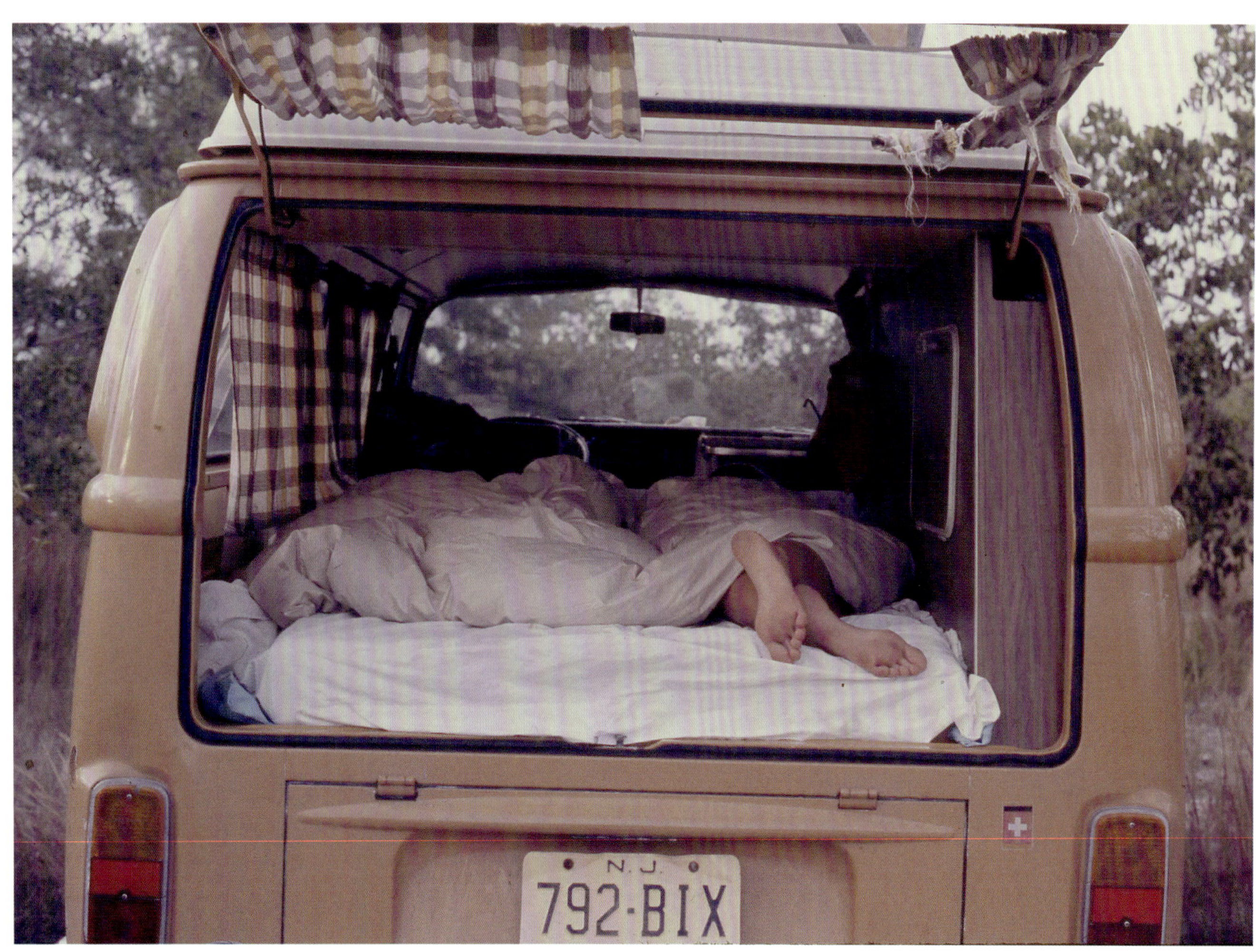

SEPTEMBER 1976. GREENPORT, NY

VW camper van. Some great years of camping and traveling up and down the coast. Lots of travel and surf destinations. Nancy getting some extra z's. I lived in this van the entire summer of '75, while working on Plum Island, off Orient Point.

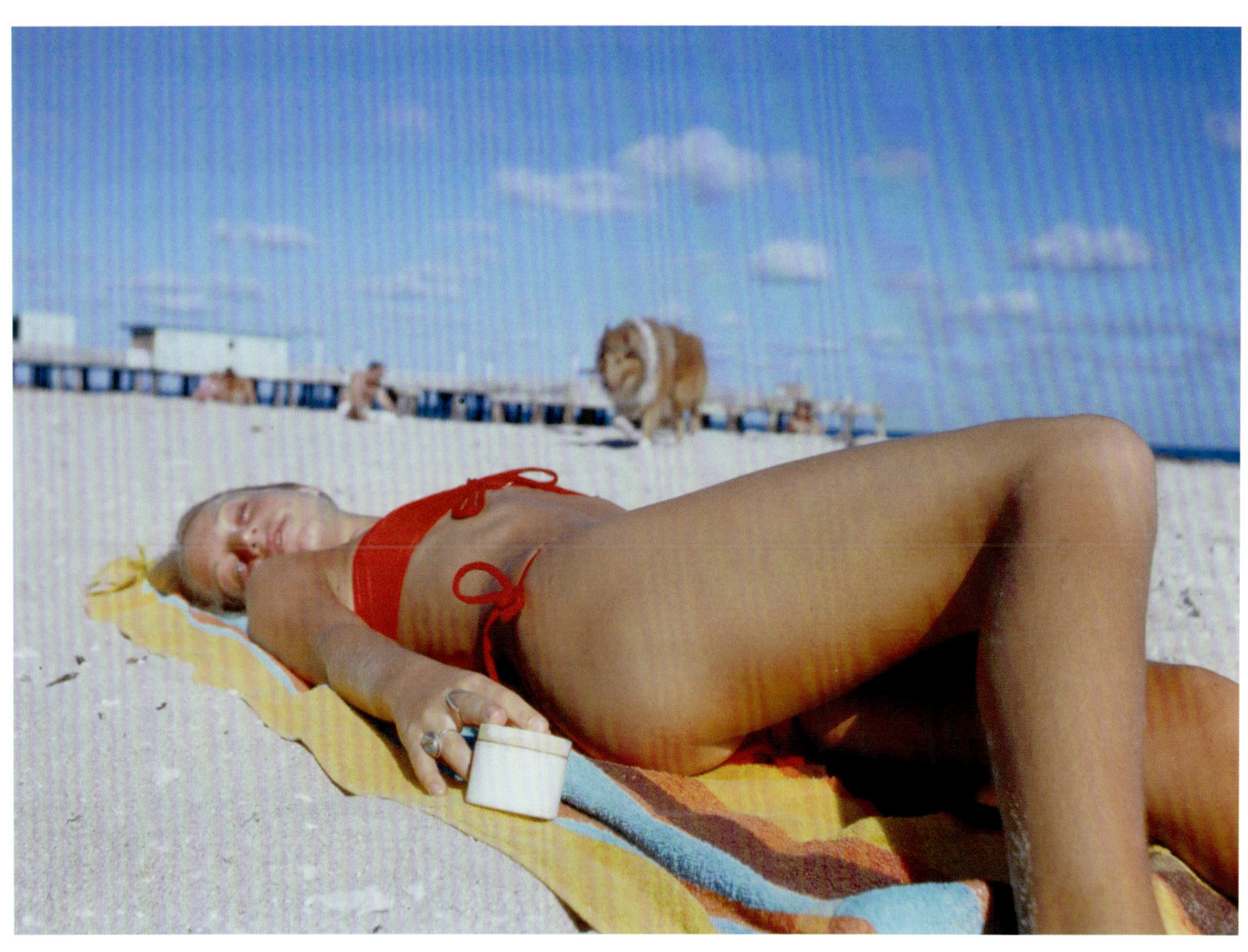

SUMMER 1977

Judy Ashner loving the sunshine and beach.

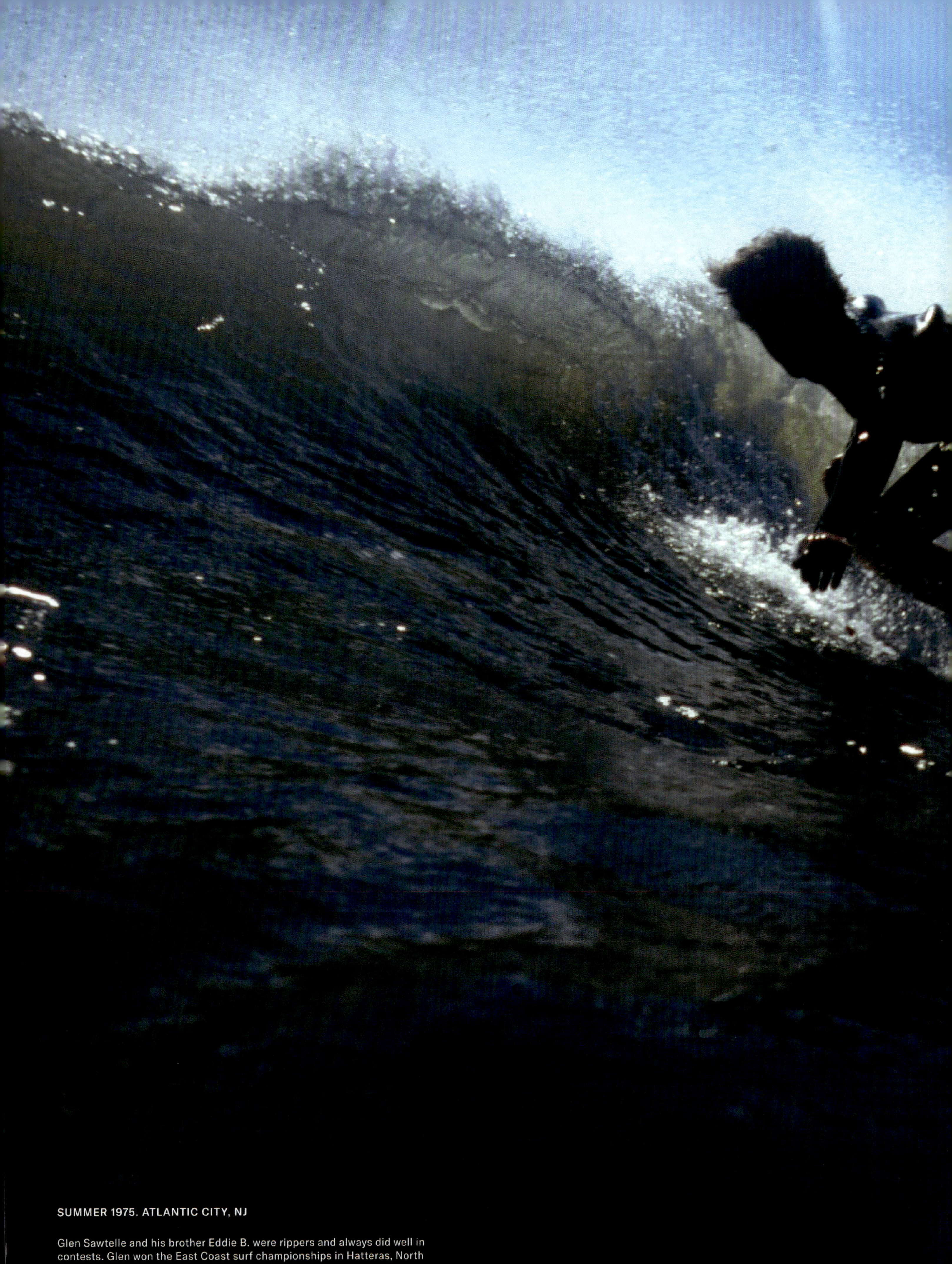

SUMMER 1975. ATLANTIC CITY, NJ

Glen Sawtelle and his brother Eddie B. were rippers and always did well in contests. Glen won the East Coast surf championships in Hatteras, North Carolina, in 1972, on his blue board shown in this photo.

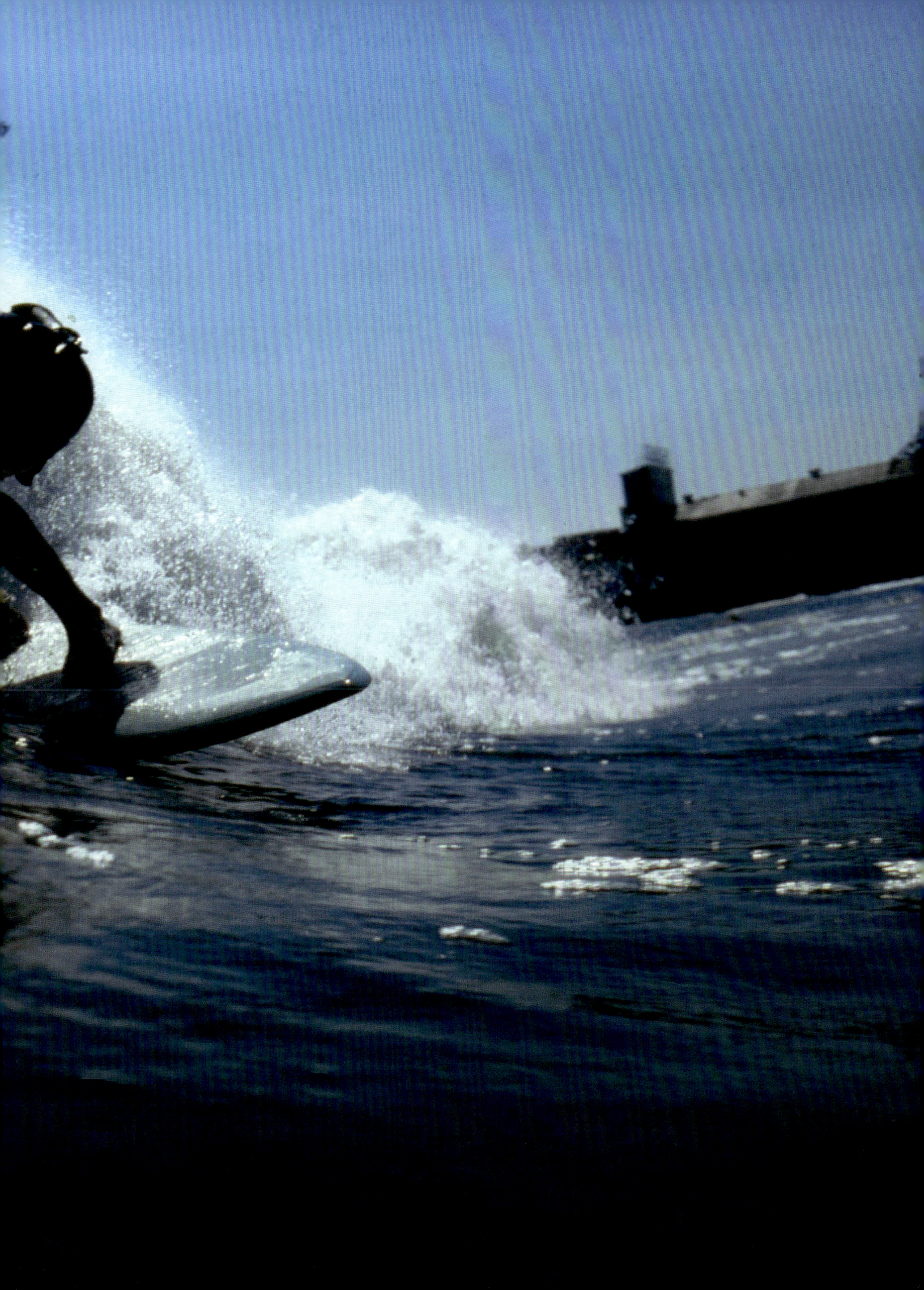

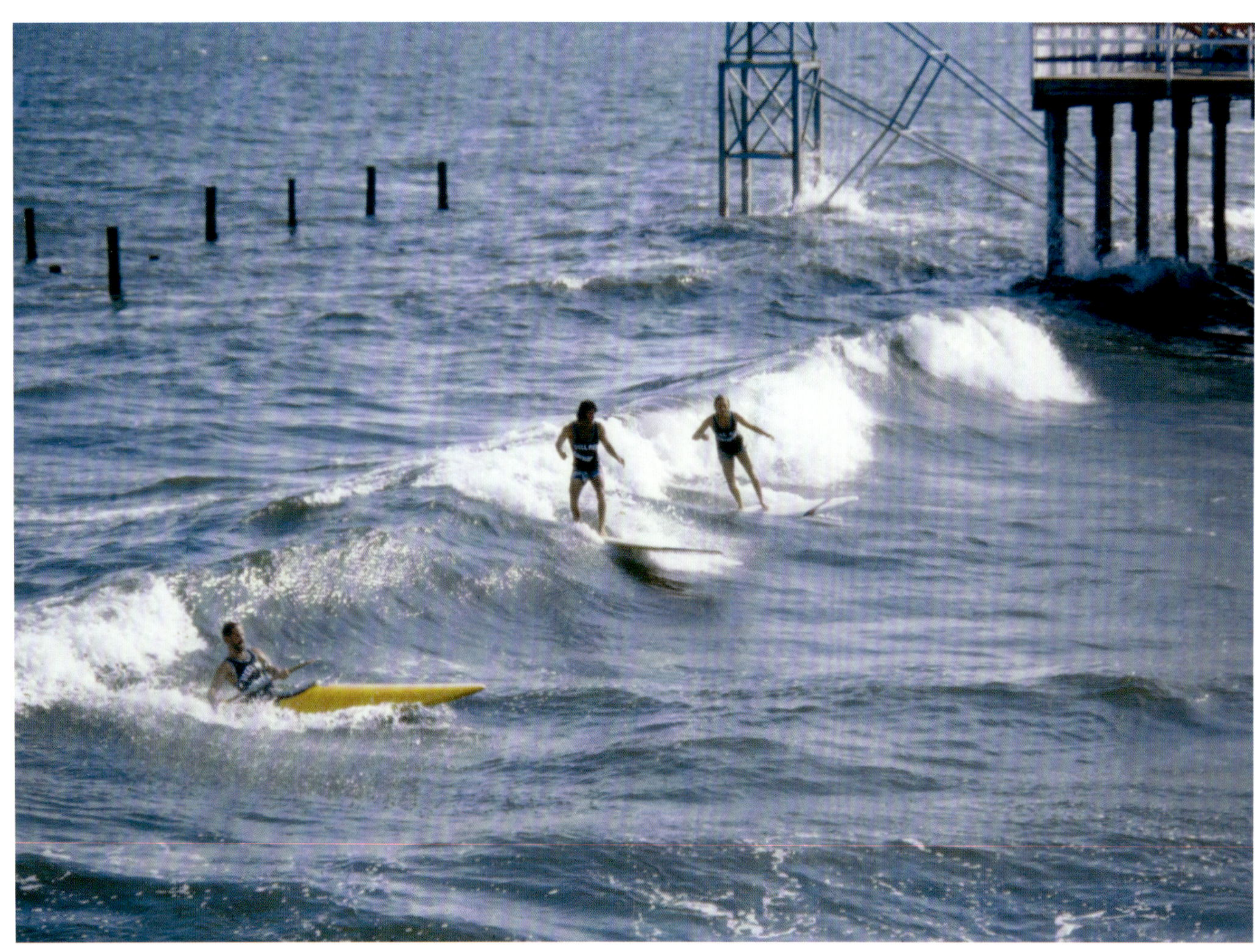

JUNE 1975. ATLANTIC CITY, NJ

(LEFT TO RIGHT) Joel Fogel (kayak), Mark Neustadter (longboard), and Linda Davoli. This was a show I produced for the Steel Pier. We were called the "Steel Pier Surf Riders." Visitors and locals would watch us surf on the side of the pier, and Chuckie Klotz was the announcer.

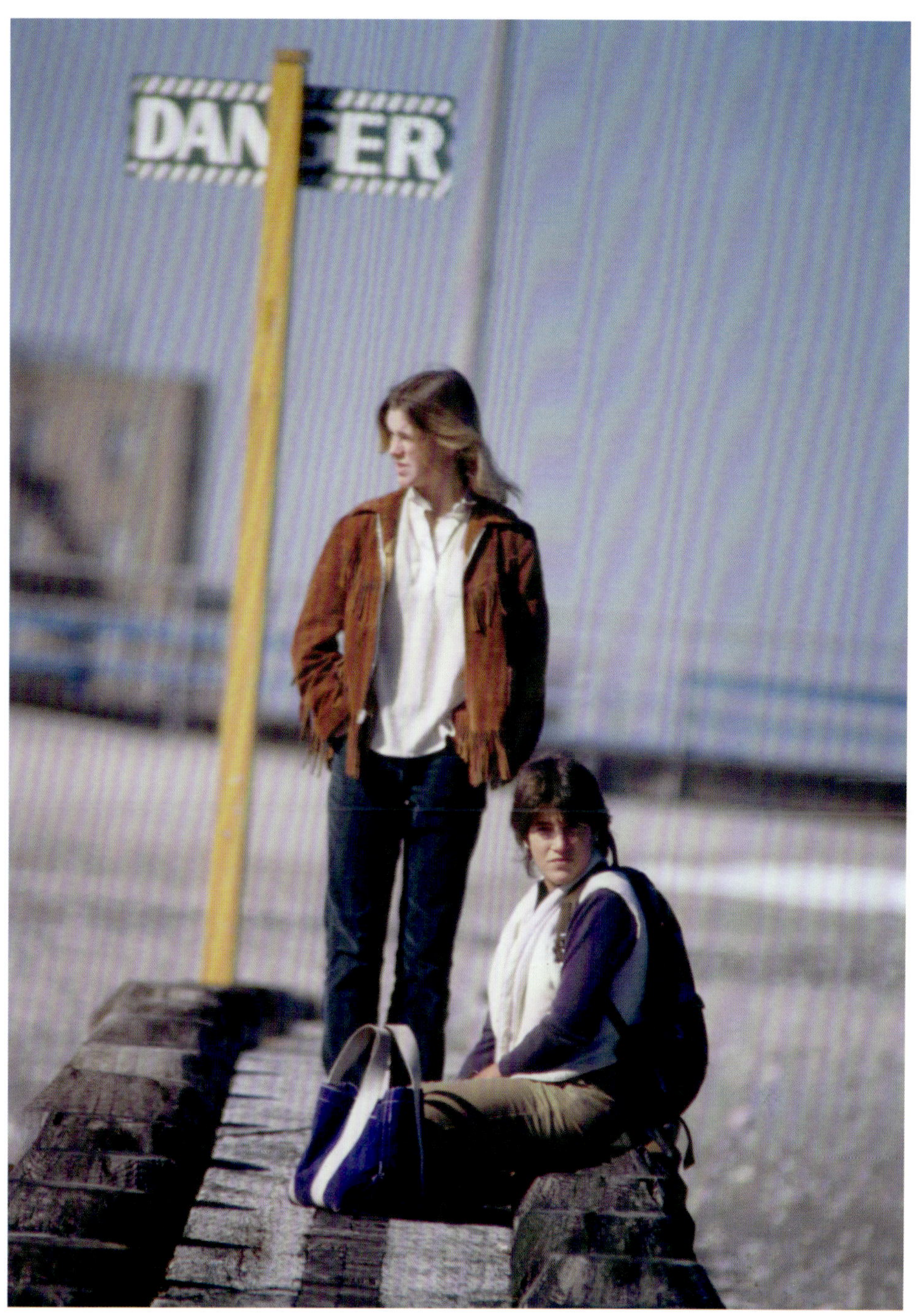

MARCH 1979. ATLANTIC CITY, NJ

Suzanne Steinberg and her friend hanging out on one of the massive jetties that always had a good wave off of it.

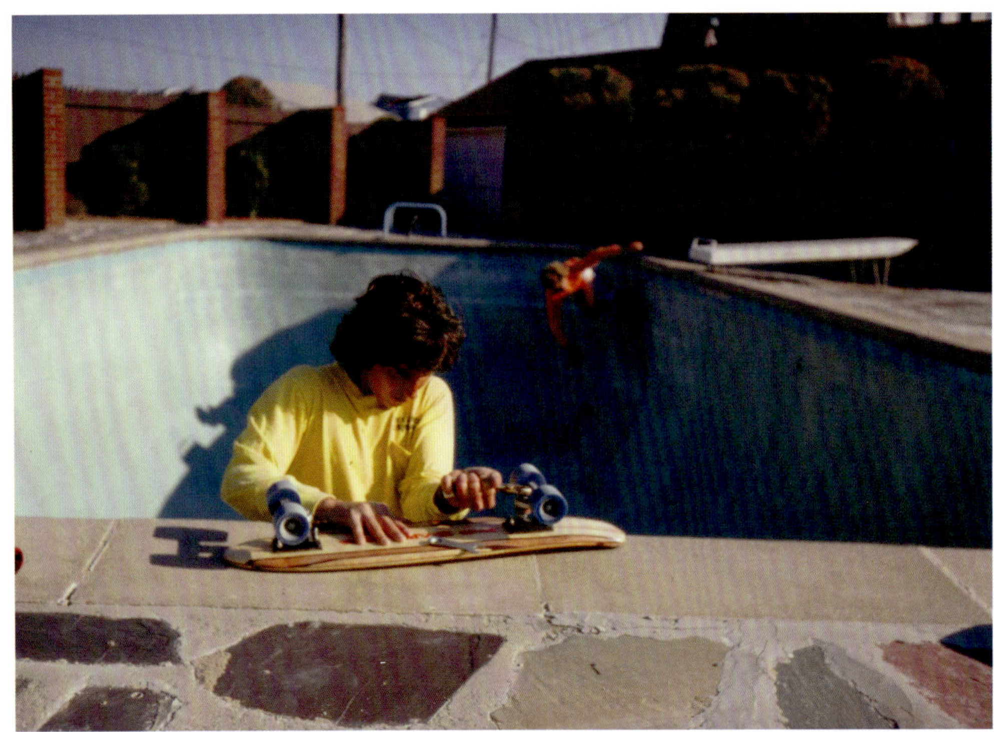

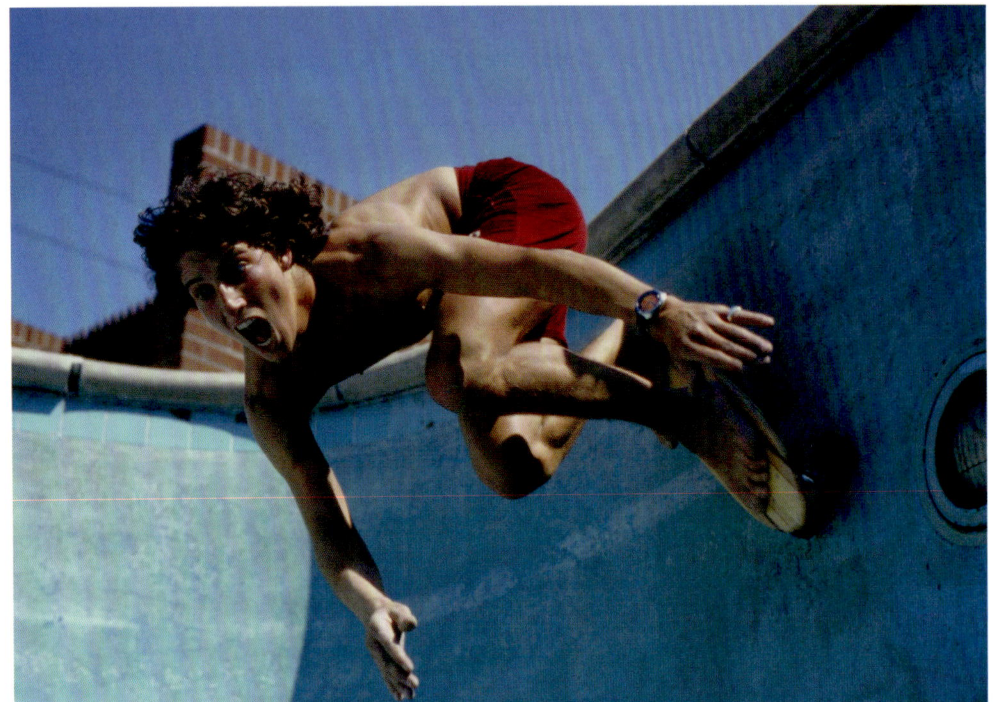

MAY 1977. LONGPORT, NJ

Sonny Mattola in the foreground, tightening up his trucks, while his best friend, pool ripper Jimmy Blair, flies high off the corner. These two skaters had their New Jersey version of Dogtown right in their backyard in Longport. The house belonged to the owner of the Ice Capades, who later donated the house to a group of nuns.

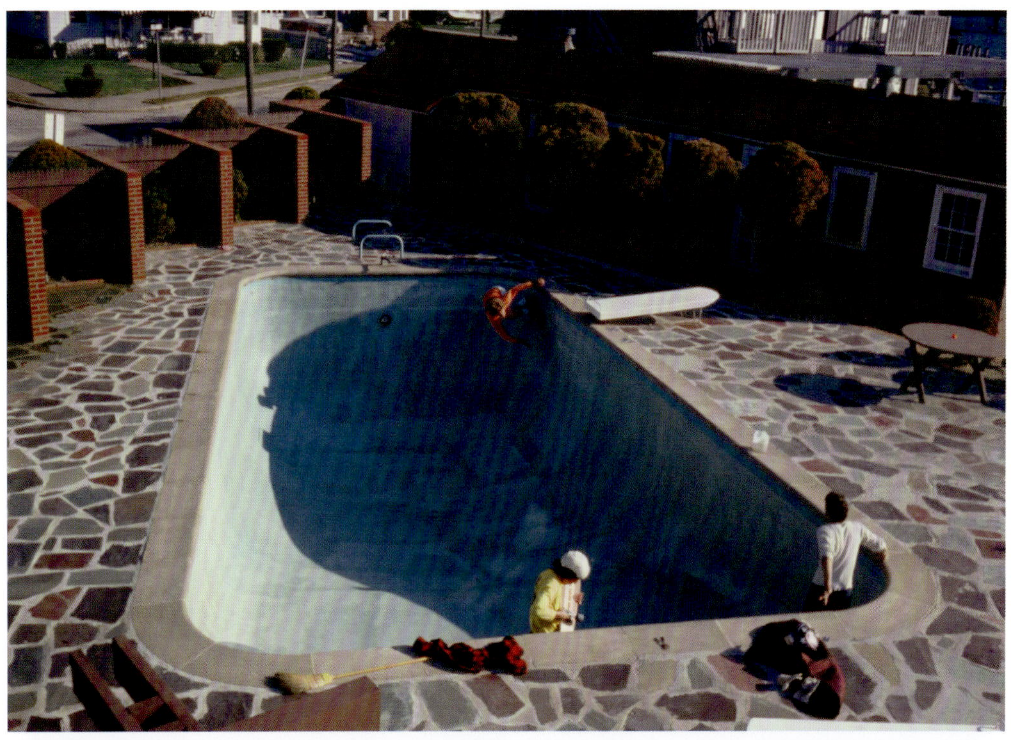

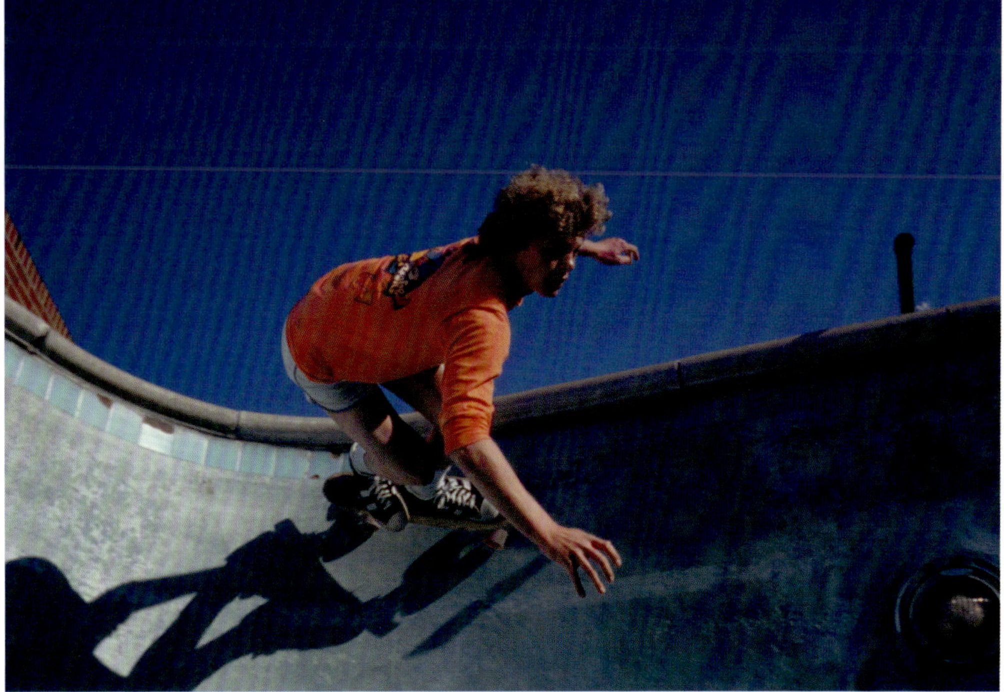

MAY 1977. LONGPORT, NJ

Overview shot of this great pool that Jimmy Blair (upper corner in background) and Sonny Mattola (foreground) drained, maintained, and shredded for years. A little piece of skate heaven for these two lucky locals.

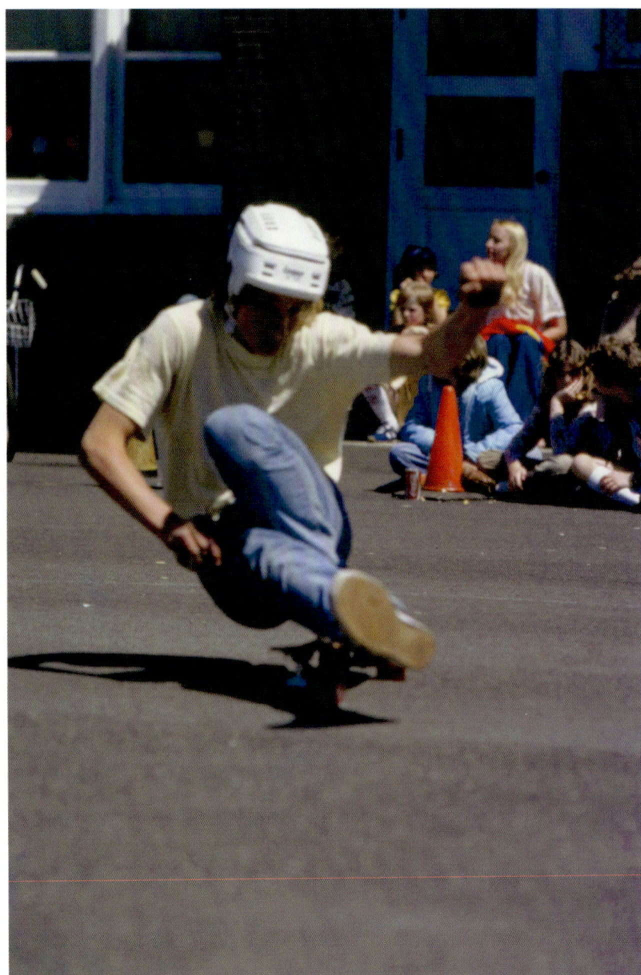

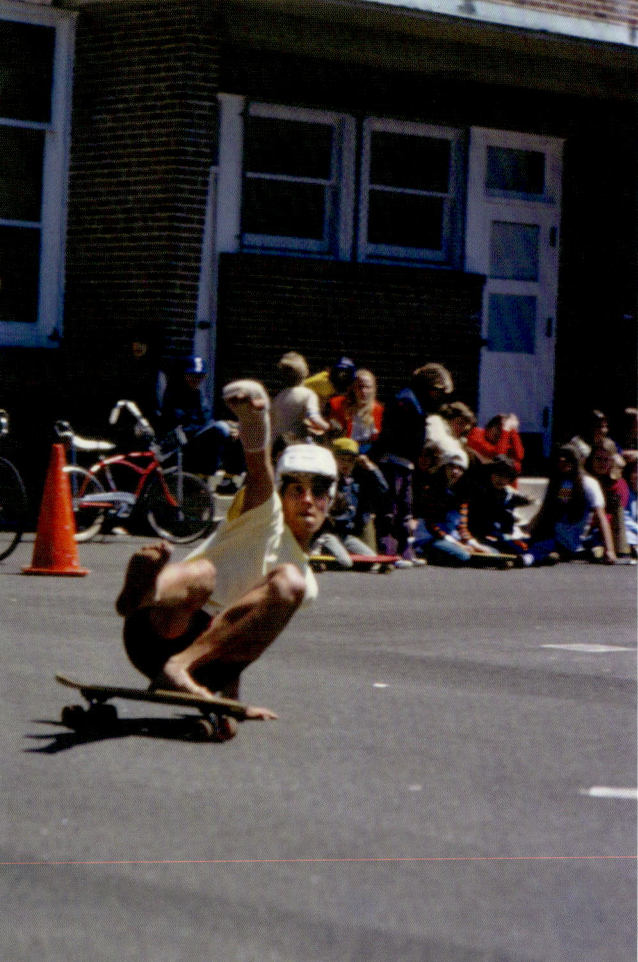

APRIL 1977. SONNY MATTOLA, UNION AVENUE
SKATEBOARD COMPETITION, MARGATE, NJ

No shoes, broken arm, but wearing his helmet. This competition was sponsored by Jim Earle's Reef Surf Shop, where Sonny was a skate team member.

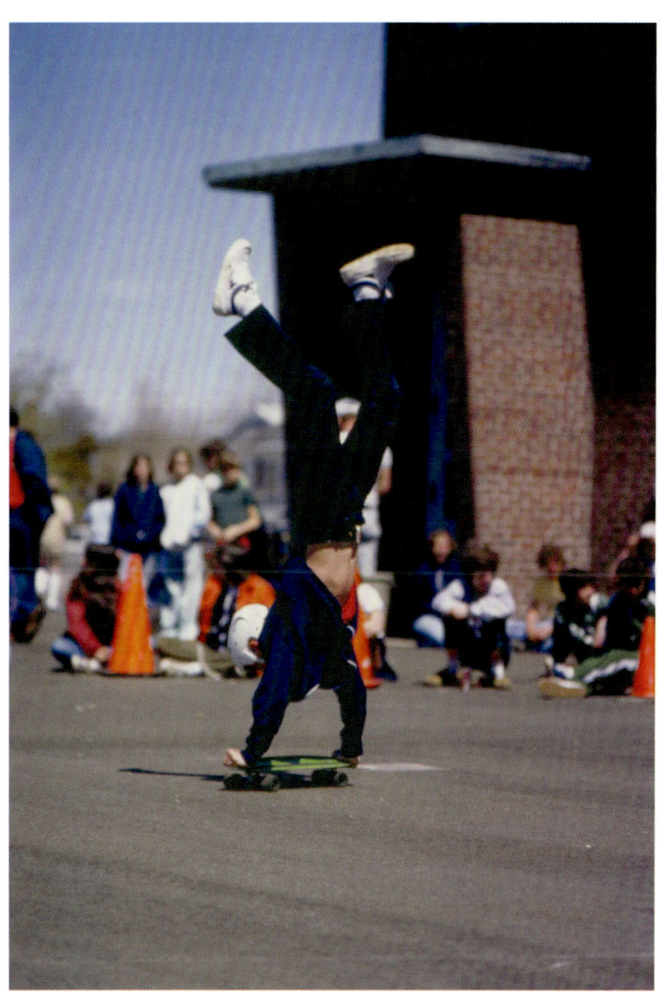

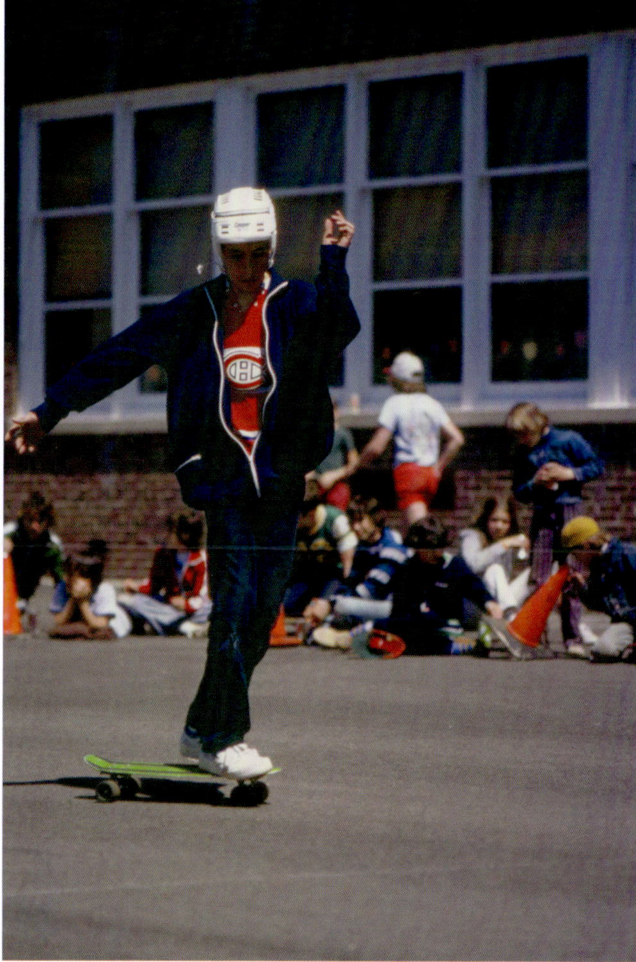

APRIL 1977. UNION AVENUE
SKATEBOARD COMPETITION, MARGATE, NJ

Handstands were always a crowd favorite.

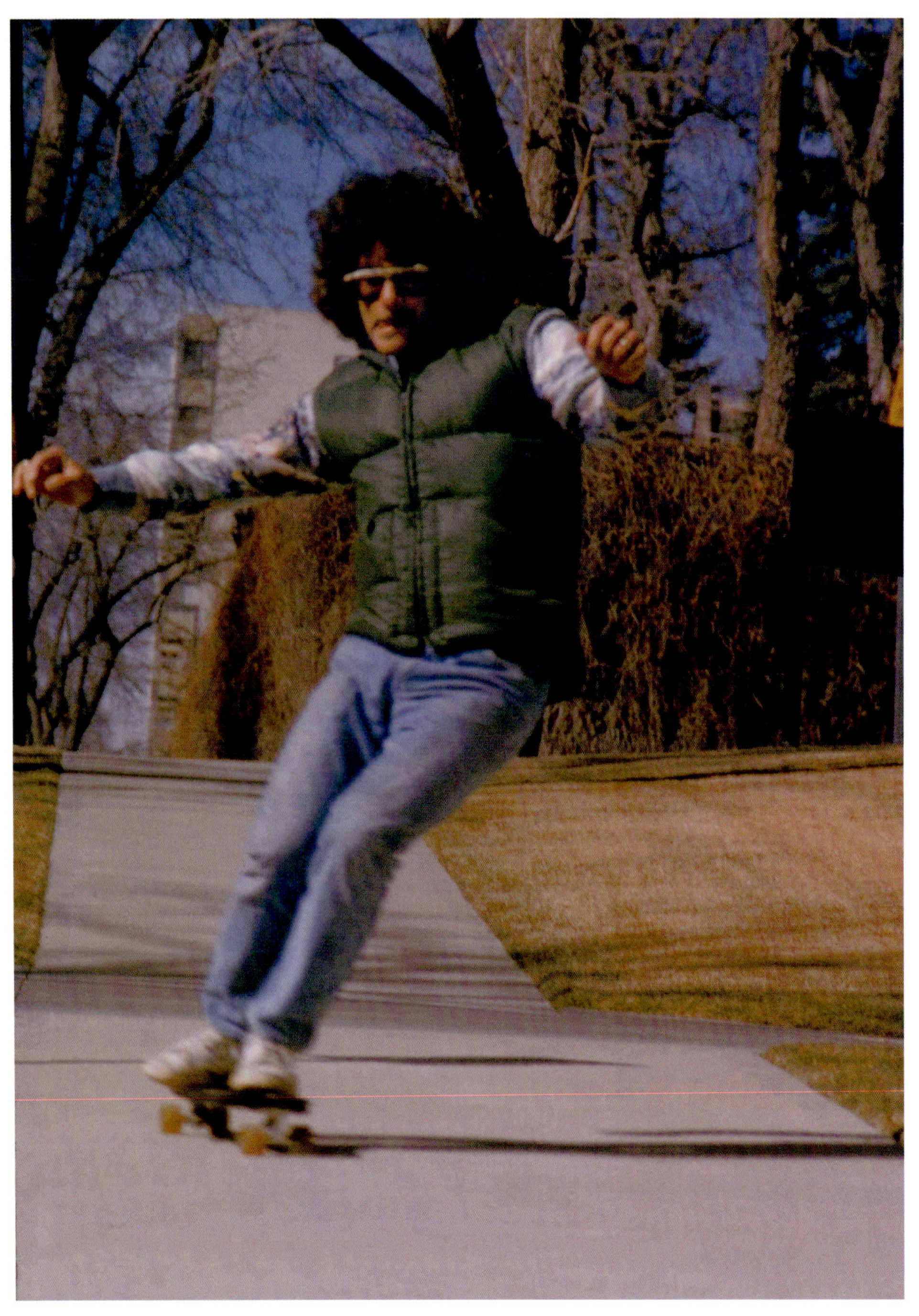

1976. POMONA, NJ

Me at Stockton State College—skateboard competition 1976—1st place.
Photographed by Mark Birnbach.

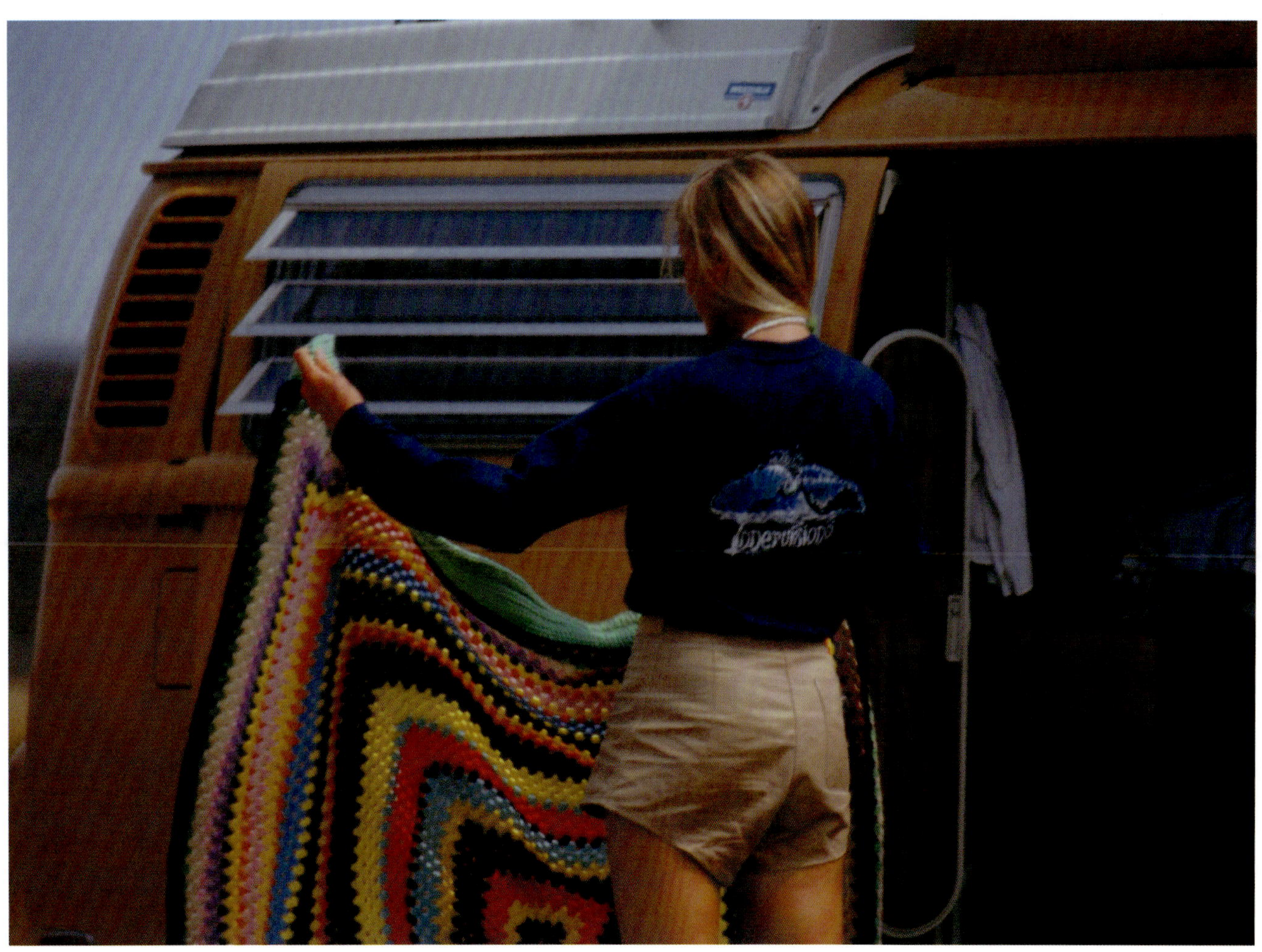

SEPTEMBER 1976

Nancy Hyde Gudauskas doing a little housekeeping on the road, camping, folding her handmade afghan. Her T-shirt is from Innervisions Surfboards, designed by me.

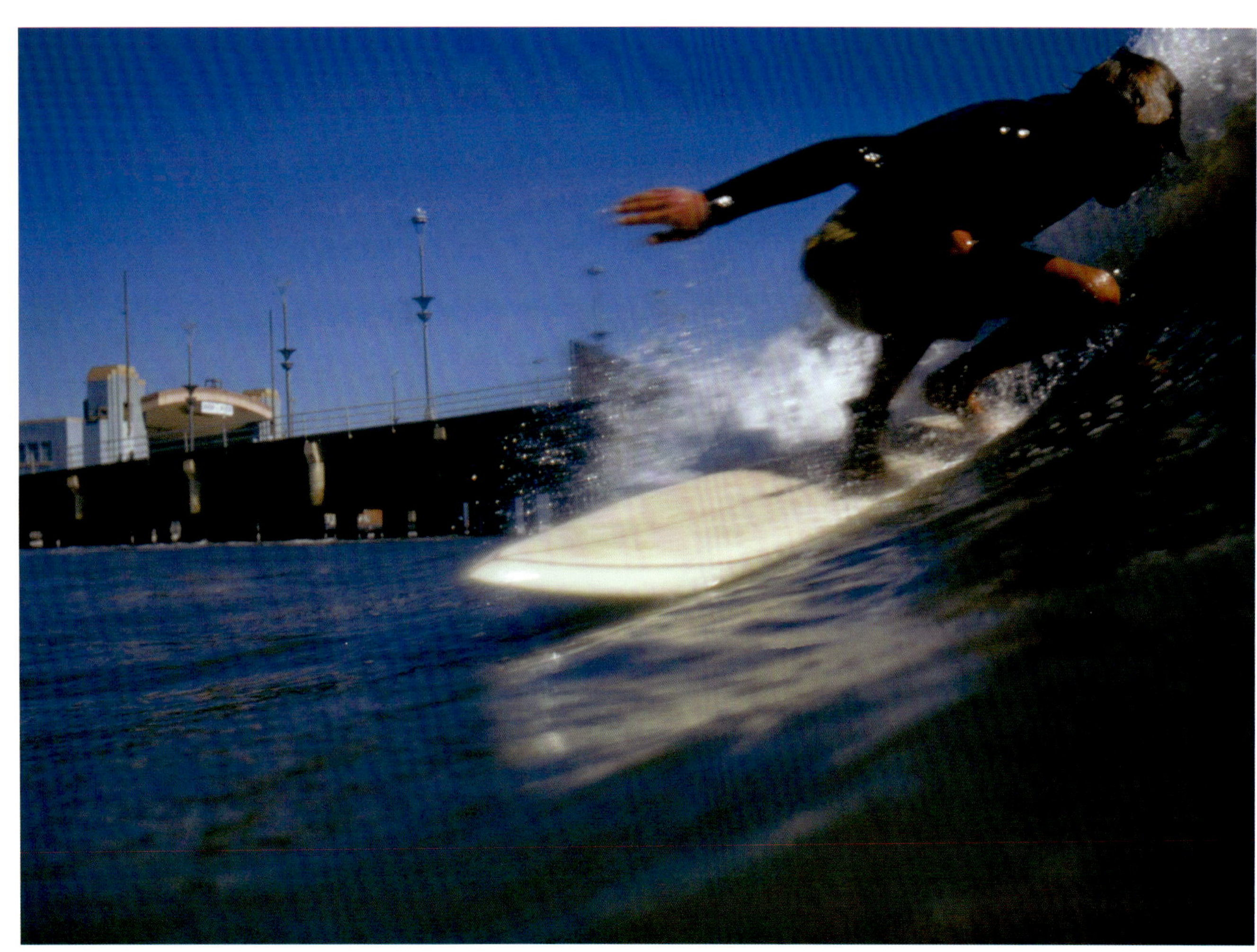

OCTOBER 1975. GENE SYKES, GARDEN PIER, ATLANTIC CITY, NJ

He was a regular foot, but he could switch stance to goofy pretty well. He was part of a big surfing family, with lots of cousins who ripped and were good all-around watermen and lifeguards. Garden Pier was one of many piers that had good surf in Atlantic City.

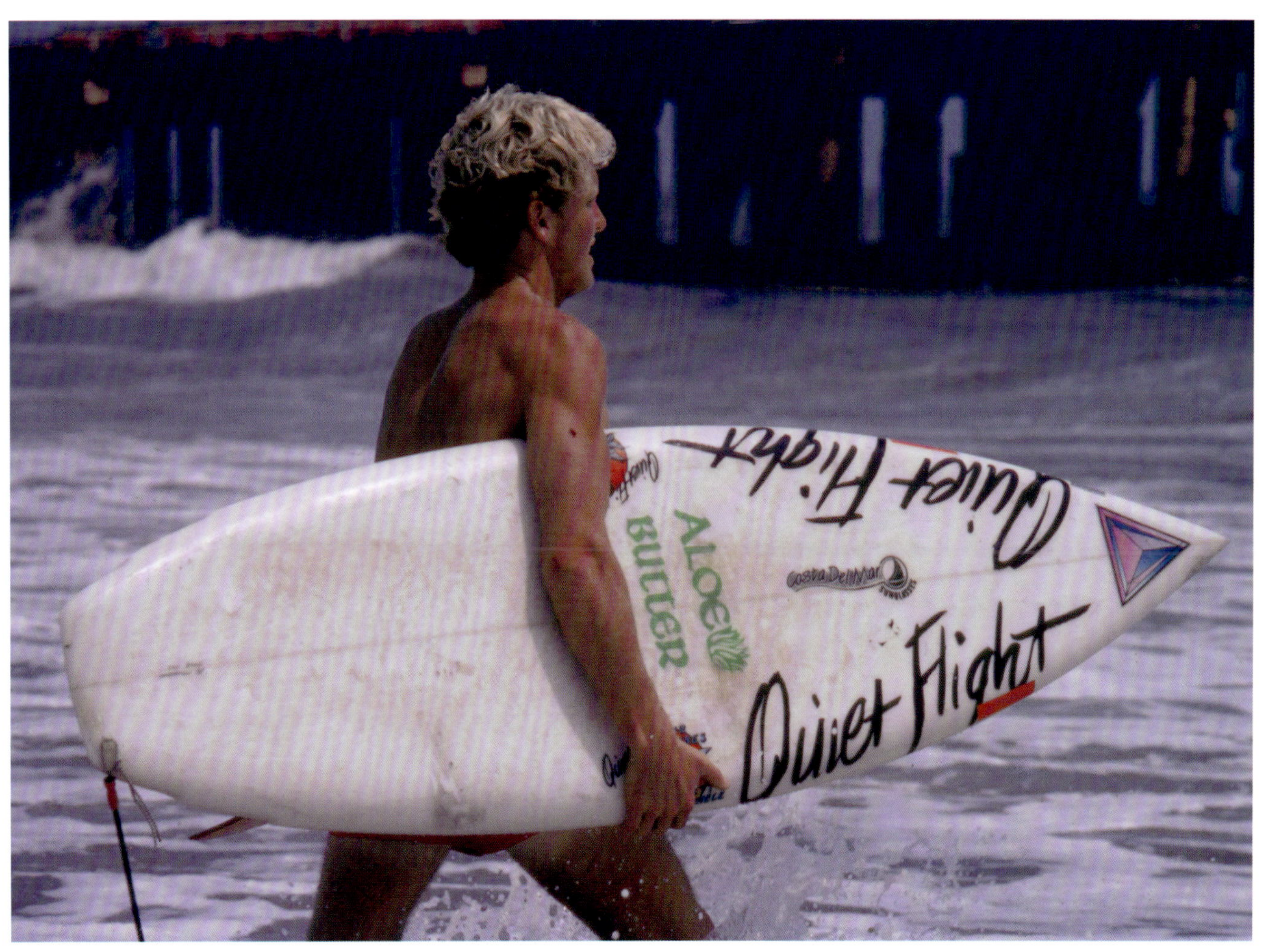

AUGUST 1983

Matt Kechele of Florida on the surf contest scene in New Jersey.
He is a legendary surfer, huge talent, and early mentor of Kelly Slater.

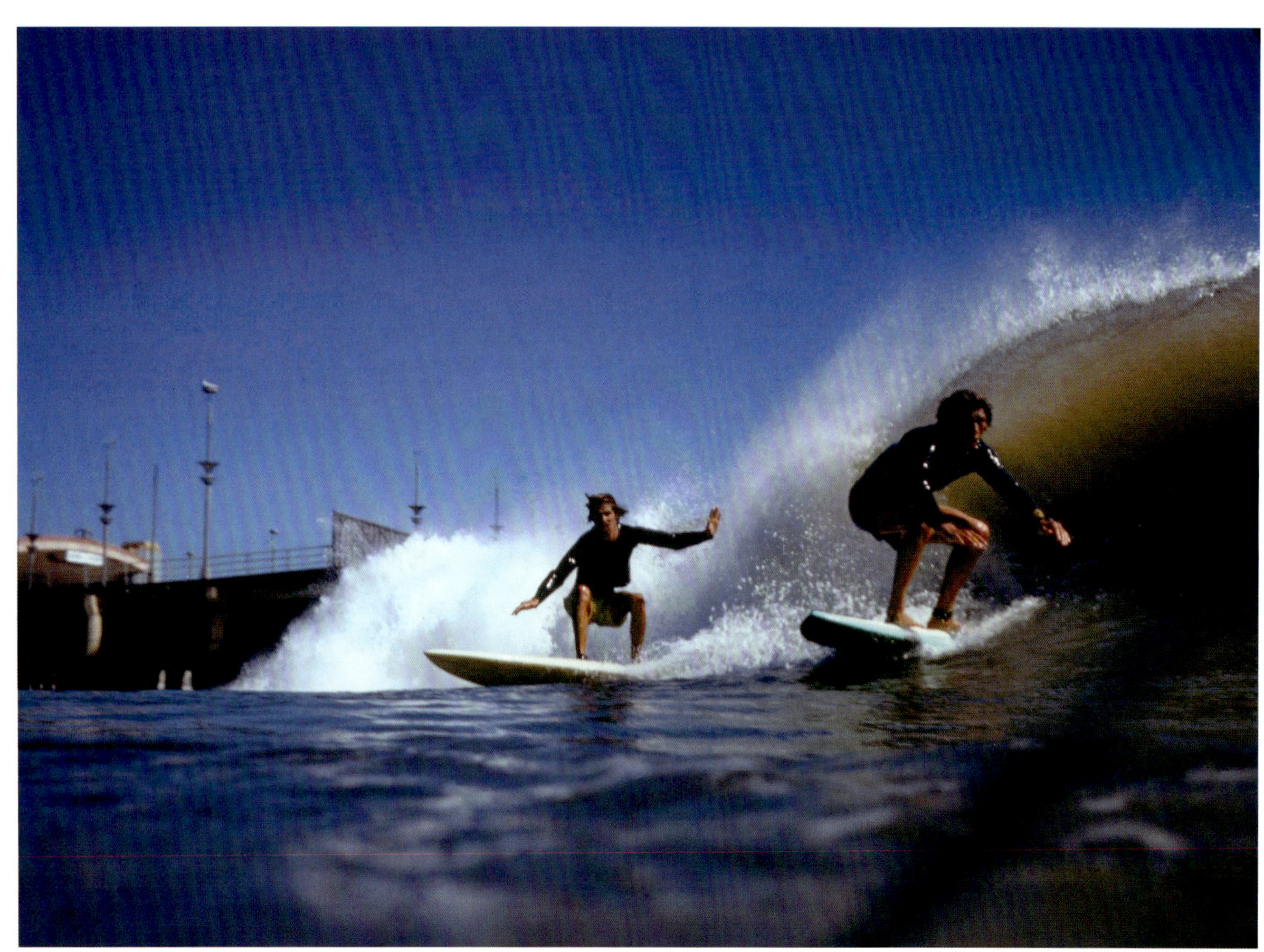

OCTOBER 1975. ATLANTIC CITY, NJ

Steve Alper (foreground) at Garden Pier, Atlantic City, New Jersey.
Gene Sykes in back—most famous drop-in quote of all time: "I didn't see you."

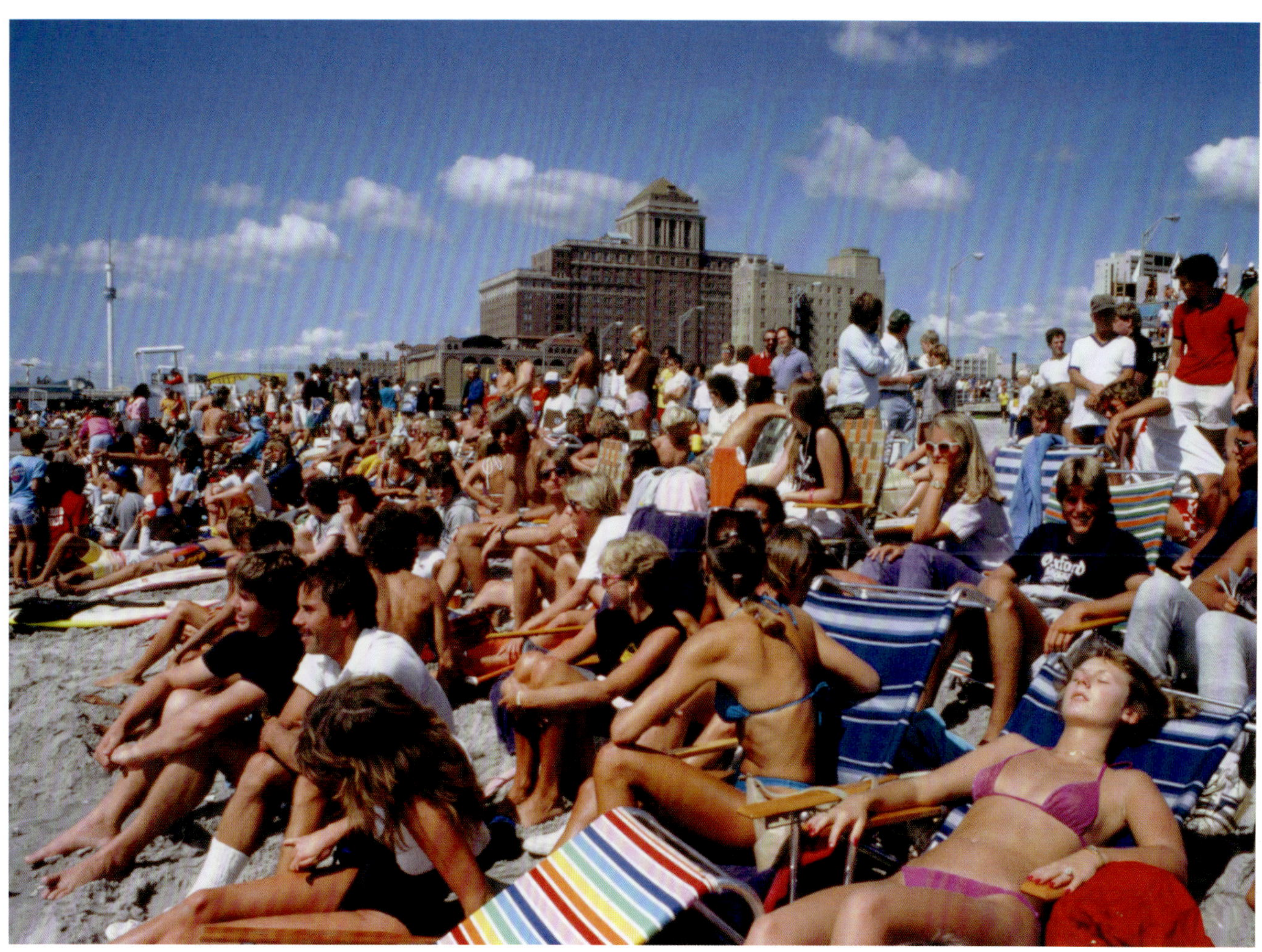

AUGUST 1983. ATLANTIC CITY, NJ

OP East Professional World Tour Contest, Atlantic City, New Jersey. This was the biggest surf contest in New Jersey—still is to this day. It was a big deal that every top surferfrom around the world came to Atlantic City. This was in the early casino days. Atlantic City's first casino, Resorts International, is in the background. The skinny needle in the background was a tourist attraction that later was torn down.

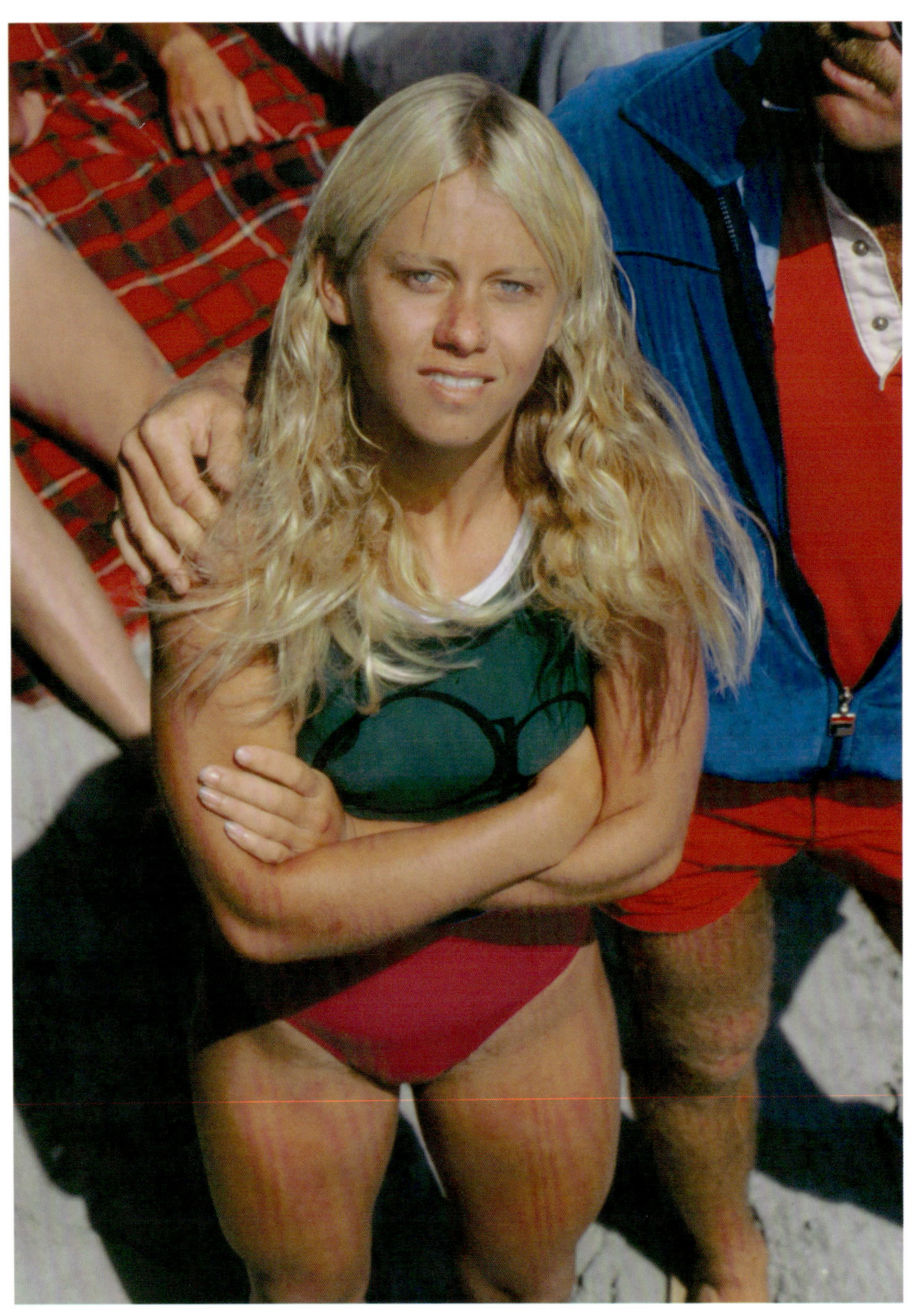

AUGUST 1983. ATLANTIC CITY, NJ

Frieda Zamba, OP Pro. She was a four-time world surf champion from Florida.

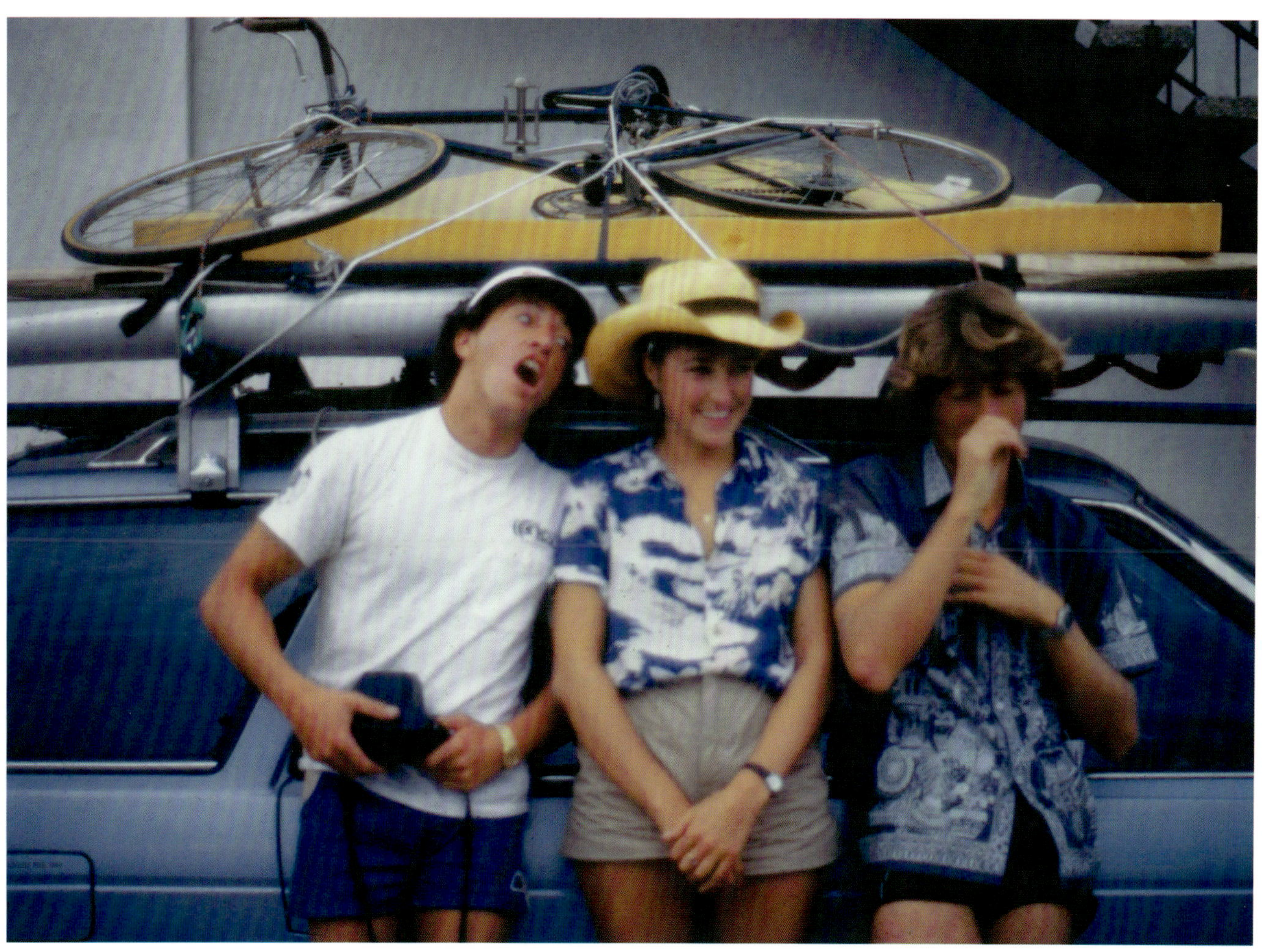

OCTOBER 1982

My car was packed up for my move back to New Jersey from California. I was relocating to the East Coast to head up sales for Rip Curl. At right, Derek Hynd, with Sandra Herman, and, at left, Derek's wingman/copilot. Derek and his Aussie mate drove my car cross-country to New Jersey.

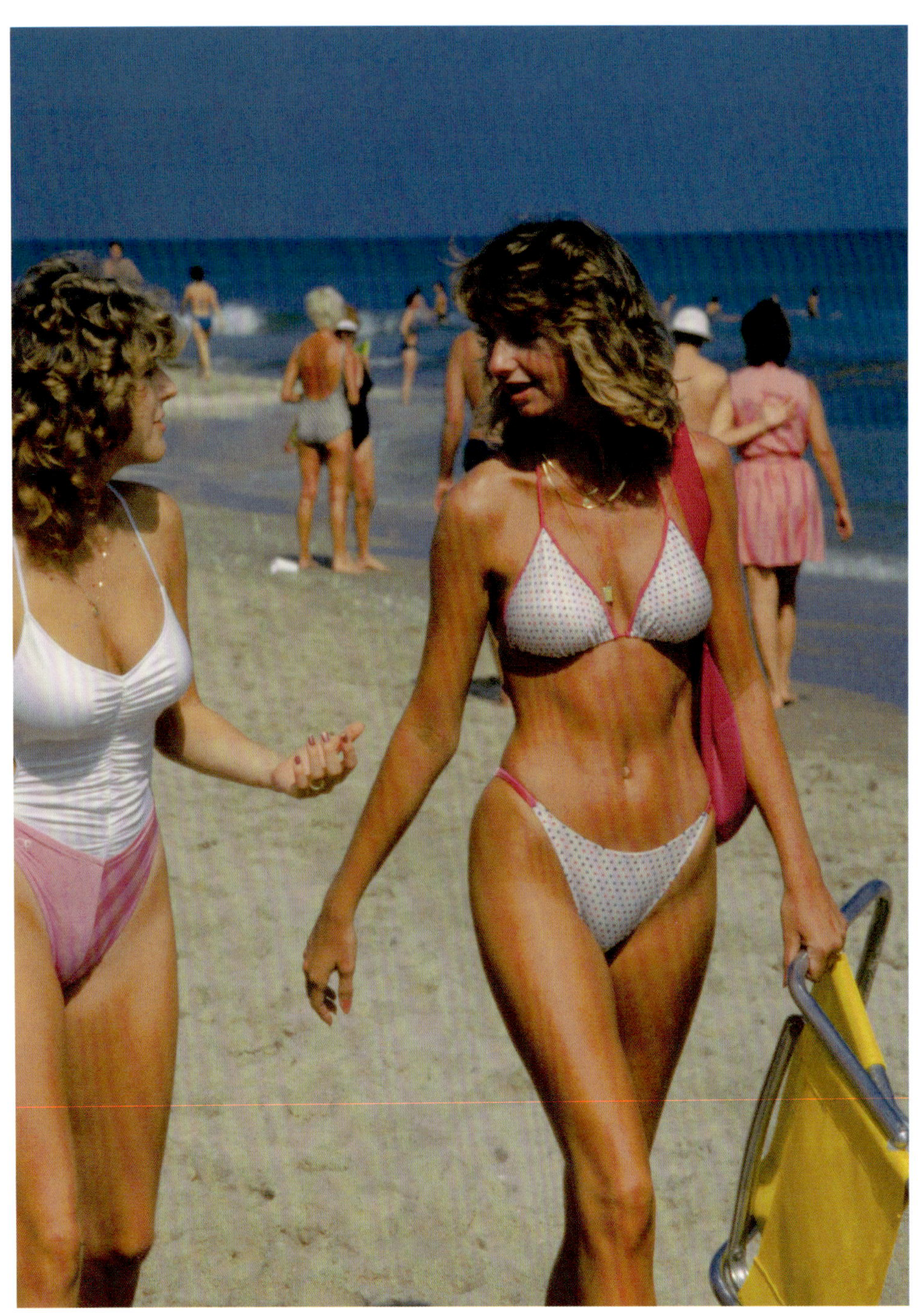

AUGUST 1983

Summertime at the Jersey Shore.

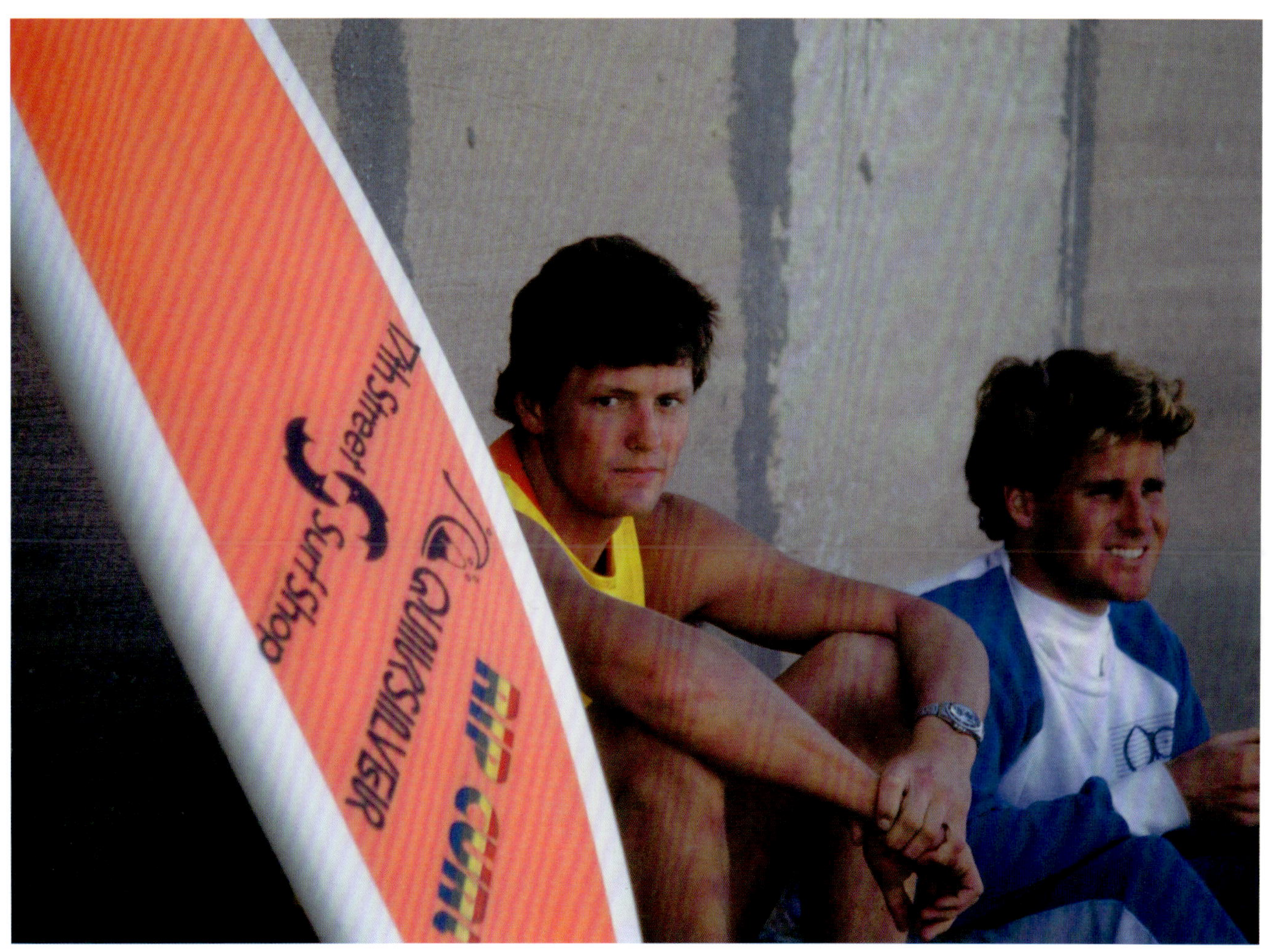

AUGUST 1983

Wes Laine, pro surfer from Virginia Beach, Virginia. He won the OP Pro Atlantic City. Sitting here with David Barr.

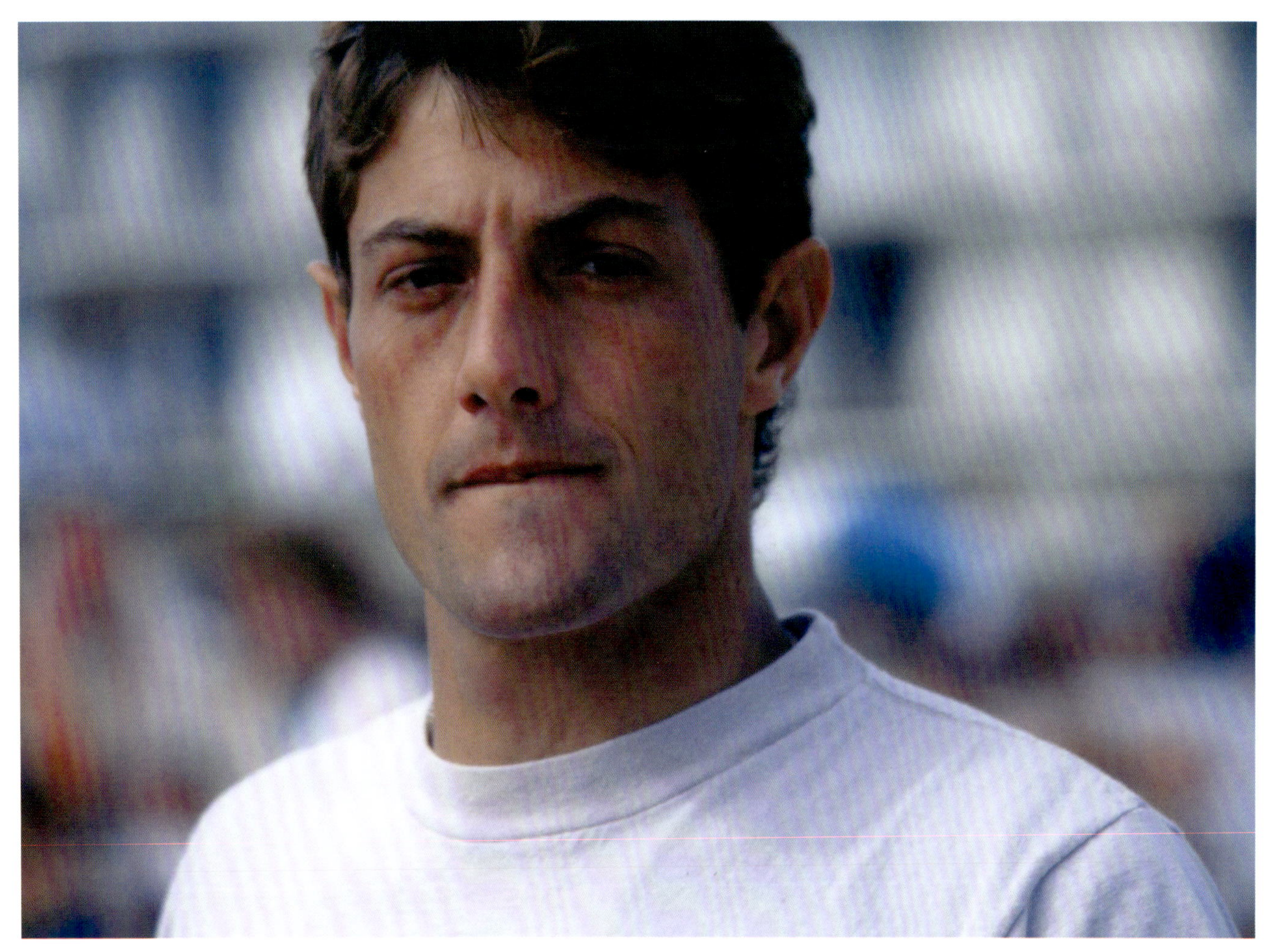

AUGUST 1983. ATLANTIC CITY, NJ

Shaun Tomson, Jersey Shore—1977 World Surf Champion.

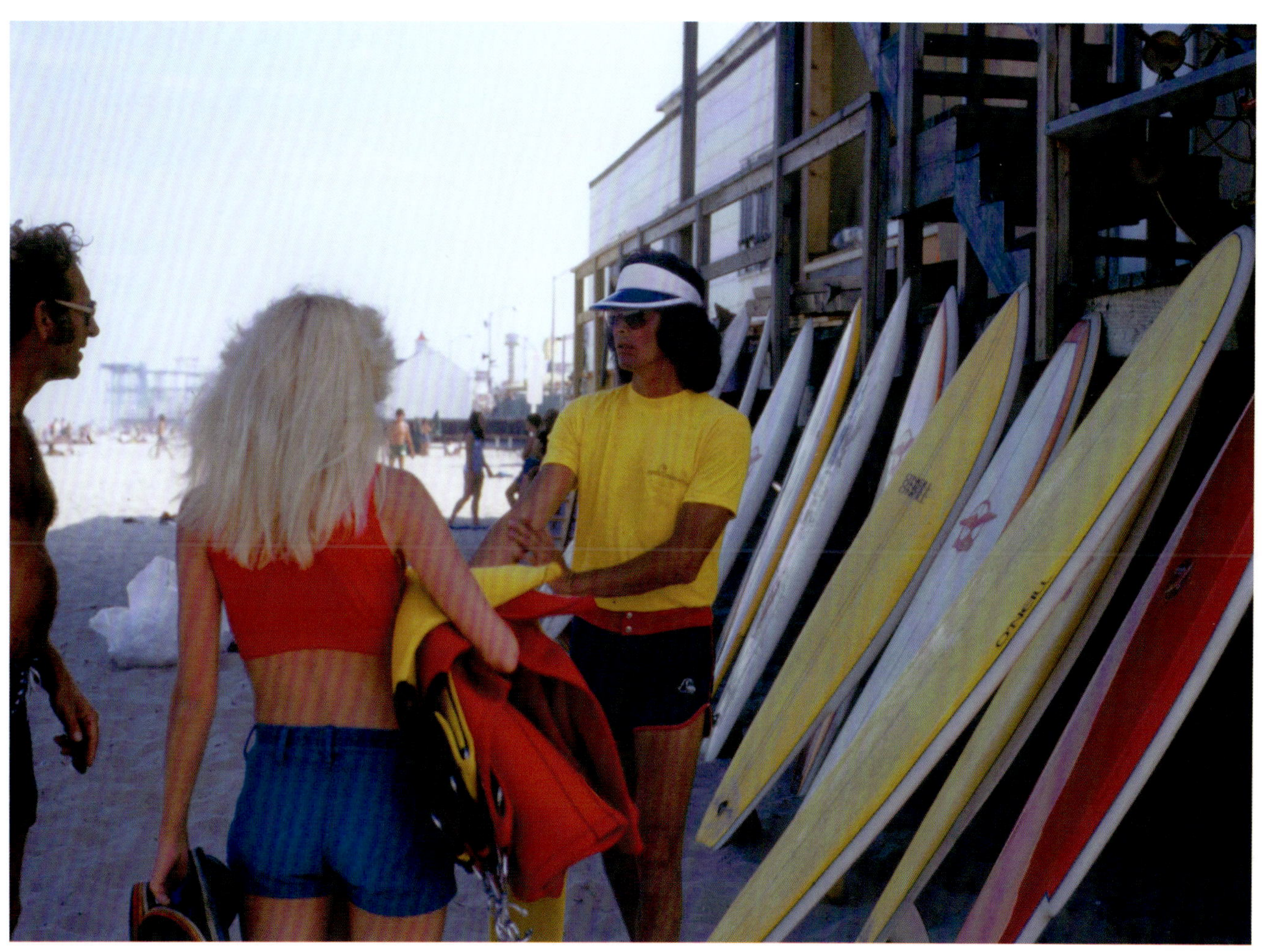

JULY 1977. SEASIDE HEIGHTS, NJ

David Nuuhiwa in yellow shirt with visor, talking to the Godfather of East Coast surfing, Dick Catri from Florida, at the Grog's Seaside Pro contest. Check out those boards lined up.

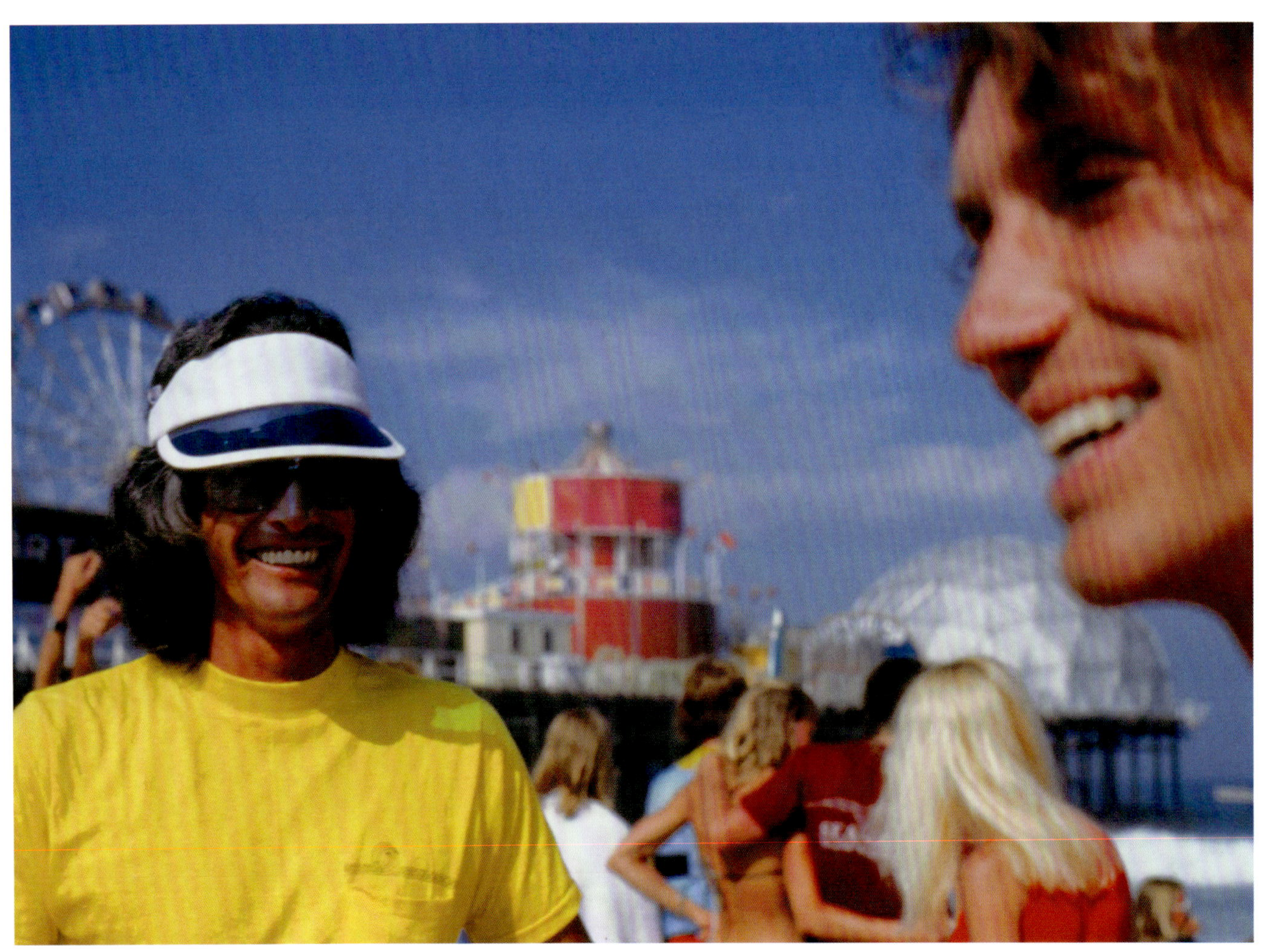

JULY 1977. SEASIDE HEIGHTS, NJ

Greg "Grog" Mesanko in foreground, having a laugh with David Nuuhiwa, at the Grog's Seaside Pro contest. Casino Pier in the background.

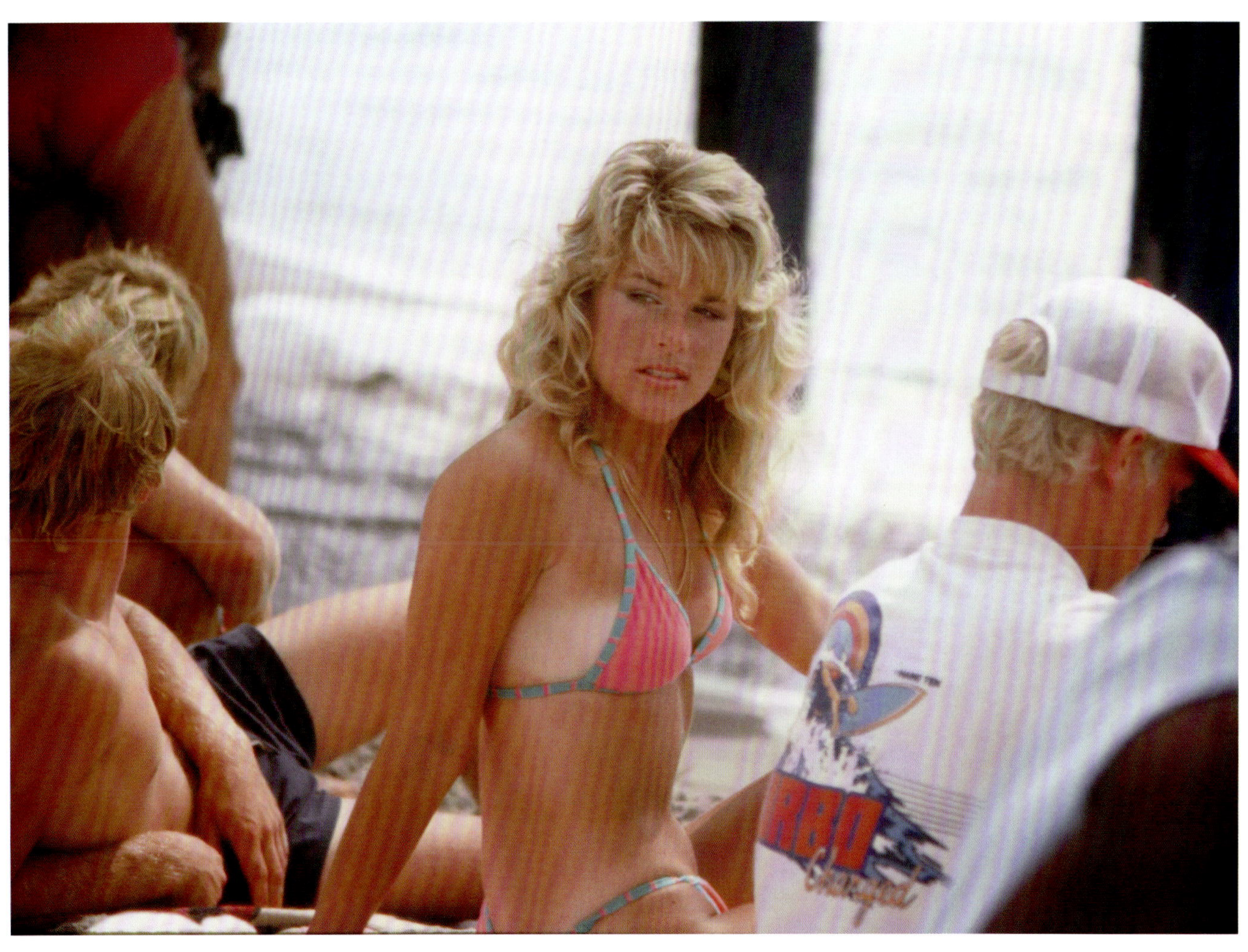

AUGUST 1983. OP PRO, ATLANTIC CITY, NJ

Taking in the contest, with Joey Buran at right.

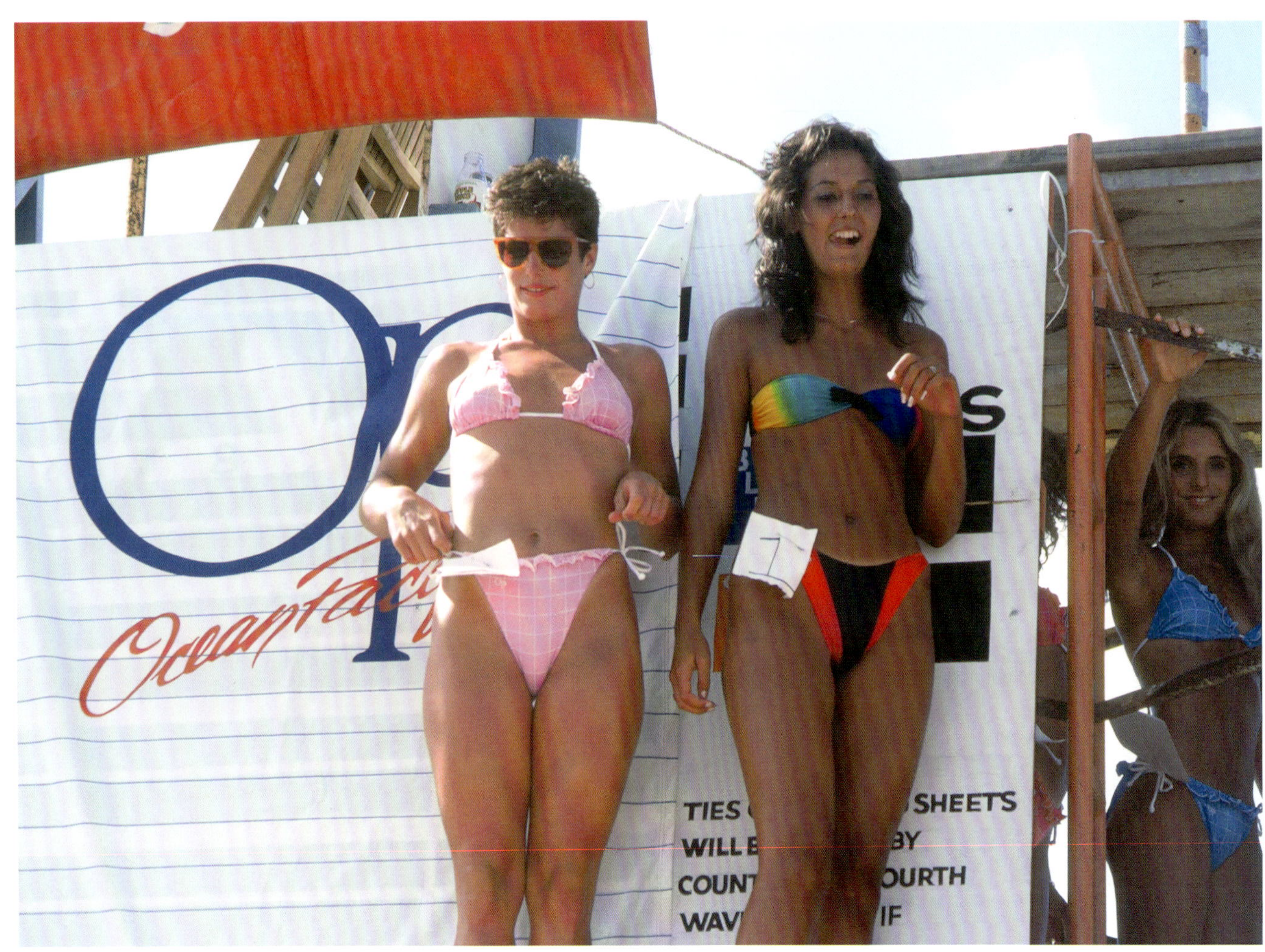

AUGUST 1983. OP PRO, ATLANTIC CITY, NJ

Karen Keough on left, with unidentified bikini contestant and Heidi Wentz in background.

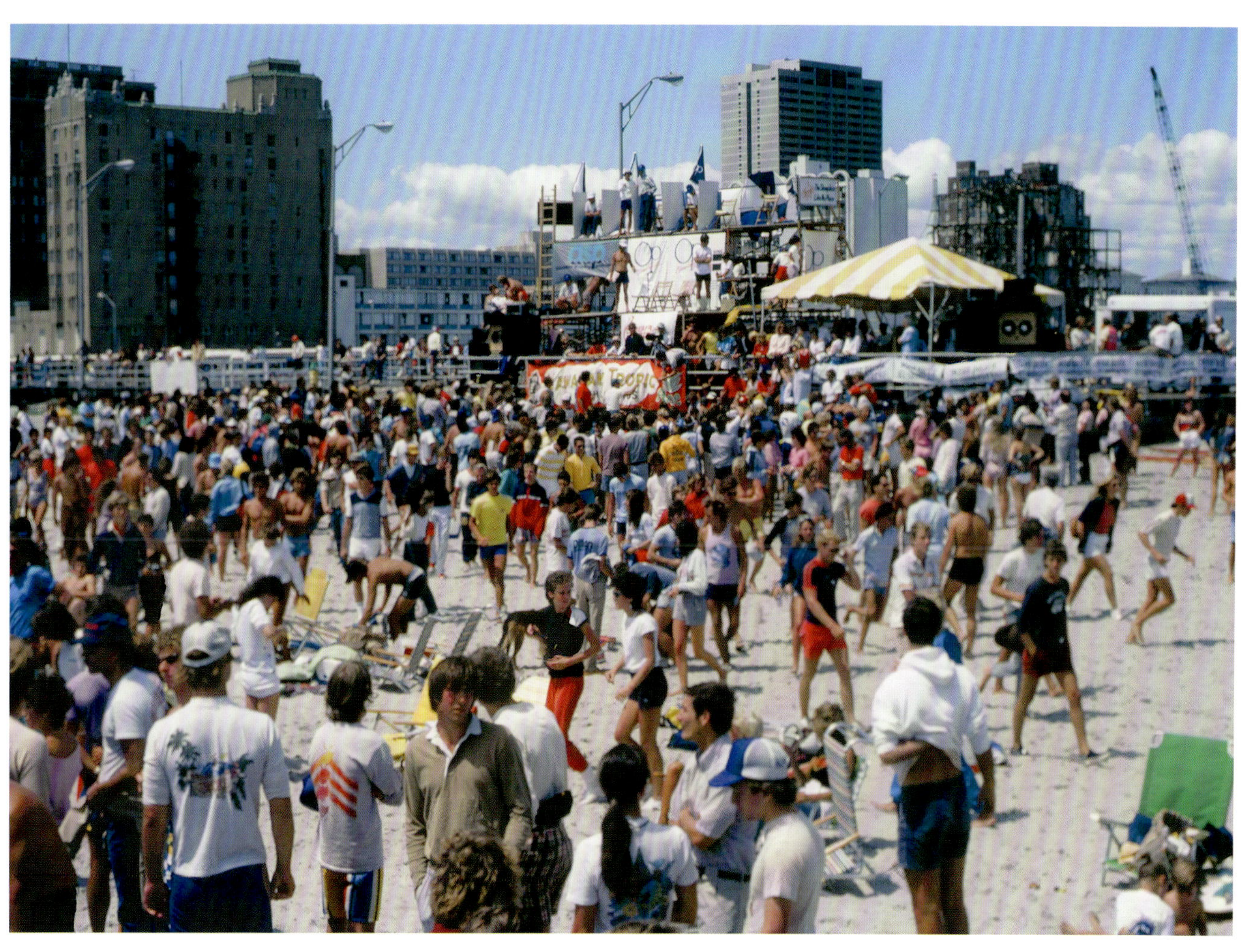

AUGUST 1983. OP PRO, ATLANTIC CITY, NJ

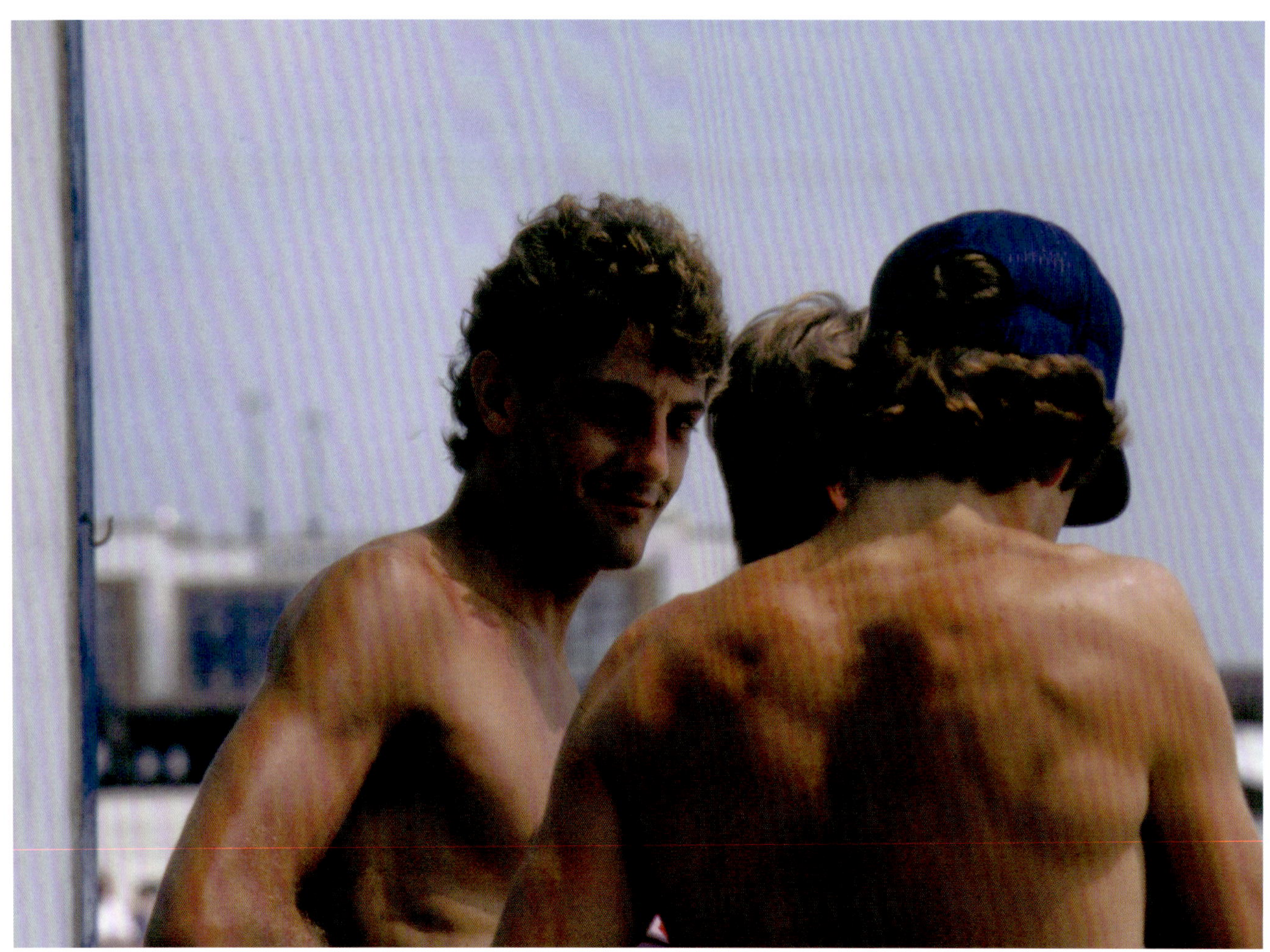

AUGUST 1983. ATLANTIC CITY, NJ

Shaun Tomson, '77 World Champion on the States Avenue lifeguard tower in Atlantic City, discussing the day with fellow competitors.

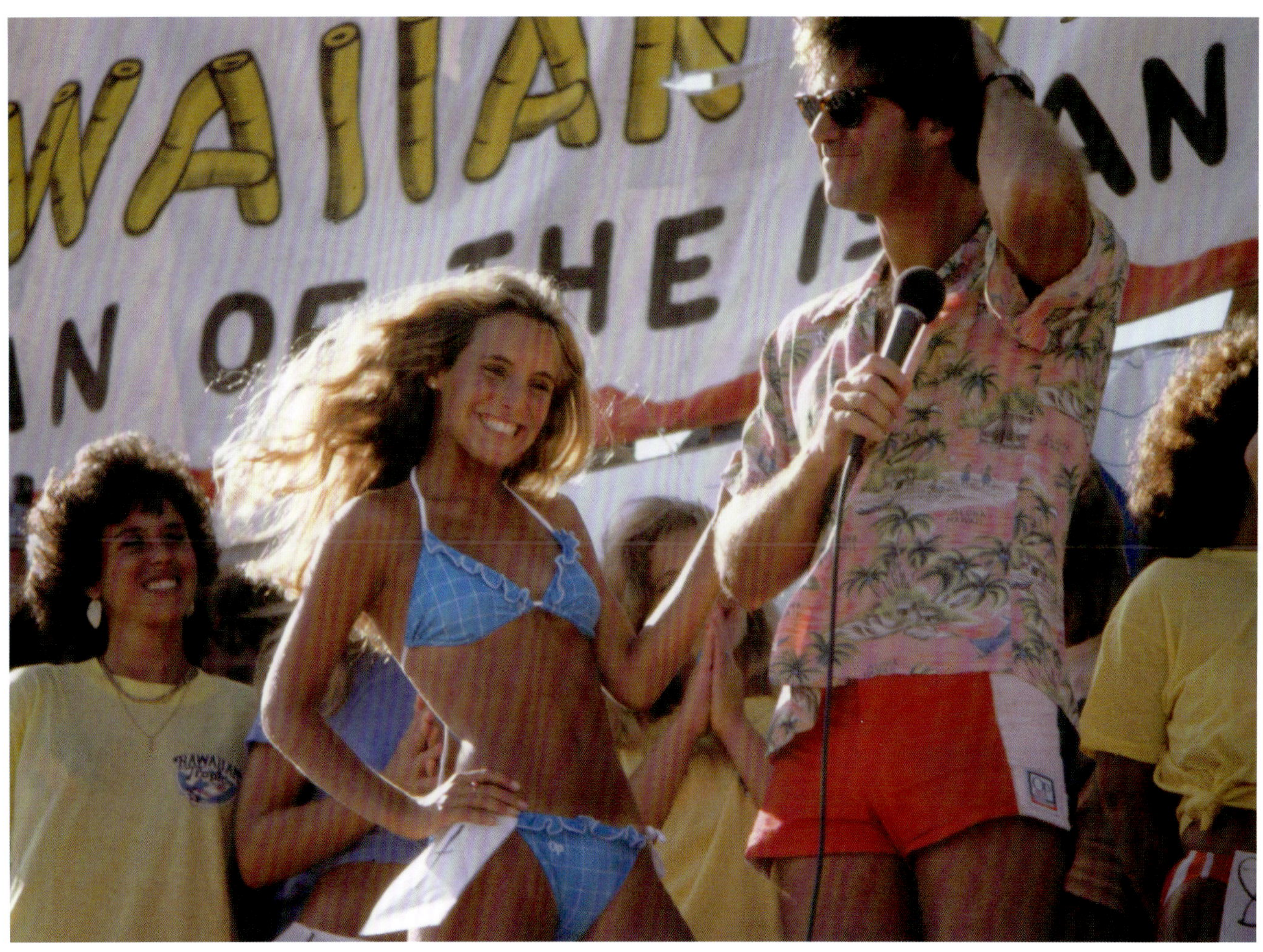

AUGUST 1983. ATLANTIC CITY, NJ

OP Pro bikini contest. D. David Moran, and local bikini contest standout Heidi Wentz.

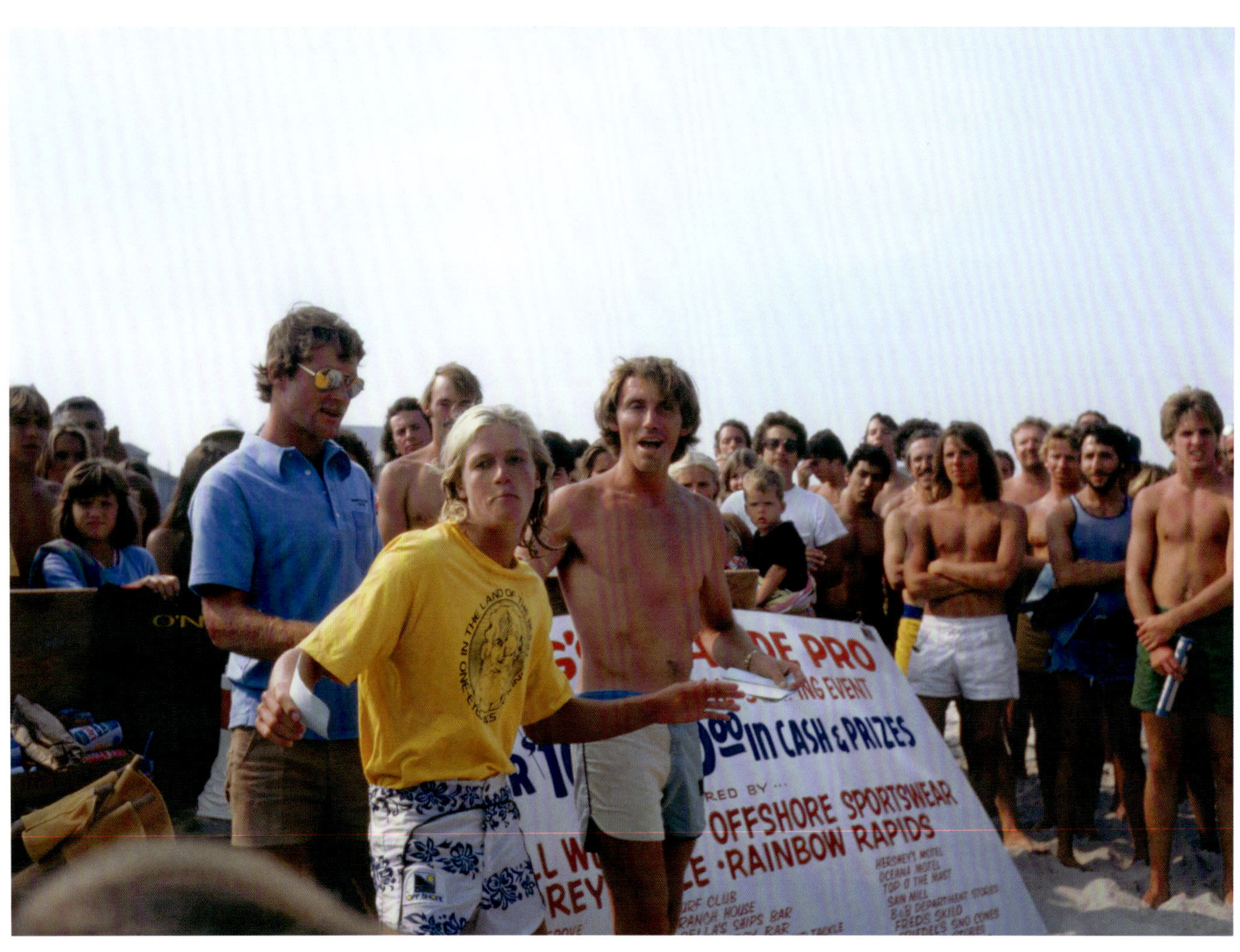

AUGUST 1978. GROG'S SEASIDE PRO, SEASIDE HEIGHTS, NJ

Randy Rarick (left, in blue), director of the World Surf Tour; Greg "Grog" Mesanko (right), contest promoter; and Pat Mulhern (in yellow), receiving his 2nd-place check. The contest was held in Seaside Heights. On the finals day, the city said it was too crowded on the beach, and the contest was moved, last minute, down to Meters in Seaside Park. They left behind all judging and spectator stands, grabbed the sign, and mobilized to finish the contest in the new location a few miles down the beach.

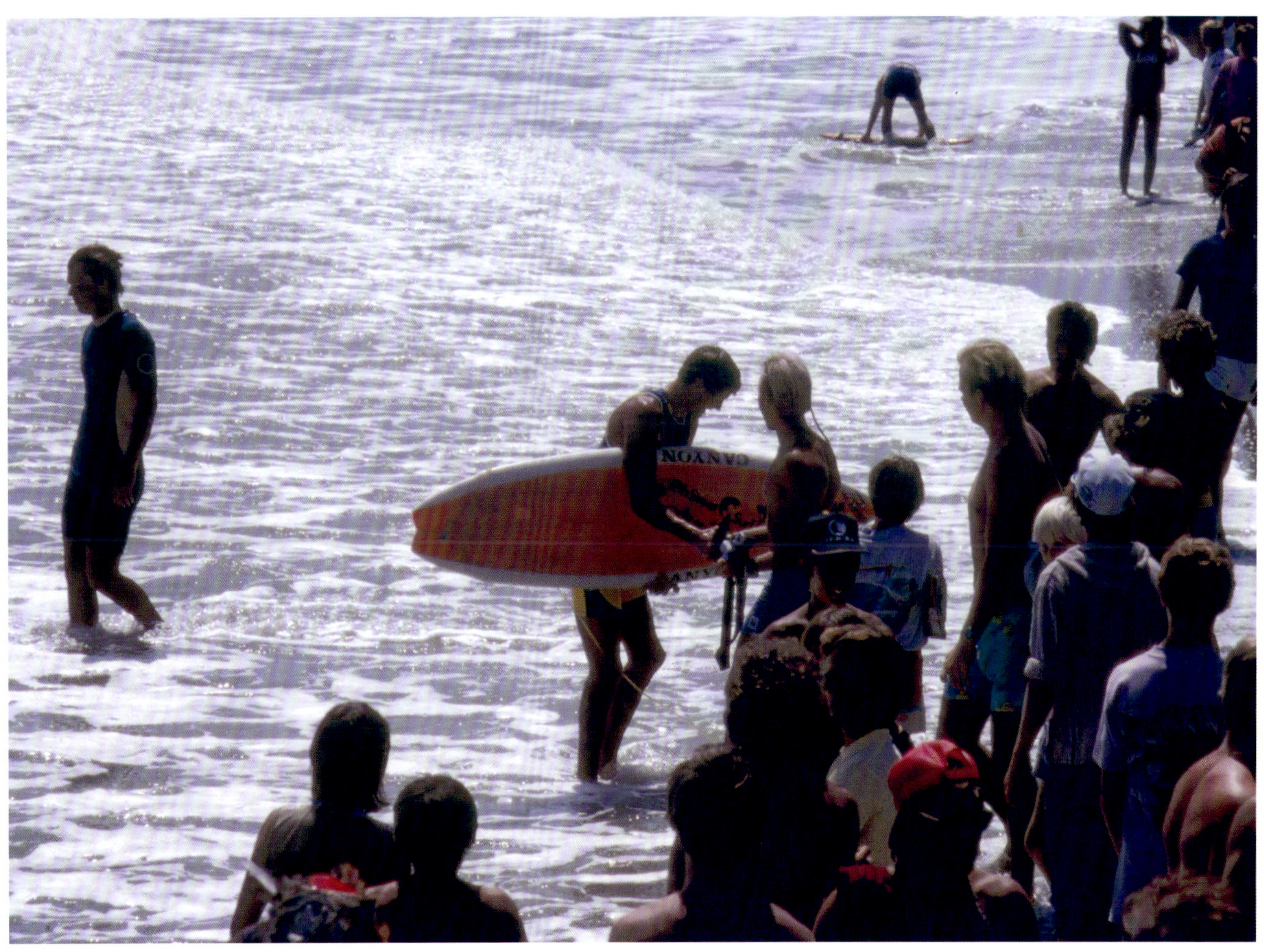

AUGUST 1983

Wes Laine of Virginia Beach, coming out of the water. He was the winner of the OP Pro Atlantic City. This was one of Wes's few world tour wins. He had an epic final with Bud Llamas of Huntington Beach, California.

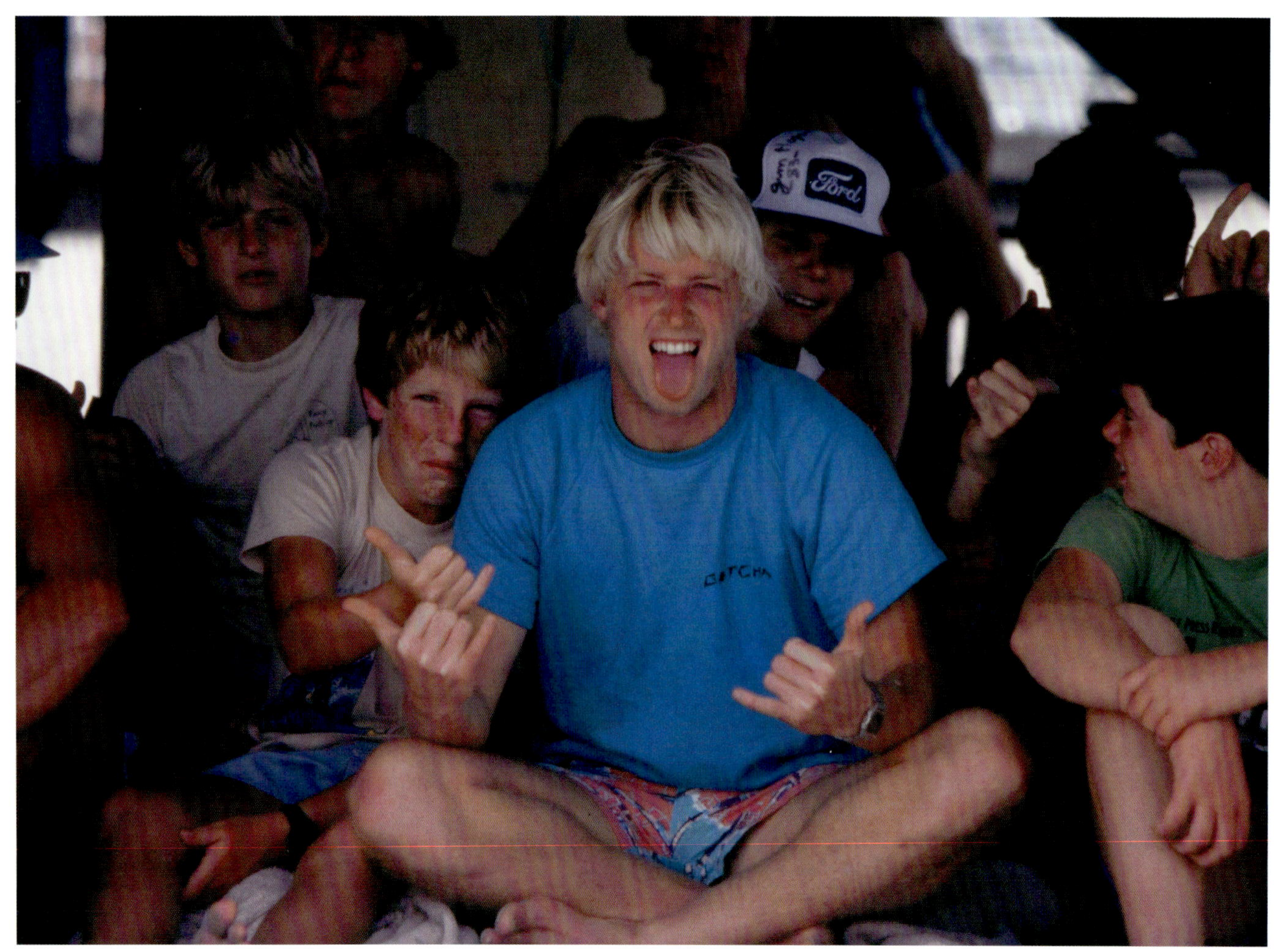

AUGUST 1983. OP PRO, ATLANTIC CITY, NJ

Cheyne Horan from Australia hanging out under the lifeguard tower with all the local groms at the OP Pro Atlantic City. Cheyne was an incredible competitor and all-around surfer, who was a four-time runner-up to World Champion Mark Richards every time.

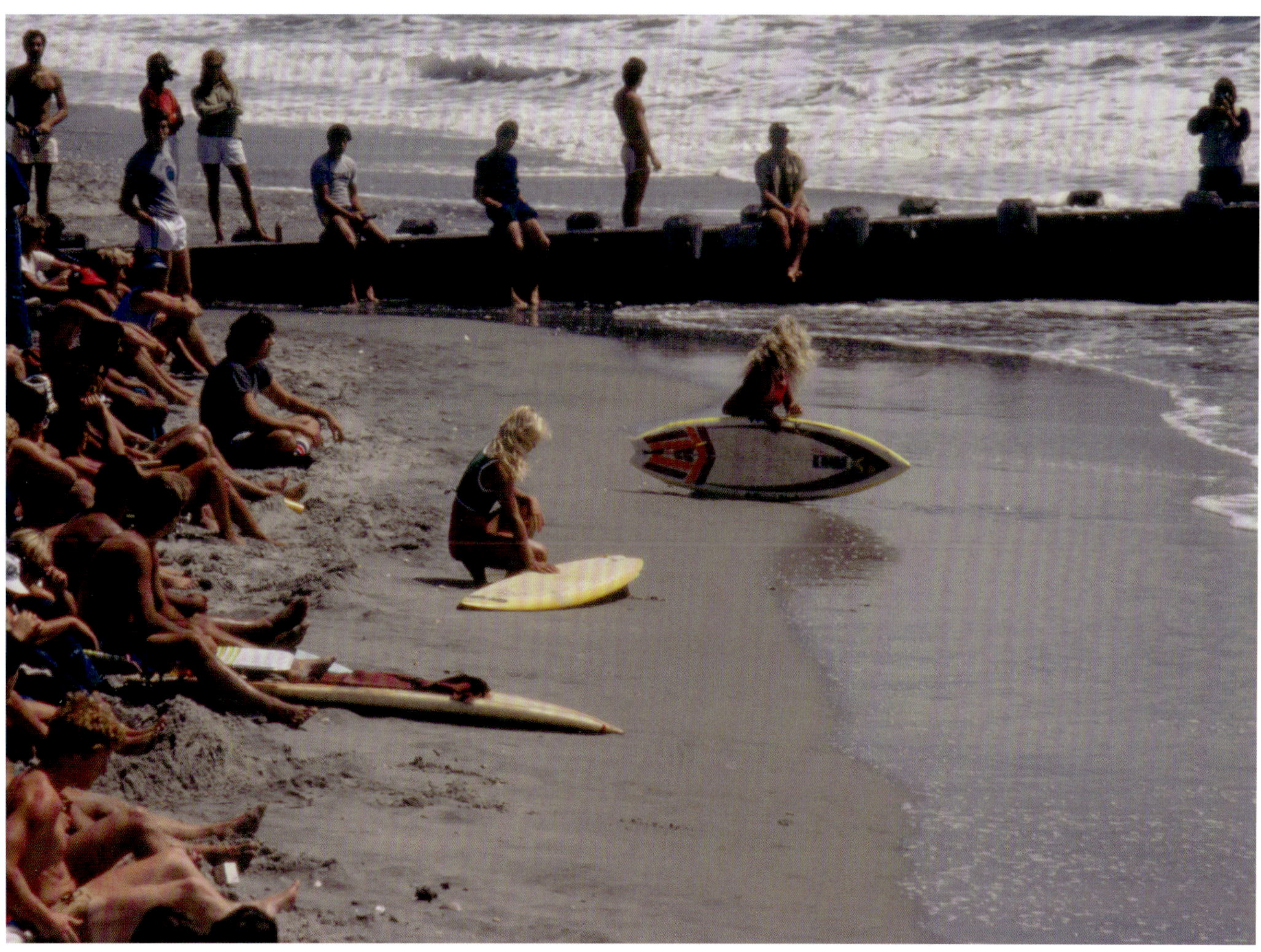

AUGUST 1983. OP PRO, ATLANTIC CITY, NJ

Florida's Frieda Zamba, left, and Kim Mearig, right, from Santa Barbara, California, get ready for their heat at the OP Pro Atlantic City. I believe this was the final, and Frieda won.

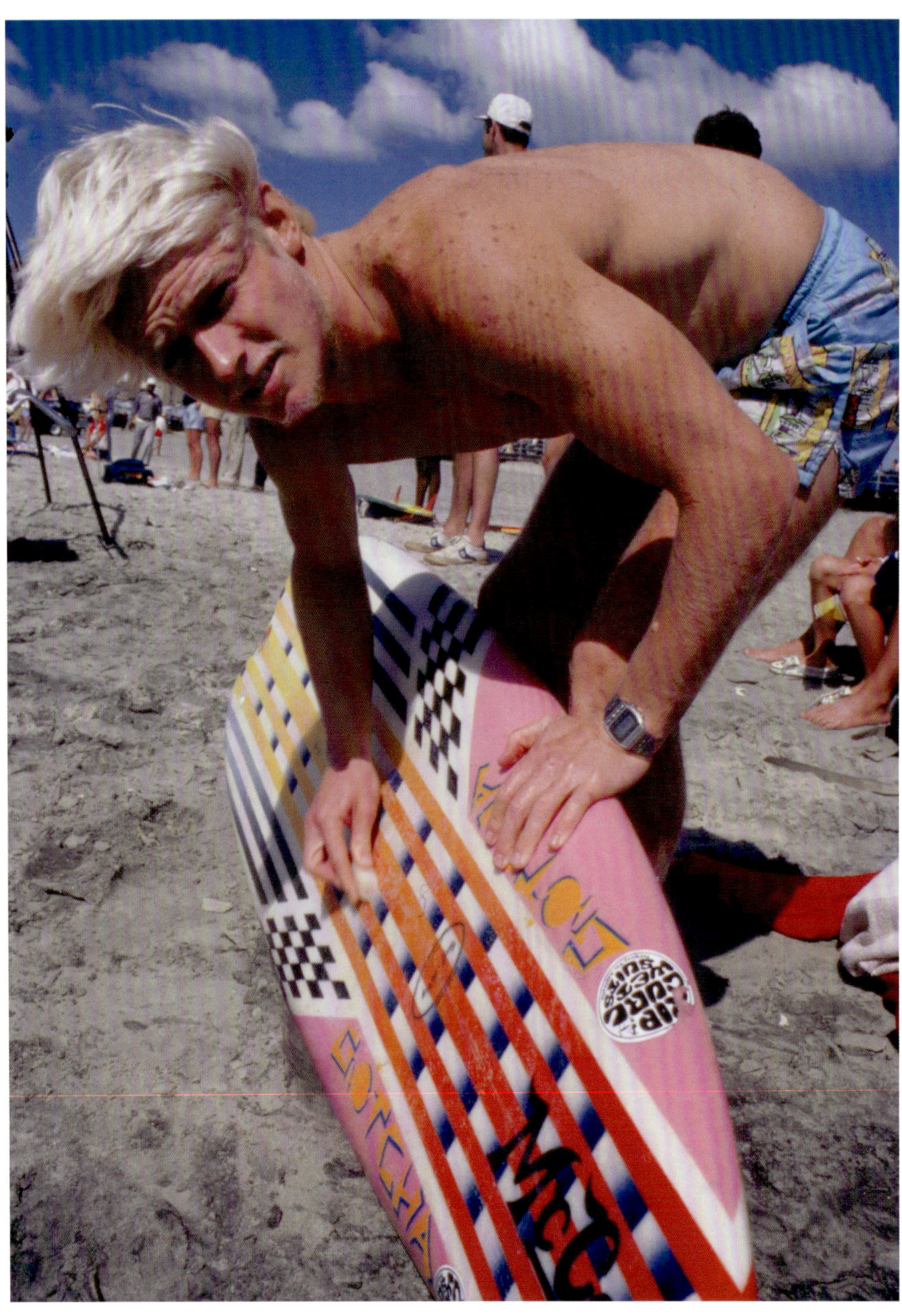

AUGUST 1983. OP PRO, ATLANTIC CITY, NJ

Cheyne Horan from Bondi Beach, Australia. In his early days he was a young gun on the "Bronzed Aussies" surf team. Some of the other members were Peter "PT" Townend, Ian Cairns, Jim Banks, and Mark Warren.

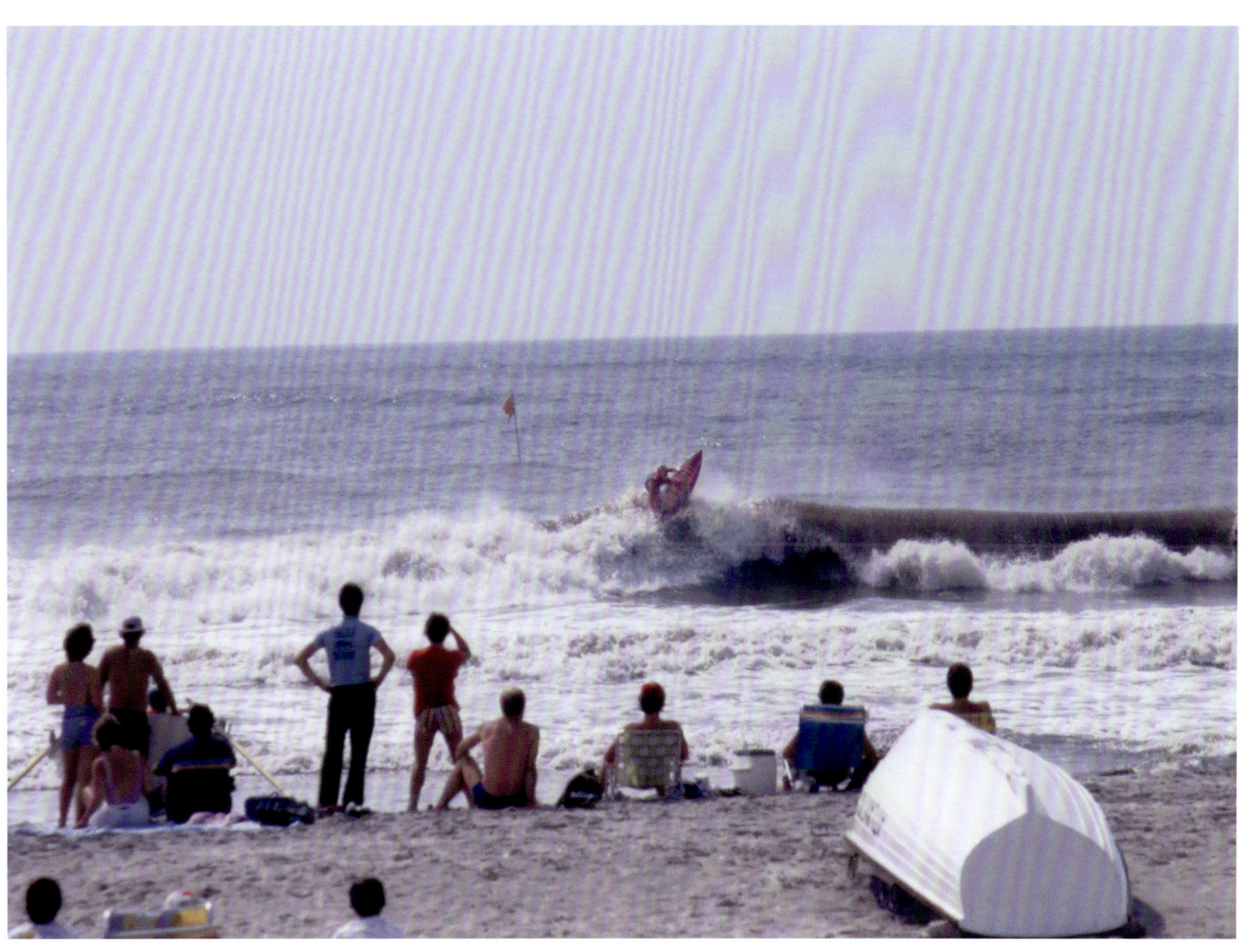

AUGUST 1983. CHEYNE HORAN, OP PRO, ATLANTIC CITY, NJ

A huge backside off the lip.

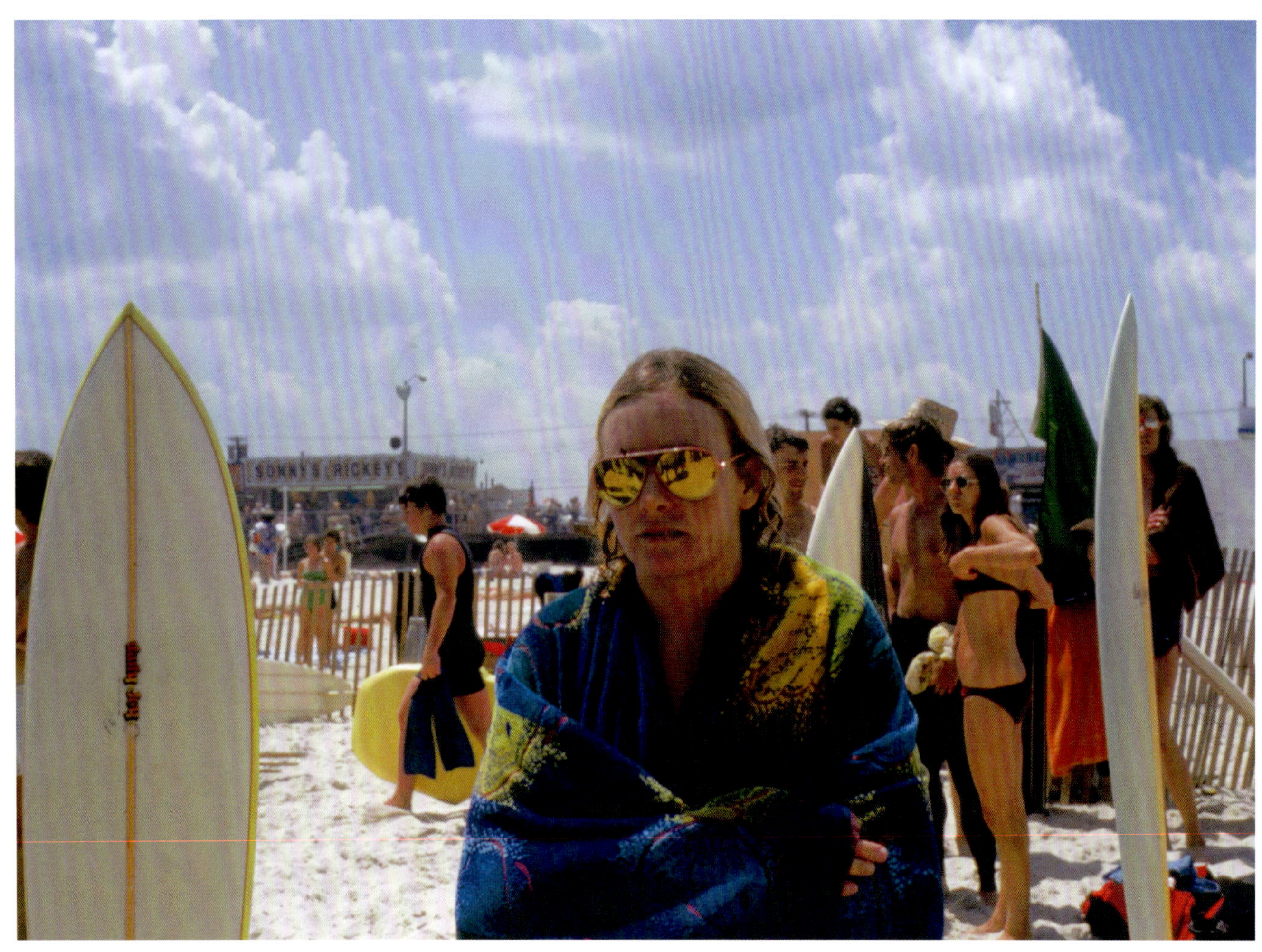

JUNE 1977. LINDA DAVOLI, SEASIDE HEIGHTS, NJ

Linda was the first East Coast surfer to win an ASP-ranked pro event, winning the 1981 Bells Beach contest in Australia. That year, she was runner-up to the world champion, Margo Oberg.

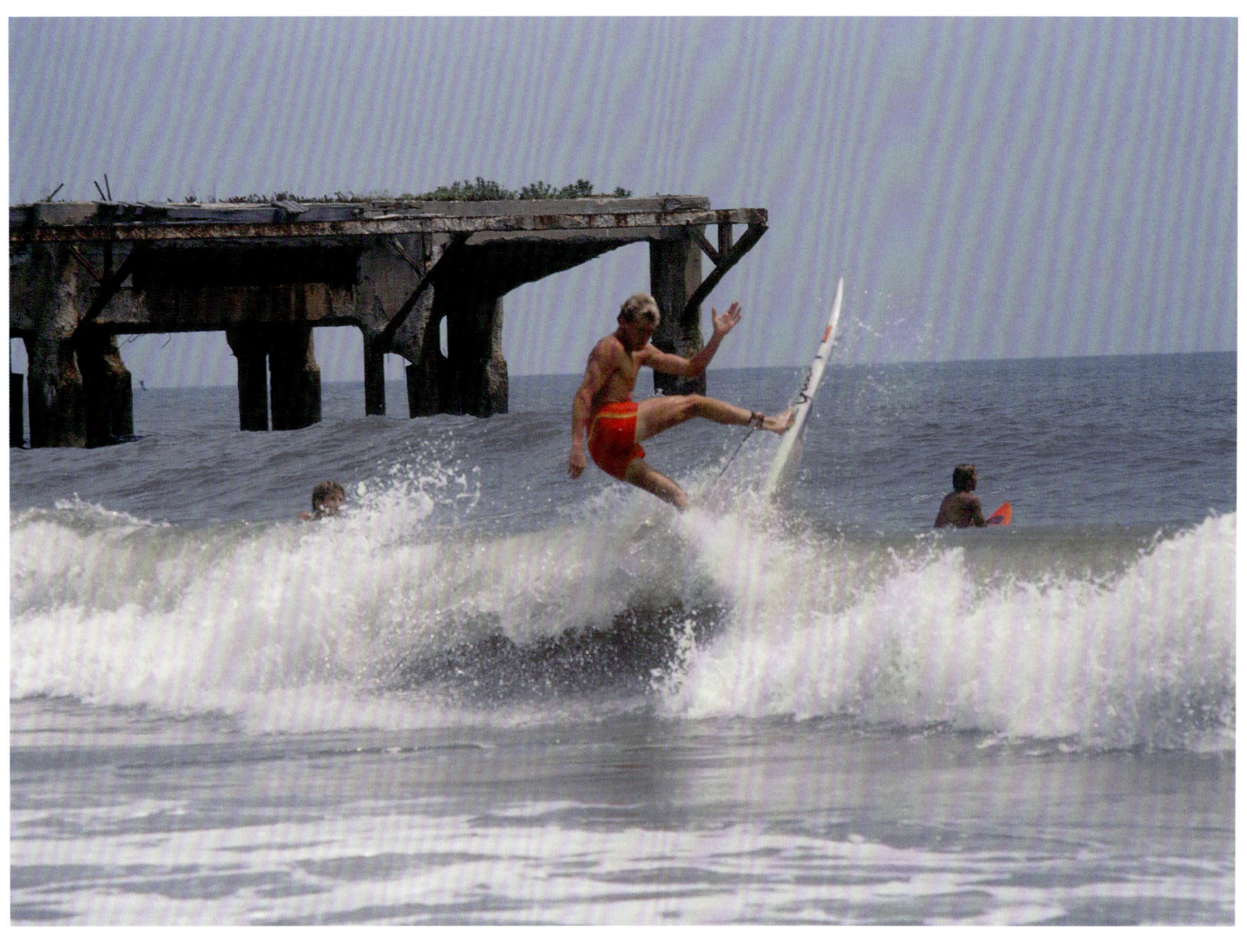

JUNE 1977

Floridian Matt Kechele.

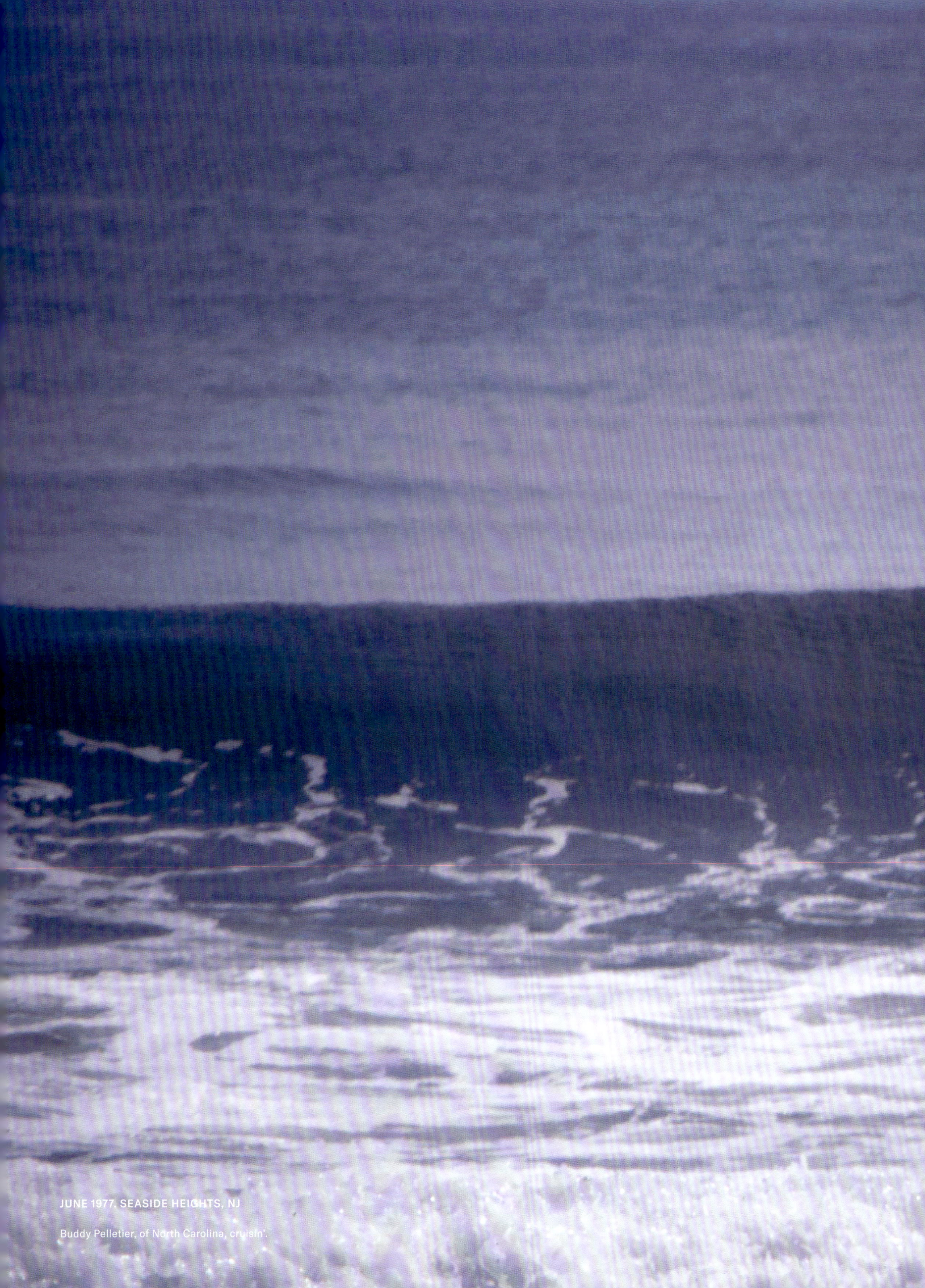

JUNE 1977, SEASIDE HEIGHTS, NJ

Buddy Pelletier, of North Carolina, cruisin'.

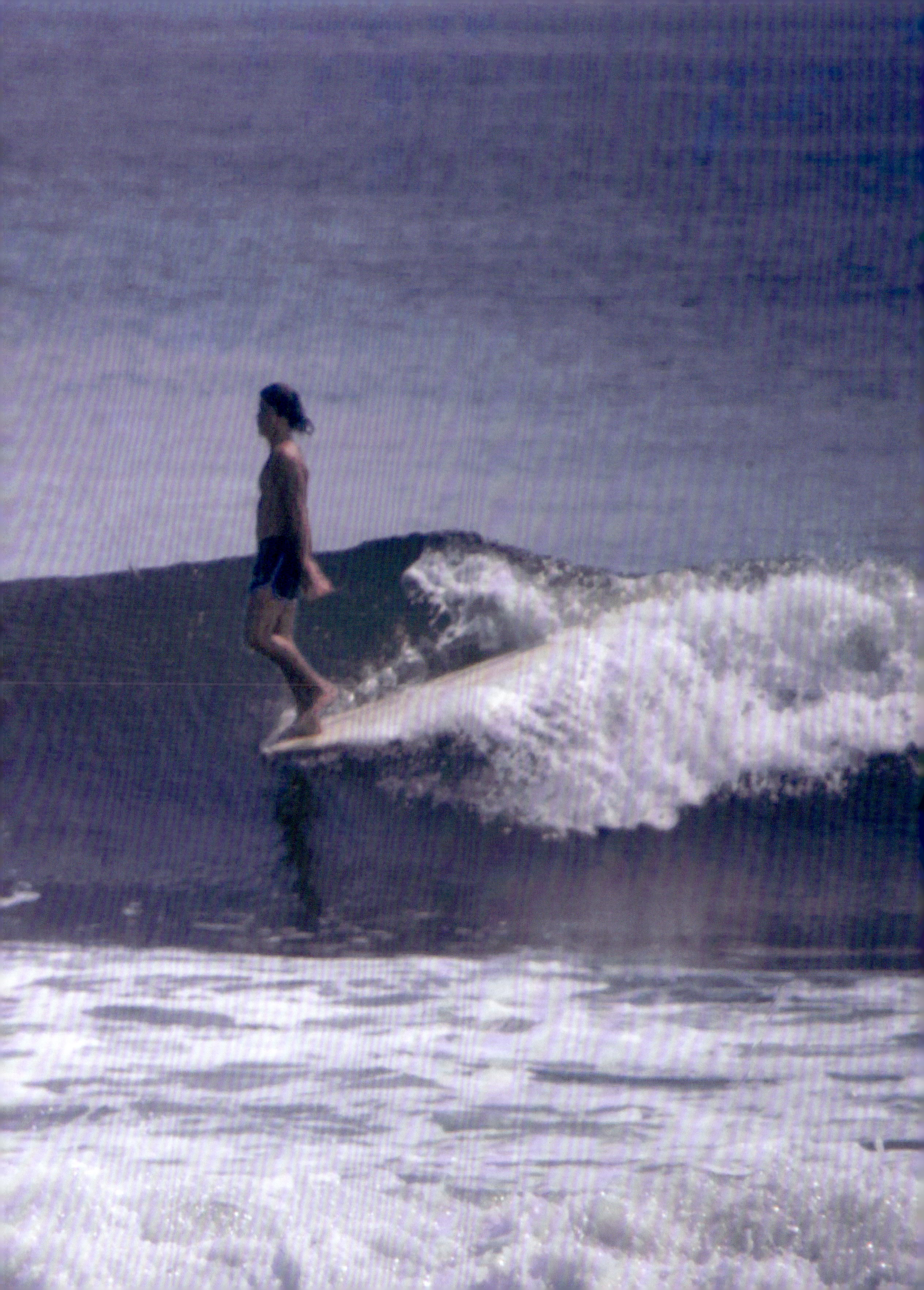

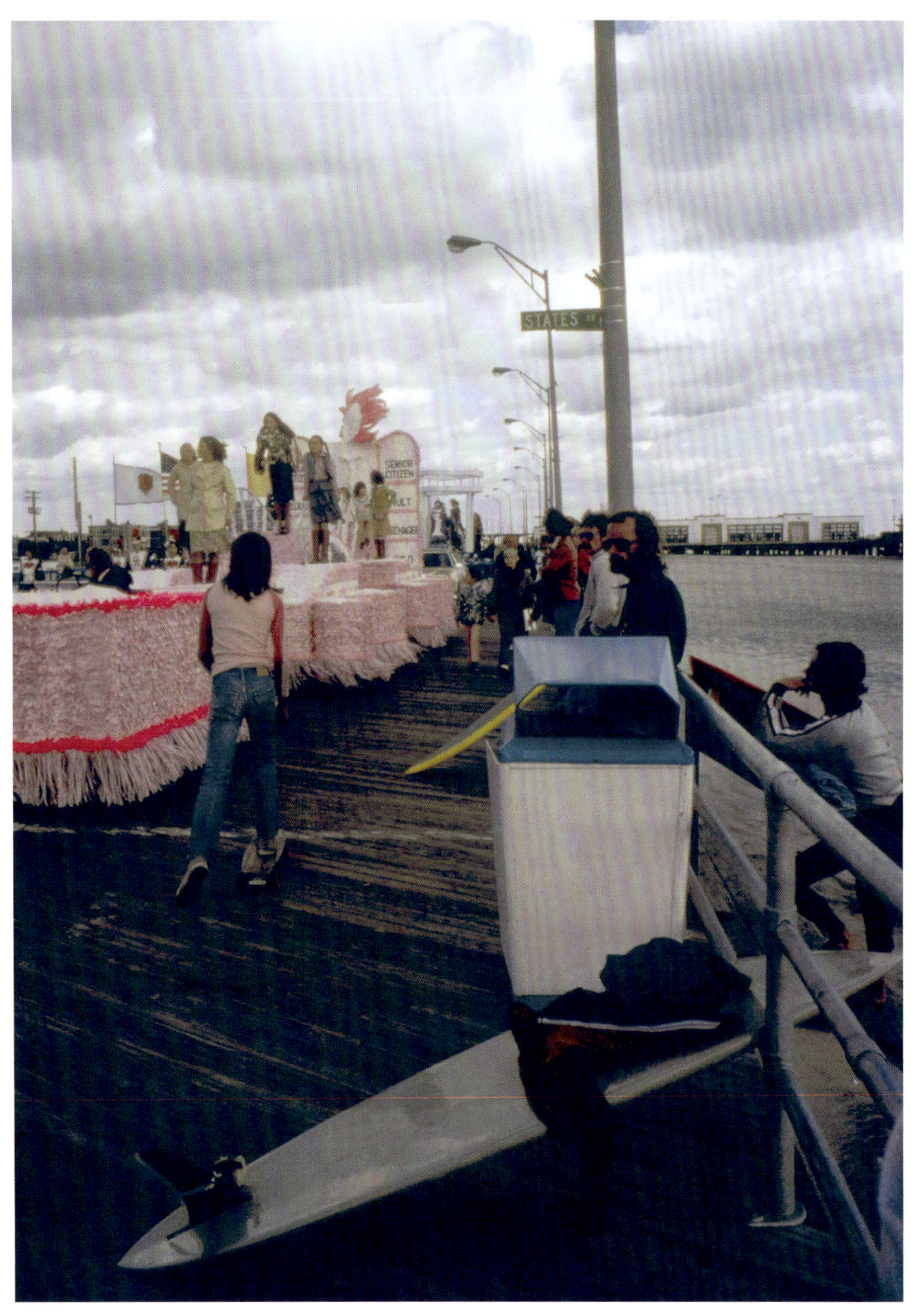

OCTOBER 1978. GAS CHAMBER, STATES AVENUE, ATLANTIC CITY, NJ

Group of surfers finishing up a session at Gas Chamber, States Avenue, watching one of many parades that ran down the Atlantic City Boardwalk.

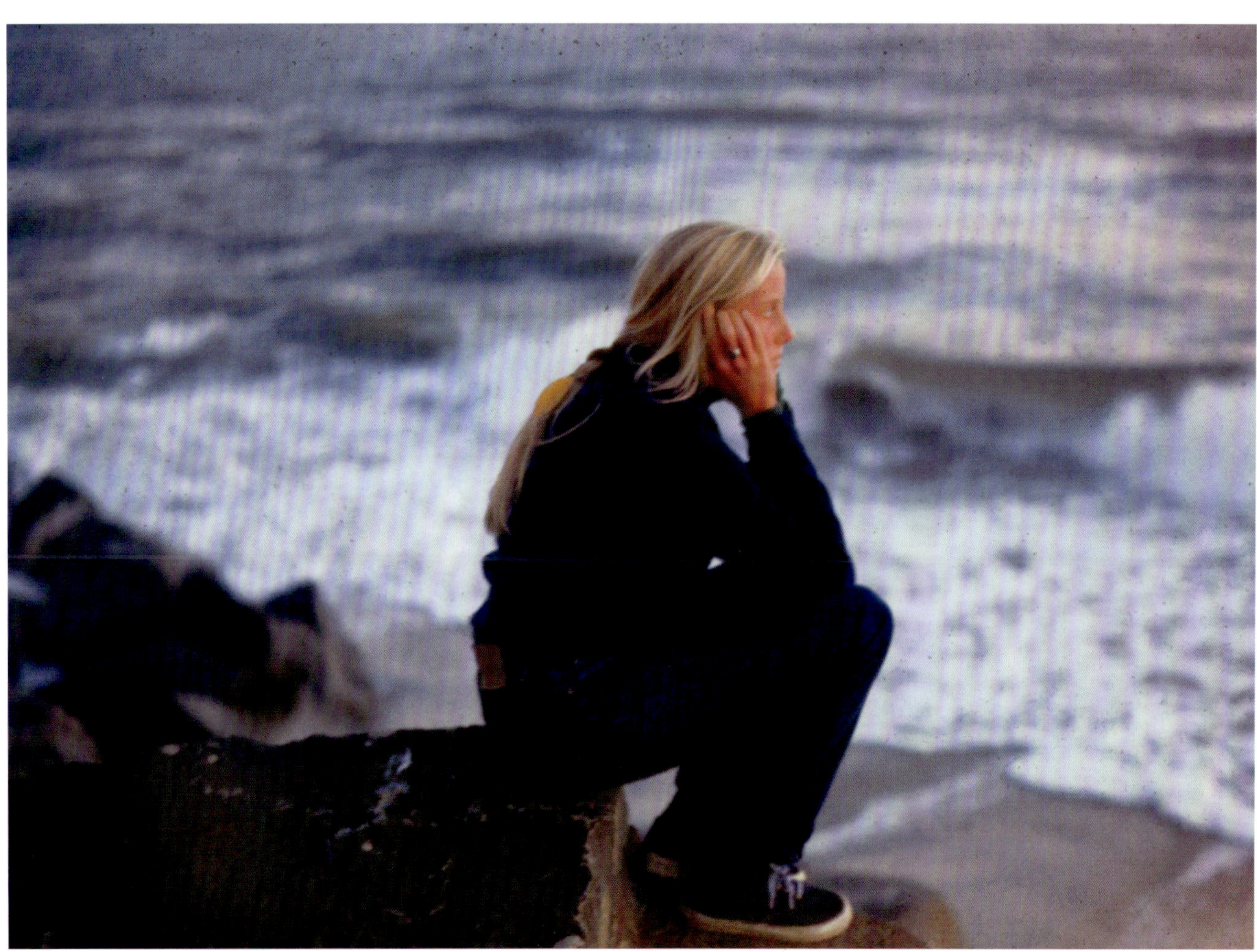

OCTOBER 1975. LONGPORT, NJ

Nancy Hyde Gudauskas in deep thought, watching the surf, at the point in Longport, New Jersey. This was a great place to watch sunsets. It was at the southern tip of the island looking over the bay at the Ocean City inlet. We both grew up on the island a few blocks from each other.

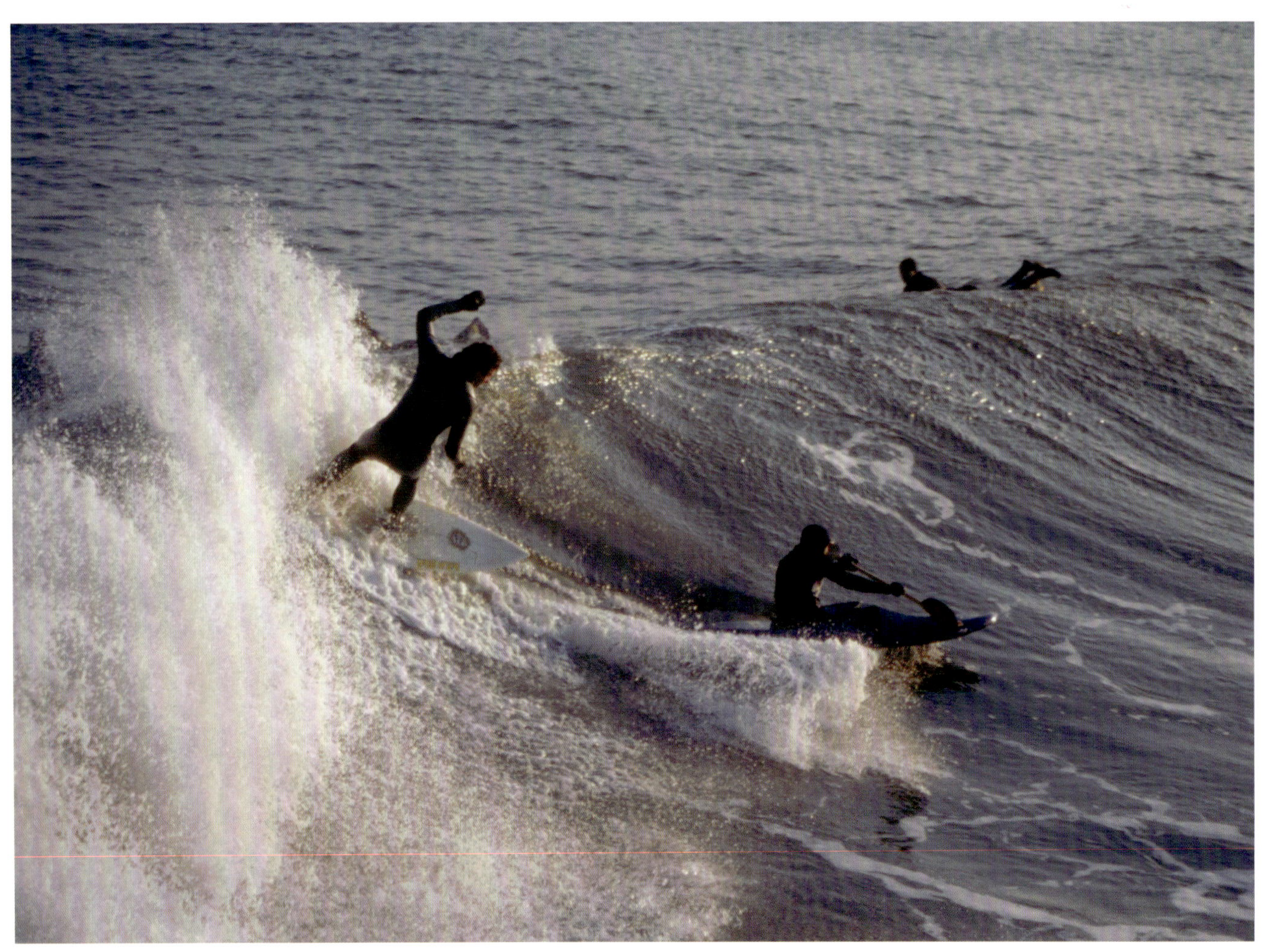

MARCH 1984. ATLANTIC CITY, NJ

This photo was taken from the end of Central Pier in Atlantic City, the famous New York Avenue left. Two of my good friends sharing a wave—flying off the top is Dave Kilpatrick dropping in on local Frank DiNoto.

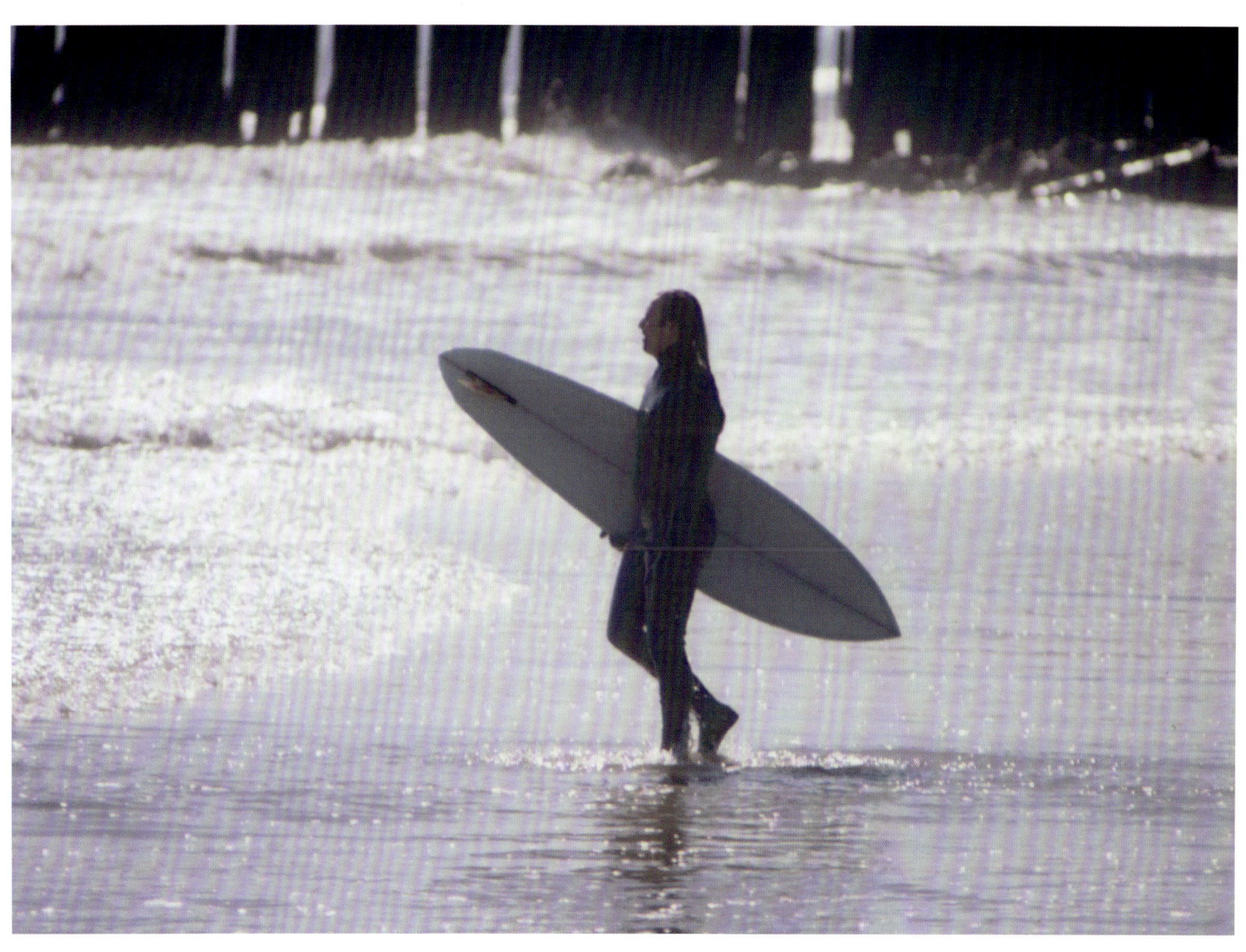

MARCH 1979. GAS CHAMBER, STATES AVENUE, ATLANTIC CITY, NJ

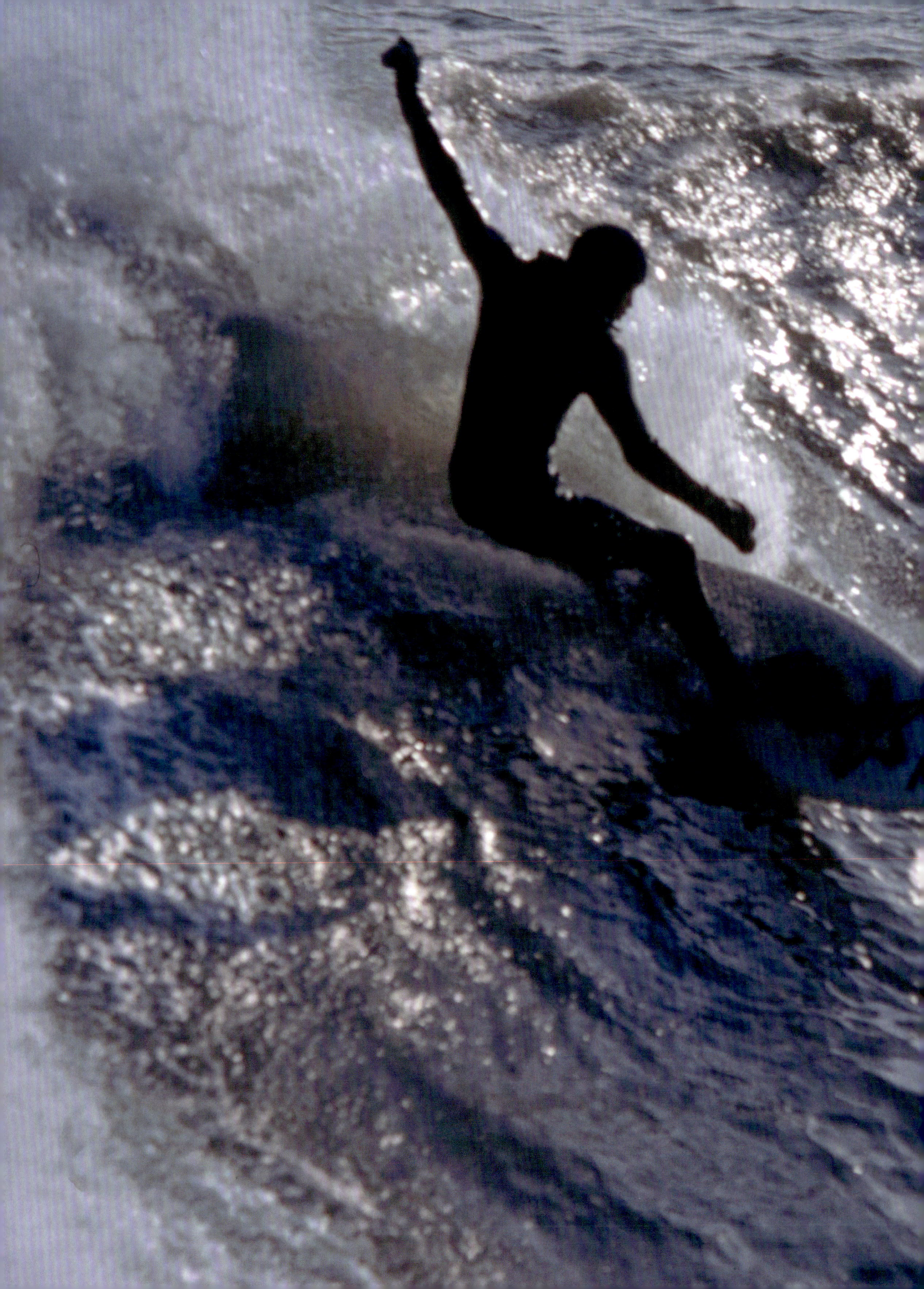

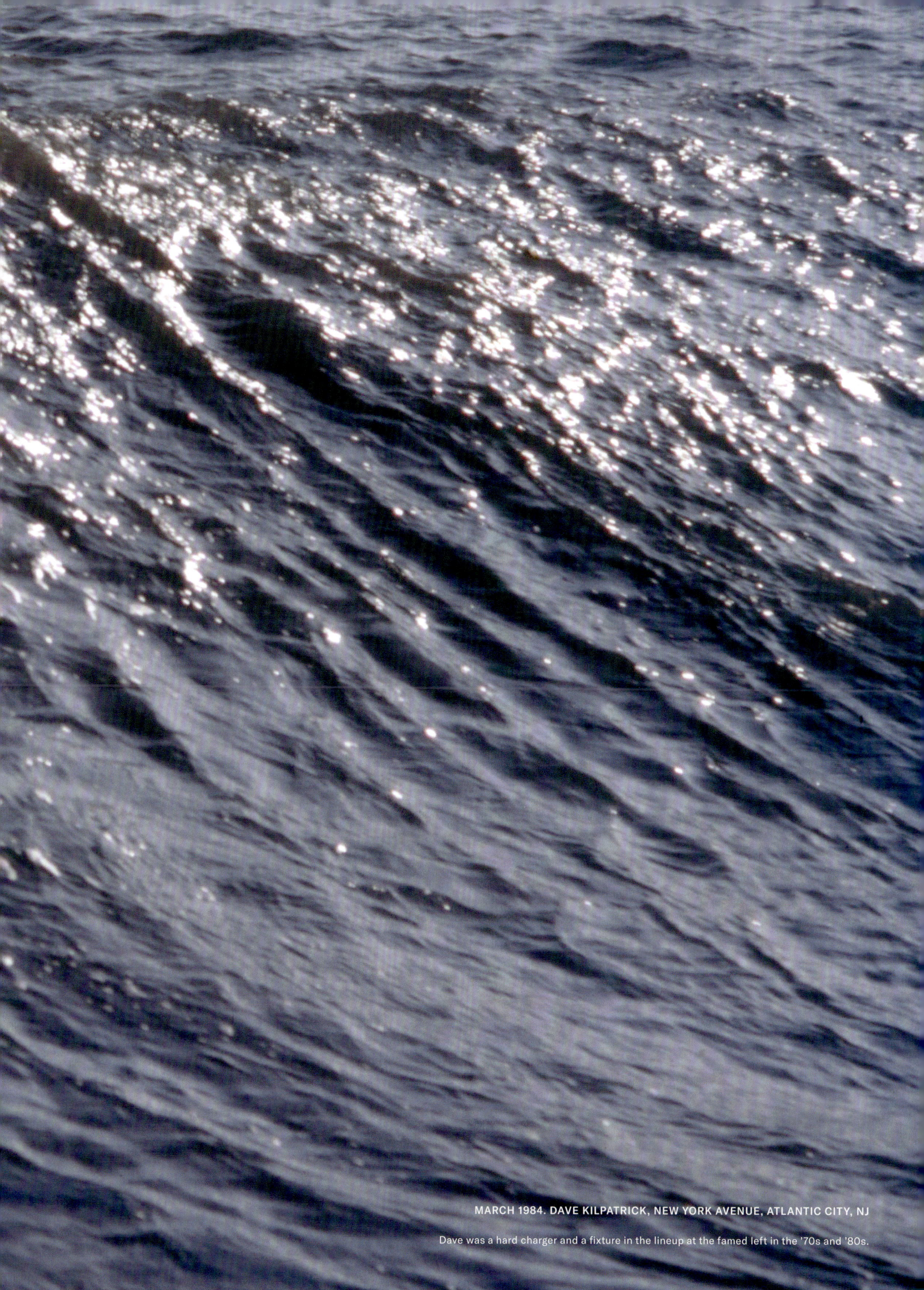

MARCH 1984. DAVE KILPATRICK, NEW YORK AVENUE, ATLANTIC CITY, NJ

Dave was a hard charger and a fixture in the lineup at the famed left in the '70s and '80s.

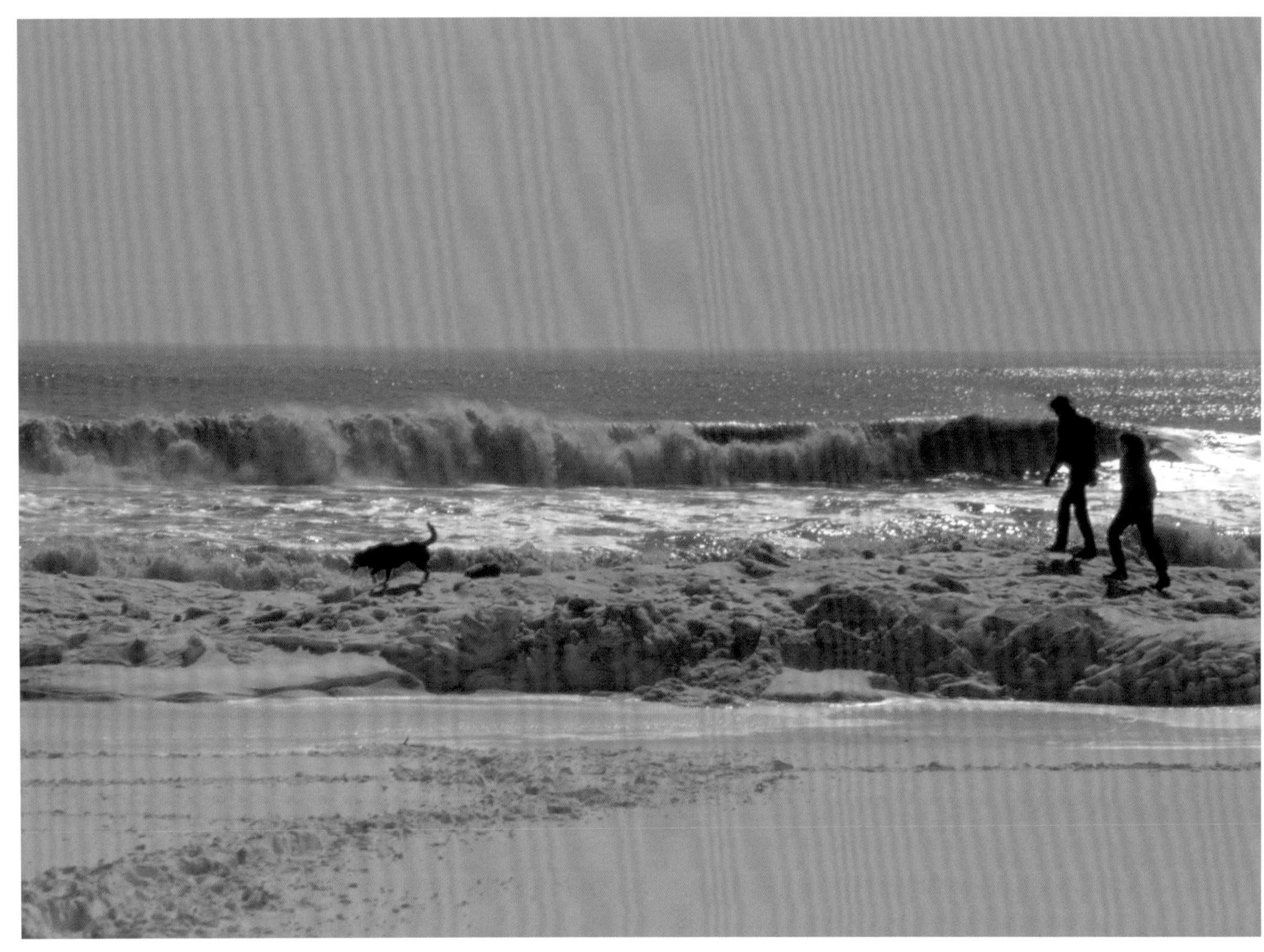

MARCH 1979. MARGATE, NJ

The day after a massive snowstorm—waves were good and a rare occasion where there was an iceberg built up at the water's edge to walk on. After the storms would pass, the sun would come out and the wind would roll offshore.

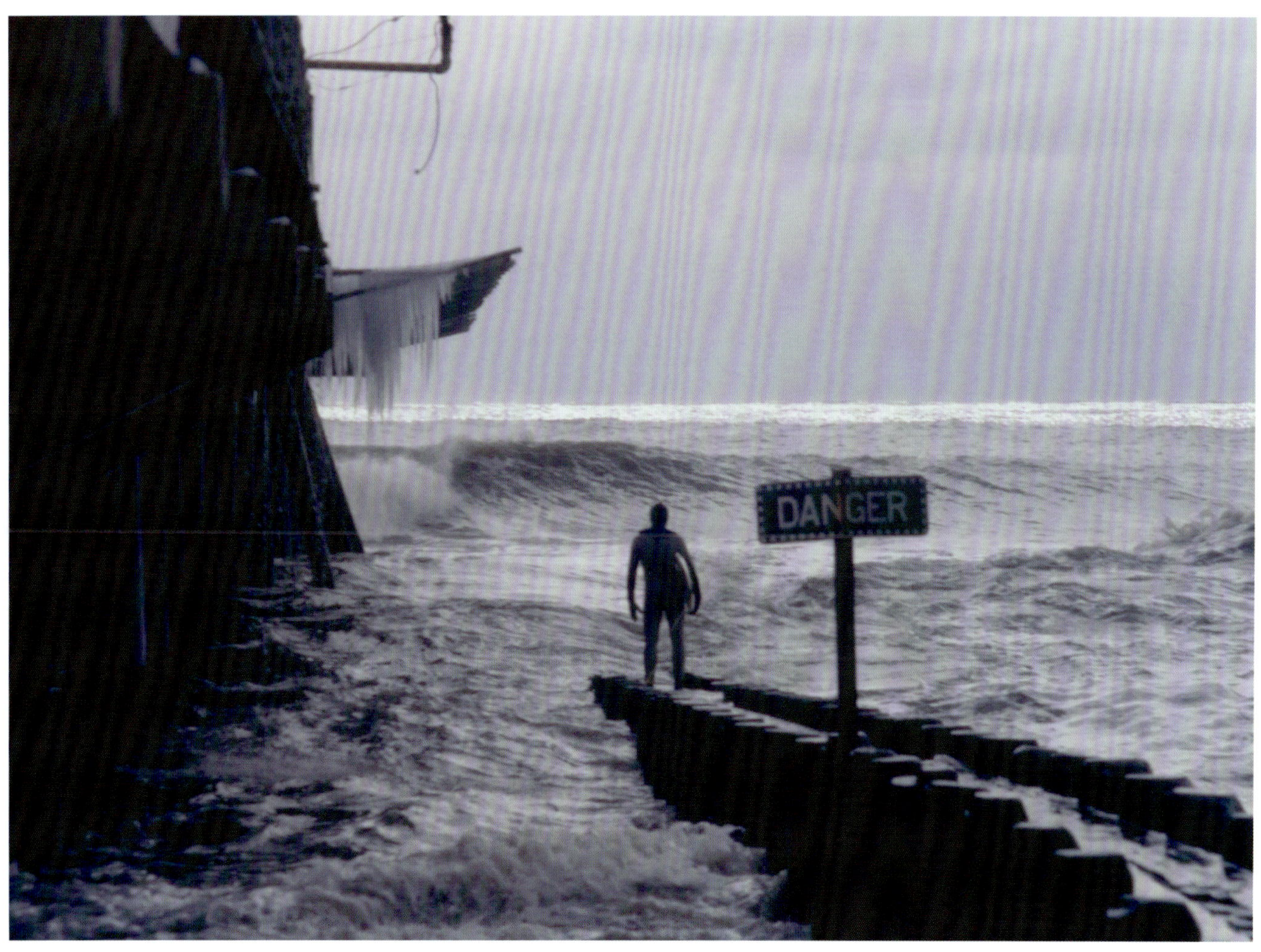

FEBRUARY 1984. ATLANTIC CITY, NJ

Dave Kilpatrick waiting for a lull to paddle out. As you can see, it was pretty cold, with icicles hanging off the pier and nobody out. We used to walk out on these jetties, as far as we could, so we could see the oncoming sets and get a jump start paddling out. The jetty was extremely slippery. The farther out you went, the worse it got.

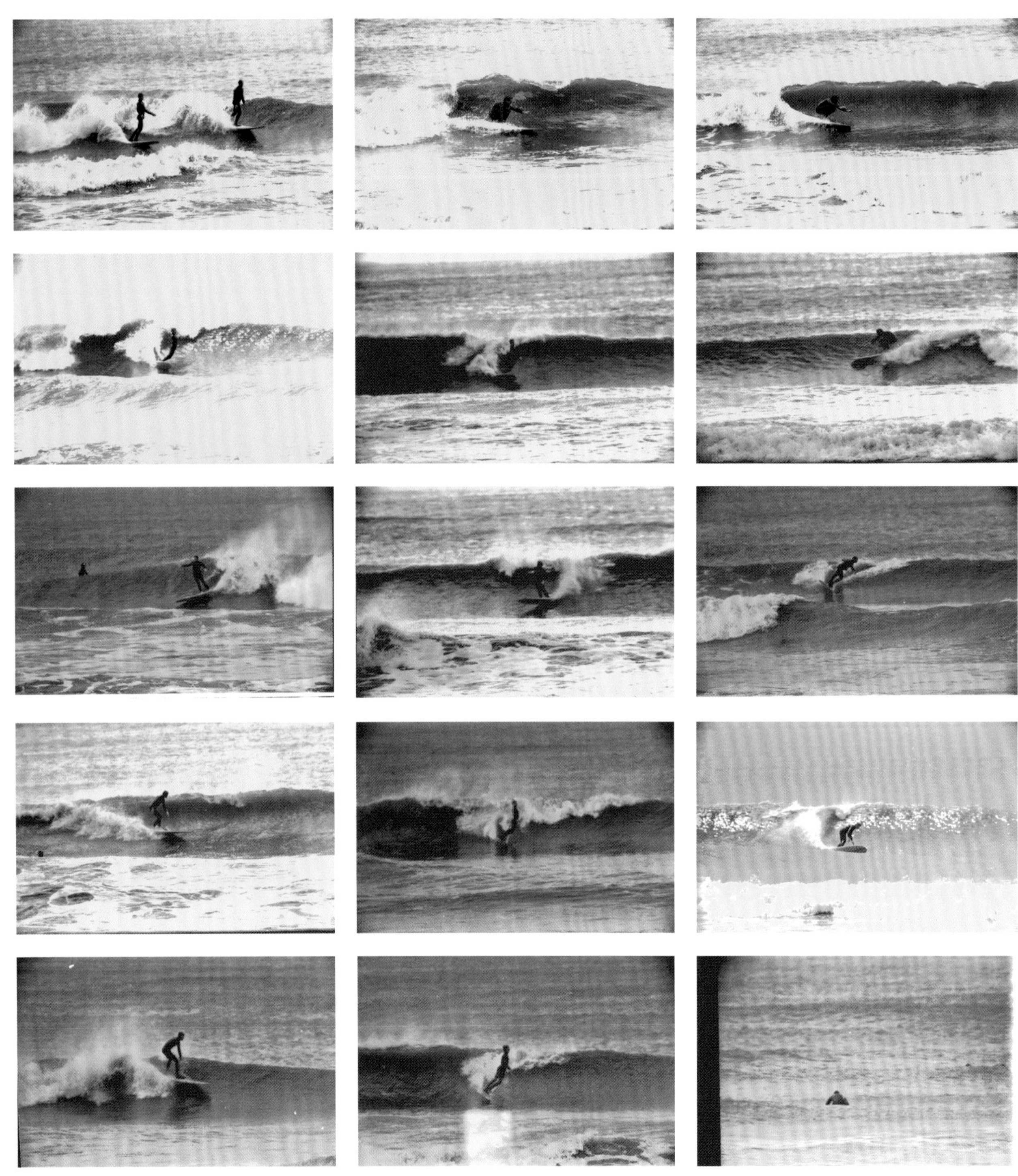

WINTER 1964. ATLANTIC CITY, NJ

Ricky Leeds
All photographs pages 136–159 by Dan Mittelman

BENEATH THE SURFING UNDERDOG

NOT WITHSTANDING THE CONSTANT UNDERDOG STATUS of the state of New Jersey within pretty much any context you choose to emphasize (rock and roll, funk, hamburgers, poetry, team sports, etc.), the impressive New Jersey accomplishments in these fields are known to locals and frequently impress outsiders.

When it comes to surfing though, New Jersey isn't even an underdog. The fact that it would be considered an underdog is truly curious to me considering the wealth of historical evidence of its vanguard status in the field. We do believe that the Sandwich Island lady rode a wave in Asbury Park circa 1888, and that Del Monte chose to advertise their fine Jersey tomato products with a cartoon of a cute young lady on a wave circa 1922.

Before that, Duke Kahanamoku, who popularized the ancient Hawaiian sport of surfing, stopped by Atlantic City in 1912 surfing a solid redwood board that his kindly brother David shipped over. His subsequent 1914 visit set off a bit of an ongoing New Jersey fascination with all matters Hawaiian. By 1917, visiting Hawaiians had constructed wooden belly boards that were in use at several Atlantic City beach hotels. In 1930, a string of "Hawaiian Hula Huts" were set up on the boardwalk bringing the exotica of island life to the Jersey Shore. And from that point, New Jersey surfing follows the developments in the rest of the surfing world pretty closely. Technological advancements, pop-culture high tides and lows, the development of a language of athleticism alongside its shadow of identity politics all intermingle in its narrative.

When Danny and I started working on this project, we were truly lucky to find these caches of unseen masterful photography, and to have been steered in the direction of treasure troves of cultural remains. This book is steeped in romanticism and the picturesque, certainly: the stuff is so cool and visual, and the photography is like stepping inside a gentler time with better clothes. But more than that, I hope this book is a useful stepping stone toward the unveiling of more and more historical and cultural narratives linked to surfing and everyday life. People might say to each other that they heard there are waves in New Jersey.

—**JOHAN KUGELBERG**

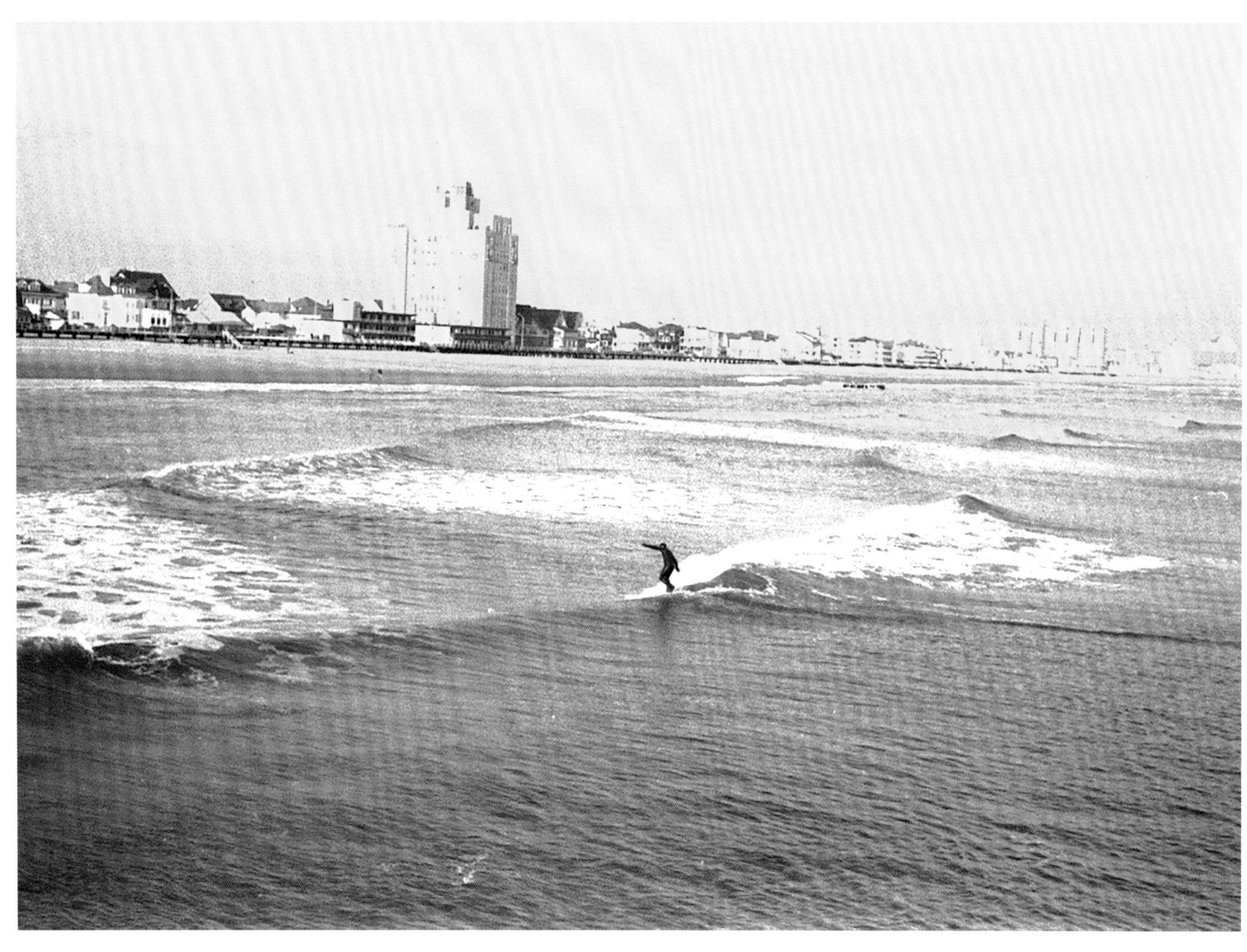

WINTER 1964. ATLANTIC CITY, NJ

Ronnie Perr

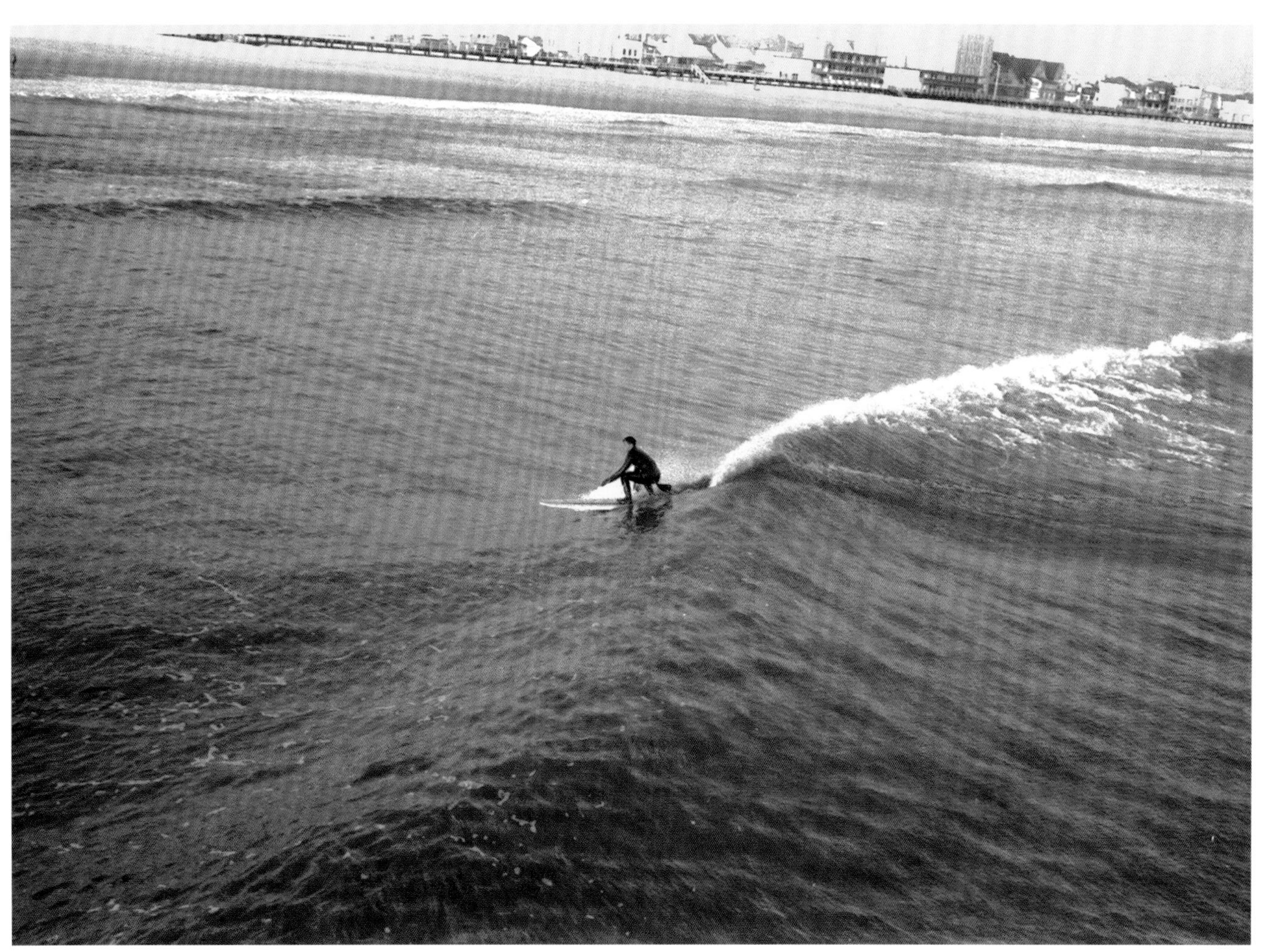

WINTER 1964. ATLANTIC CITY, NJ

Glenn Klotz

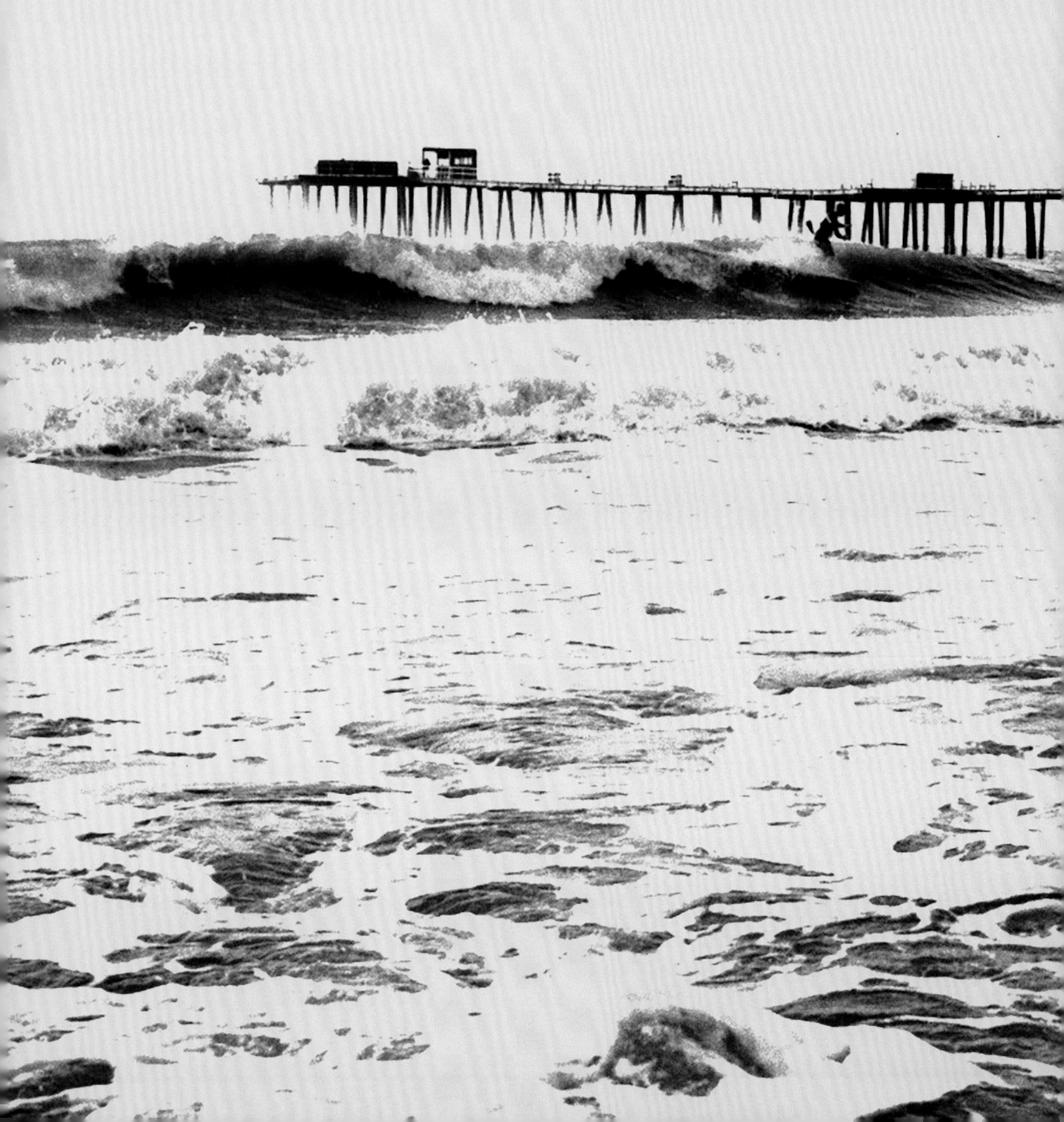

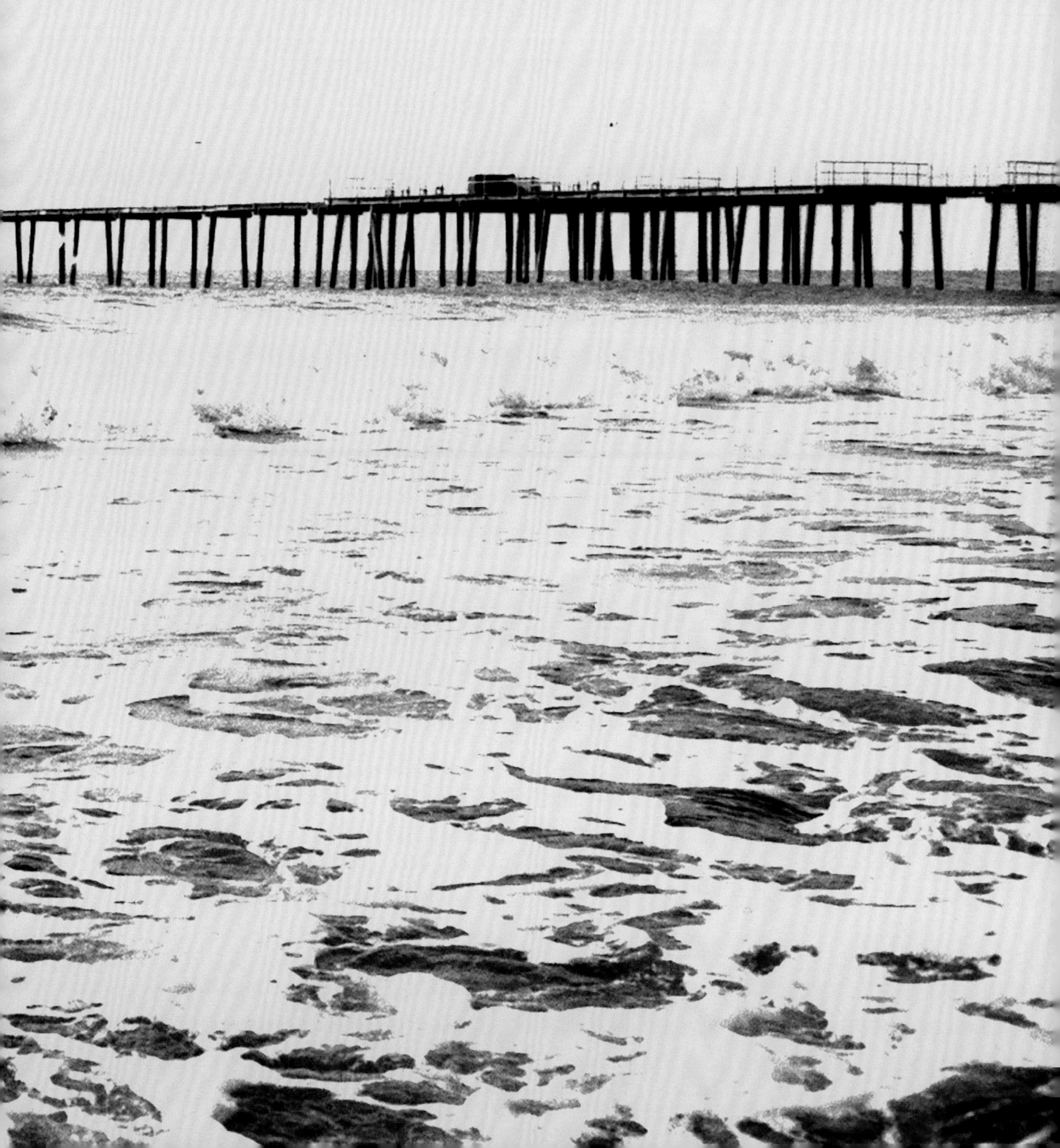

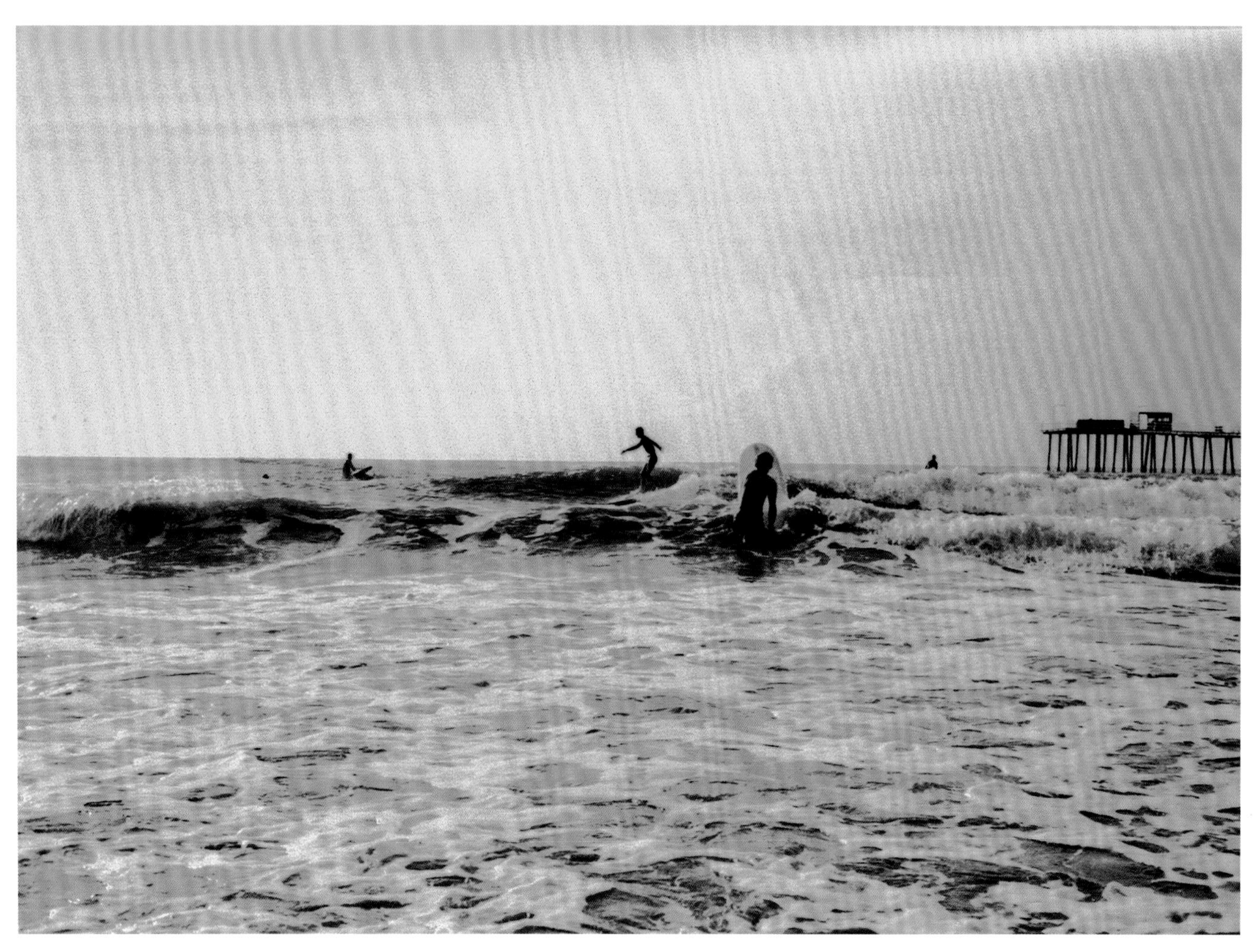

WINTER 1964. ATLANTIC CITY, NJ

Glenn Klotz

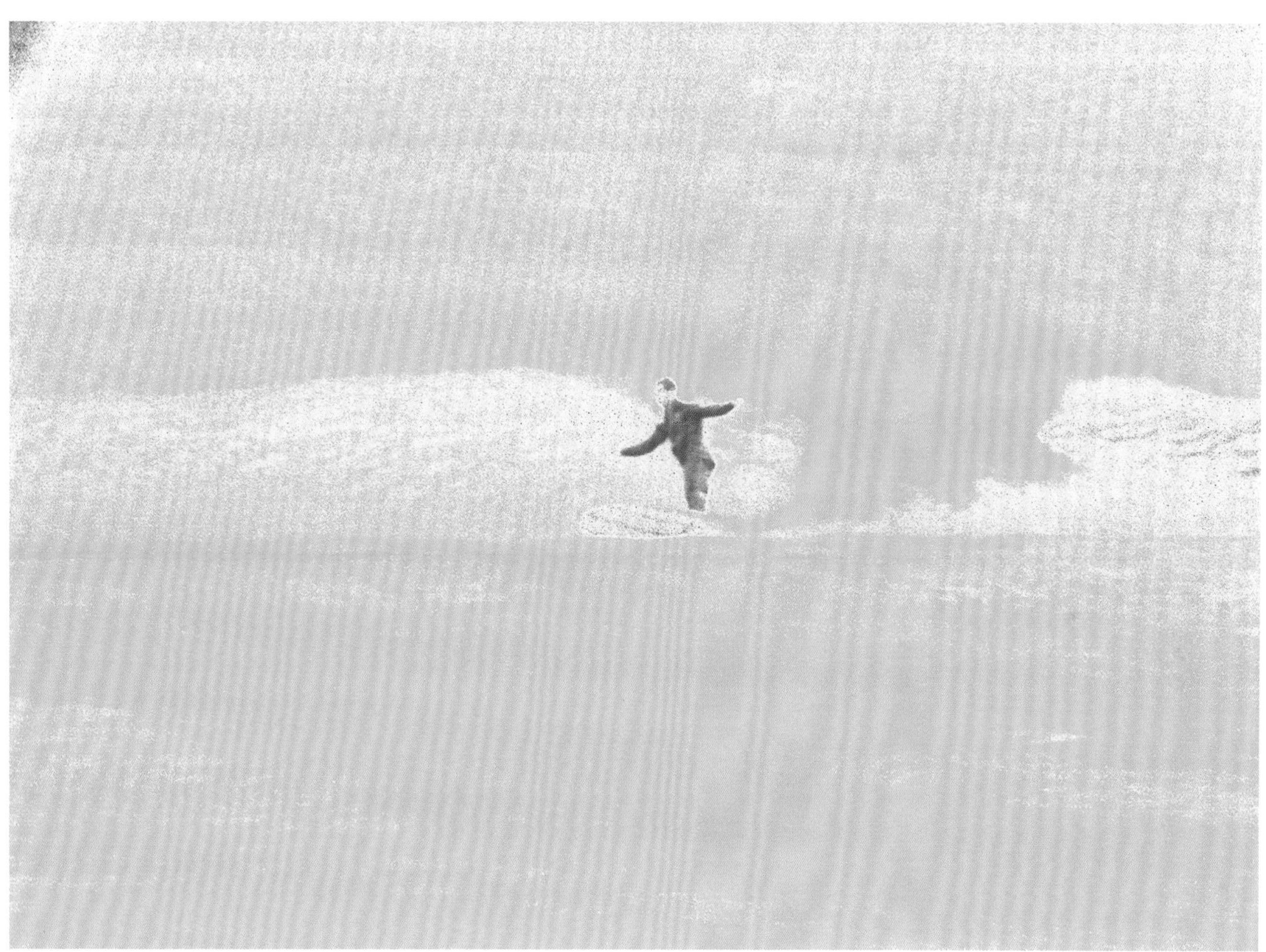

WINTER 1964. ATLANTIC CITY, NJ

Art Nahas

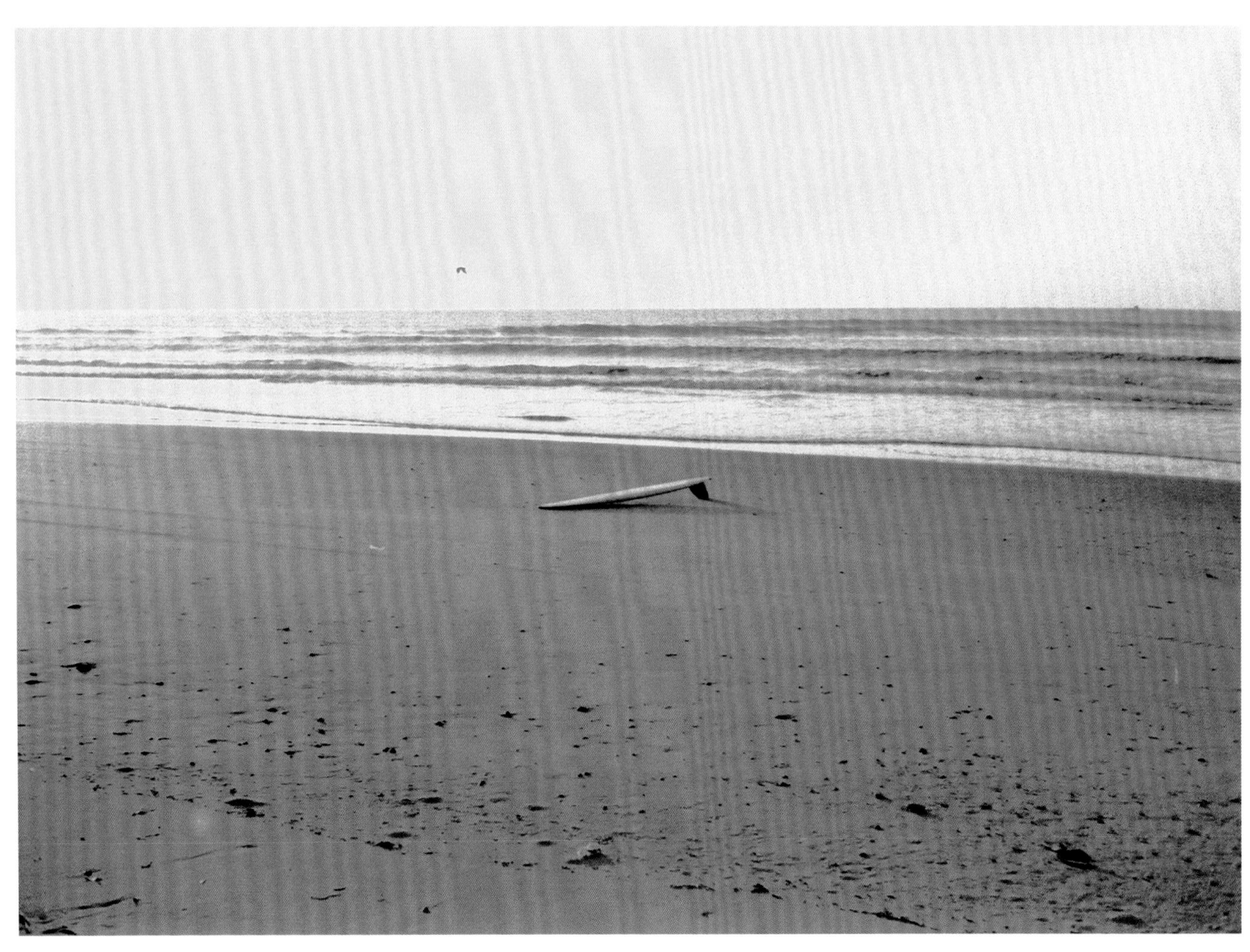

WINTER 1964. ATLANTIC CITY, NJ

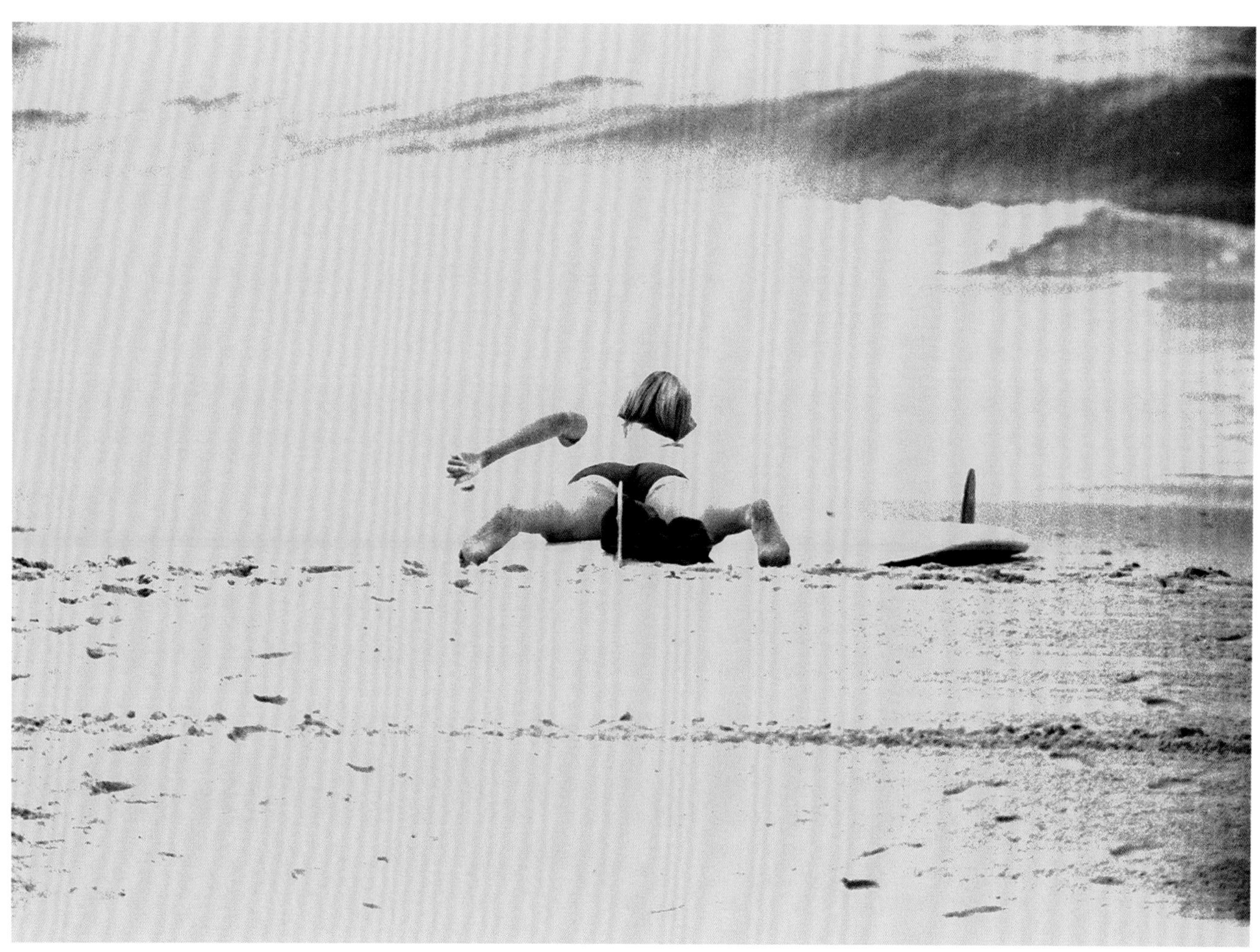

WINTER 1964. ATLANTIC CITY, NJ

Ernie Rettberg

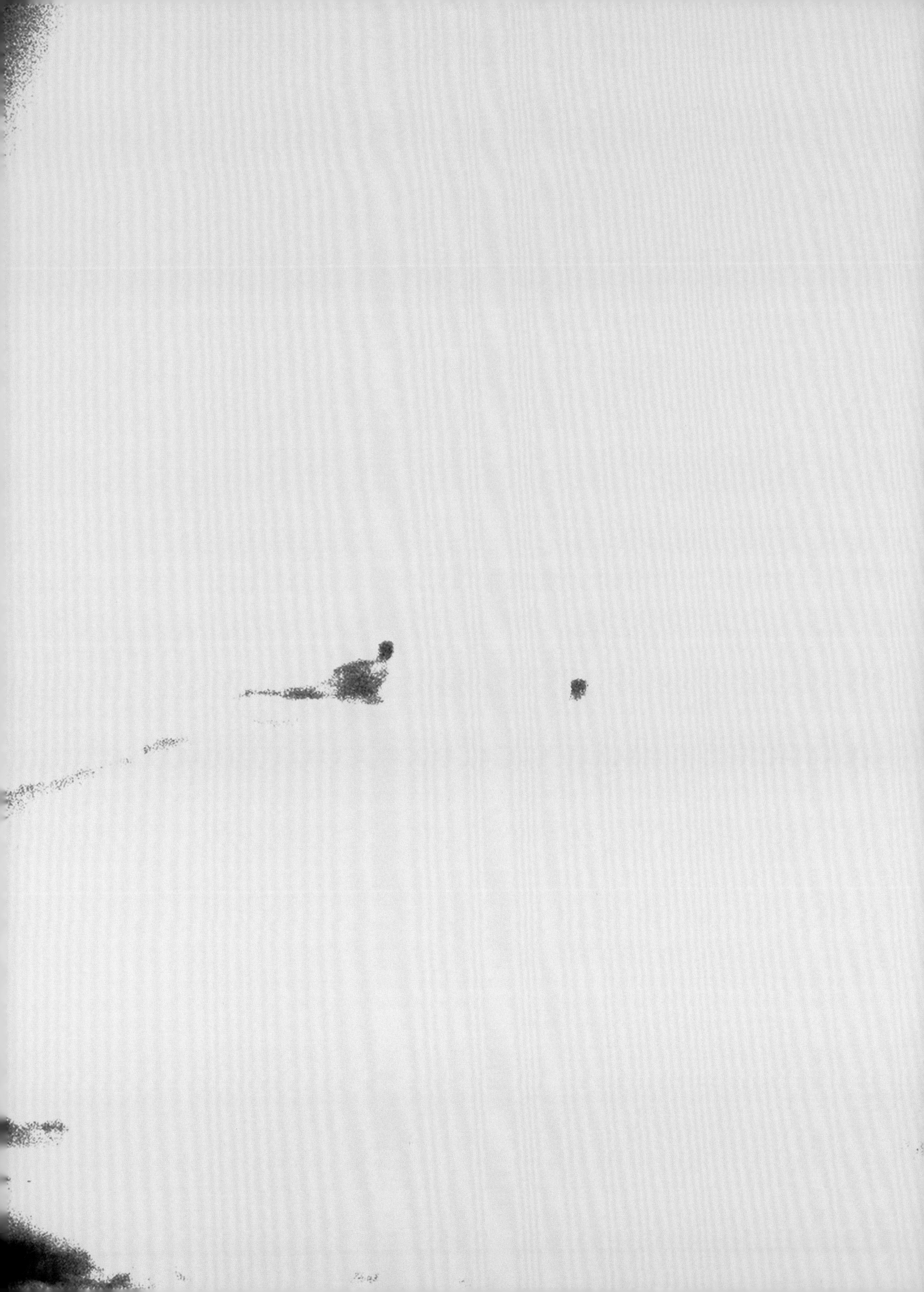

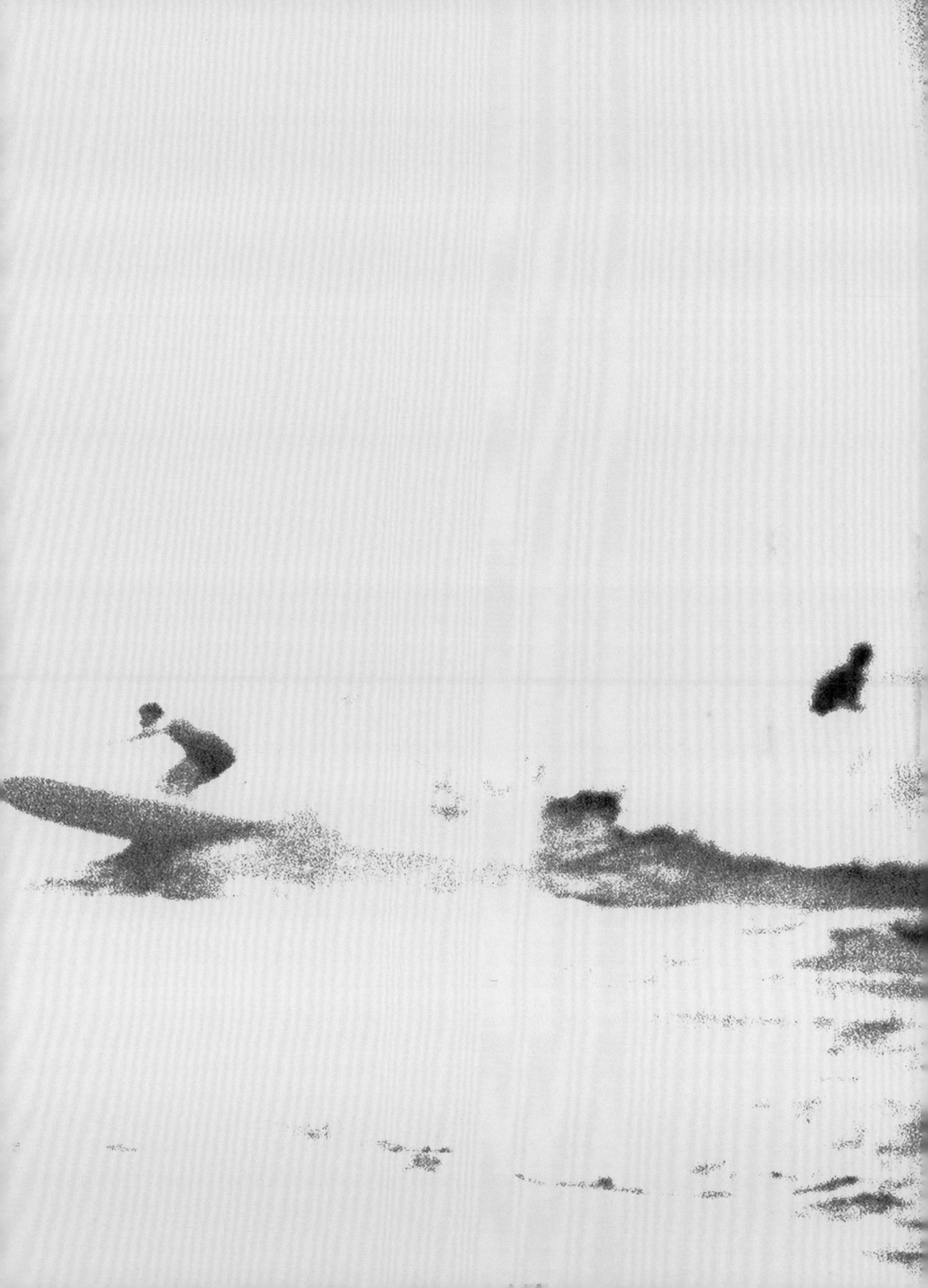

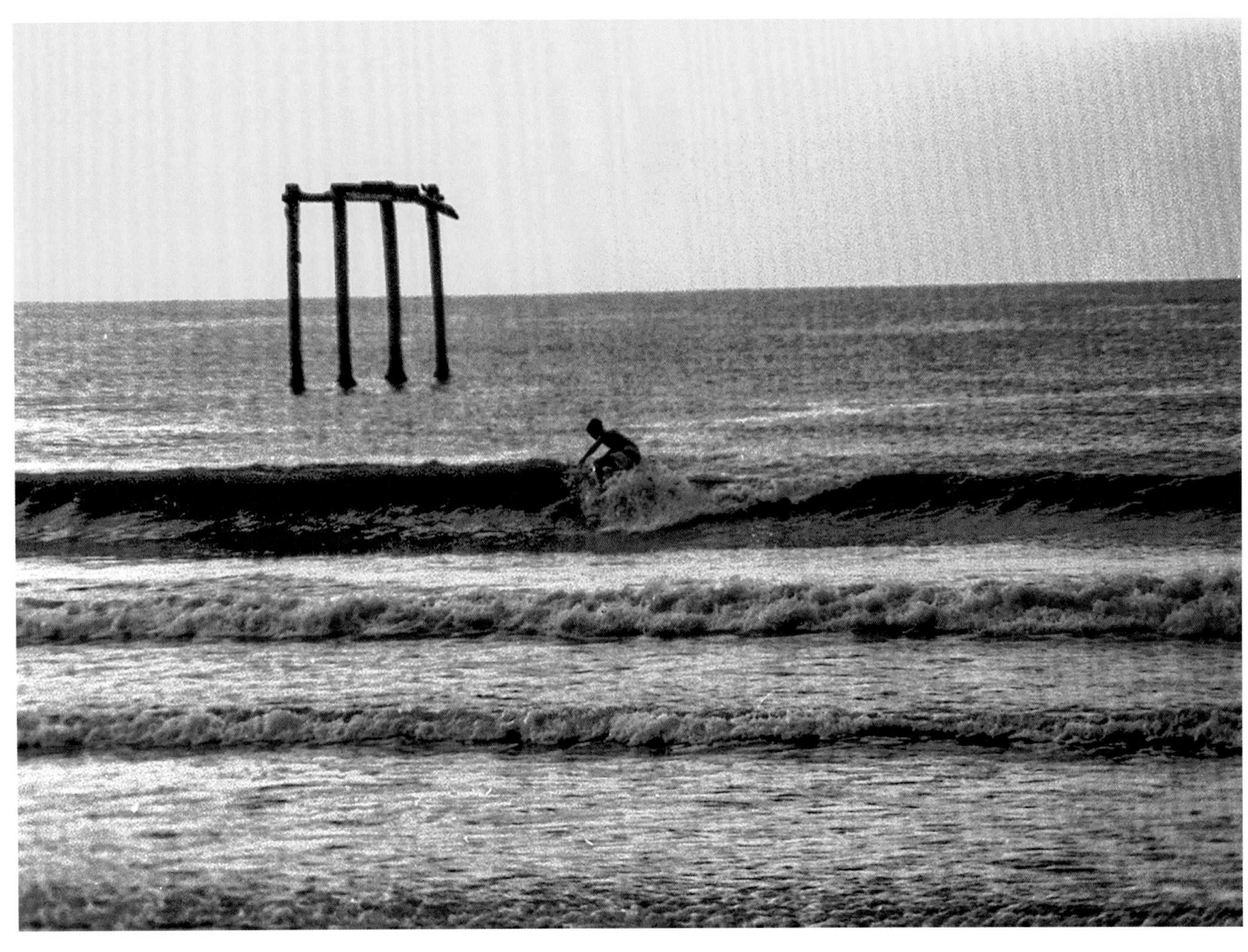

FALL 1964. ATLANTIC CITY, NJ

Ricky Leeds

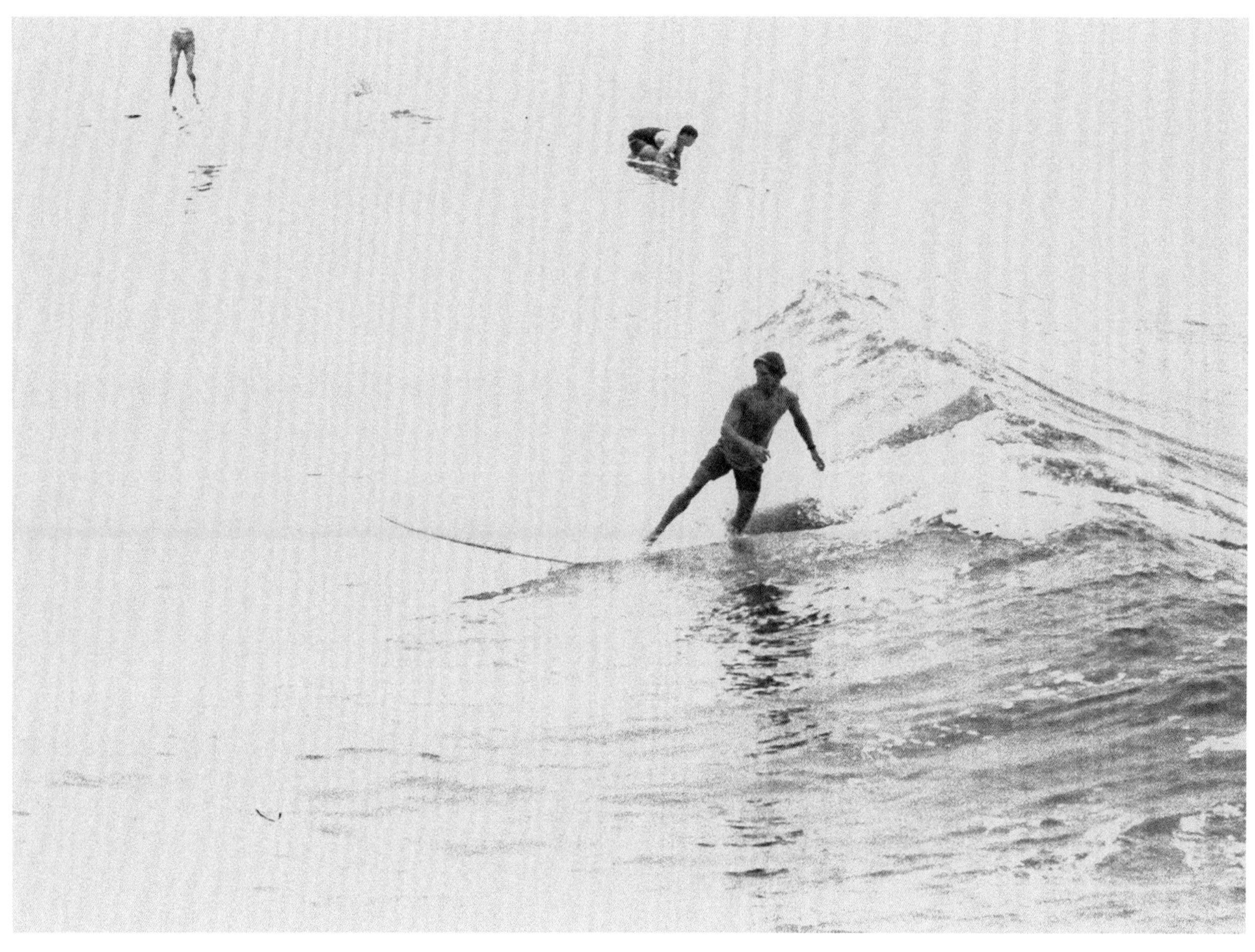

FALL 1964. ATLANTIC CITY, NJ

Bruce Dougherty

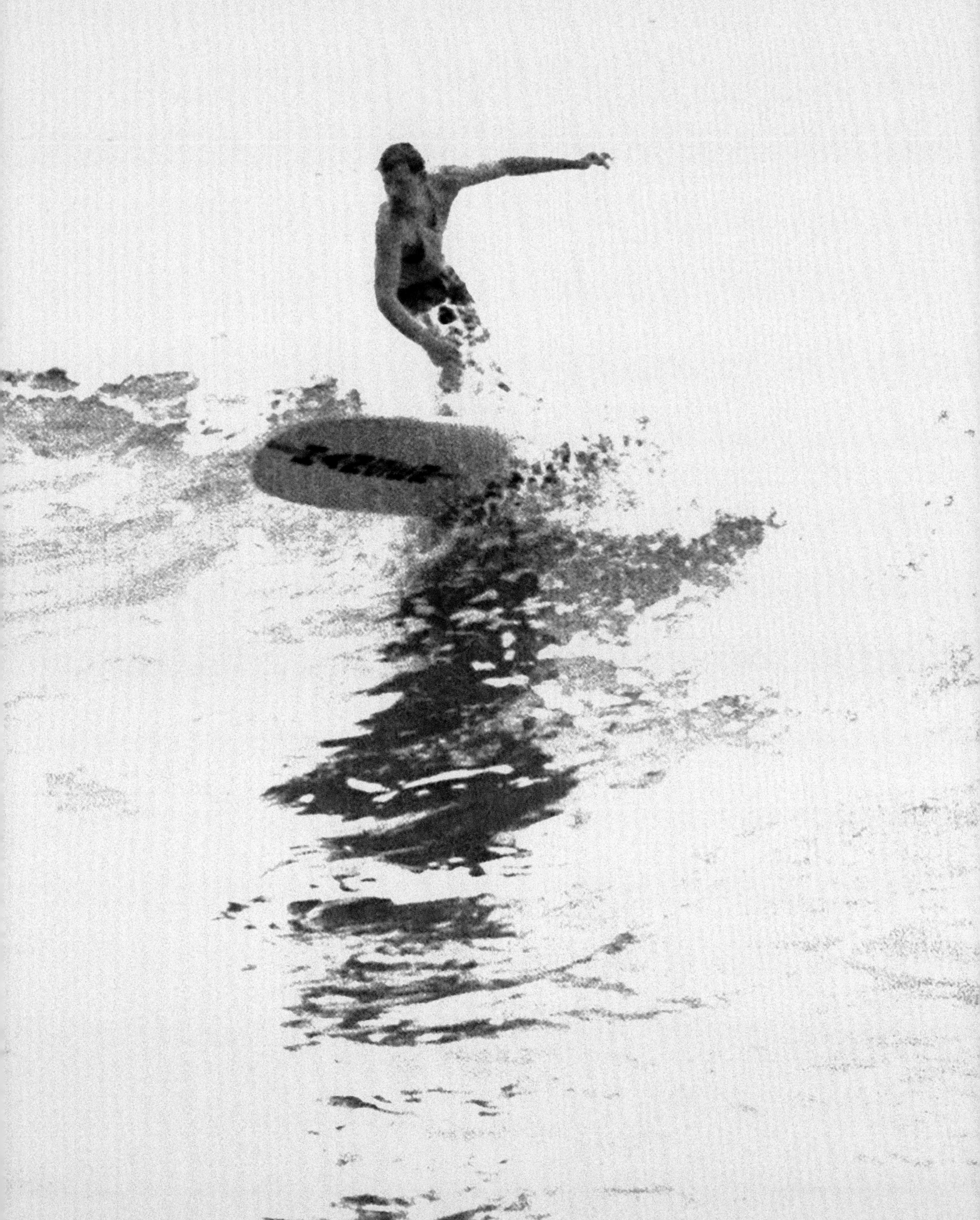

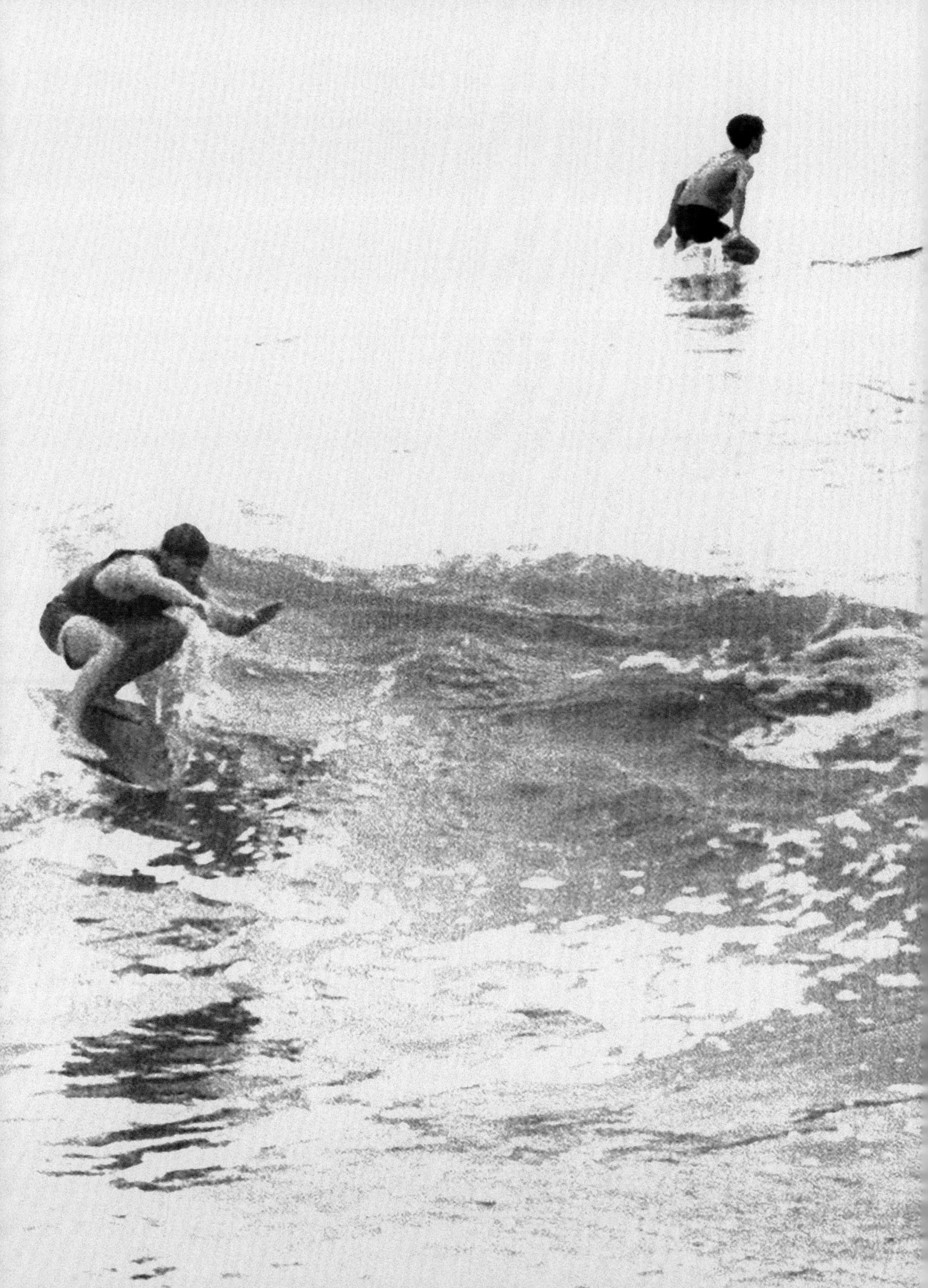

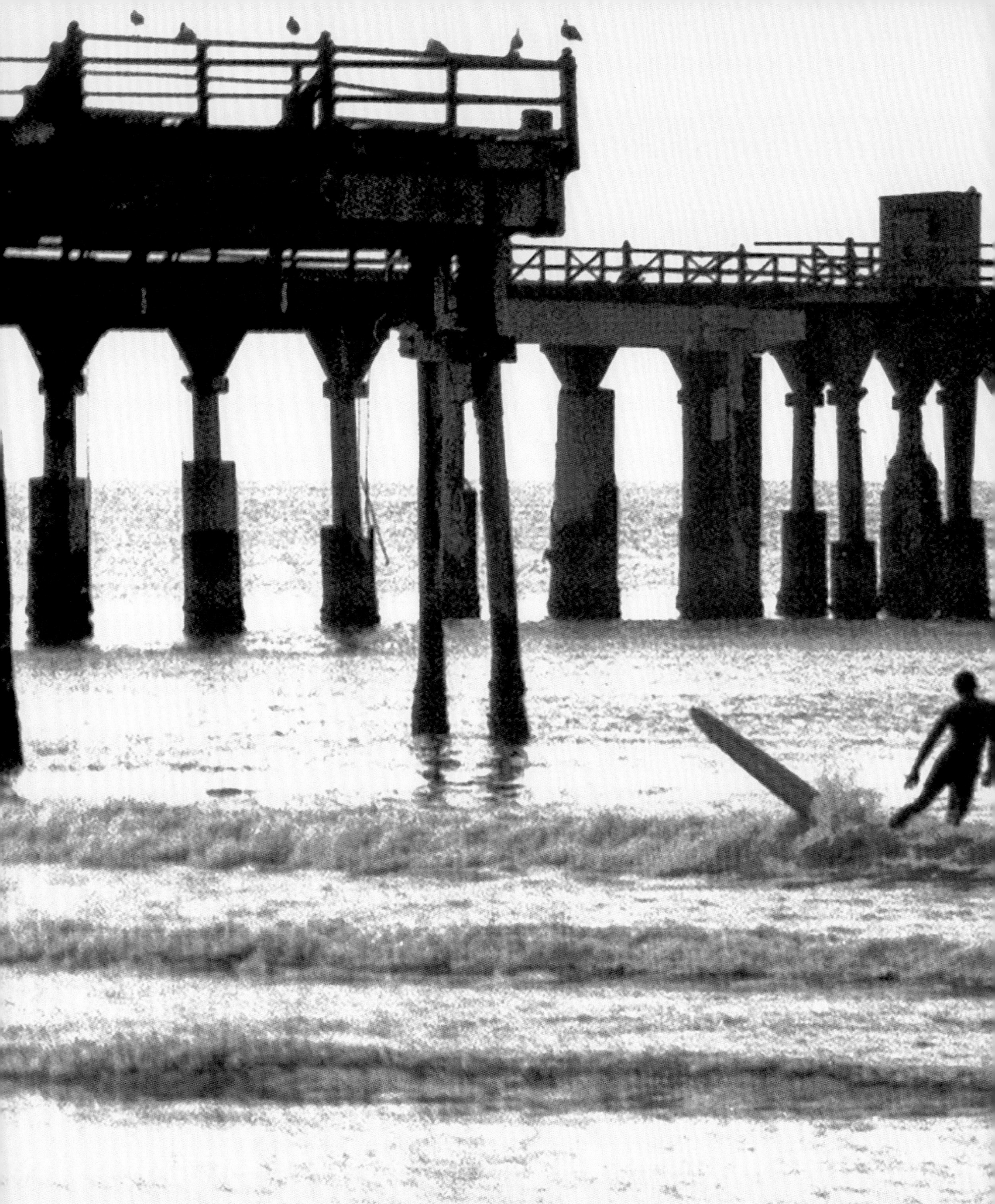

WINTER 1964, ATLANTIC CITY, NJ

Ricky Leeds

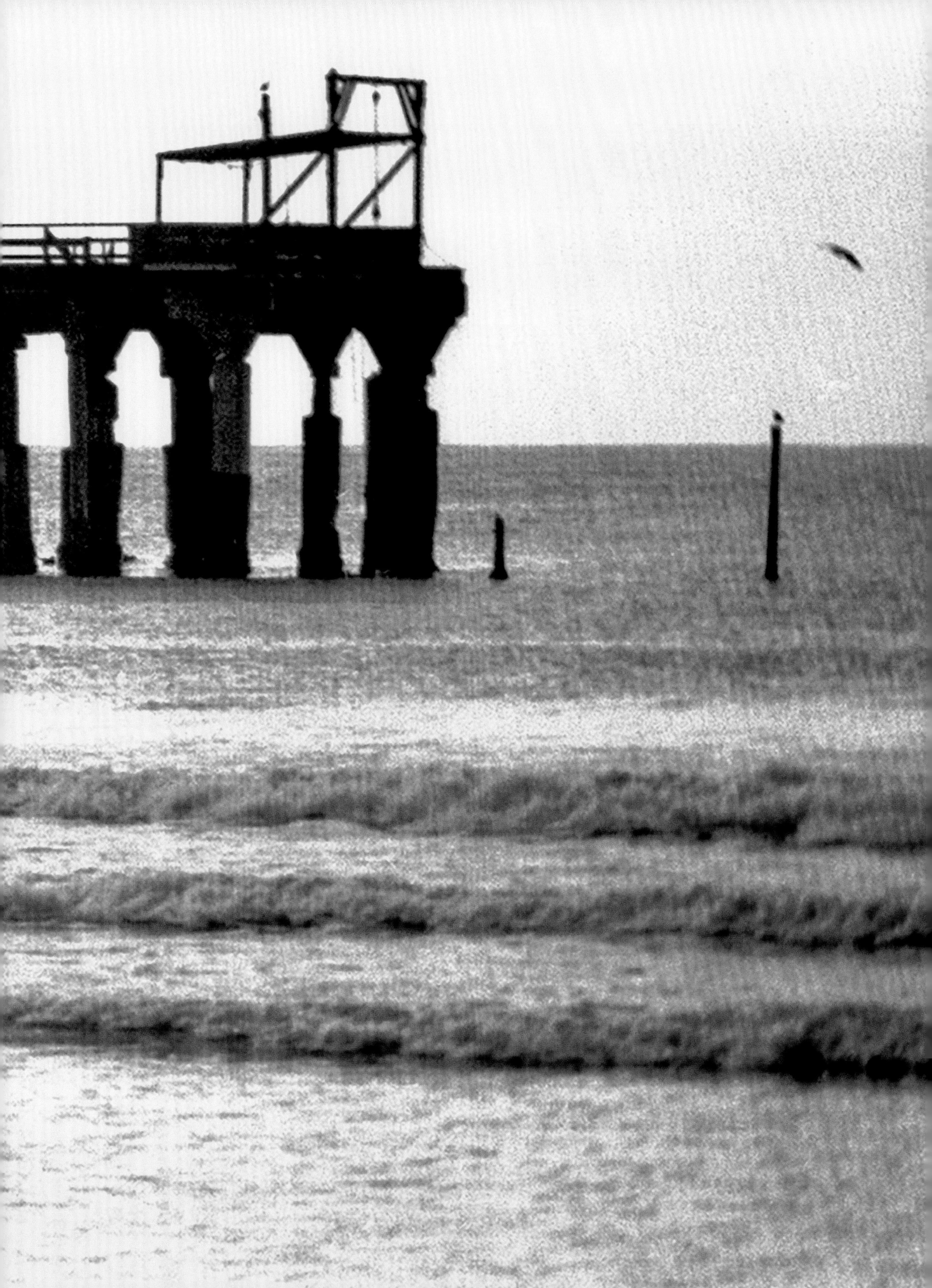

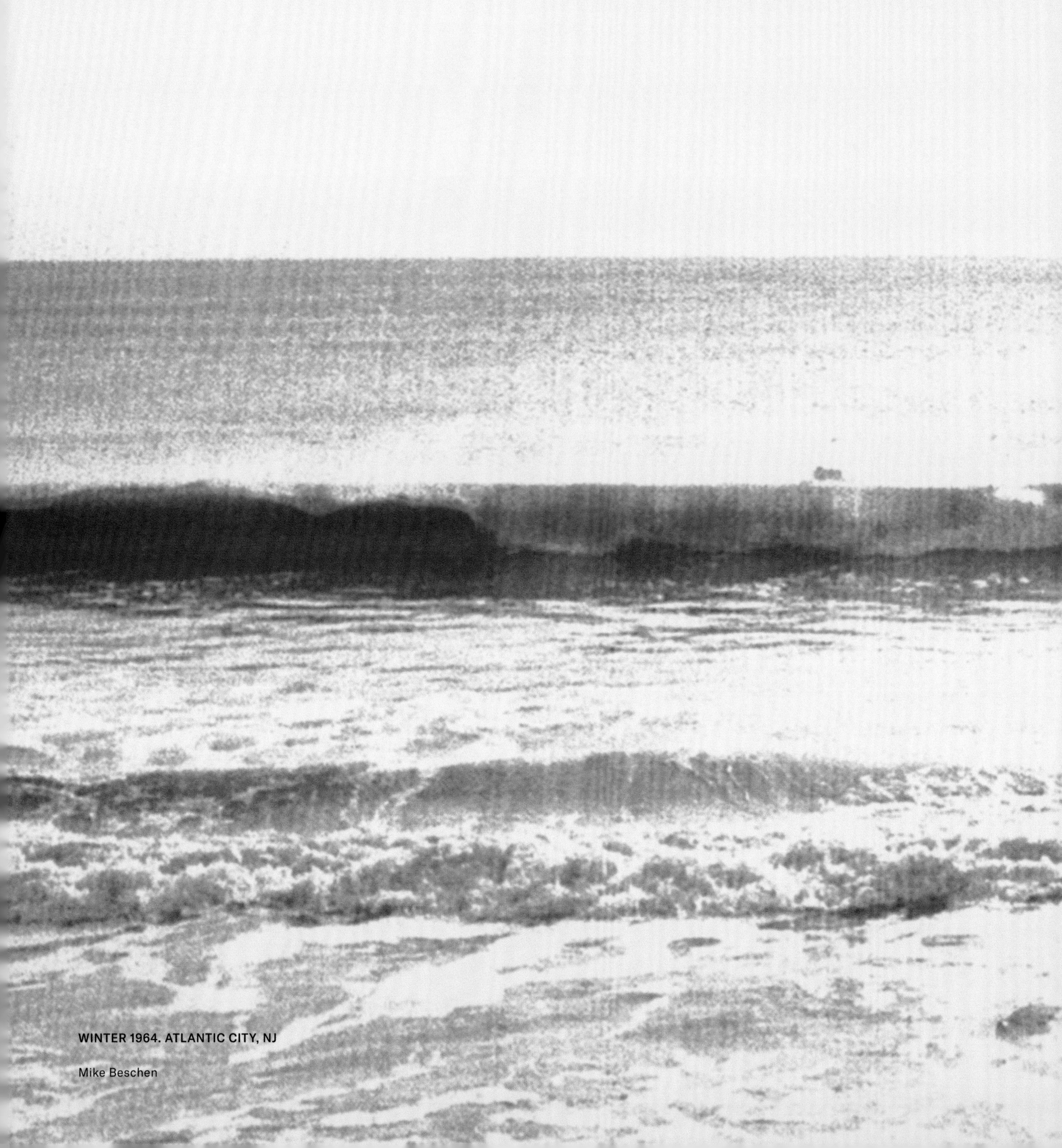

WINTER 1964. ATLANTIC CITY, NJ

Mike Beschen

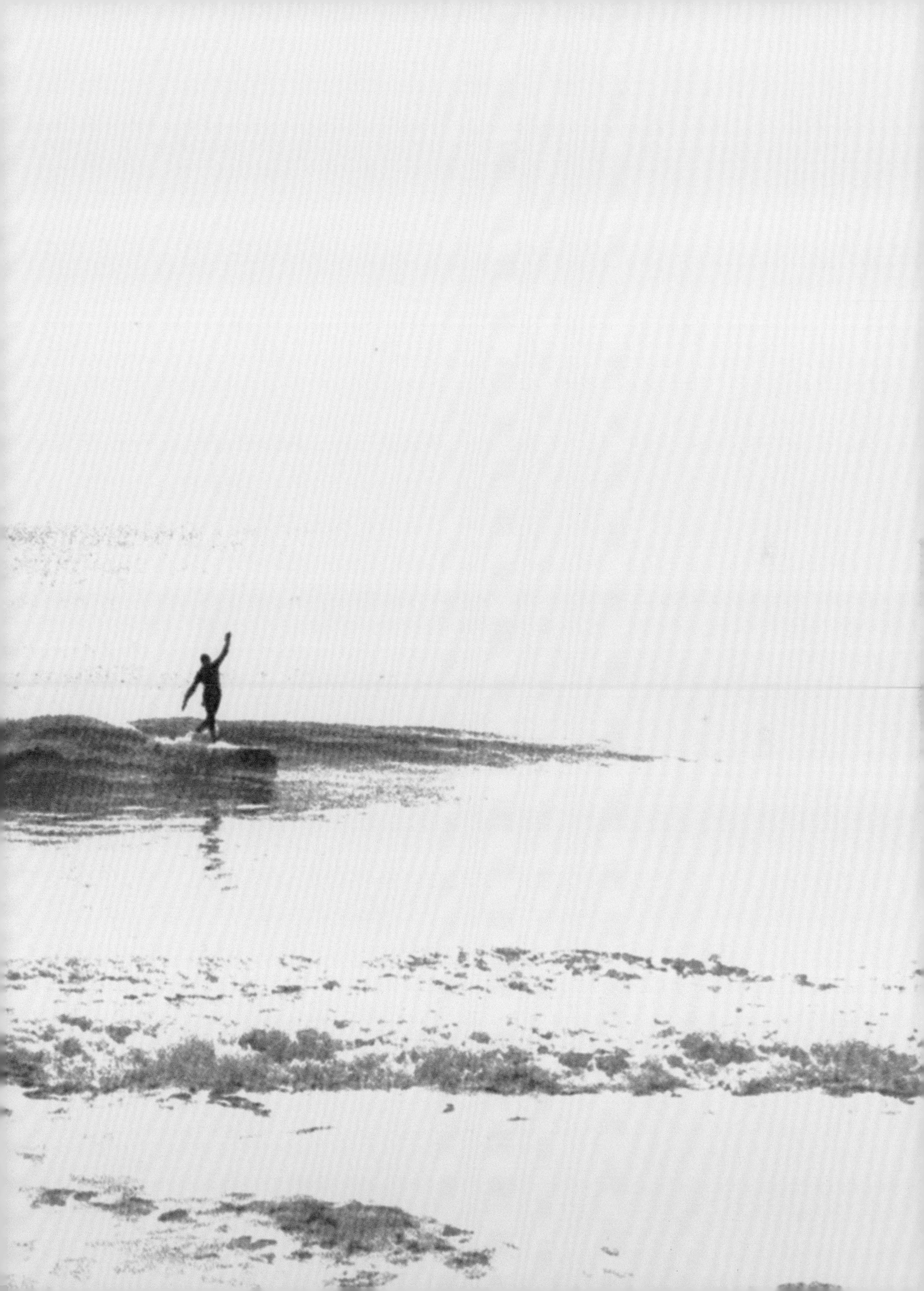

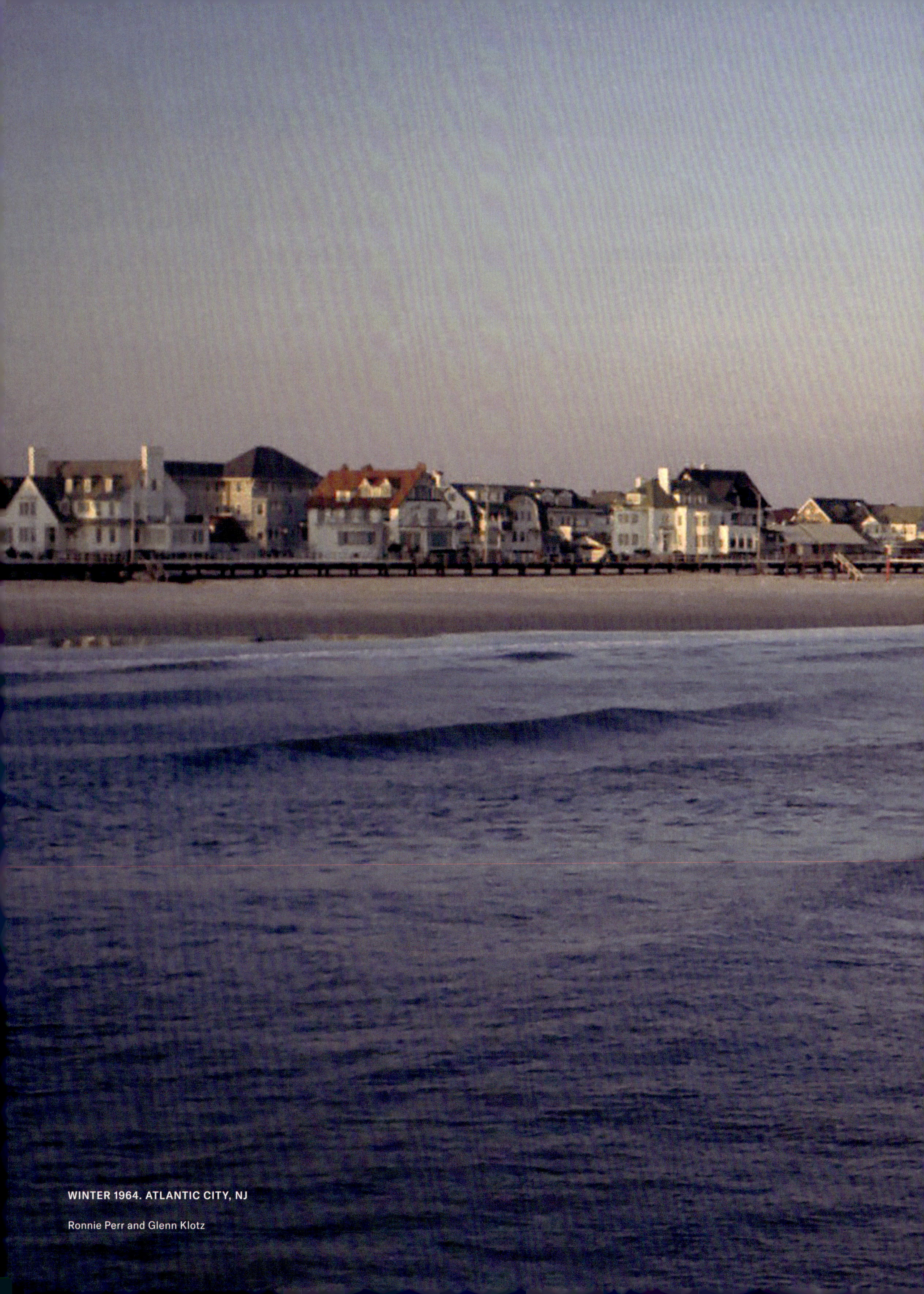

WINTER 1964. ATLANTIC CITY, NJ

Ronnie Perr and Glenn Klotz

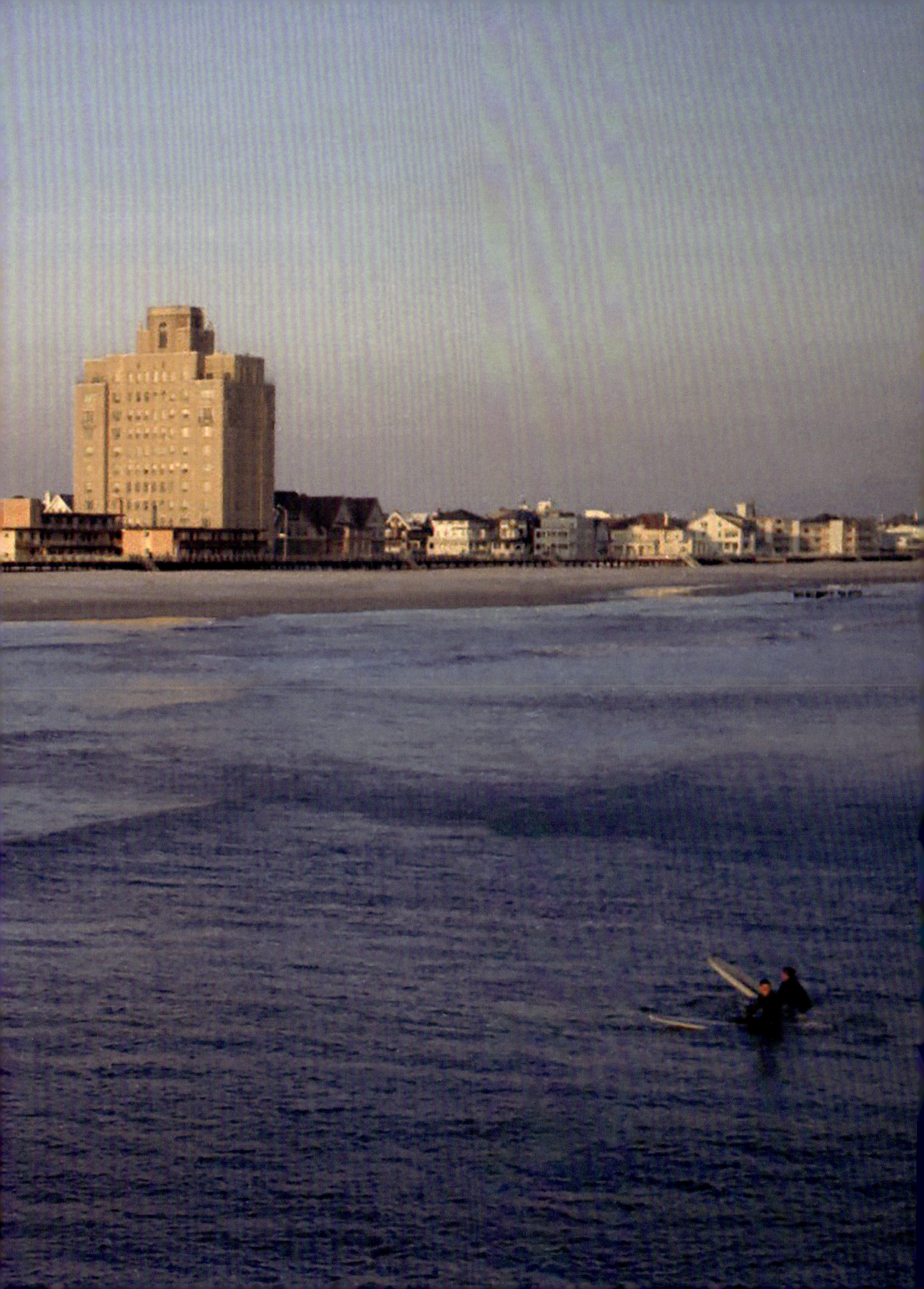

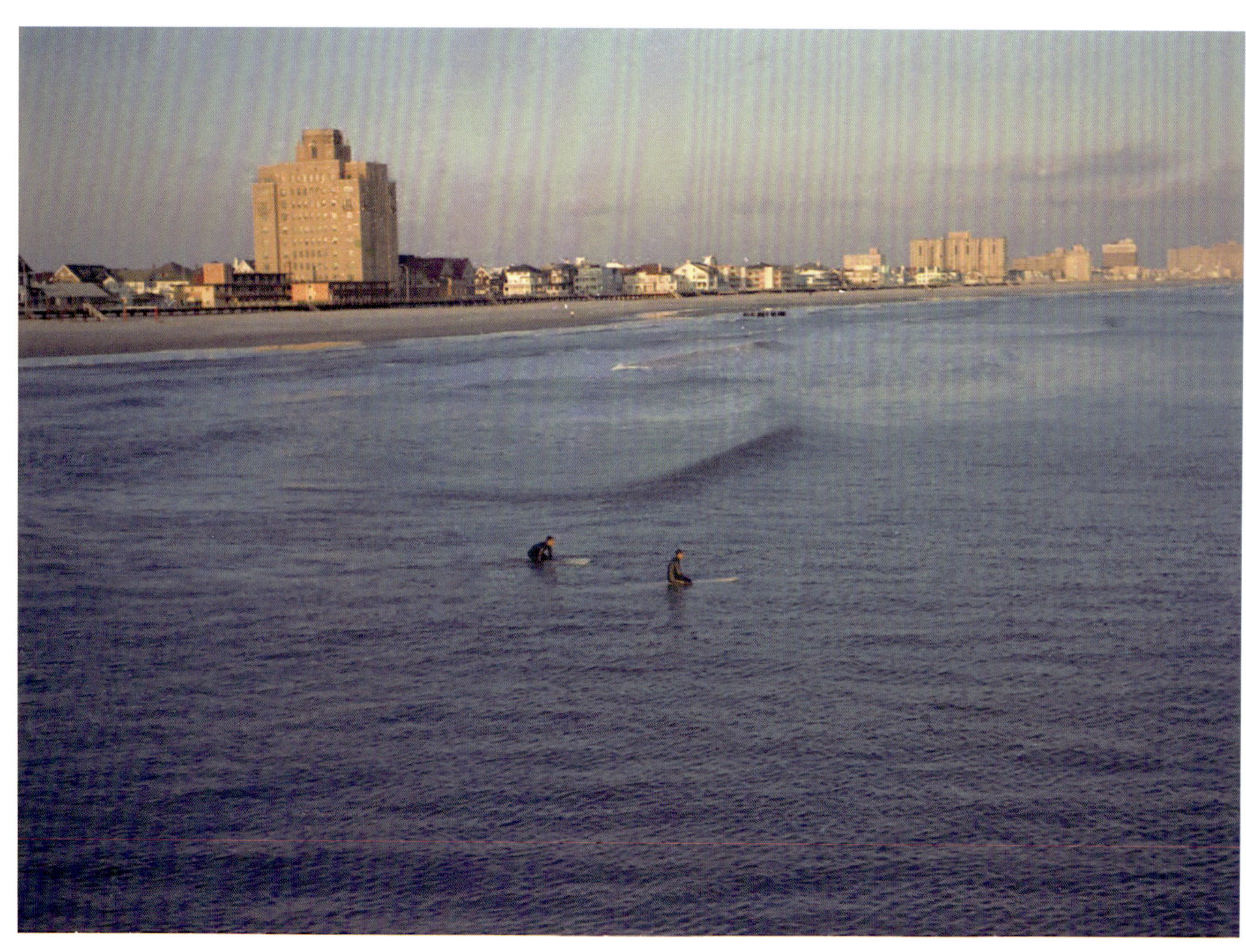

WINTER 1964. ATLANTIC CITY, NJ

Ronnie Perr and Glenn Klotz

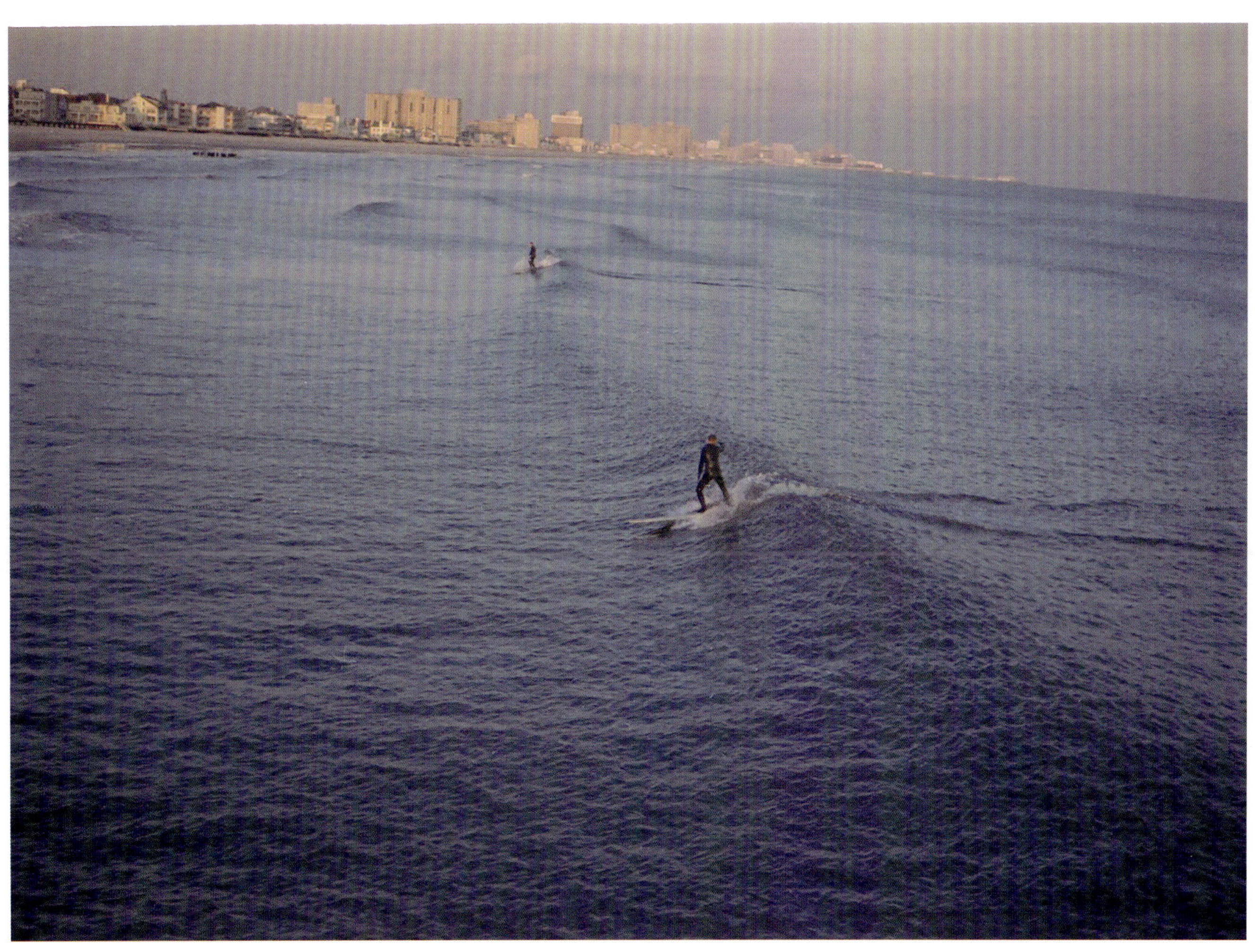

WINTER 1964. ATLANTIC CITY, NJ

Glenn Klotz

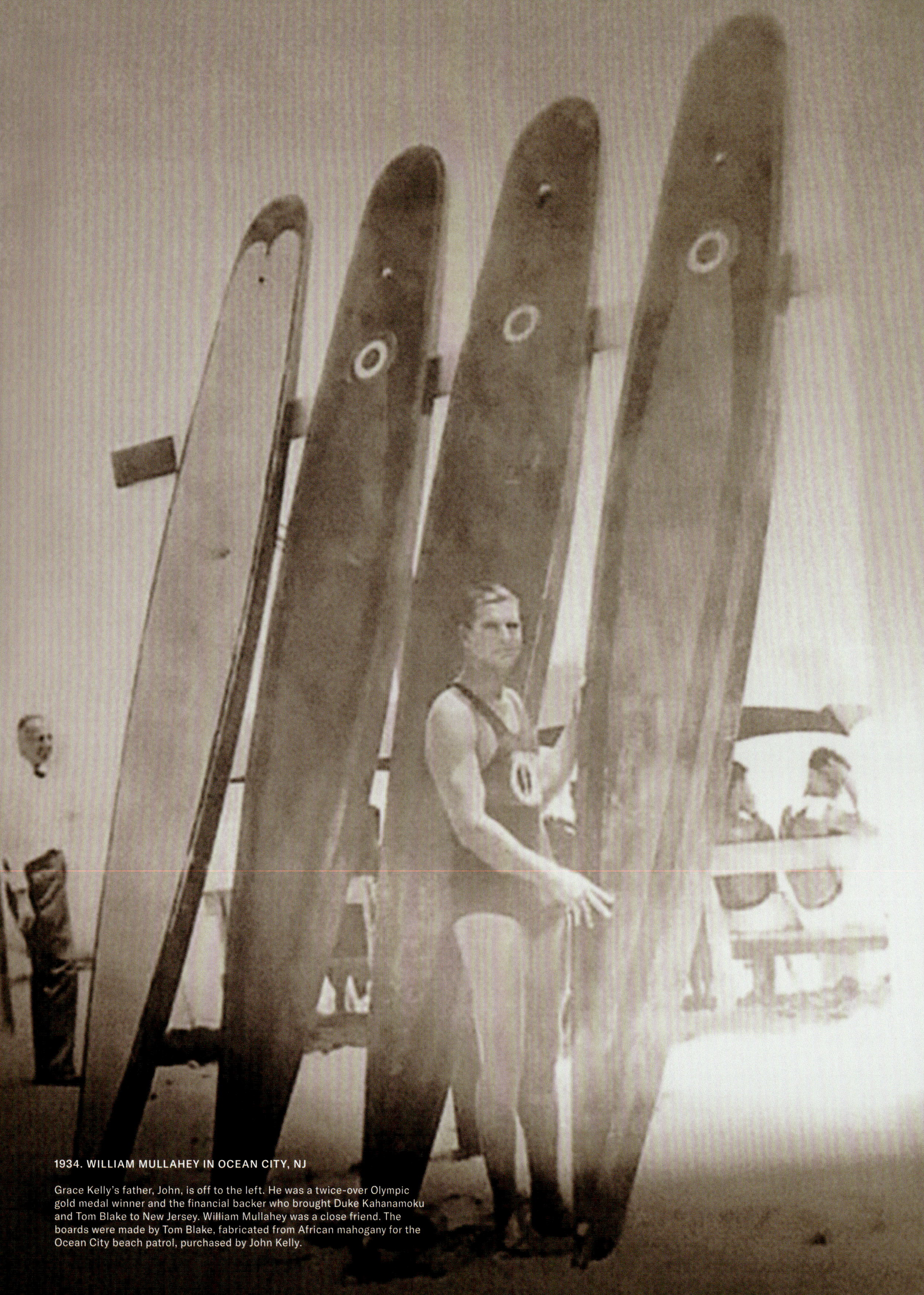

1934. WILLIAM MULLAHEY IN OCEAN CITY, NJ

Grace Kelly's father, John, is off to the left. He was a twice-over Olympic gold medal winner and the financial backer who brought Duke Kahanamoku and Tom Blake to New Jersey. William Mullahey was a close friend. The boards were made by Tom Blake, fabricated from African mahogany for the Ocean City beach patrol, purchased by John Kelly.

EPHEMERA

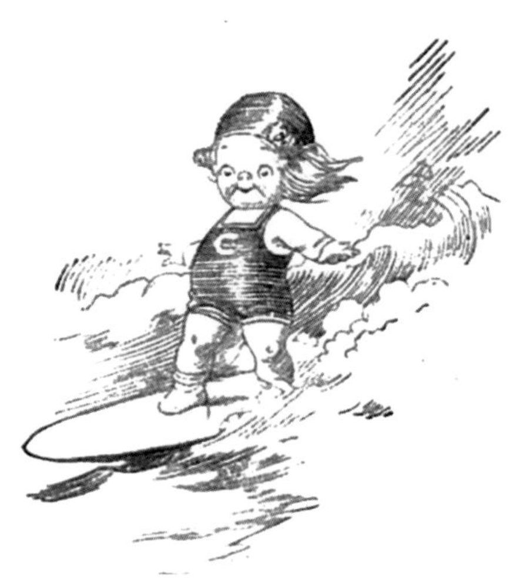

EPHEMERA COURTESY OF THE NEW JERSEY SURF MUSEUM AND THE NEW JERSEY SURFING HALL OF FAME AT THE TUCKERTON SEAPORT AND BAYMEN'S MUSEUM.

THE CURIOUS CAN FIND an extraordinary gathering of New Jersey surfing history at the Tuckerton Seaport. Behind the main building, down a path, past well-kept historical structures, you can find a large cabin filled with the most extraordinary selection of original surfboards, photographs, publications, clothing, and ephemera highlighting the history and legacy of surfing in New Jersey. Without this wonderful historical depository, our book would have been so much less. We are truly grateful to the New Jersey Surf Museum and the New Jersey Surfing Hall of Fame for not only their accommodating kindness alongside their expert stewardship of this cultural narrative, but furthermore for giving us access to their archives for the purpose of bringing another dimension of phenomenal visuals to this book.

—**JOHAN KUGELBERG & DANNY DIMAURO**

SOUNDS FROM THE SEA.

MANY WAYS OF ENJOYING LIFE AT THE RESORTS.

The Greatest Girl Bather—Some of the Celebrities Who Take a Dip in the Surf.

SHE WILL BE drowned." "No, she cannot drown. She must be a sea nymph." "Nothing so classic as a sea nymph. Simply a South Sea Island woman."

A group of summer loungers on the beach at Asbury park were watching the antics of a dark-eyed, bronze-faced girl in the sea this morning. The object of all this interest and solicitude was beyond the line of breakers and standing on a plank that rose and fell with the swelling waves. Her bathing dress was of some dark material, fitting close to the figure, the skirts reaching scarce to the knee. Her stockings were of amber hue, adorned with what from the shore seemed to be vines and roses in colored embroidery. She wore no hat or cap. Her hair bound across the forehead and above the ears by a silver fillet turned down upon her shoulders or streamed out upon the wind in black and shining profusion. Her tunic was quite sleeveless, and one could scarcely fail to observe the perfect development and grace of her arms. As a wave larger than those which had gone before slowly lifted the plank upon its swelling surface, she poised herself daintily upon the support, her round arms stretched out and her body swinging to and fro in harmony with the motion of the waters. As the wave reached its fullest volume she suddenly, quick as thought and with a laugh that rang full into shore, drew herself together, sprang into the air, and, her hands clasped together and clearing her way, plunged into the rolling sea. There was a little cry from timid feminine watchers on the sand, but the smiling face was above water again while they cried, and the daring Triton was up on the plank again in another moment and waiting for a second high roller. So she has been amusing herself and interesting the mob for three mornings. She is as completely at ease in the sea as you or I on land, and the broad plank obeys her slightest touch. When she has had enough of it she will bring the plank into shore, she riding upon the further end and guiding it like a goddess over the crests and through the foam of the biggest breakers. She comes from the Sandwich Islands and is making a tour of the country. Her father is an enormously rich planter. She arrived in the park a week ago with the family of a wealthy New York importer. She is at a fashionable hotel, and is one of the most charming dancers at the hotel hops, as well as the most daring swimmer on the Jersey coast. She is well educated and accomplished, and, of course, speaks English perfectly, and with a swell British accent that is the despair of the dudes. She learned to be mistress of the waves in her childhood at her native home by the sea, where, she modestly says, all the girls learn swimming as a matter of course, quite as much as girls in this country learn tennis and croquet.

JULY 31, 1888. THE PITTSBURGH PRESS

First Girl Surfer.

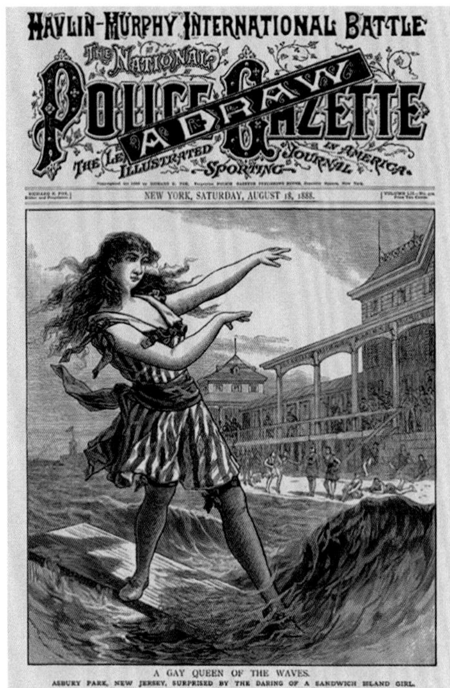
HAVLIN-MURPHY INTERNATIONAL BATTLE

THE NATIONAL POLICE GAZETTE

THE LEADING ILLUSTRATED SPORTING JOURNAL IN AMERICA.

NEW YORK, SATURDAY, AUGUST 18, 1888.

A GAY QUEEN OF THE WAVES.

ASBURY PARK, NEW JERSEY, SURPRISED BY THE DARING OF A SANDWICH ISLAND GIRL.

AUGUST 18, 1888. THE POLICE GAZETTE

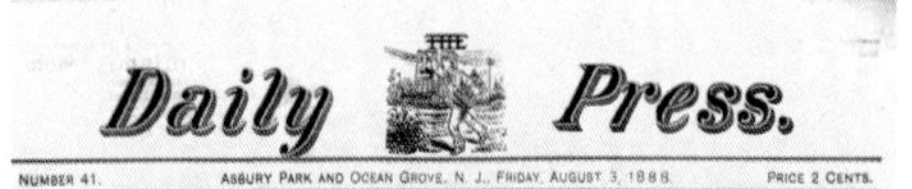
THE Daily Press.

NUMBER 41. ASBURY PARK AND OCEAN GROVE, N. J., FRIDAY, AUGUST 3, 1888. PRICE 2 CENTS.

Will the Search be Successful.

Yesterday a gentleman called at THE DAILY PRESS office and said that he had seen in one of the New York papers a personal notice of the arrival in Asbury Park of a young lady from the Sandwich Islands. His home was located there—he knew the young lady and desired to find her, and accordingly placed an advertisement in this paper asking for her whereabouts.

AUGUST 3, 1888. THE DAILY PRESS

Printed in the classified ads in the *Asbury Park Press* after the Sandwich Island story made it to the New York papers.

ATLANTIC CITY DAILY PRESS WEDNESDAY, AUGUST 24, 1910

KEFCH STARTS SURF RIDING AT NIGHT

Big Search Light on Chelsea Drug Store Shows Him to Boardwalk Throng.

Alvin D. Keech, the young man from Honolulu who came here a few weeks ago to visit friends who are connected with the Hawaiian Exhibit, at the Marlborough-Blenheim, and whose performances with the surf board delighted and astonished the thousands of people who witnessed his performances during one or two afternoons, has begun a genuine novelty, in the shape of surf riding at night under the glaring rays of a searchlight.

Young Keech is said to be one of the cleverest surf riders that has ever come out of Hawaii, and those who know something of that Island, know that means a great deal. That is the home of the surf rider, and everybody down in that part of the country swims, and swims well.

When he announced a short time ago that he would given an exhibition at night for the benefit of some of his friends who are staying at the Hotel Chelsea, it was hardly believed that he would attempt it. It was during the time the sea was heaviest as a result of the Northeaster, and few believed the young man would take the risk.

But he did, and he gave a splendid exhibition. He stood up on the long plank and rode in on the crest of the big billows as gracefully as a duck swims in a pond.

ast night Mr. Keech gave another exhibition in Chelsea, and hundreds of people, having learned of his purpose, gathered on the Boardwalk to see him.

A big searchlight, atop of a drug store nearby threw its glare upon the young man, and everybody could see him as plain as day. It was a thrilling sight and none who saw it is likely to soon forget.

AUGUST 24, 1910. ATLANTIC CITY DAILY PRESS

Alvin Keech.

ATLANTIC CITY DAILY PRESS TUESDAY, JUNE 11, 1912.

Athletic young men bathers are busily engaged in launching their diving boards, a la Hawaii, these summery days down by the sea. The game is to throw the board into the shallow surf that it will float along in an inch or more of water, then to jump aboard, keeping the nose of the board elevated. The impetus given by the expert jump propels the board through fifty yards or more of surf, and the bather stops and starts all over again.

JUNE 11, 1912. ATLANTIC CITY DAILY PRESS

Skimboarding in 1912 in Atlantic City.

SUNDAY GAZETTE, ATLANTIC CITY, N. J., AUGUST 18, 1912.

SEE DUKE P. KAHANAMOKU, Hawaiian Aquatic Phenom, and World's Champion Swimmer in His Surf Board Riding Exhibitions from the Million Dollar Pier.

AUGUST 18, 1912. THE SUNDAY GAZETTE

Duke Kahanamoku surfing Young's Million Dollar Pier, Atlantic City.

ATLANTIC CITY DAILY PRESS THURSDAY, AUGUST 15, 1912

DUKE KAHANAMOKU ENTERTAINS THOUSANDS WITH AQUATIC ANTICS

Olympic Hero Paying Respects to the Shore and Is Giving Exhibitions.

Duke P. Kahanamoku, of Honolulu, Hawaii, where surf riding, on boards made for that purpose, is almost a national pastime, is giving a series of hibitions in this city on a 2½x9 foot board. His exhibitions began yesterday and will last for about ten days. He will ride the waves rom in front of the Million Dollar Pier. The Duke yesterday called upon Commissioner of Public Safety Bartlett and received a permit for his work.

Kahanamoku was a member of the Olympic team which represented the United States at the recent games in Stockholm. He won the 100-metre dash in one minute two and two-fifths seconds, thereby breaking the old and establishing a new world's record. His work so pleased the Sewdish King that he was asked by that Monarch to give an exhibition swim before him. This he did, and was publicly thanked by the King. Kahanamoku afterwards swam in Hamburg, where he bettered his former record for 100 metres by going the distance, which is equal to 109 yards and 13 inches, in one minute and three-fifteenths of a second.

The young Hawaiian is 21 years old, weighs 180 pounds and is six feet one inch in height. He states that nearly every person in his native town in Honolulu is a surf-board riding enthusiast. It is almost the national sport. The enthusiasts lie flat, face downward, on the boards and paddle out to sea as far as they care to go, Then, turning round, they come ashore on the crests of the great beach combers, traveling sometimes faster than twenty miles an hour.

As a general thing the majority of surf-board riders sit on their boards for the return trip to shore, but the more expert are able to perform many feats while gliding swiftly over the crests of the waves.

Kahanamoku, who is a member of the latter class of surf-riders, is able to stand up, stand on his head, or stand on his hands while coming back to shore. He has often carried a passenger ashore on his shoulders.

He had two boards with him but will use only the better one of these while here. This board is two and one-half feet wide, two inches thick, and nine feet long. It is made from one solid piece of California Redwood, and weighs seventy-five pounds. It was manufactured in Honolulu, and sent to America by Kahanamoku's brother.

The athlete says it is no unusual thing in his own city to see hundreds of persons shooting shorewards on surfboards, propelled by the giant waves which eventually land the intrepid riders far up on the beach, from whence they paddle back into the ocean for another ride in. Moonlight swimming and surf riding, he states, are also very popular.

Kahanamoku expects to return to Honolulu the latter part of this month. He will sail from San Francisco about August 26, and reach his home some time late in September. His trip back is in response to many letters from his family, who are enxious to see him, following his excellent work at Stockholm. He will probably return to America next spring.

Mr. and Mrs. S. D. Kock, of Allentown, Pa., are down for a week or more. They are located at the Beechwood Hotel.

Miss Madeline Early and Miss Loretta Early are among New York City visitors at the Westminster.

Mrs. Ryan and the Misses Elizabeth M. and Catherine Ryan, of Philadelphia, are other recent arrivals at the Westminster Hotel.

Mr. and Mrs. Charles Strong, of New Brunswick, are making an indefinit sojourn at the Holmhurst Hotel.

Mr. and Mrs. J. R. Scott and the Misses Scott, of Somers, Pa., are registered at the Seaside Hotel for a stay of indefinite duration.

Mr. and Mrs. T. K. McCrous have joined the Pittsburgh contingent at the Seaside House.

Mr. and Mrs. J. E. McNall, of Wilmington, Del., have come to the shore for a week or more, establishing their headquarters at the Continental Hotel.

Dr. H. B. Cox, of Philadelphia, has left professional cares at home and is here recuperating. He is accompanied by Mrs. Cook at Young's Hotel.

Mrs. W. T. Welsh and Dr. B. B. Miller are visitors from Washington, D. C., at the Bouvier.

At the Chetwoode are Mr. Stephen S. Enright and Mr. J. Rohr, of Chicago. Mr. Enright is accompanied by his wife and nieces, Miss Mae Devine, of Washington, D. C., also Miss Mae Fohey, of Chicago.

Mis Devine is a beautiful debutante

Mr. P. A. Barron, prominent silk importer of New York City, his mother and sister, Mrs. Mary McBride, are also at the Chetwode.

Mr. and Mrs. Allan McFadden, of Pittsburgh, Pa., have been entertaining their two nieces, Mrs. I. Miller and Miss Dobie, of Aberdour, Scotland, for two months, visiting some of the principal cities, after staying a week at the Hotel Morton, they returned on the S. S. California for home.

OCEAN CITY, Aug. 14.—The

AUGUST 15, 1912. ATLANTIC CITY DAILY PRESS

The Duke surfs New Jersey.

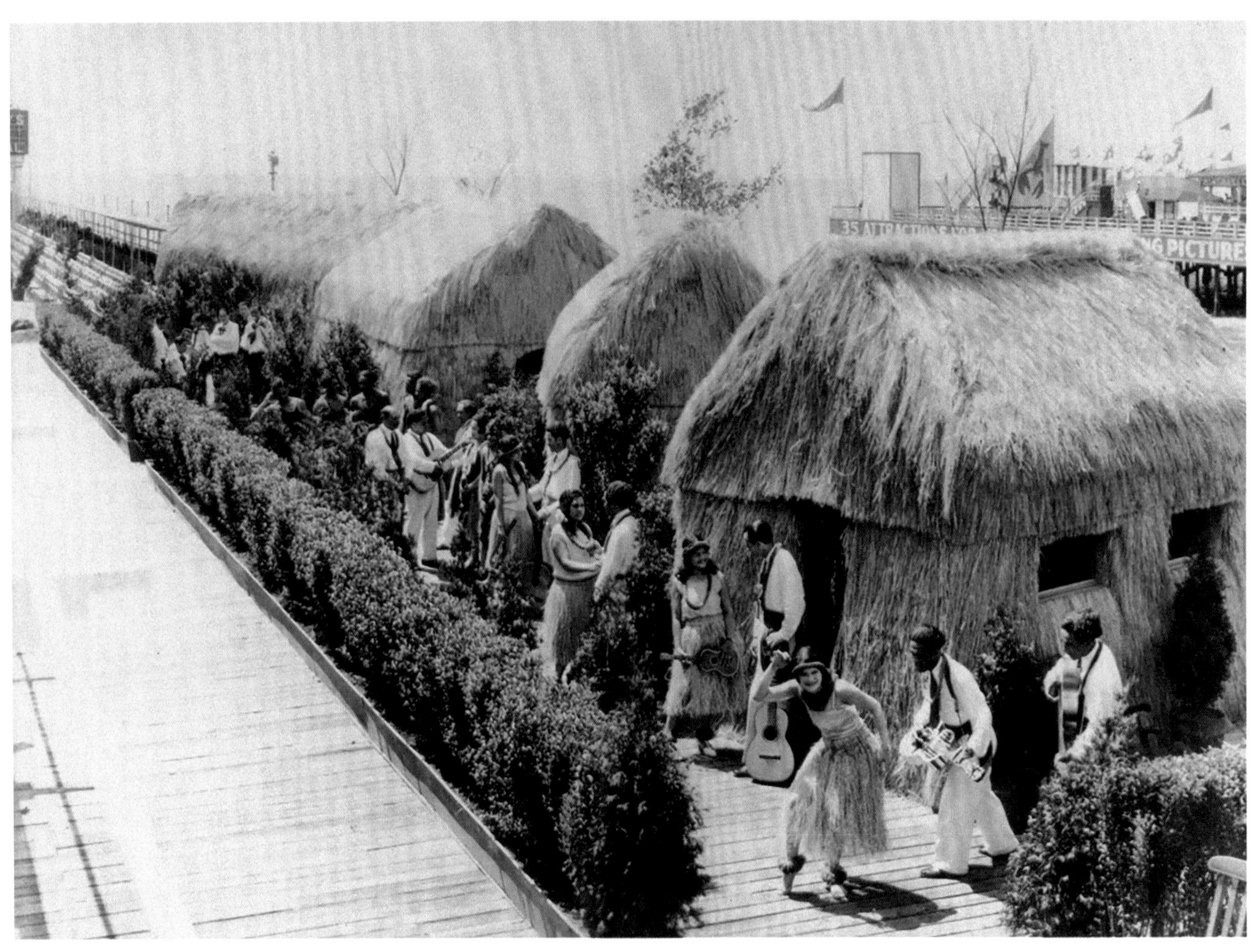

1930S. HAWAIIAN HULA HUTS, ATLANTIC CITY, NJ

Hawaiian Hula Huts were set up on the boardwalk to showcase music, life, and water sports, including the famed high diving that took place at Steel Pier.

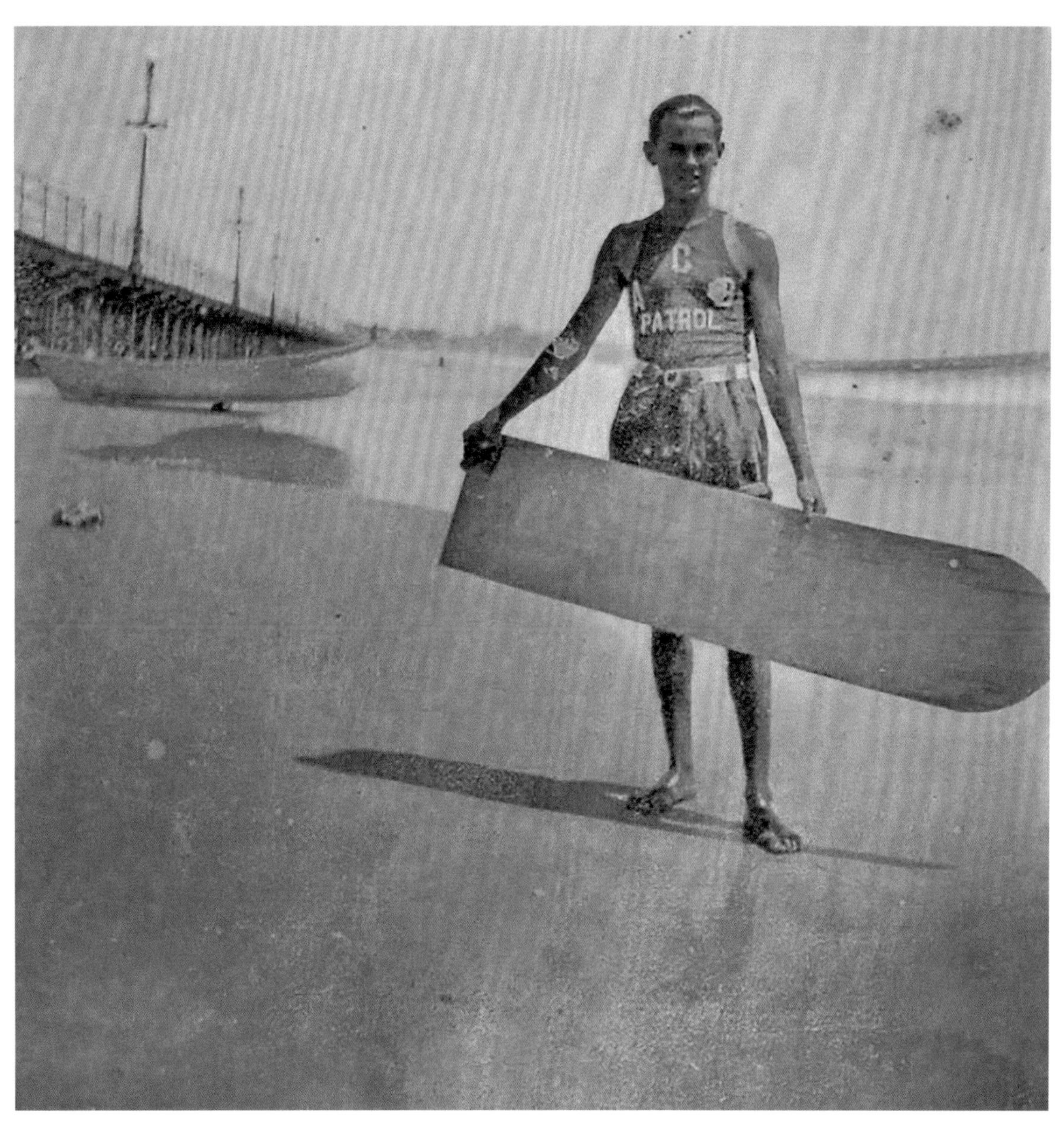

1920S. ATLANTIC CITY, NJ

Atlantic City lifeguard, circa 1920s.

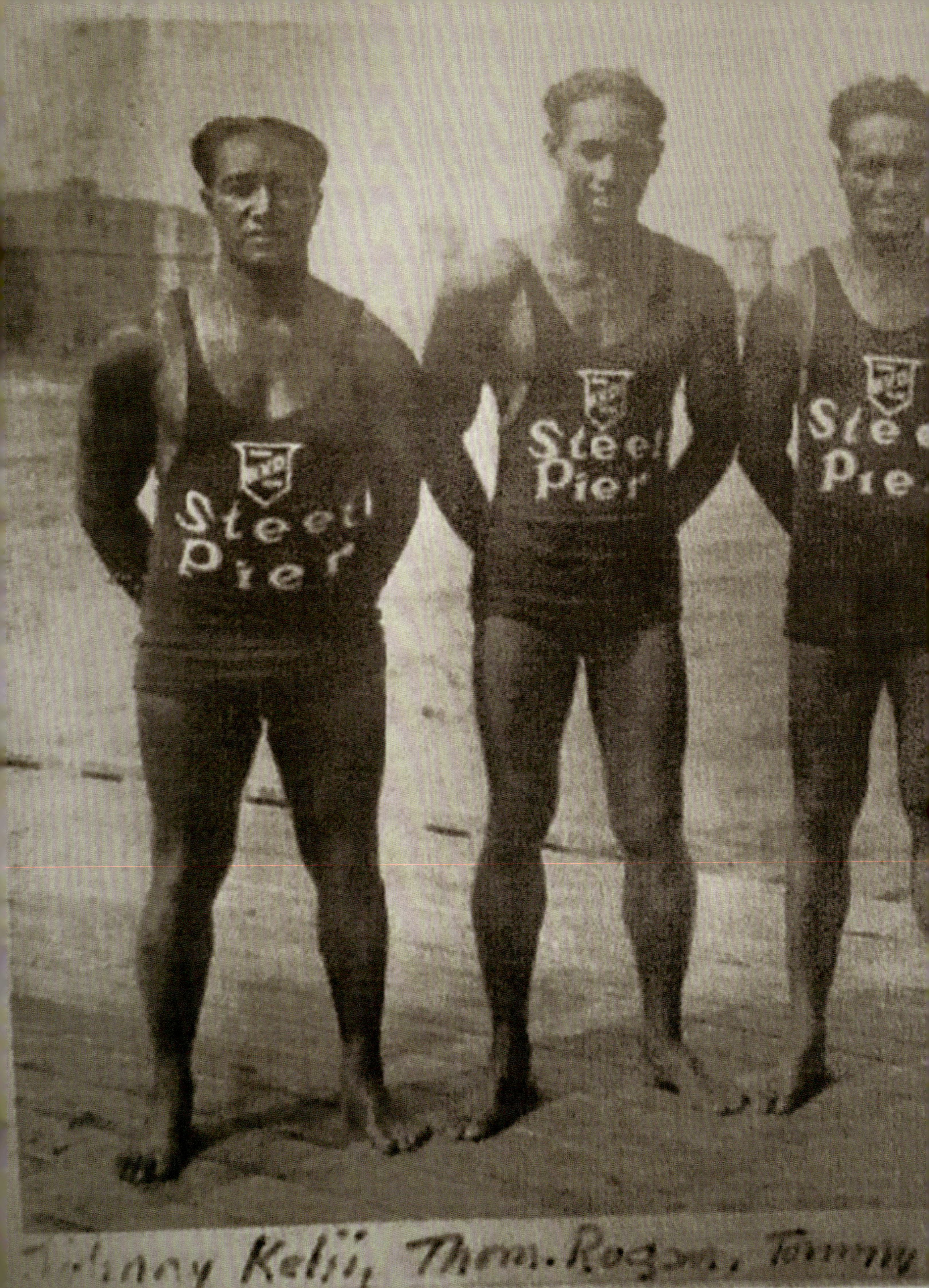
Steel Pier
Steel Pier
Johnny Kelii, Thom. Rogan, Tommy

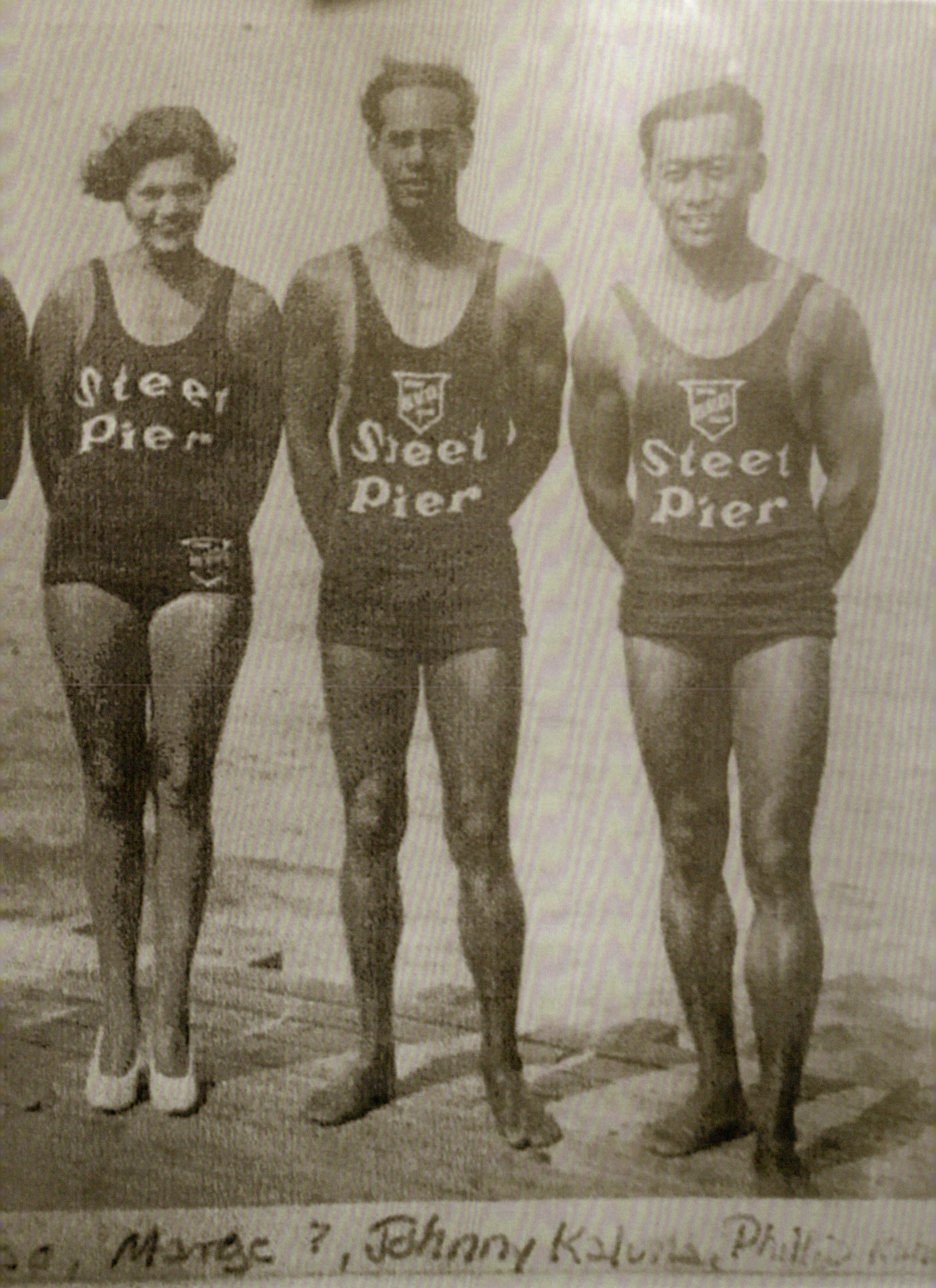
Steel Pier
Steel Pier
Steel Pier
Marge ?, Johnny Kaluna, Phillip

This Is the Advertisement You Saw in the
ASBURY PARK PRESS
Over 50,000 Copies Sold Daily

ATLANTIC STATES
SURFING CONTEST

Spring Ice Breaker

SATURDAY, APRIL 13th

Sumner Ave. at Boardwalk 8:30 A.M.

SEASIDE HEIGHTS

Open To All Ages . . .

REGISTRATION
FEE . . . $5.

Closing Date
APRIL 8, 1968

Official Eastern Surfing Association
Rules will be in effect.

Applications Available at

KELLERS SURF SHOP
Rt. 35 at New York Avenue
LAVALLETTE

or Write Seaside Heights Businessmen's
Assoc. P.O. Box 98, Seaside Heights

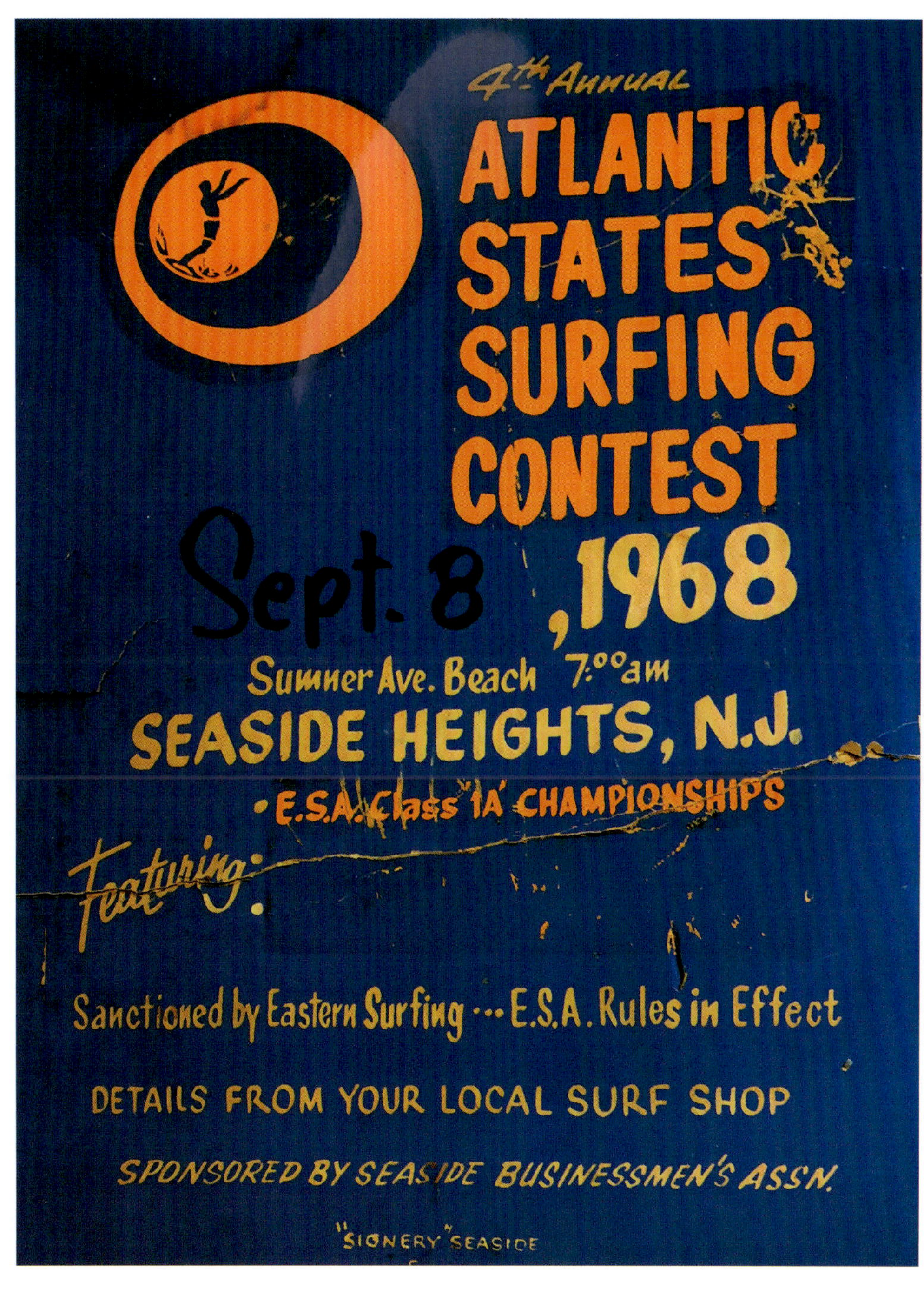
4th Annual
ATLANTIC STATES SURFING CONTEST
Sept. 8 ,1968
Sumner Ave. Beach 7:00am
SEASIDE HEIGHTS, N.J.
• E.S.A. Class 1A' CHAMPIONSHIPS
Featuring:
Sanctioned by Eastern Surfing ··· E.S.A. Rules in Effect
DETAILS FROM YOUR LOCAL SURF SHOP
SPONSORED BY SEASIDE BUSINESSMEN'S ASSN.
"SIGNERY" SEASIDE

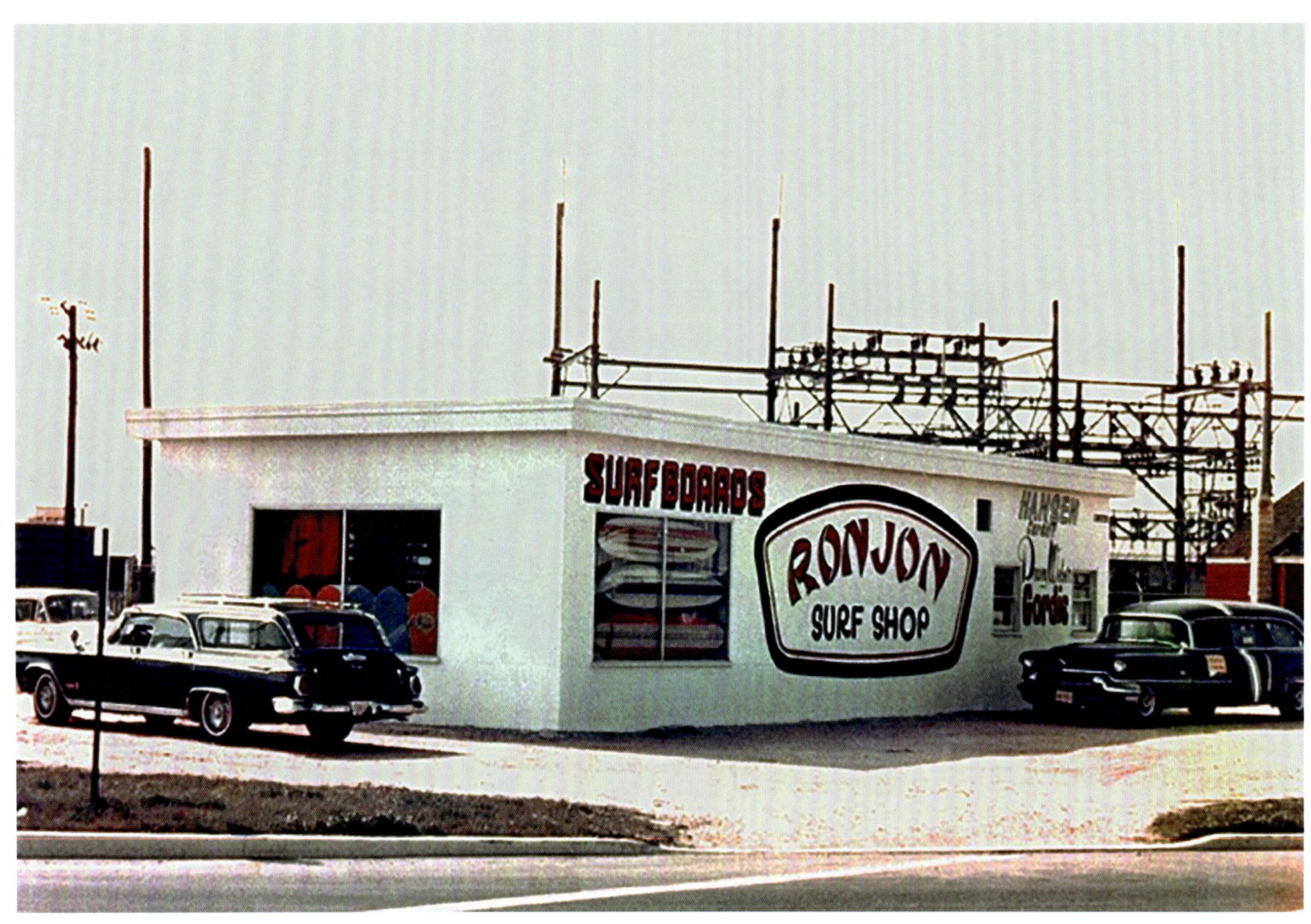

1961. RON JON SURF SHOP, SHIP BOTTOM, LONG ISLAND BEACH, NJ

Ron DiMenna opens Ron John Surf Shop in a trailer park in Ship Bottom, Long Island Beach, New Jersey. Ron Jon Surf shop is the one of the oldest and most iconic shops in the United States.

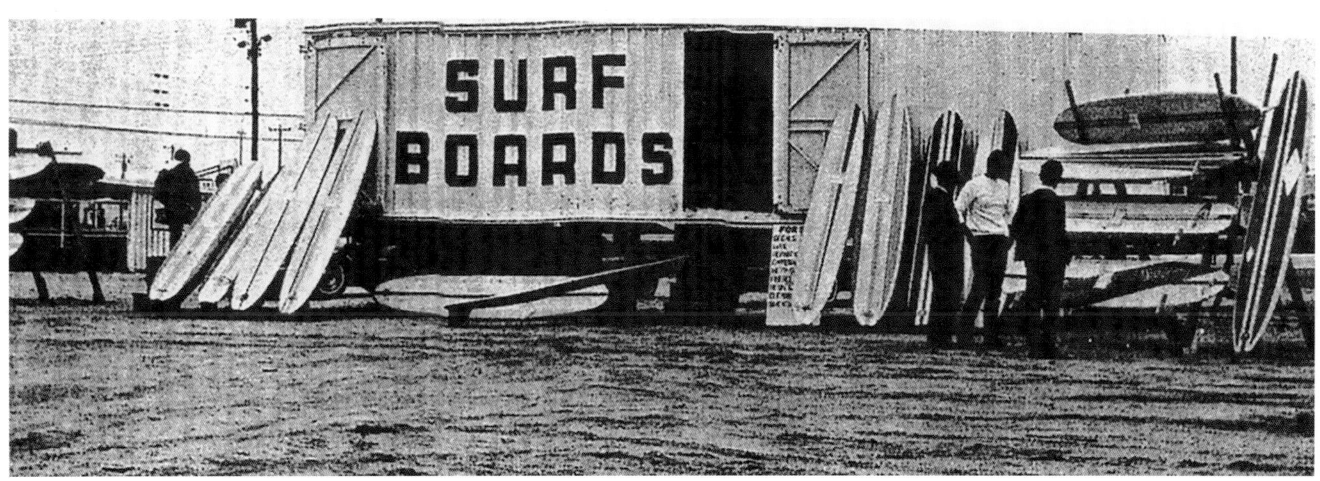
SURF
BOARDS

NEW JERSEY Surfers

Make your First stop

the Custom Surf Shop

East Coast Headquarters for:

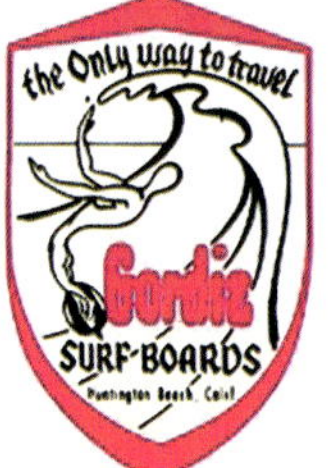

&

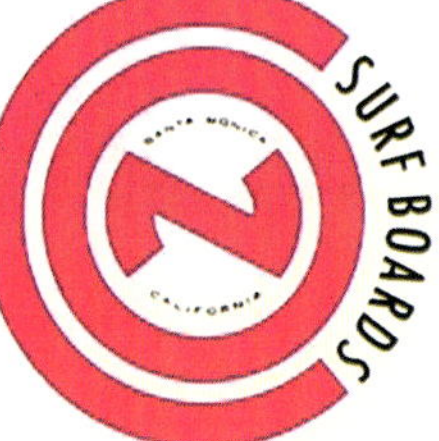

Custom Surf Shop, 507 Grand Central Ave., Lavalette, New Jersey
(across from Post Office)

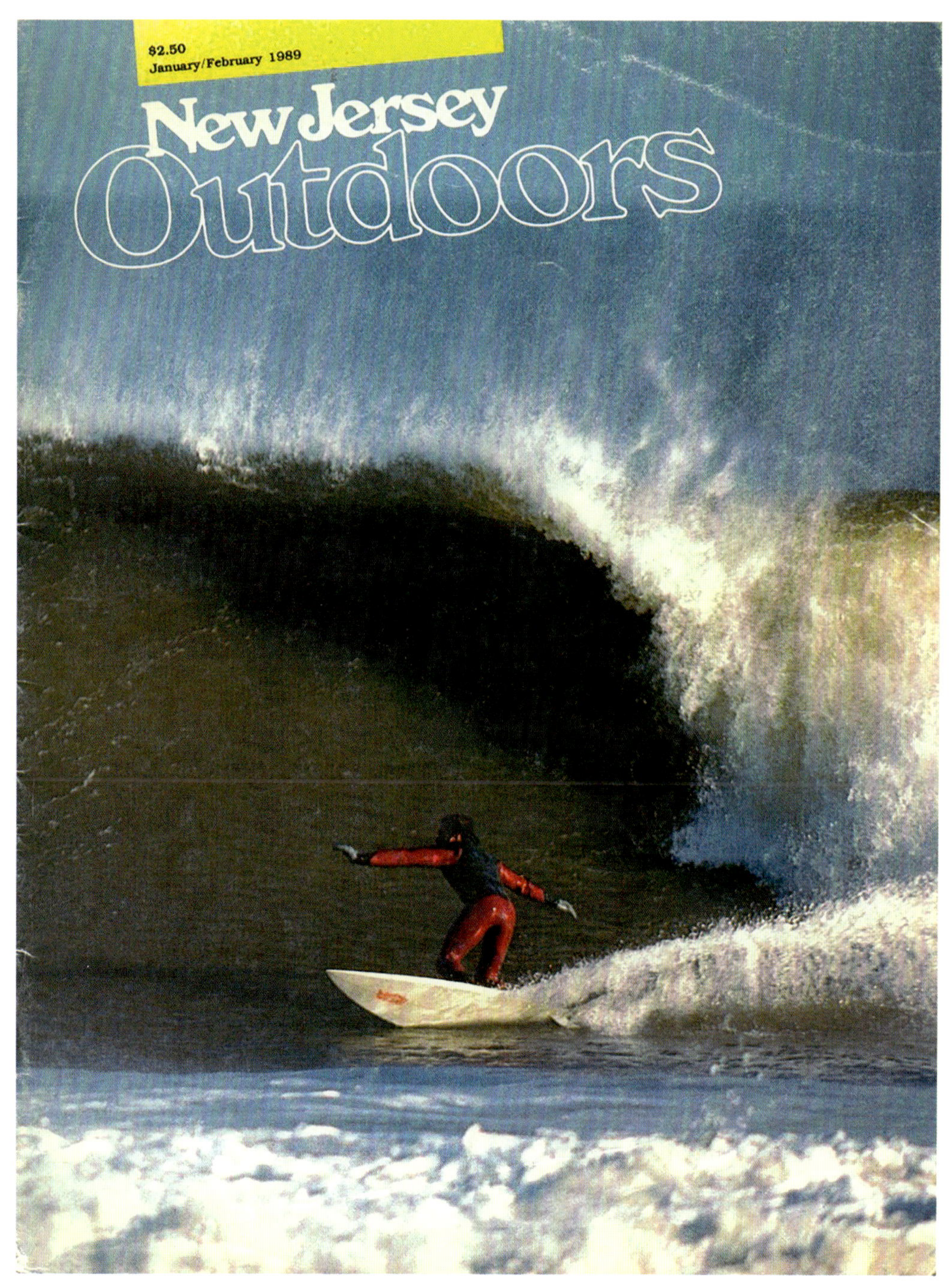
$2.50
January/February 1989
New Jersey
Outdoors

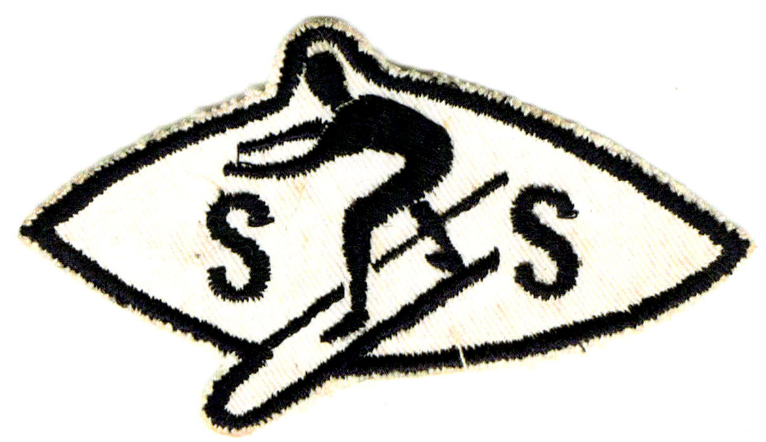

1960S. SURFERS SUPPLIES PATCH, OCEAN CITY, NJ

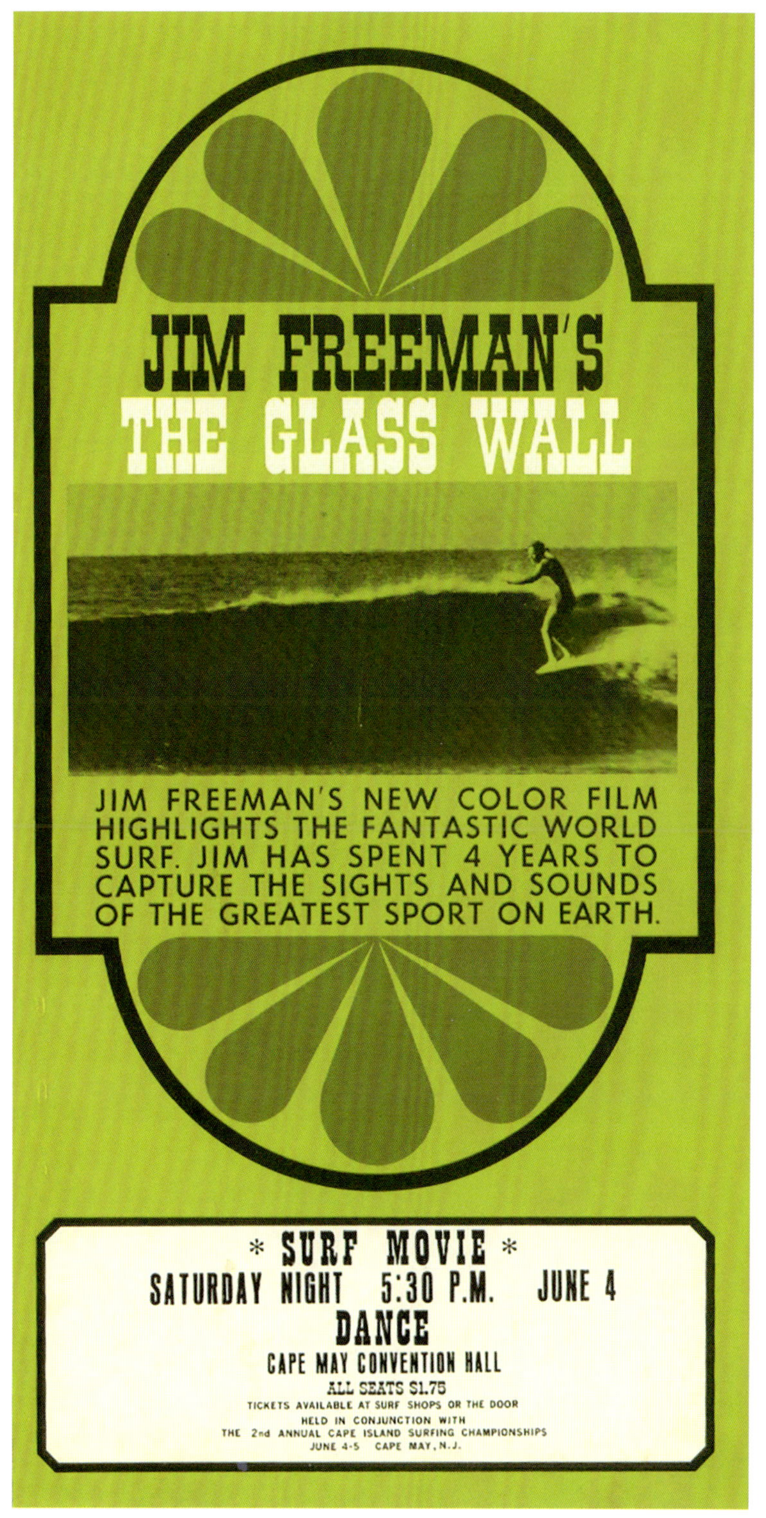
JIM FREEMAN'S
THE GLASS WALL
JIM FREEMAN'S NEW COLOR FILM HIGHLIGHTS THE FANTASTIC WORLD SURF. JIM HAS SPENT 4 YEARS TO CAPTURE THE SIGHTS AND SOUNDS OF THE GREATEST SPORT ON EARTH.
* SURF MOVIE *
SATURDAY NIGHT 5:30 P.M. JUNE 4
DANCE
CAPE MAY CONVENTION HALL
ALL SEATS $1.75
TICKETS AVAILABLE AT SURF SHOPS OR THE DOOR
HELD IN CONJUNCTION WITH
THE 2nd ANNUAL CAPE ISLAND SURFING CHAMPIONSHIPS
JUNE 4-5 CAPE MAY, N.J.

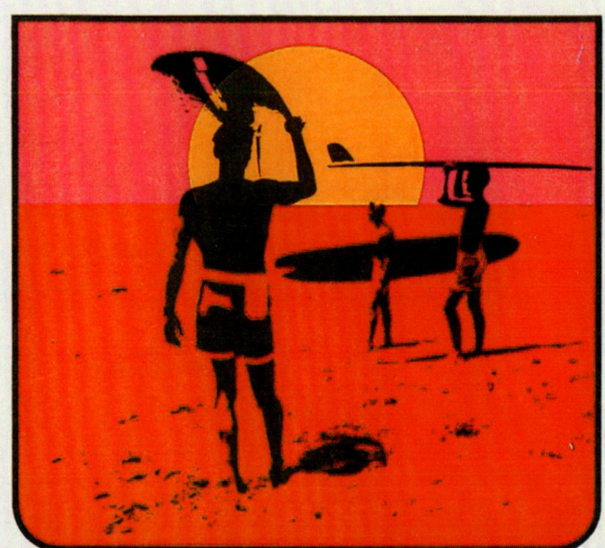

The Endless Summer

On any day of the year it's summer somewhere in the world. Bruce Brown's latest color film highlights the adventures of two young American surfers, Robert August and Mike Hynson who follow this everlasting summer around the world. Their unique expedition takes them to Senegal, Ghana, Nigeria, South Africa, Australia, New Zealand, Tahiti, Hawaii and California. Share their experiences as they search the world for that perfect wave which may be forming just over the next Horizon.

BRUCE BROWN FILMS

Bruce Brown Films the producer of "Slippery When Wet," "Surf Crazy," "Barefoot Adventure," "Surfing Hollow Days," "Waterlogged" and "The Endless Summer."

BRUCE BROWN NARRATING IN PERSON . . .
STRAIGHT from EXCLUSIVE Hollywood Premiere!!

PLUS—MEET THE WORLD'S GREATEST SURFERS
IN PERSON . . .

PHIL EDWARDS — "World's Best Surfer"
(Surfer Magazine Poll)
JOEY CABELL — Hawaii's Makaha Champion
HOBIE ALTER — Tandem Surfing Champion
CORKY CARROLL — Pacific Coast Jr. Champion
MIKE HYNSON—Featured surfer in "The Endless Summer'

Don't Miss the Special Surfing Demonstrations
By These Top Surfers at
CONVENTION HALL BEACH
WEDNESDAY, JULY 1 at 10:00 A.M.

THEY WILL ALSO BE AT FILM SHOWING
TO ANSWER ANY QUESTIONS

FREE
to be given away at show

$140.00 CUSTOM HOBIE SURFBOARD
HANG-TEN SURFWEAR (the surfer's surfwear)
AND . . . TO THE FIRST THOUSAND PATRONS
A COPY OF SURFER MAGAZINE

ONE NIGHT ONLY
ASBURY PARK CONVENTION HALL
THURSDAY —-JULY 2 — 8:30 P.M.
All tickets $1.50 at door or in advance from
MANATEE SEA CENTER, 12th & Ocean Ave., Belmar
Phone — 681-3947

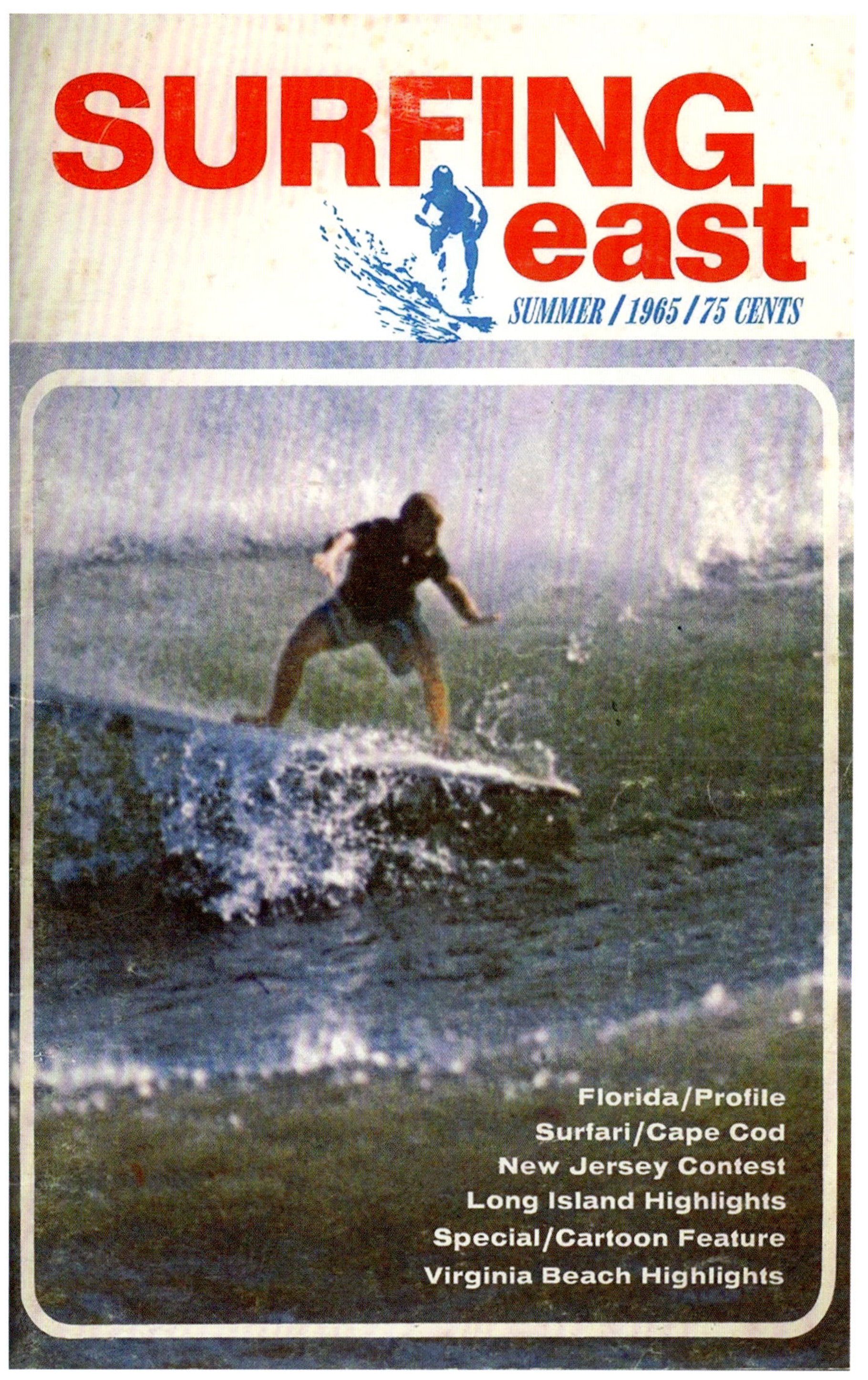
SURFING east
SUMMER / 1965 / 75 CENTS
Florida/Profile
Surfari/Cape Cod
New Jersey Contest
Long Island Highlights
Special/Cartoon Feature
Virginia Beach Highlights

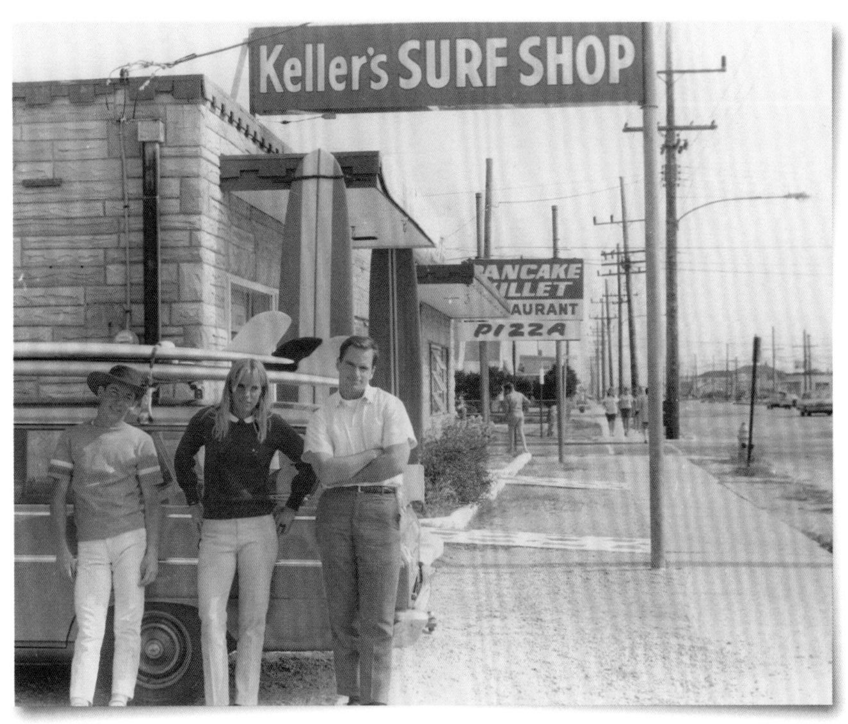

1966. KELLER'S SURF SHOP, LAVALLETTE, NJ

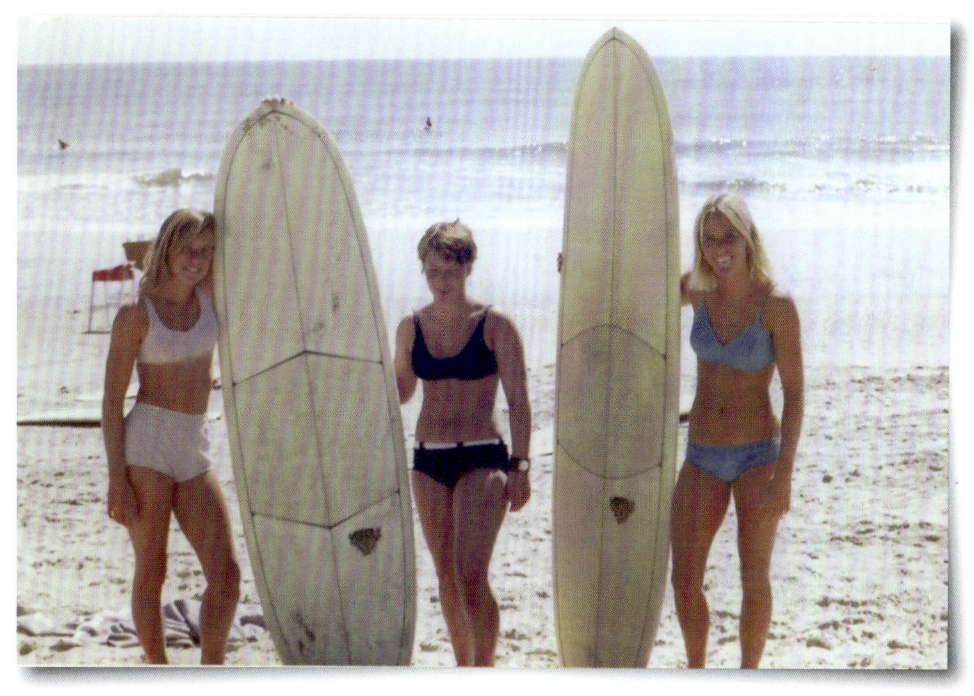

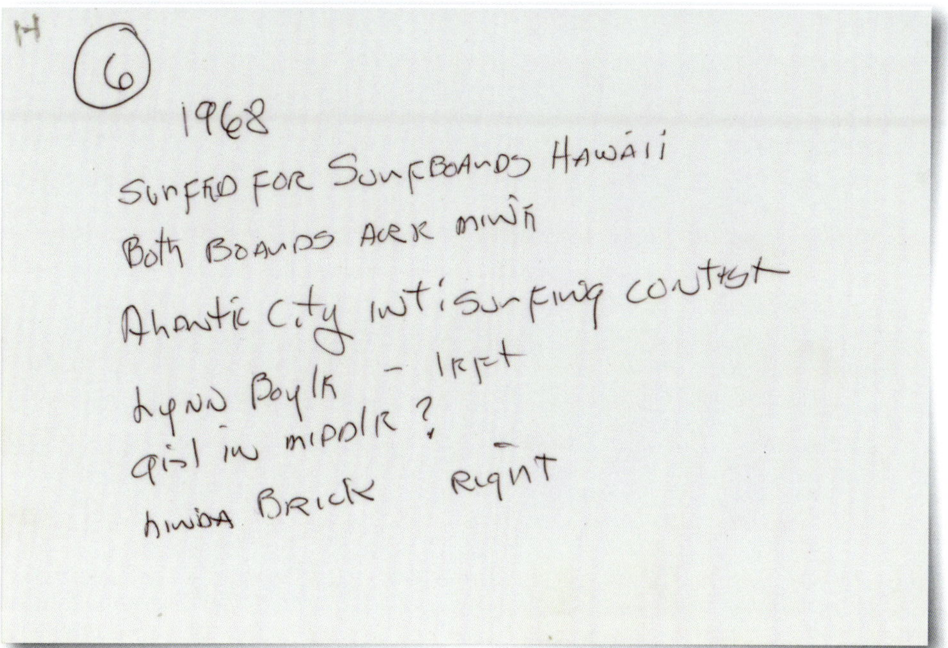

H

(6)

1968

Surfed for Surfboards Hawaii

Both boards are mine

Atlantic City int'l surfing contest

Lynn Boyle - left

girl in middle?

Linda Brick right

1968. ATLANTIC CITY INTERNATIONAL SURFING CONTEST, ATLANTIC CITY, NJ

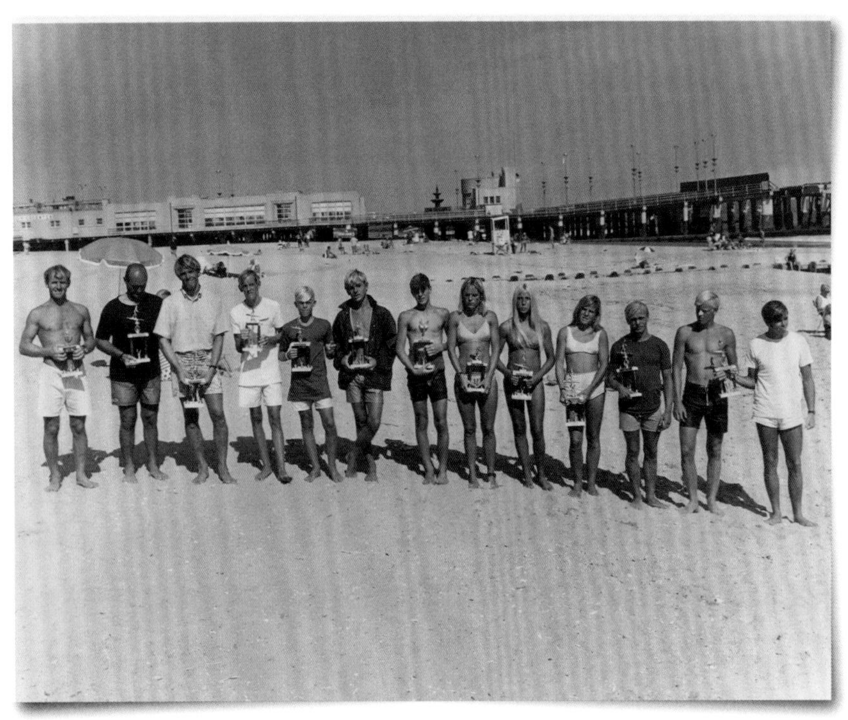

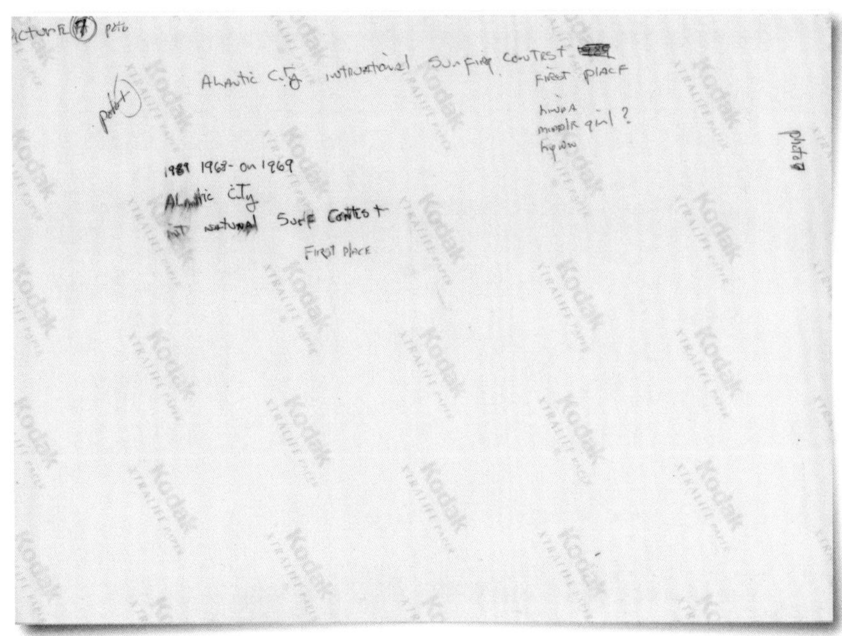

1968. ATLANTIC CITY INTERNATIONAL SURFING CONTEST, ATLANTIC CITY, NJ

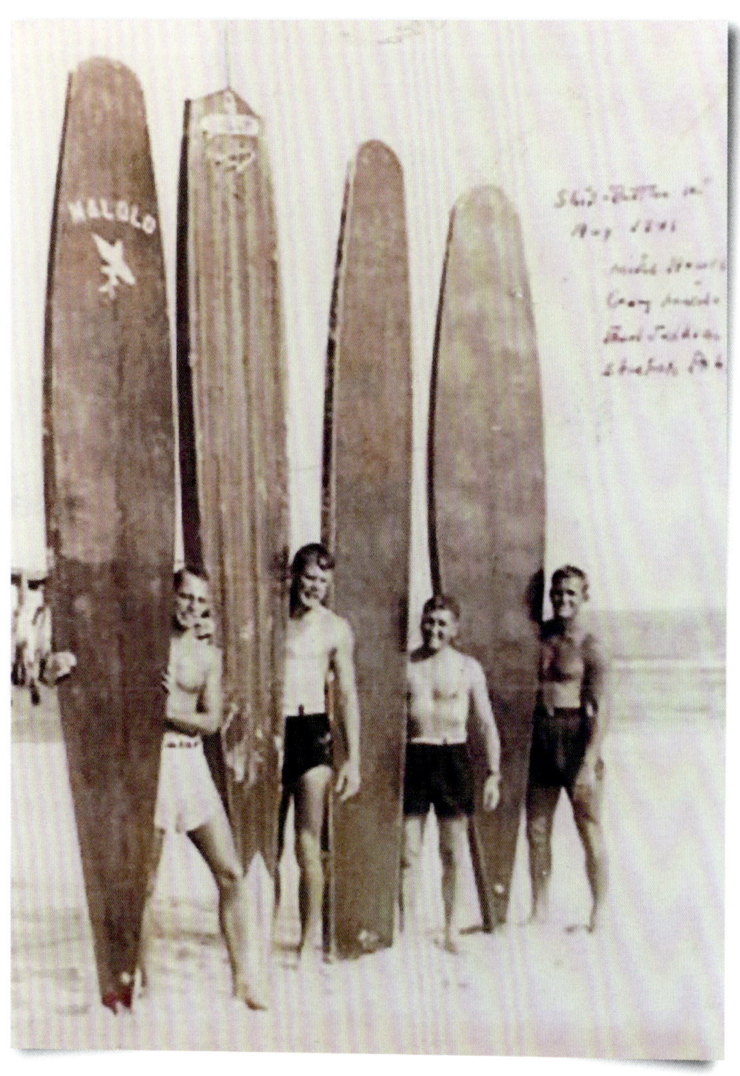

1941. MALOLO-AKULA SURFBOARD CLUB, SHIP BOTTOM, NJ

Wrights Pier at 20th Street, Ship Bottom, New Jersey. The club was formed in the 1930s. Pictured left to right: Mike Howes, Cary Lincoln, Erle Jackson, and Stretch Pohl.

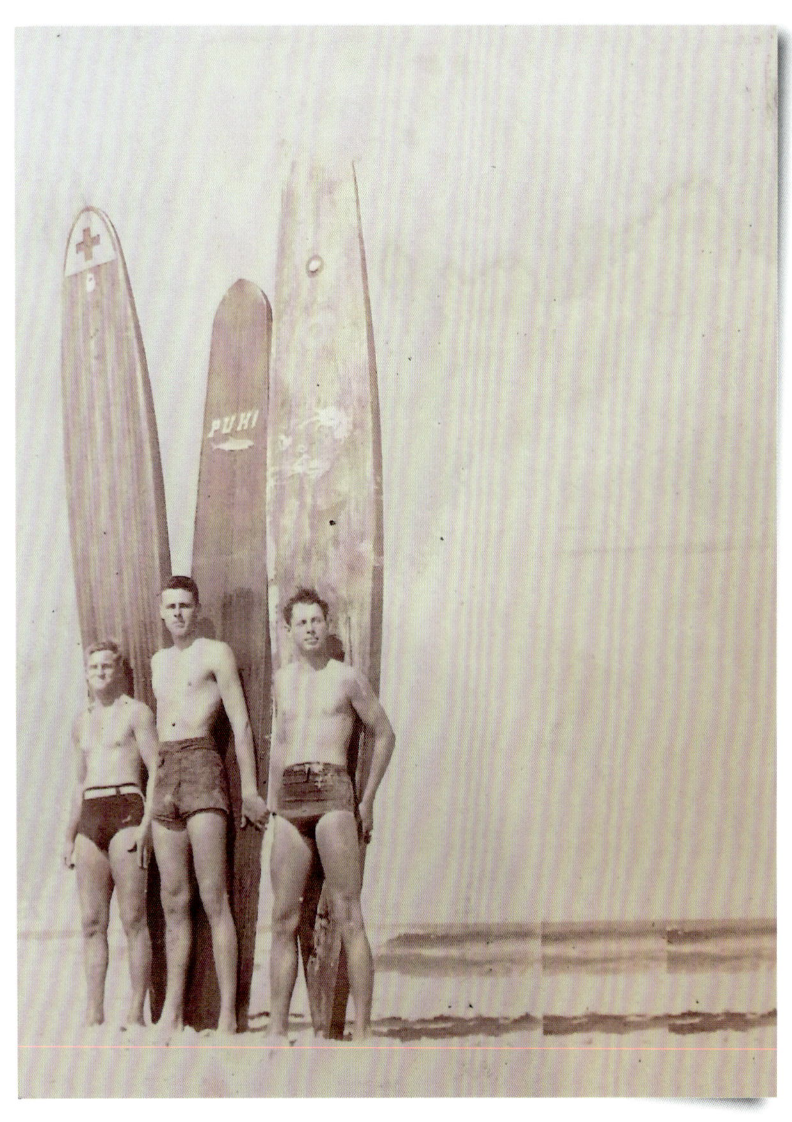

1935. ORTLEY BEACH, NJ

Henry "Stretch" Pohl, Bob Hensler, and Mike Howes.

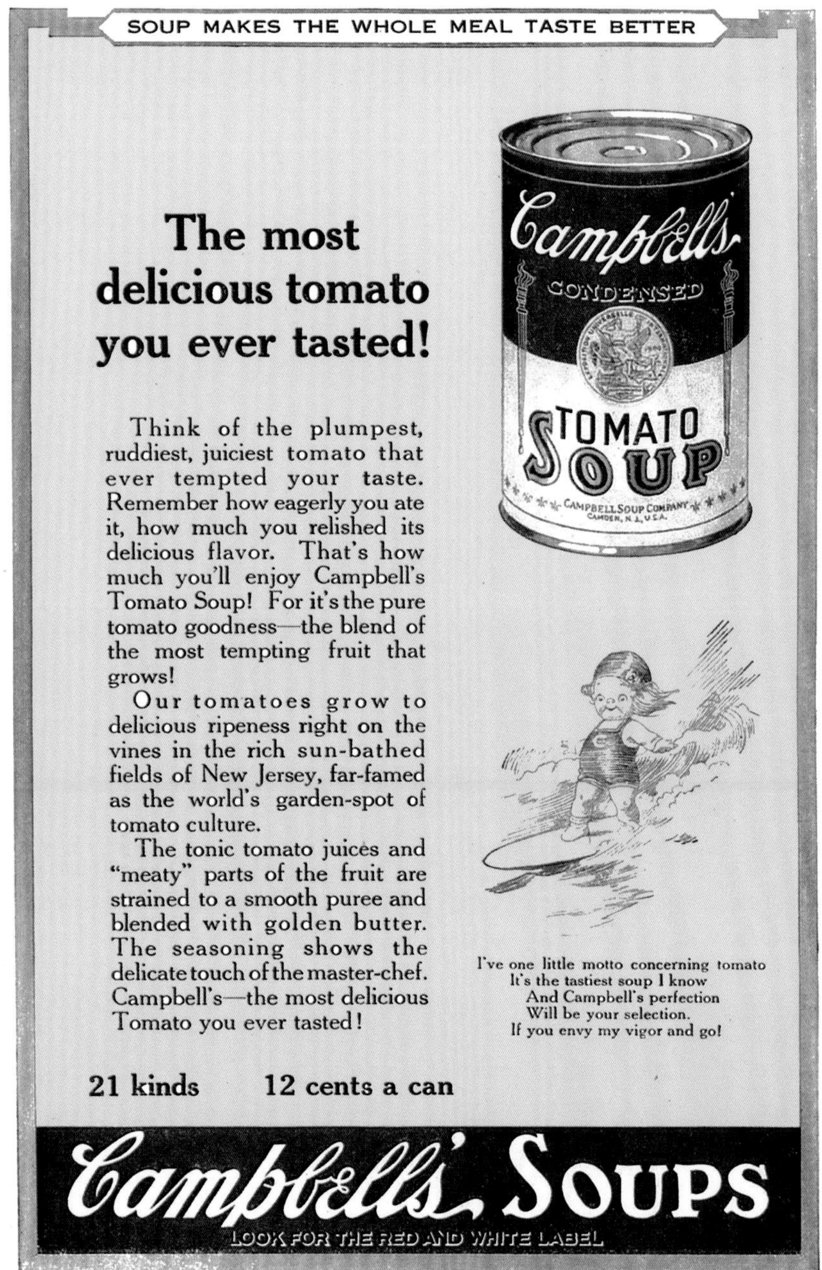

CIRCA 1920S

Celebrating New Jersey tomatoes with a cartoon of a surfer girl.

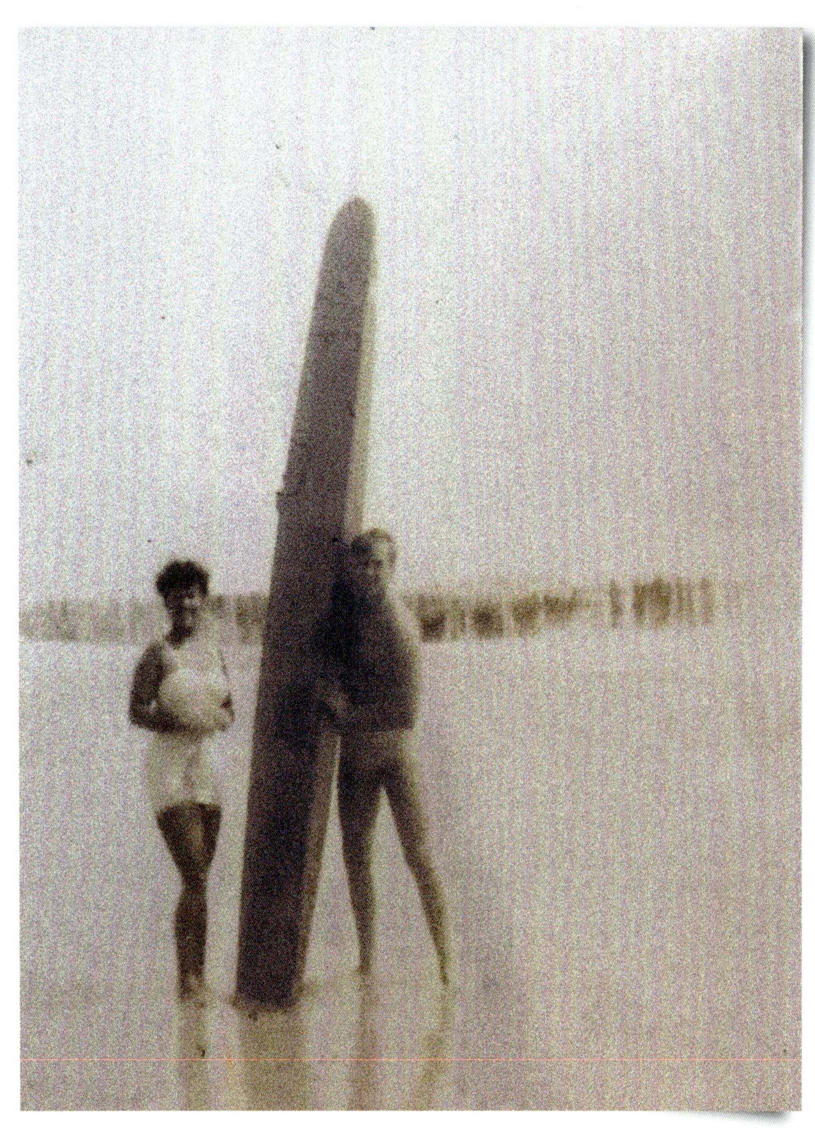

1952. RICHARD LISIEWSKI AND HIS WIFE, PAULINE, HOLGATE, NJ

On the beach in Holgate.

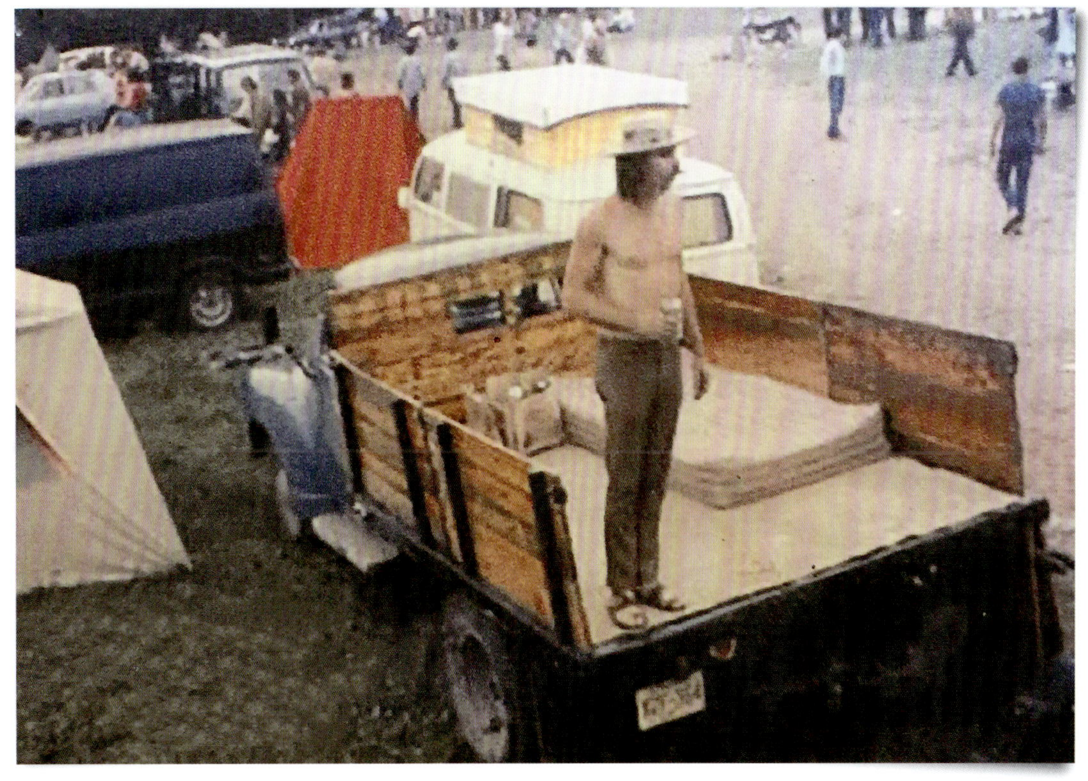

1969. WOODSTOCK, NY

Tinker and his infamous stake body truck at Woodstock.

Atlantic City, U.S. - Internationals

SURF CONTEST

JUNE 28, 29, 30-JULY 1, 1966

Sponsored by
CITY OF ATLANTIC CITY, N. J.

Co-Sponsored by
DOWNBEACH SURF CLUB

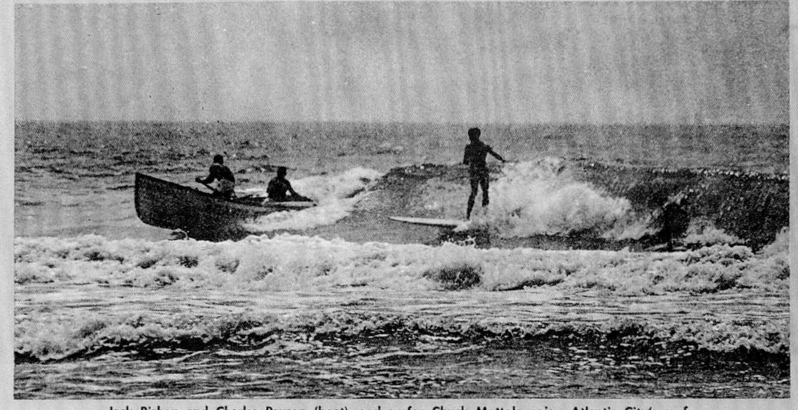

Jack Bishop and Charles Paxson (boat), and surfer Chuck Mottola enjoy Atlantic City's surf.

Information: **MICKEY L. GOSE, Director**

SURF TOURNAMENT HEADQUARTERS

2300 PACIFIC AVENUE **ATLANTIC CITY, N. J. 08401**

Comments

June 28 – 8:00 A.M. to 12:00 P.M. – Atlantic City Closed
(Brigantine, Atlantic City, Ventnor, Margate, Longport and Ocean City) LOCAL ENTRIES ONLY

June 29 – 8:00 A.M. to 6:00 P.M. – New Jersey Closed
NEW JERSEY ENTRIES ONLY

June 30 – 8:00 A.M. to 6:00 P.M. – U.S.-International Opens
(Semi-Finals) WORLD-WIDE ENTRY

July 1 – 8:00 A.M. to 6:00 P.M. – U.S.-International Opens
(Finals – Trophies and Awards Presentation) WORLD-WIDE ENTRY

sea of joy

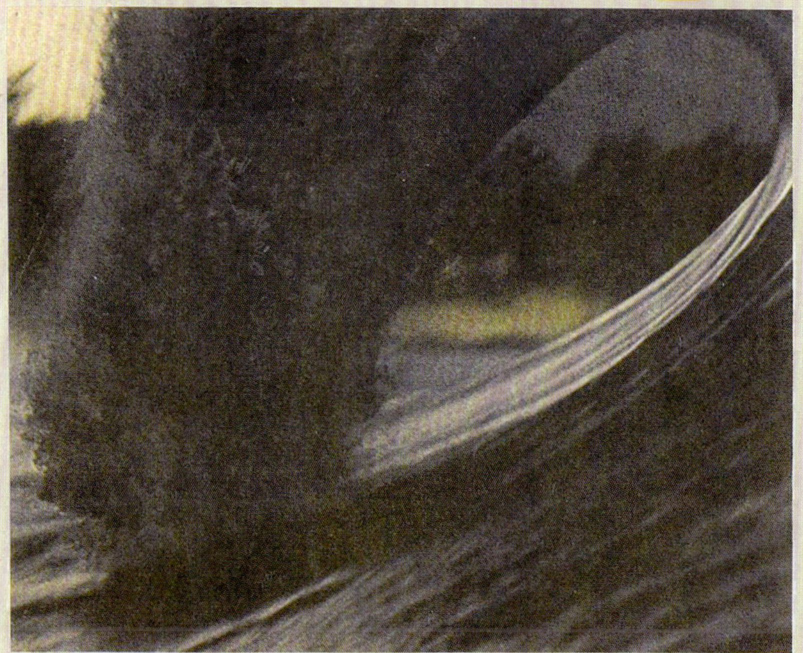

a new film by paul witzig
(producer of "evolution")
released by macgillivray-freeman

EAST COAST PREMIER

OCEAN CITY, N. J. – FRIDAY & SATURDAY, AUGUST 6 & 7
ST. AUGUSTINES YOUTH CENTER

MARGATE, N. J. SUNDAY & MONDAY, AUGUST 8 & 9
REEF SURF SHOP

**PLUS – From Hal Jepson, the maker of "The Cosmic Children"
"THE THIRD REEL"
'70-'71 Hawaii Footage – Pipeline, Sunset, Haleiwa, Honolua Bay
Jeff, Barry, Tiger, Owl, Jay and a cast of thousands

Screentime 8:30 p.m. 2 Hour Show Admission $2.50

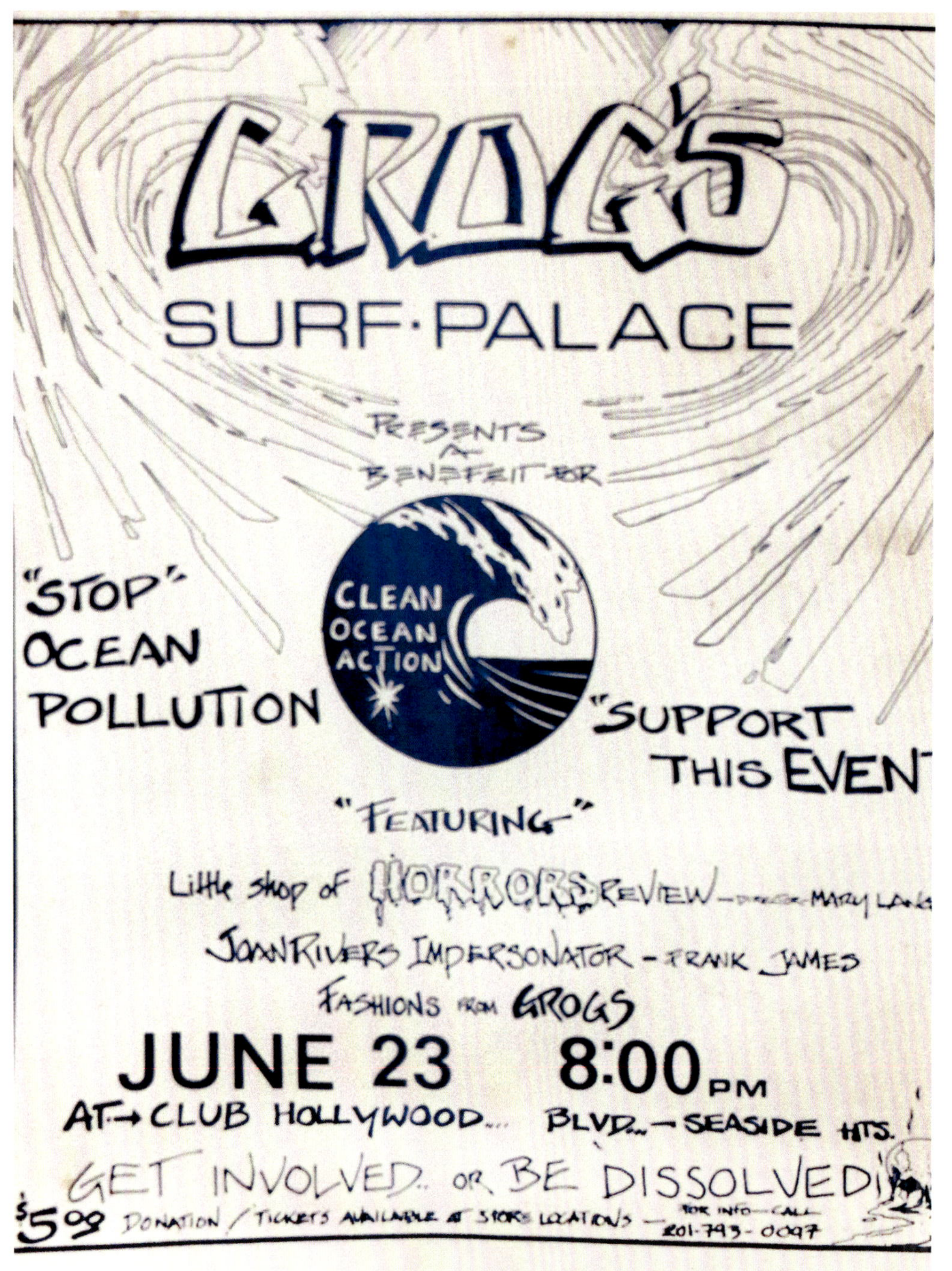
GROG'S
SURF·PALACE
PRESENTS
A
BENEFIT FOR
CLEAN
OCEAN
ACTION
"STOP"
OCEAN
POLLUTION
"SUPPORT
THIS EVENT
"FEATURING"
Little shop of HORRORS REVIEW — MARY LANG
JOAN RIVERS IMPERSONATOR — FRANK JAMES
FASHIONS FROM GROGS
JUNE 23 8:00 PM
AT → CLUB HOLLYWOOD... BLVD... — SEASIDE HTS.
GET INVOLVED.. OR BE DISSOLVED!
$5.00 DONATION / TICKETS AVAILABLE AT STORE LOCATIONS — FOR INFO — CALL 201-793-0097

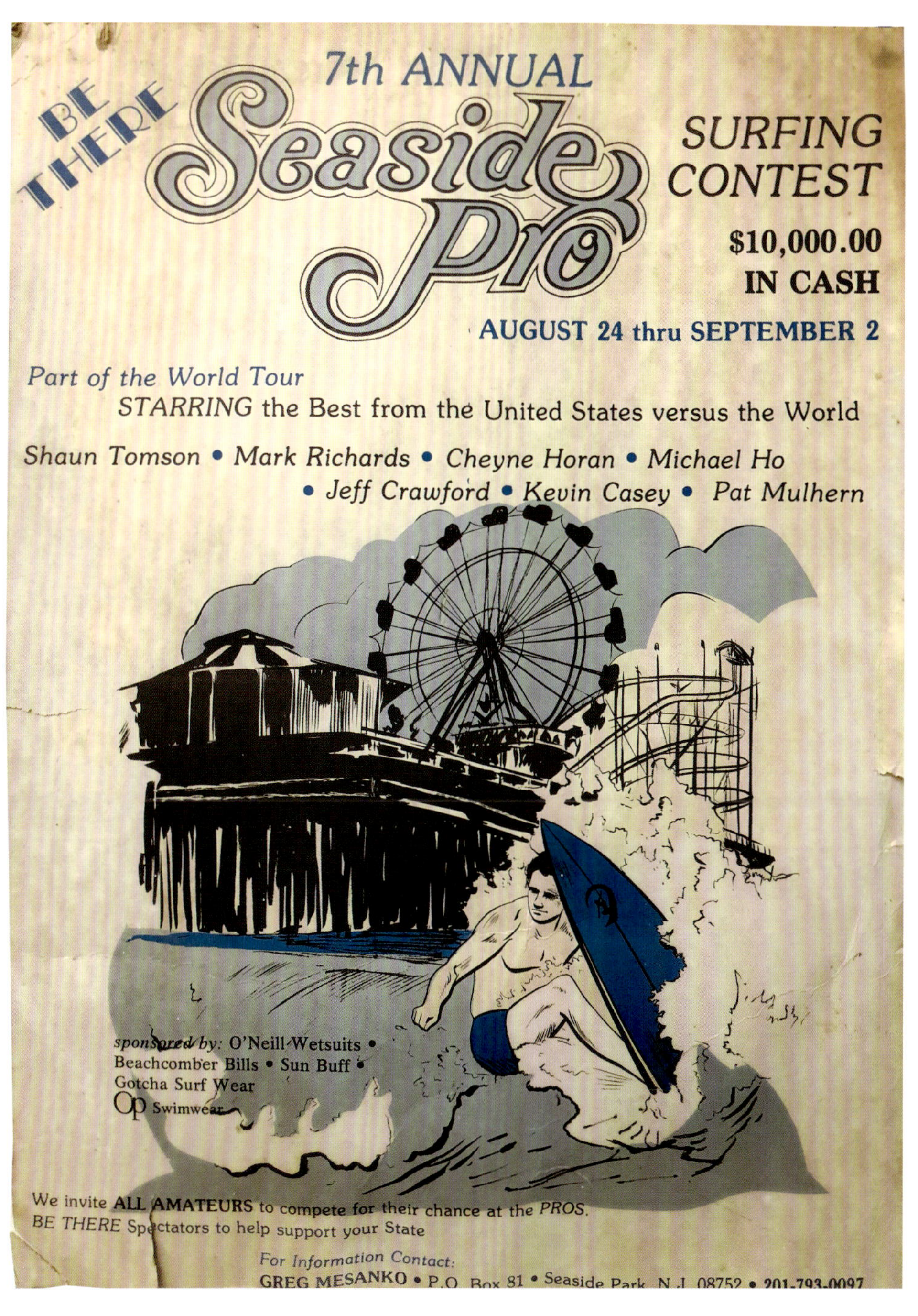
BE THERE
7th ANNUAL
Seaside Pro
SURFING CONTEST
$10,000.00
IN CASH
AUGUST 24 thru SEPTEMBER 2
Part of the World Tour
STARRING the Best from the United States versus the World
Shaun Tomson • Mark Richards • Cheyne Horan • Michael Ho
• Jeff Crawford • Kevin Casey • Pat Mulhern
sponsored by: O'Neill Wetsuits •
Beachcomber Bills • Sun Buff •
Gotcha Surf Wear
Op Swimwear
We invite ALL AMATEURS to compete for their chance at the PROS.
BE THERE Spectators to help support your State
For Information Contact:
GREG MESANKO • P.O. Box 81 • Seaside Park, N.J. 08752 • 201-793-0097

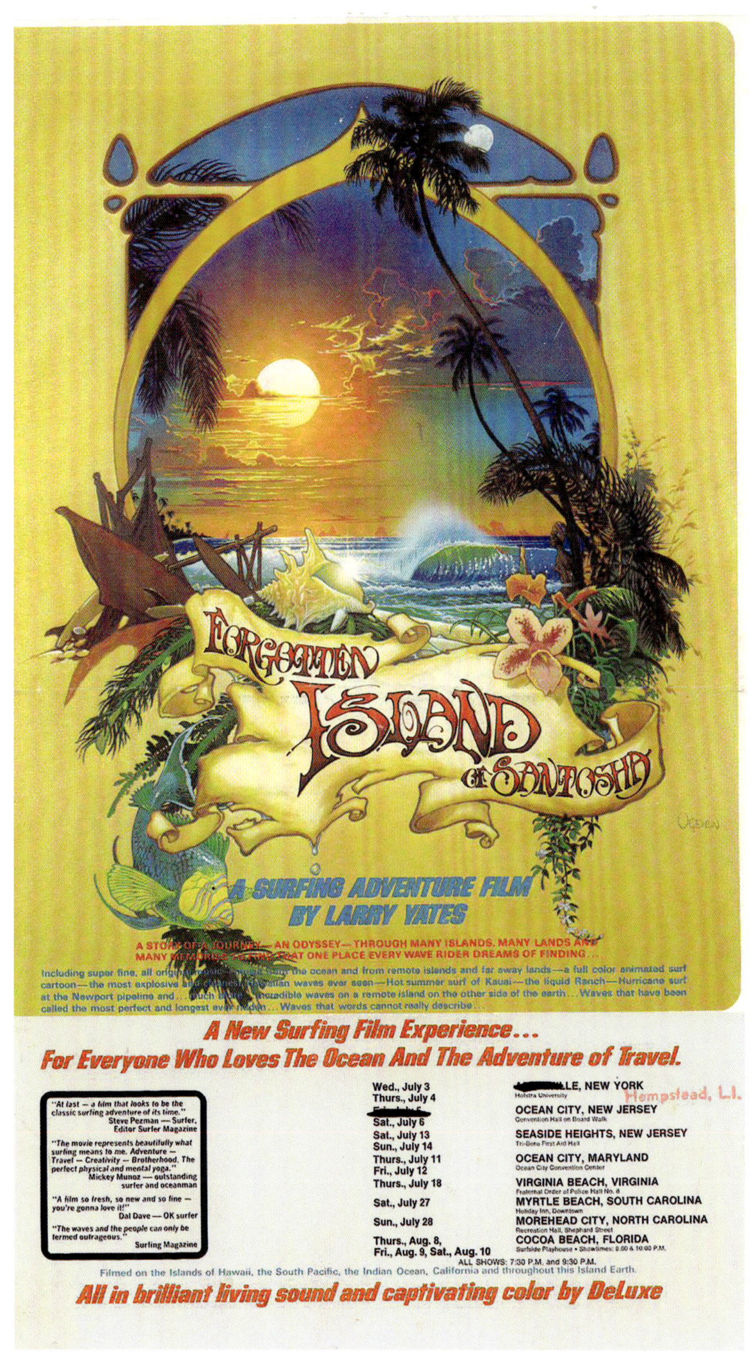
FORGOTTEN ISLAND OF SANTOSHA
A SURFING ADVENTURE FILM
BY LARRY YATES
AN ODYSSEY—THROUGH MANY ISLANDS, MANY LANDS
THAT ONE PLACE EVERY WAVE RIDER DREAMS OF FINDING...
the ocean and from remote islands and far away lands—a full color animated surf
waves ever seen—Hot summer surf of Kauai—the liquid Ranch—Hurricane surf
at the Newport pipeline and...
incredible waves on a remote island on the other side of the earth... Waves that have been
called the most perfect and longest
Waves that words cannot really describe...
A New Surfing Film Experience...
For Everyone Who Loves The Ocean And The Adventure of Travel.
"At last — a film that looks to be the classic surfing adventure of its time."
Steve Pezman — Surfer, Editor Surfer Magazine
"The movie represents beautifully what surfing means to me. Adventure — Travel — Creativity — Brotherhood. The perfect physical and mental yoga."
Mickey Munoz — outstanding surfer and oceanman
"A film so fresh, so new and so fine — you're gonna love it!"
Dal Dave — OK surfer
"The waves and the people can only be termed outrageous."
Surfing Magazine
Wed., July 3
Thurs., July 4
LE, NEW YORK
Hofstra University
Hempstead, L.I.
Sat., July 6
OCEAN CITY, NEW JERSEY
Convention Hall on Board Walk
Sat., July 13
Sun., July 14
SEASIDE HEIGHTS, NEW JERSEY
Tri-Boro First Aid Hall
Thurs., July 11
Fri., July 12
OCEAN CITY, MARYLAND
Ocean City Convention Center
Thurs., July 18
VIRGINIA BEACH, VIRGINIA
Fraternal Order of Police Hall No. 8
Sat., July 27
MYRTLE BEACH, SOUTH CAROLINA
Holiday Inn, Downtown
Sun., July 28
MOREHEAD CITY, NORTH CAROLINA
Recreation Hall, Shephard Street
Thurs., Aug. 8,
Fri., Aug. 9, Sat., Aug. 10
COCOA BEACH, FLORIDA
Surfside Playhouse • Showtimes: 8:00 & 10:00 P.M.
ALL SHOWS: 7:30 P.M. and 9:30 P.M.
Filmed on the Islands of Hawaii, the South Pacific, the Indian Ocean, California and throughout this Island Earth.
All in brilliant living sound and captivating color by DeLuxe

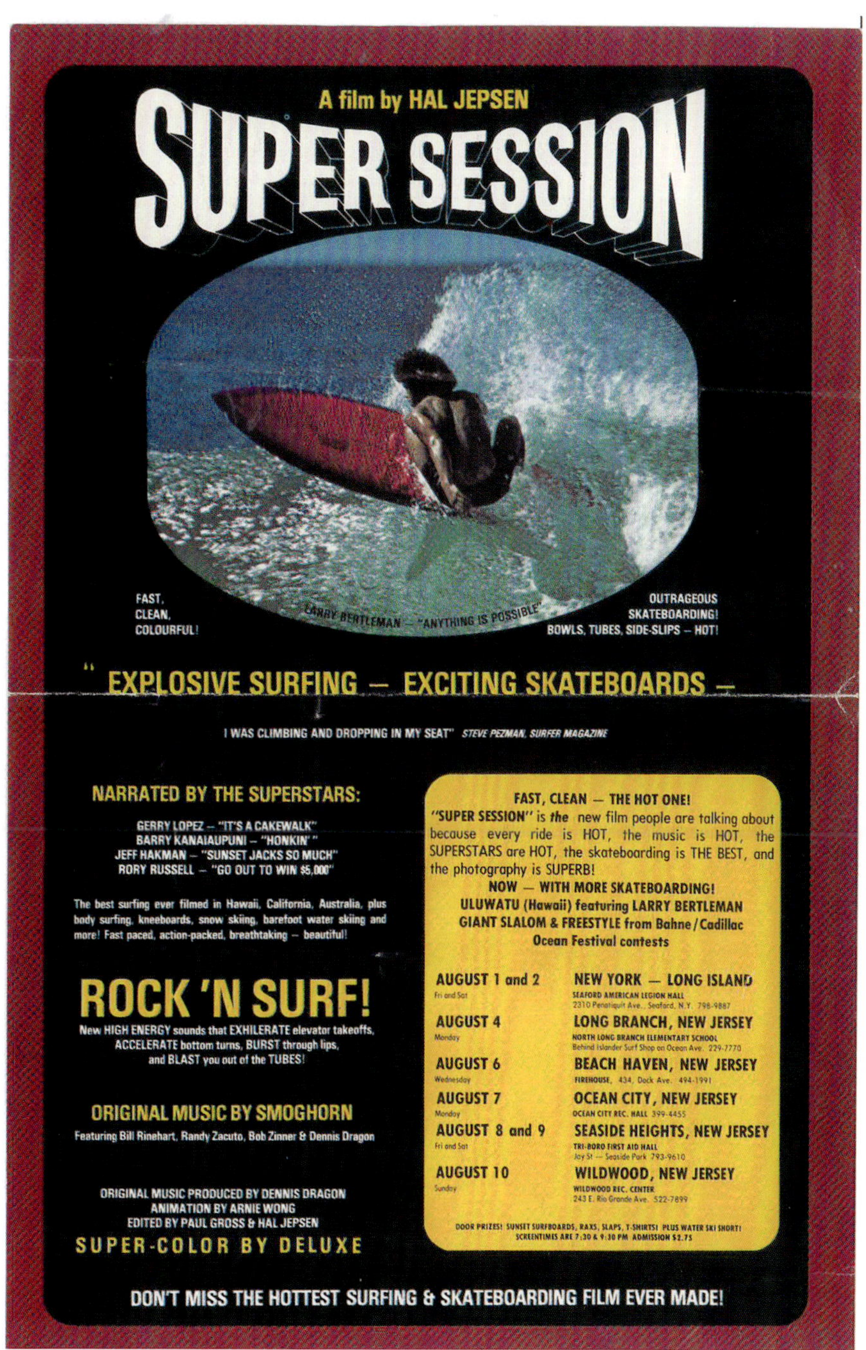
A film by HAL JEPSEN
SUPER SESSION
FAST,
CLEAN,
COLOURFUL!
LARRY BERTLEMAN — "ANYTHING IS POSSIBLE"
OUTRAGEOUS
SKATEBOARDING!
BOWLS, TUBES, SIDE-SLIPS — HOT!
"EXPLOSIVE SURFING — EXCITING SKATEBOARDS —
I WAS CLIMBING AND DROPPING IN MY SEAT" STEVE PEZMAN, SURFER MAGAZINE
NARRATED BY THE SUPERSTARS:
GERRY LOPEZ – "IT'S A CAKEWALK"
BARRY KANAIAUPUNI – "HONKIN' "
JEFF HAKMAN – "SUNSET JACKS SO MUCH"
RORY RUSSELL – "GO OUT TO WIN $5,000"
The best surfing ever filmed in Hawaii, California, Australia, plus body surfing, kneeboards, snow skiing, barefoot water skiing and more! Fast paced, action-packed, breathtaking – beautiful!
ROCK 'N SURF!
New HIGH ENERGY sounds that EXHILERATE elevator takeoffs, ACCELERATE bottom turns, BURST through lips, and BLAST you out of the TUBES!
ORIGINAL MUSIC BY SMOGHORN
Featuring Bill Rinehart, Randy Zacuto, Bob Zinner & Dennis Dragon
ORIGINAL MUSIC PRODUCED BY DENNIS DRAGON
ANIMATION BY ARNIE WONG
EDITED BY PAUL GROSS & HAL JEPSEN
SUPER-COLOR BY DELUXE
FAST, CLEAN — THE HOT ONE!
"SUPER SESSION" is the new film people are talking about because every ride is HOT, the music is HOT, the SUPERSTARS are HOT, the skateboarding is THE BEST, and the photography is SUPERB!
NOW — WITH MORE SKATEBOARDING!
ULUWATU (Hawaii) featuring LARRY BERTLEMAN
GIANT SLALOM & FREESTYLE from Bahne/Cadillac
Ocean Festival contests
AUGUST 1 and 2 Fri and Sat
NEW YORK — LONG ISLAND
SEAFORD AMERICAN LEGION HALL
2310 Penatiquit Ave., Seaford, N.Y. 798-9887
AUGUST 4 Monday
LONG BRANCH, NEW JERSEY
NORTH LONG BRANCH ELEMENTARY SCHOOL
Behind Islander Surf Shop on Ocean Ave. 229-7770
AUGUST 6 Wednesday
BEACH HAVEN, NEW JERSEY
FIREHOUSE, 434, Dock Ave. 494-1991
AUGUST 7 Monday
OCEAN CITY, NEW JERSEY
OCEAN CITY REC. HALL 399-4455
AUGUST 8 and 9 Fri and Sat
SEASIDE HEIGHTS, NEW JERSEY
TRI-BORO FIRST AID HALL
Joy St — Seaside Park 793-9610
AUGUST 10 Sunday
WILDWOOD, NEW JERSEY
WILDWOOD REC. CENTER
243 E. Rio Grande Ave. 522-7899
DOOR PRIZES! SUNSET SURFBOARDS, RAXS, SLAPS, T-SHIRTS! PLUS WATER SKI SHORT!
SCREENTIMES ARE 7:30 & 9:30 PM ADMISSION $2.75
DON'T MISS THE HOTTEST SURFING & SKATEBOARDING FILM EVER MADE!

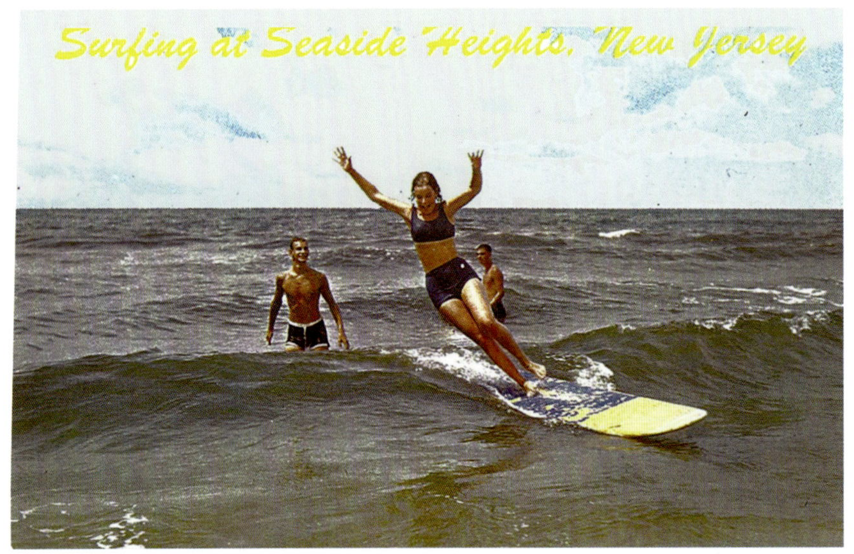
Surfing at Seaside Heights, New Jersey

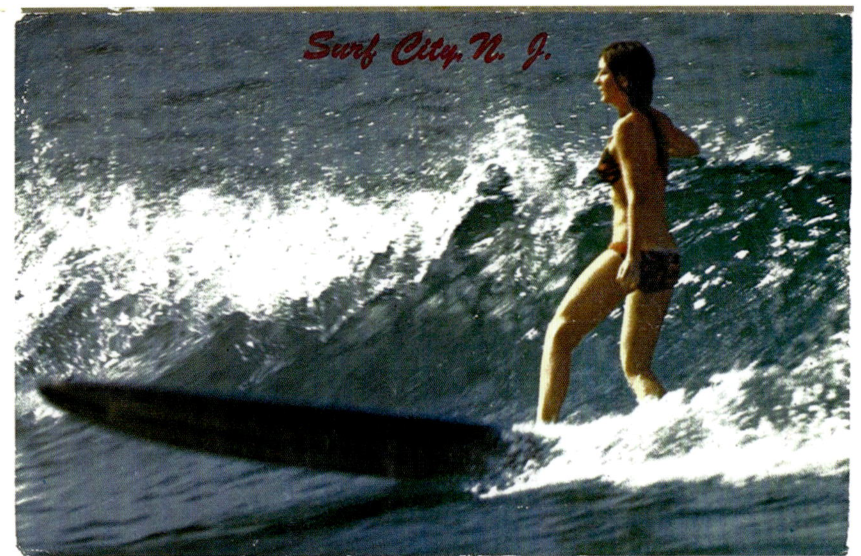
Surf City, N. J.

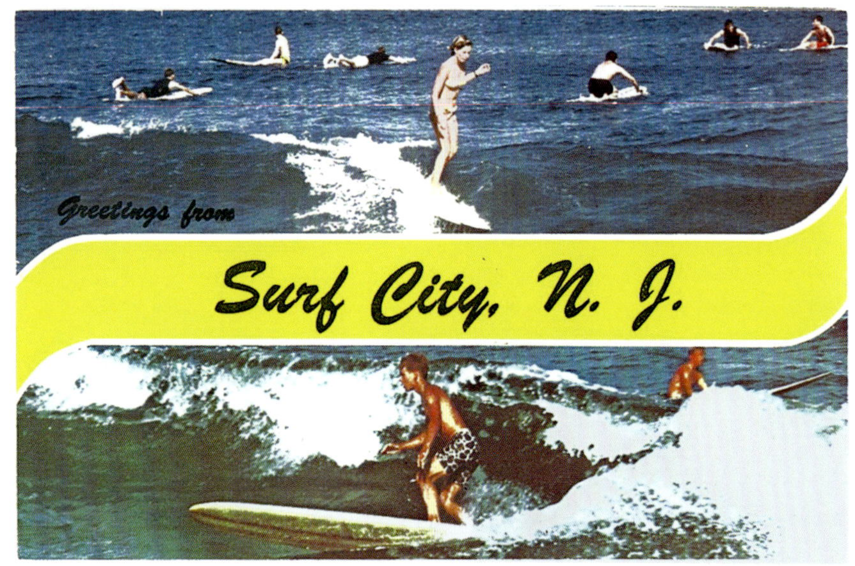
Greetings from
Surf City, N. J.

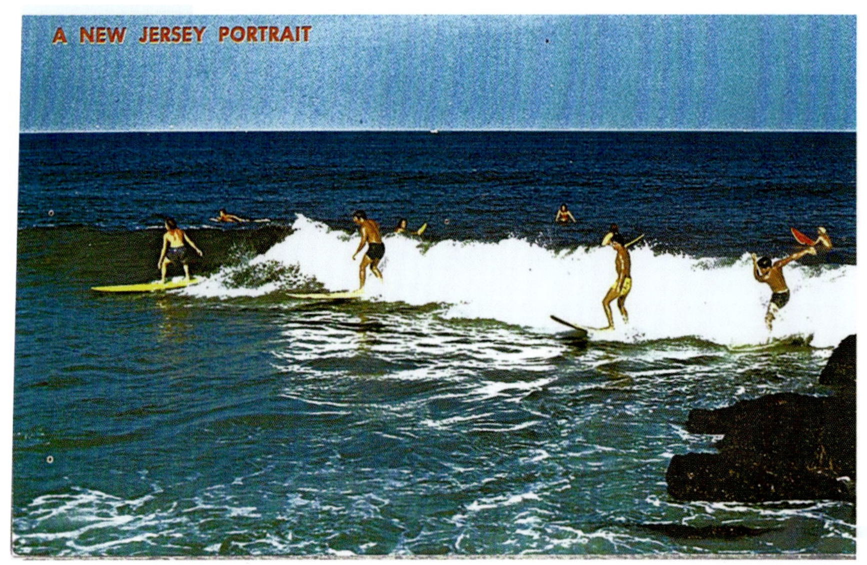
A NEW JERSEY PORTRAIT

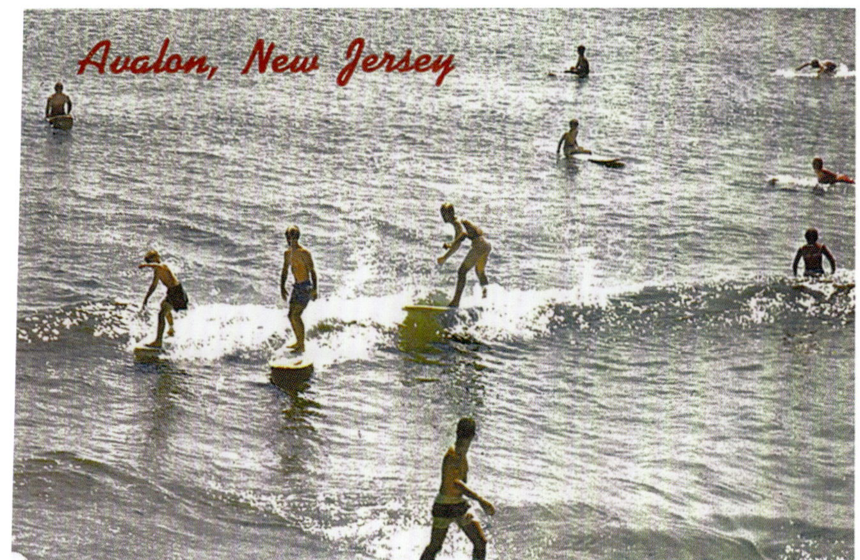
Avalon, New Jersey

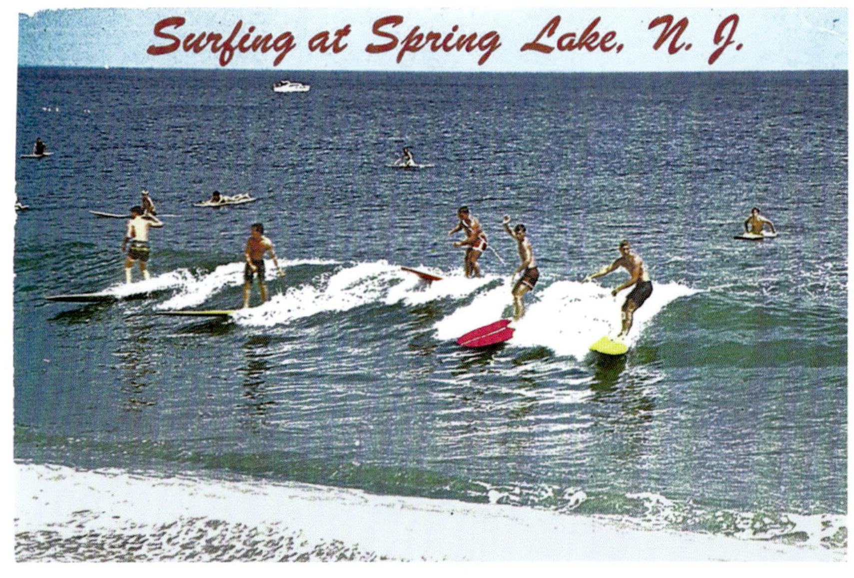
Surfing at Spring Lake, N. J.

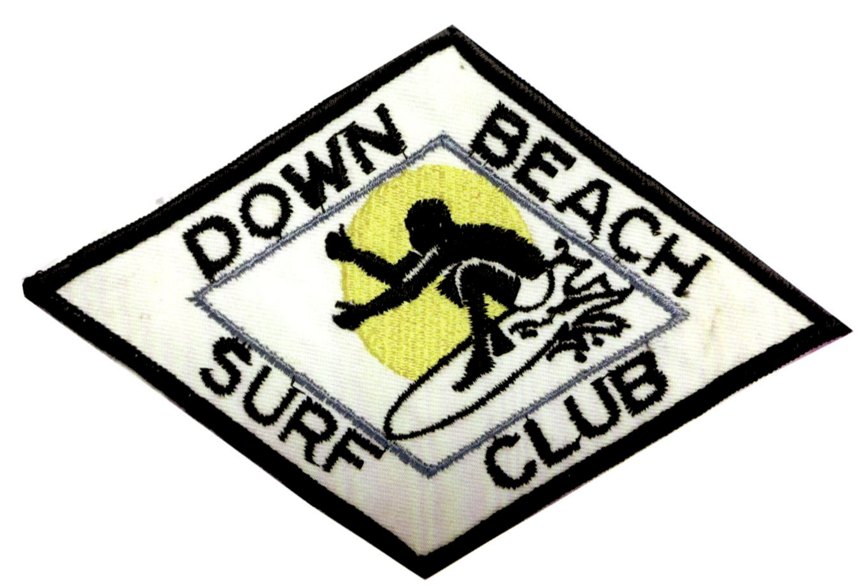

CIRCA 1960S. DOWN BEACH SURF CLUB PATCH, MARGATE, NJ

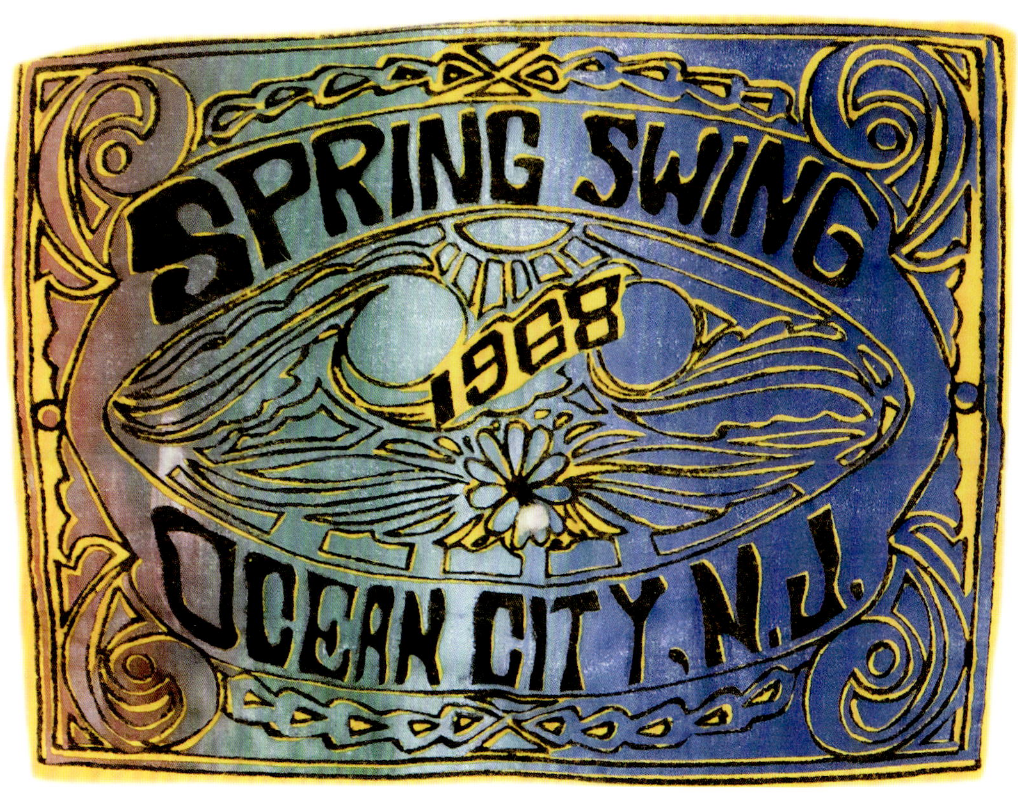

1968. SPRING SWING, OCEAN CITY, NJ

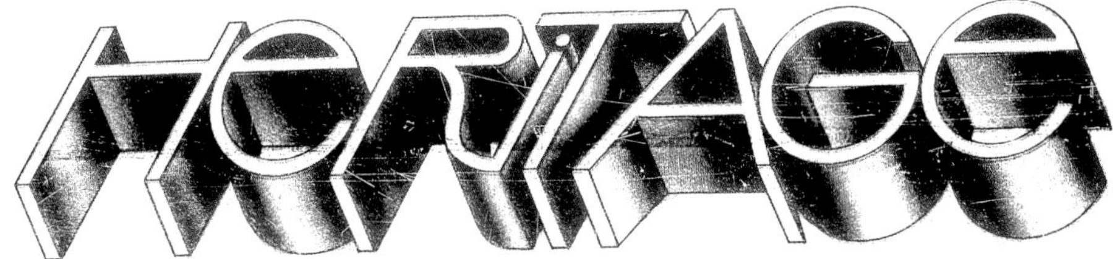

CIRCA 1970S. HERITAGE SURFBOARDS LOGO

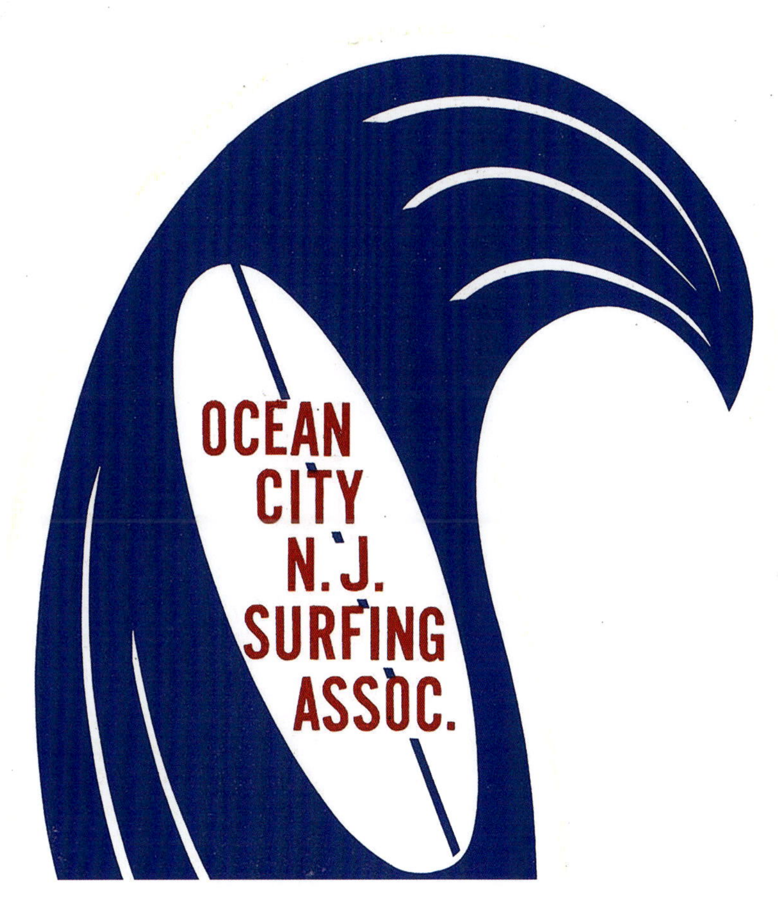

1960S. OCEAN CITY NJ SURFING ASSOCIATION DECAL

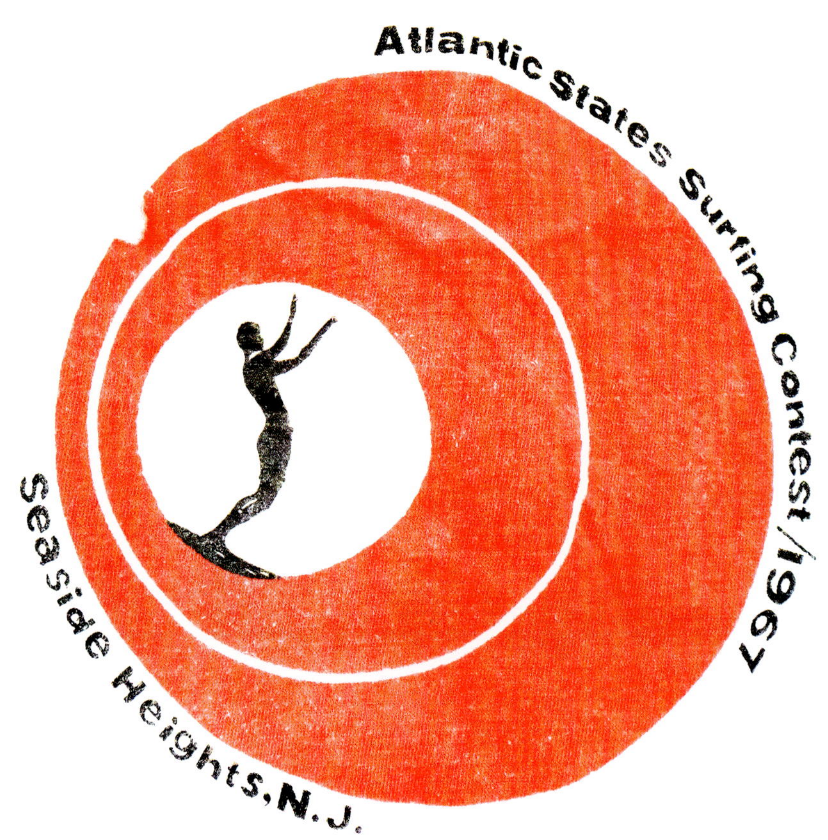
Atlantic States Surfing Contest/1967
Seaside Heights, N.J.

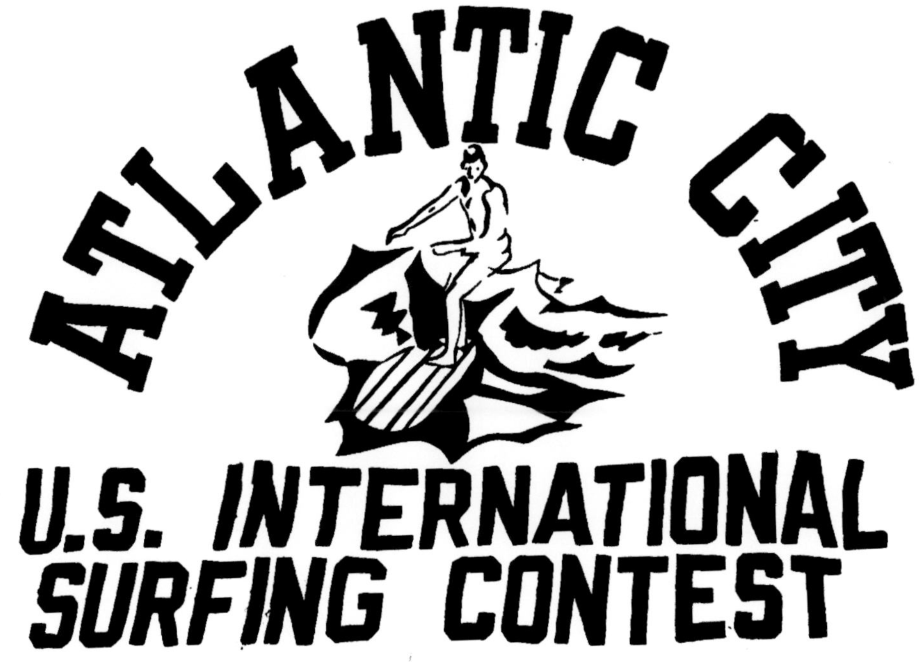
ATLANTIC CITY
U.S. INTERNATIONAL
SURFING CONTEST

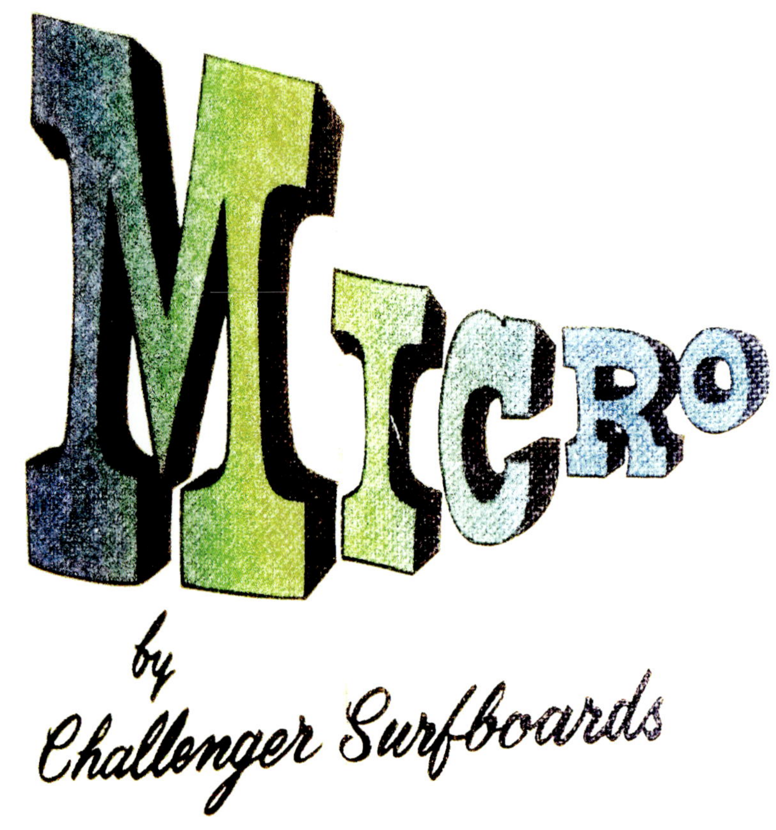

CIRCA 1960S. CHALLENGER SURFBOARDS LOGO

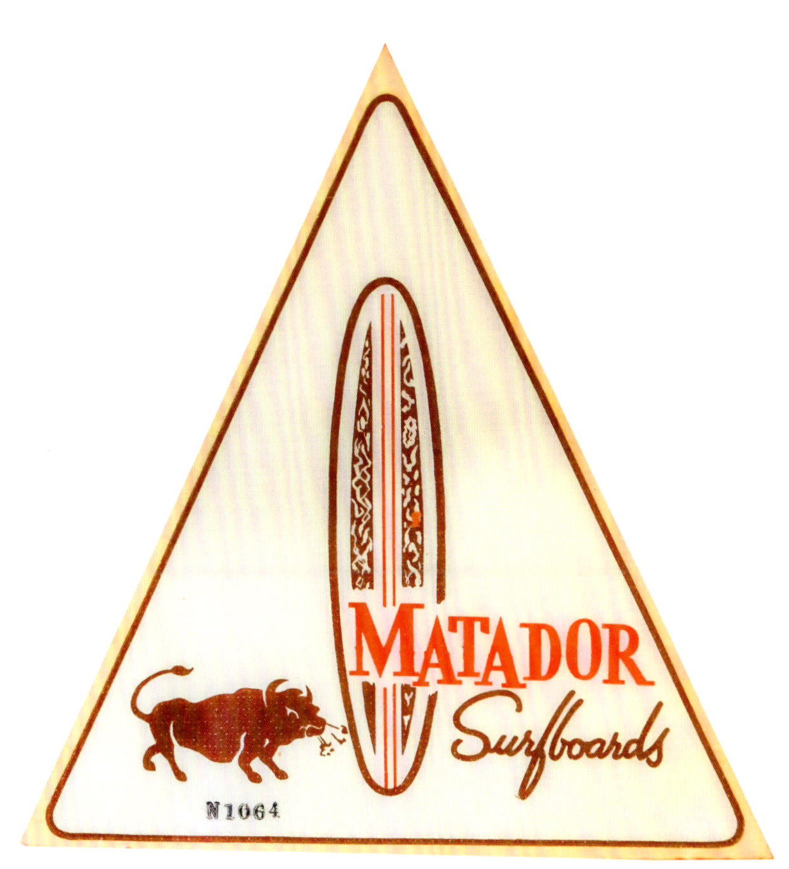

CIRCA 1960S. MATADOR SURFBOARDS LOGO

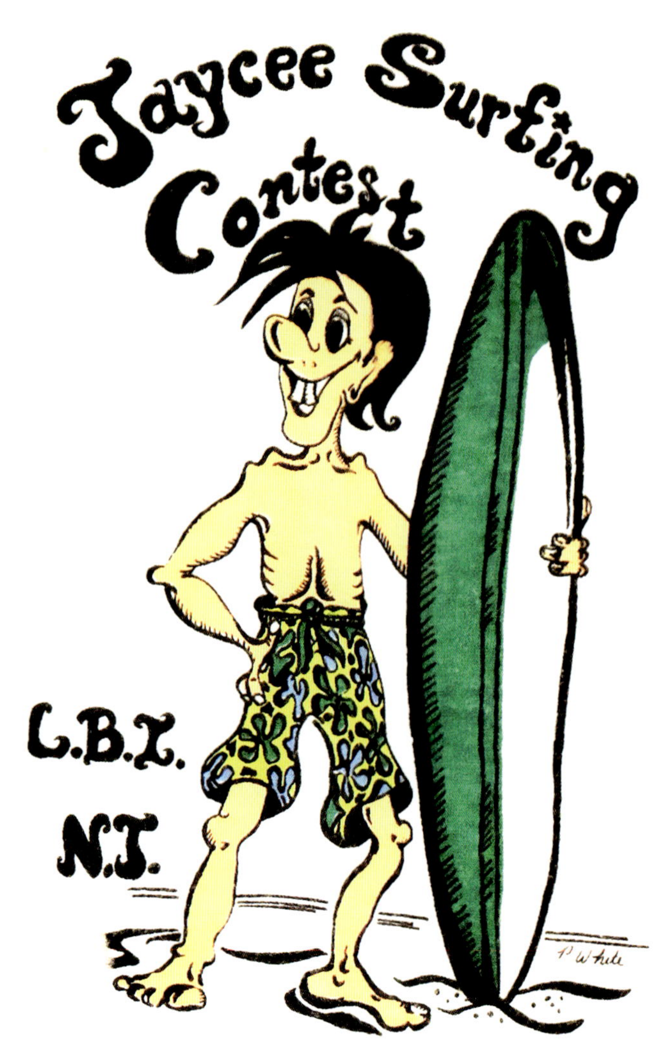
Jaycee Surfing
Contest
L.B.I.
N.J.

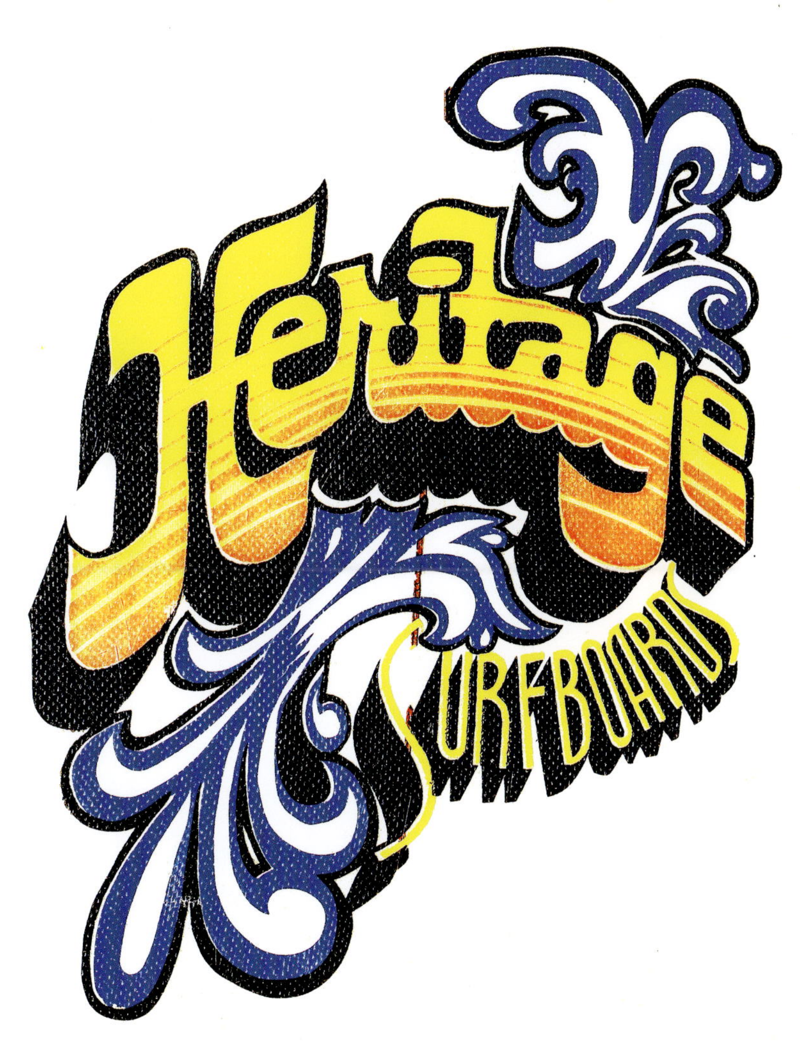
Heritage
SURFBOARDS

2nd
ANNUAL FERNDOCKS
SURFING CONTEST
OCEANSIDE SURF CLUB
SEA BRIGHT, N. J.

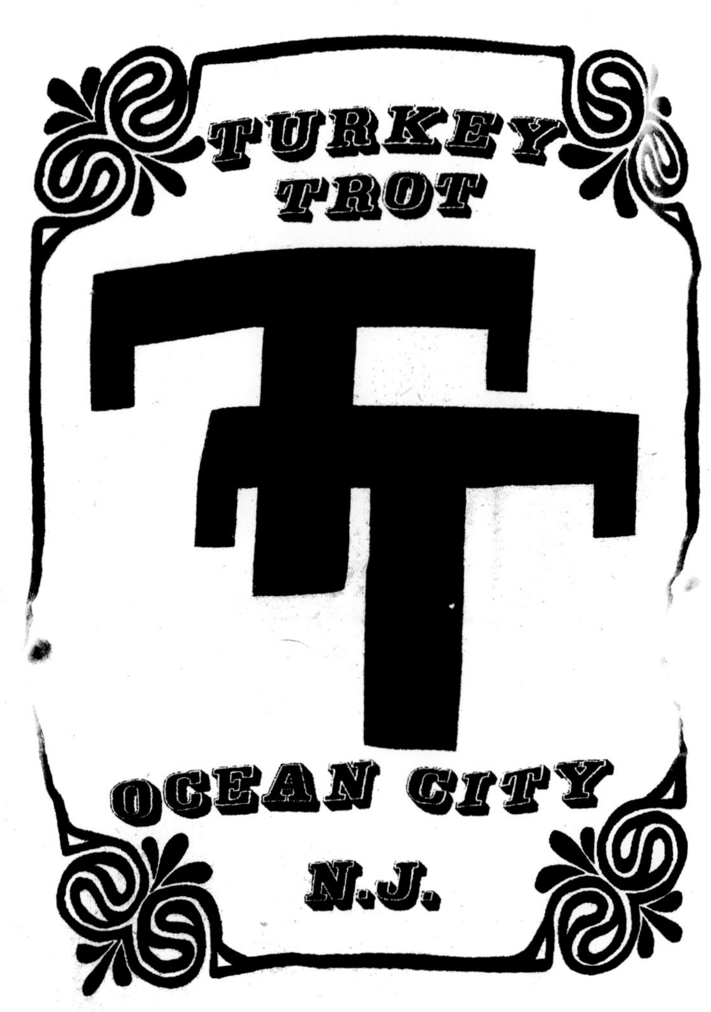
TURKEY
TROT
TT
OCEAN CITY
N.J.

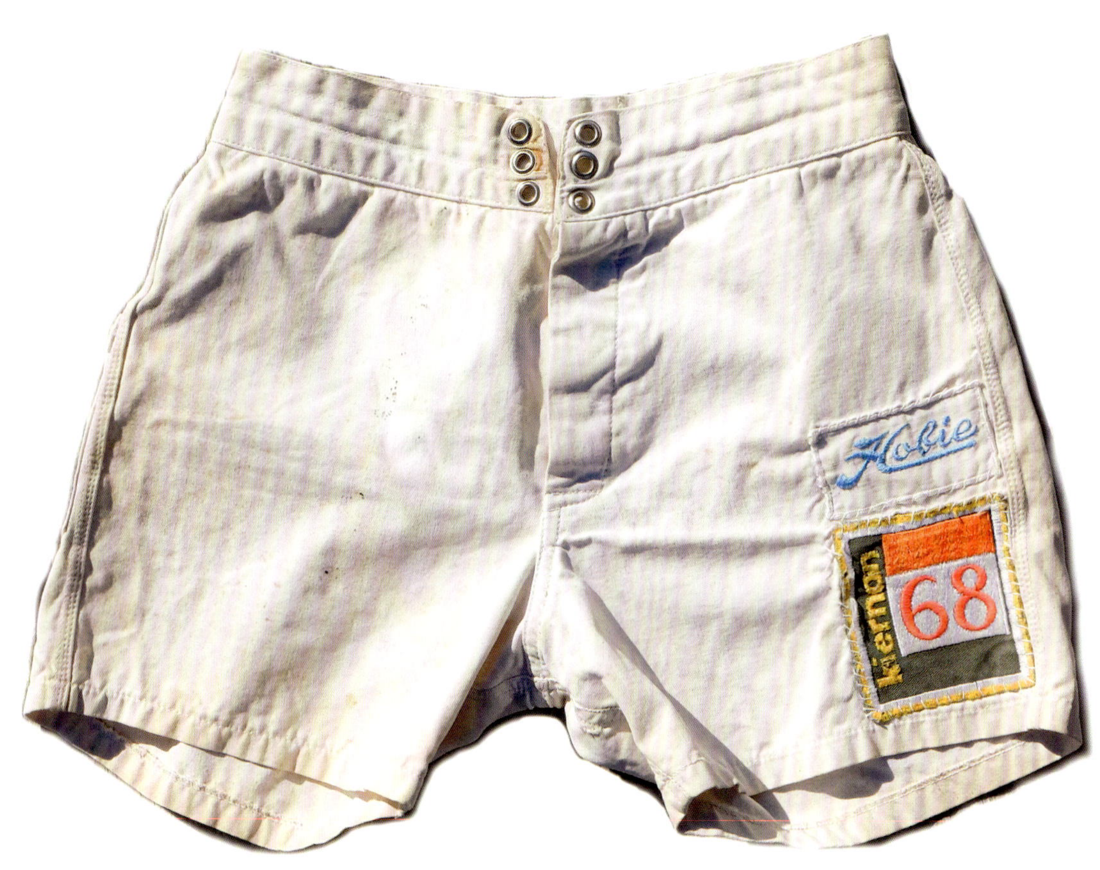
Hobie
kiernan
68

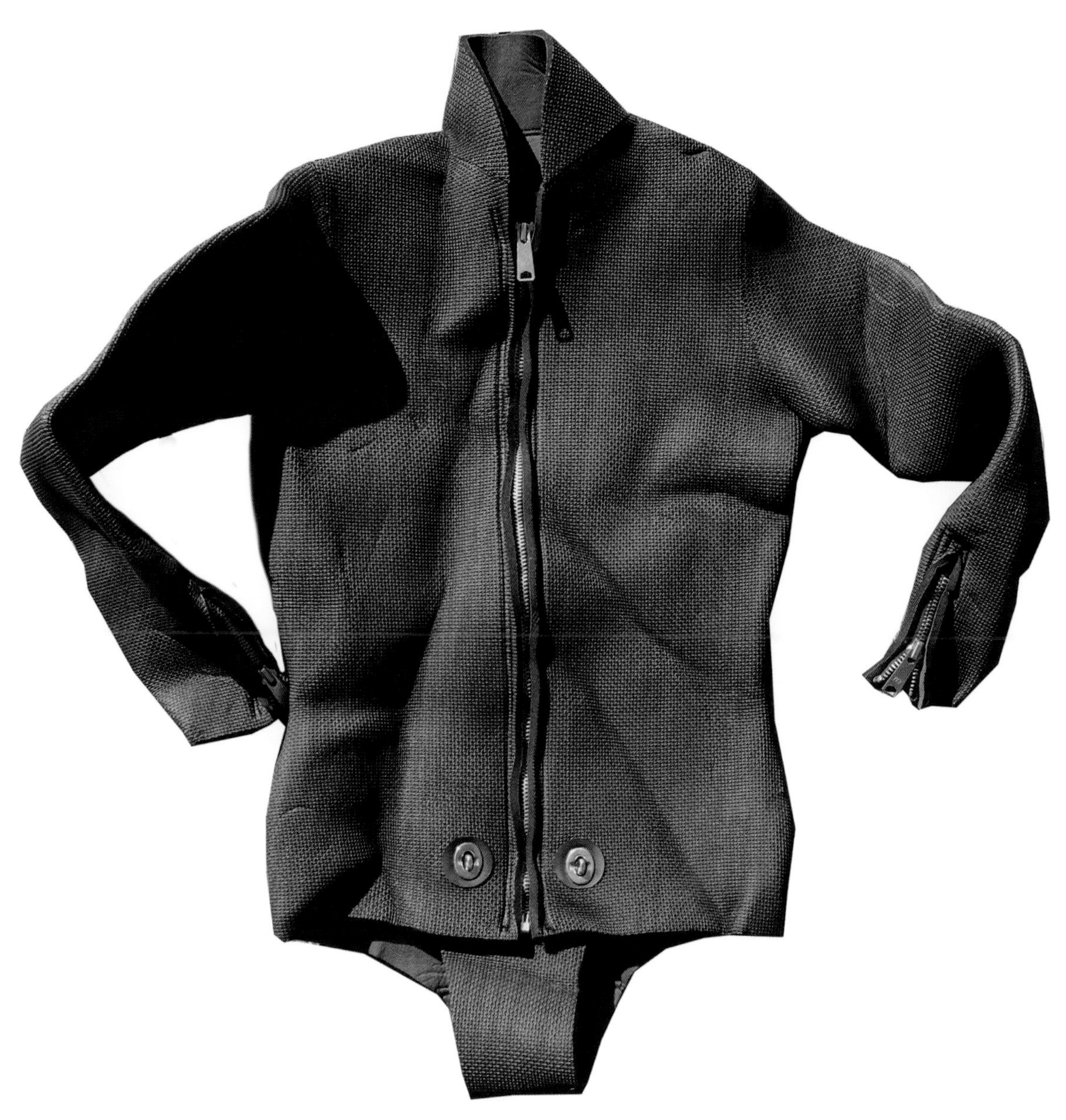

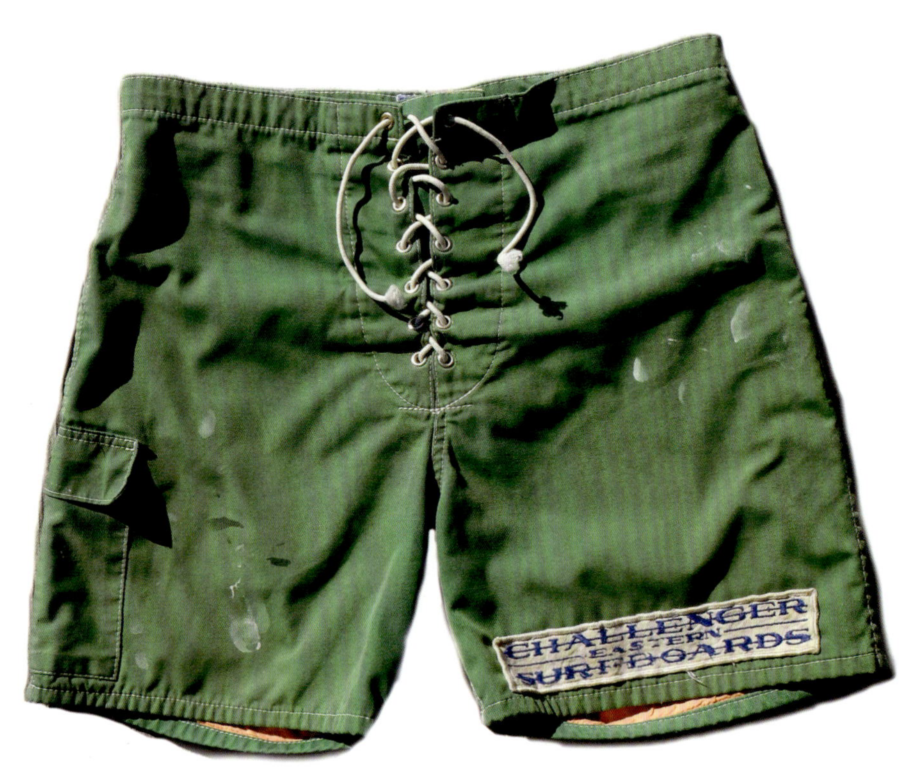

CIRCA 1960S. CHALLENGER EAST TEAM BOARDSHORTS

1966. CHALLENGER EAST FIBERGLASS SKATEBOARD MADE BY MICHEL JUNOD

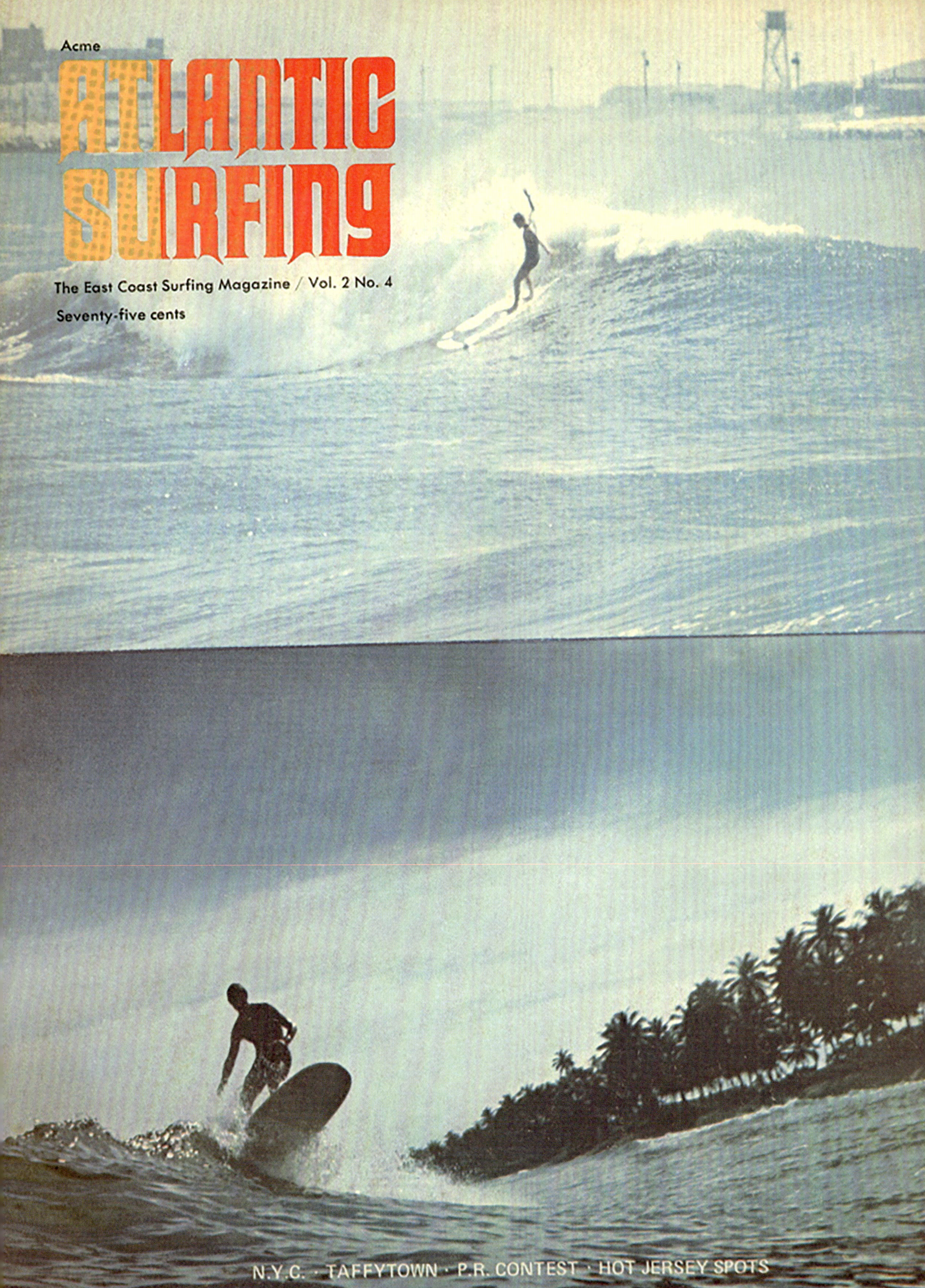

Acme
ATLANTIC SURFING
The East Coast Surfing Magazine / Vol. 2 No. 4
Seventy-five cents
N.Y.C. · TAFFYTOWN · P.R. CONTEST · HOT JERSEY SPOTS

There's an unmistakable
sound to the sea when
the wind slips off shore.
A [illegible]
wave [illegible]
ward and [illegible]
spits angrily. [illegible]
many feel the bl[illegible]ng
of those waves, [illegible]
anxiety of sightless[illegible]
then the power of a d[illegible]
and resurging confidenc[illegible]
Something, somewhere,
intended me to be, and b[illegible]
[illegible] on a beach, accompli[illegible]
to winging gulls and forlor[illegible]
[illegible] Lumps swallowed
[illegible]roat countless times
[illegible]e trust the oceans
[illegible] The sea se[illegible]nd
[illegible] Sand was made
[illegible]on and sation,
[illegible]ders reflection[illegible]
[illegible]ors. The beach i[illegible]
[illegible]point from which to
contemplate the universe.

[illegible]im Earle

REIGNS SUPREME

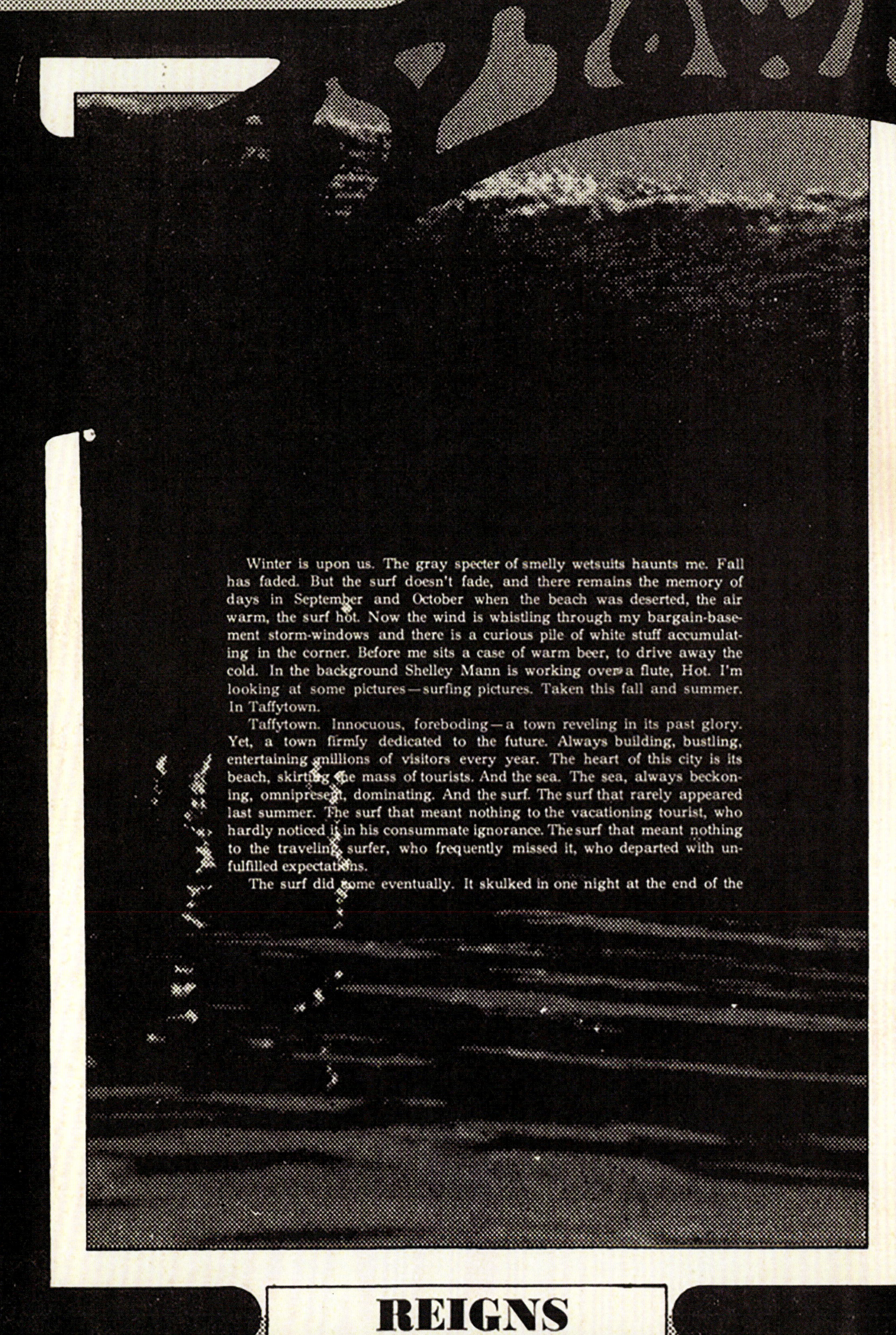

Winter is upon us. The gray specter of smelly wetsuits haunts me. Fall has faded. But the surf doesn't fade, and there remains the memory of days in September and October when the beach was deserted, the air warm, the surf hot. Now the wind is whistling through my bargain-basement storm-windows and there is a curious pile of white stuff accumulating in the corner. Before me sits a case of warm beer, to drive away the cold. In the background Shelley Mann is working over a flute, Hot. I'm looking at some pictures—surfing pictures. Taken this fall and summer. In Taffytown.

Taffytown. Innocuous, foreboding—a town reveling in its past glory. Yet, a town firmly dedicated to the future. Always building, bustling, entertaining millions of visitors every year. The heart of this city is its beach, skirting the mass of tourists. And the sea. The sea, always beckoning, omnipresent, dominating. And the surf. The surf that rarely appeared last summer. The surf that meant nothing to the vacationing tourist, who hardly noticed it in his consummate ignorance. The surf that meant nothing to the traveling surfer, who frequently missed it, who departed with unfulfilled expectations.

The surf did come eventually. It skulked in one night at the end of the

REIGNS

SUPREME

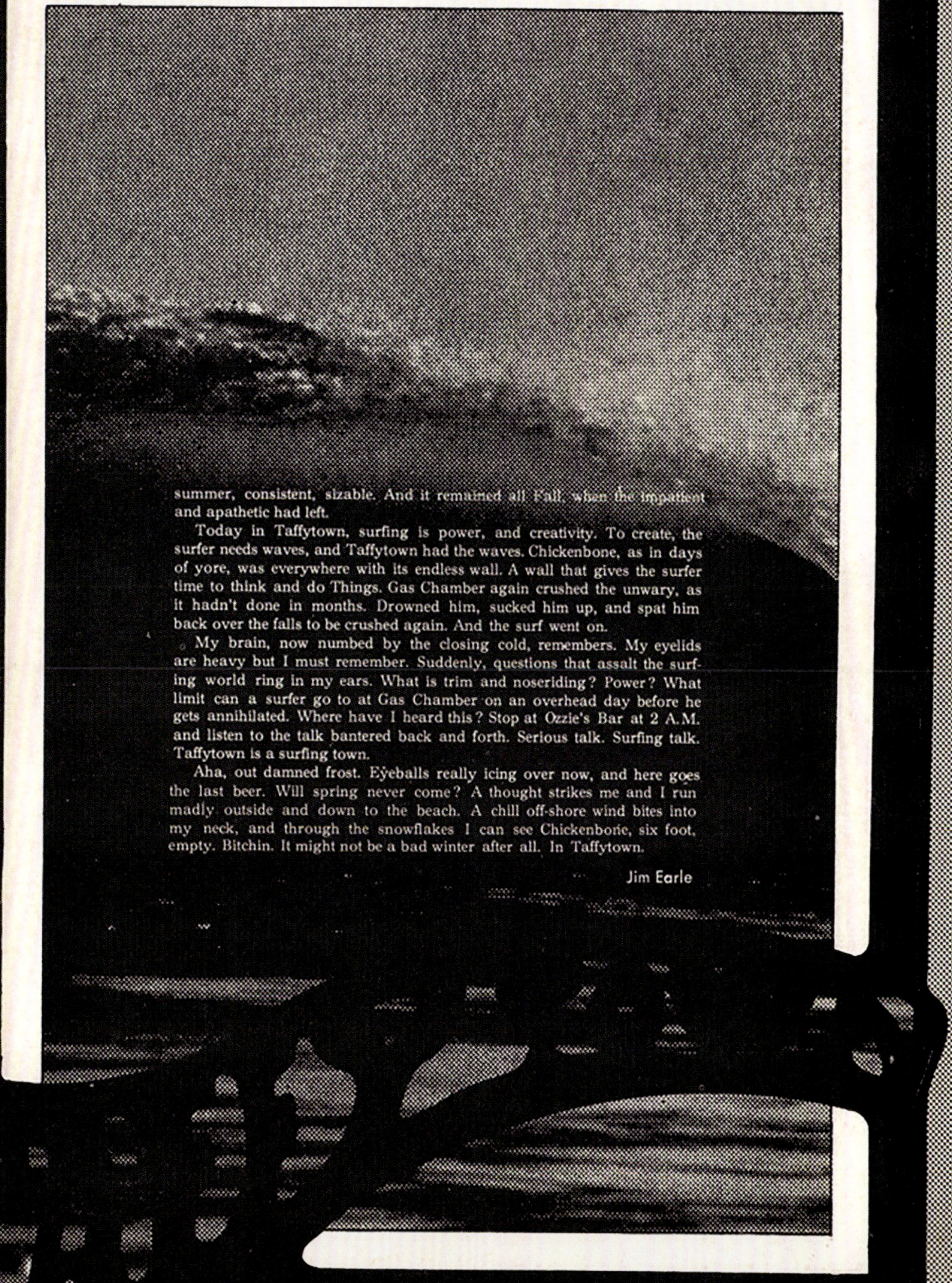

summer, consistent, sizable. And it remained all Fall, when the impatient and apathetic had left.

Today in Taffytown, surfing is power, and creativity. To create, the surfer needs waves, and Taffytown had the waves. Chickenbone, as in days of yore, was everywhere with its endless wall. A wall that gives the surfer time to think and do Things. Gas Chamber again crushed the unwary, as it hadn't done in months. Drowned him, sucked him up, and spat him back over the falls to be crushed again. And the surf went on.

My brain, now numbed by the closing cold, remembers. My eyelids are heavy but I must remember. Suddenly, questions that assault the surfing world ring in my ears. What is trim and noseriding? Power? What limit can a surfer go to at Gas Chamber on an overhead day before he gets annihilated. Where have I heard this? Stop at Ozzie's Bar at 2 A.M. and listen to the talk bantered back and forth. Serious talk. Surfing talk. Taffytown is a surfing town.

Aha, out damned frost. Eyeballs really icing over now, and here goes the last beer. Will spring never come? A thought strikes me and I run madly outside and down to the beach. A chill off-shore wind bites into my neck, and through the snowflakes I can see Chickenbone, six foot, empty. Bitchin. It might not be a bad winter after all. In Taffytown.

Jim Earle

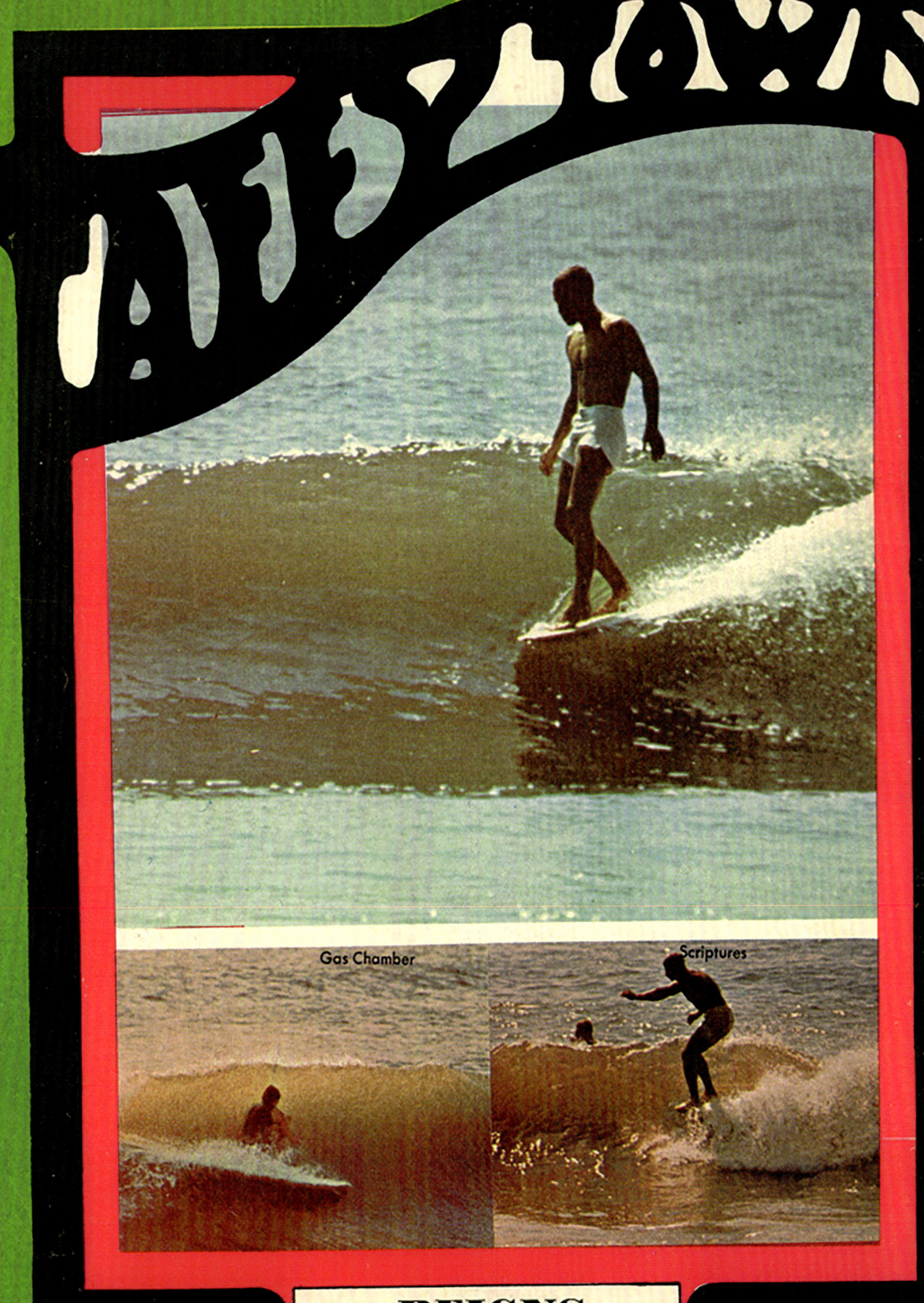
Gas Chamber
Scriptures
REIGNS

SUPREME

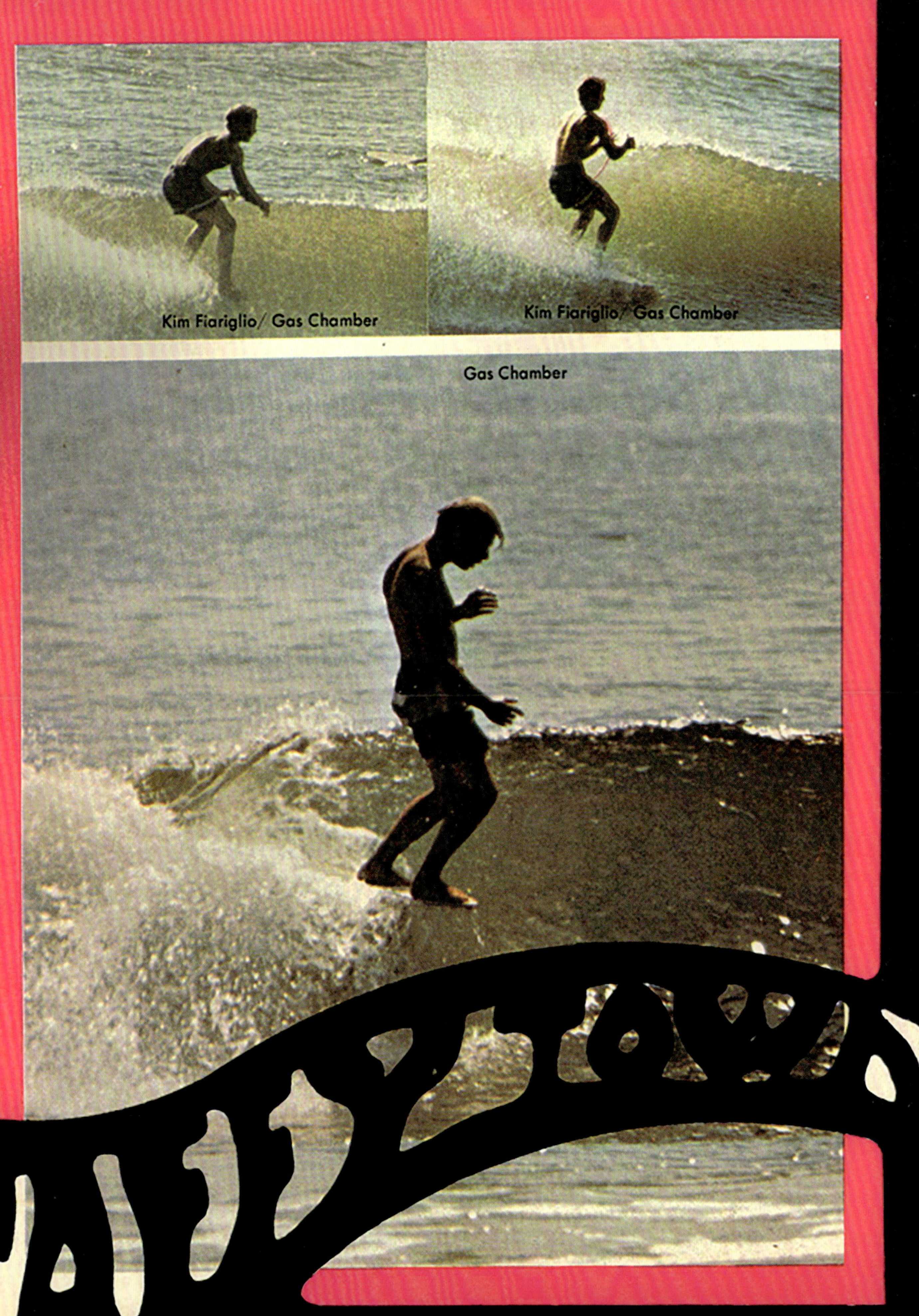

Kim Fiariglio/ Gas Chamber

Kim Fiariglio/ Gas Chamber

Gas Chamber

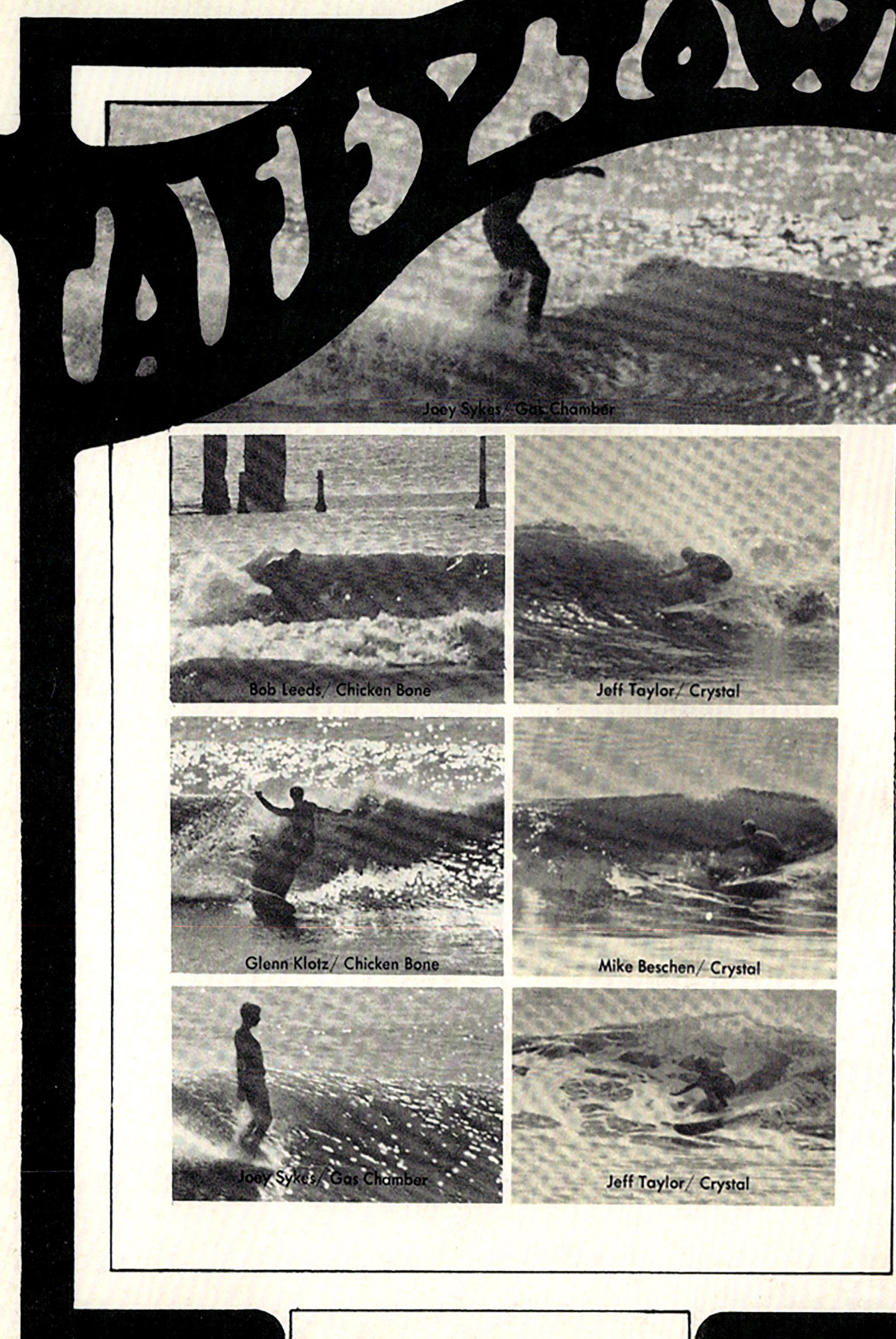

Joey Sykes / Gas Chamber

Bob Leeds/ Chicken Bone

Jeff Taylor/ Crystal

Glenn Klotz/ Chicken Bone

Mike Beschen/ Crystal

Joey Sykes/ Gas Chamber

Jeff Taylor/ Crystal

SUPREME

Jim Earle Chicken Bone . . . sequentially. Mike Sykes

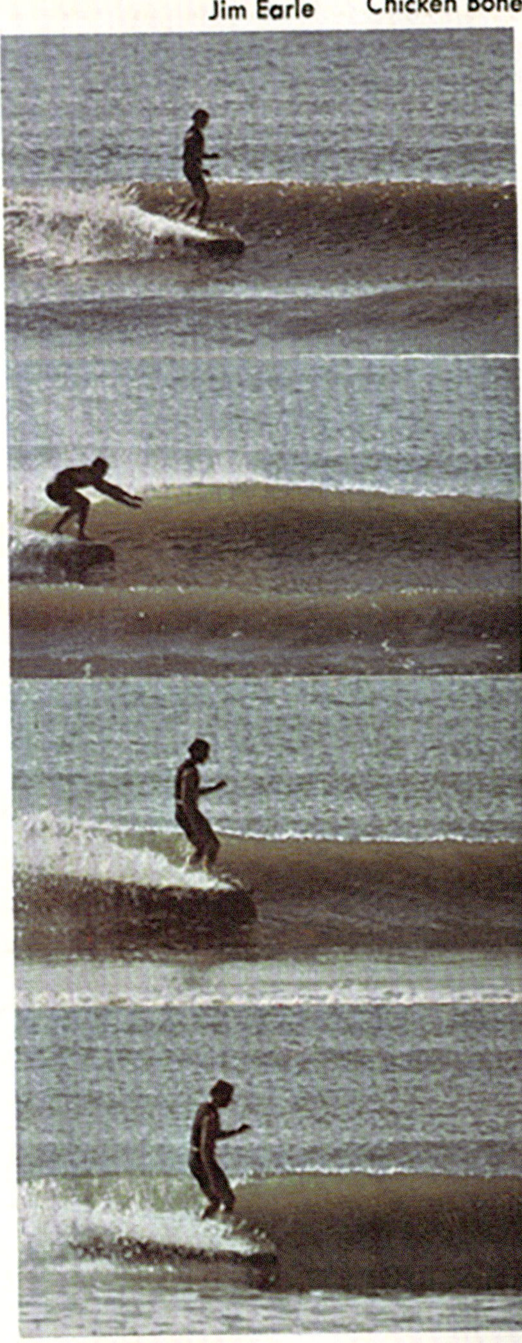

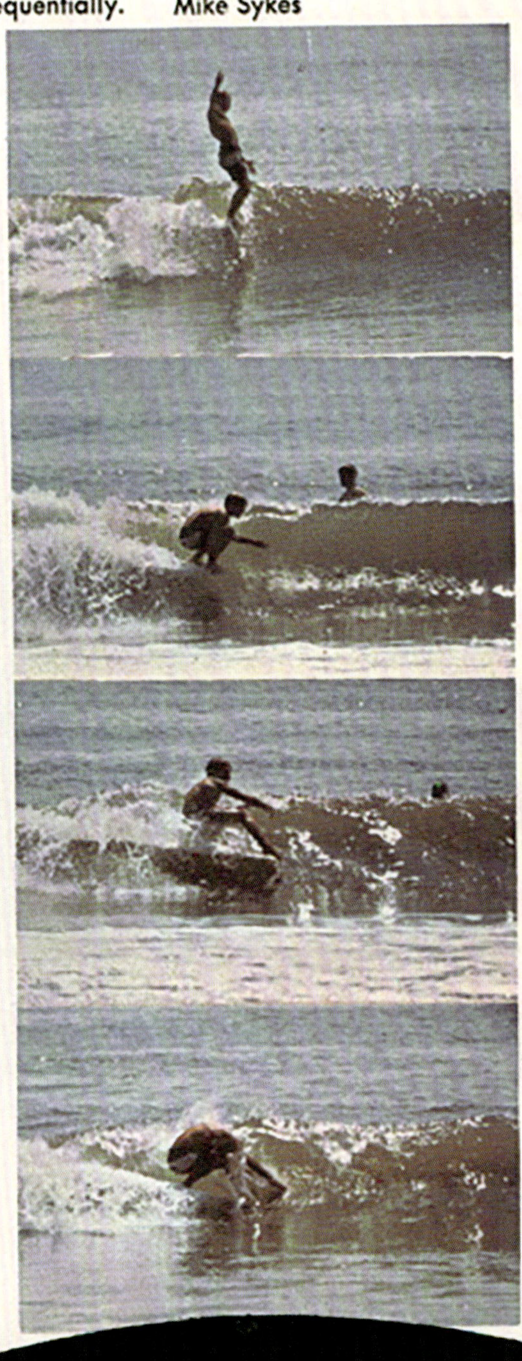

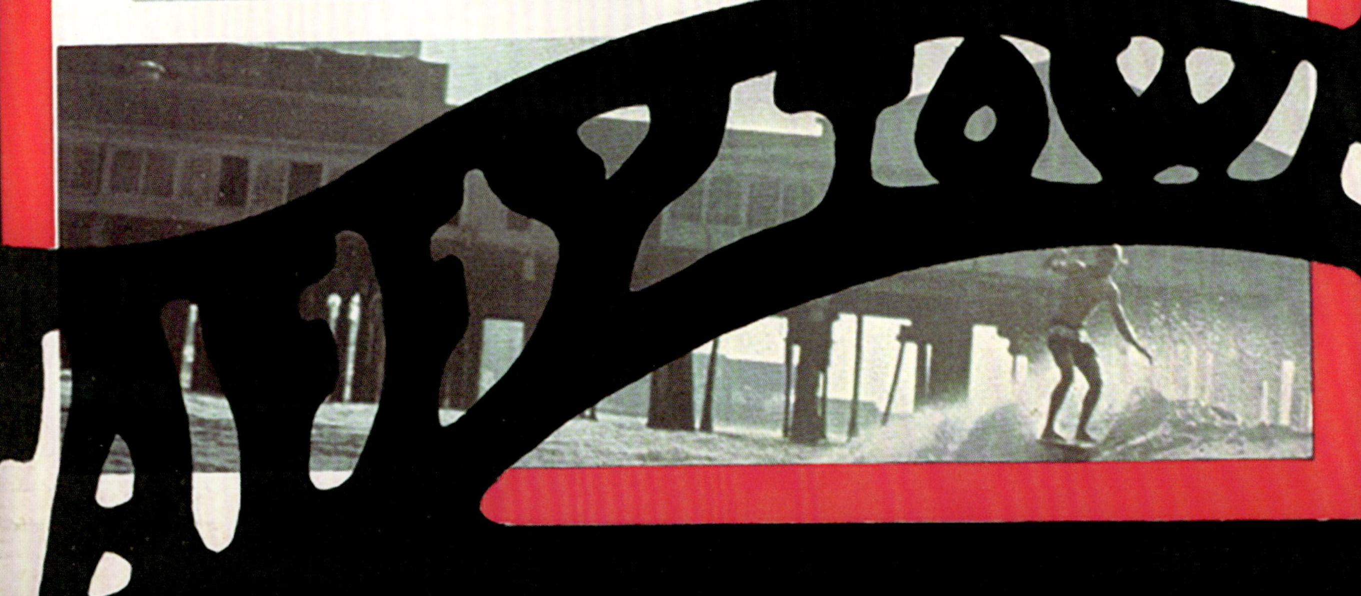

IN 1968 - PROPPER & HIS MODELS

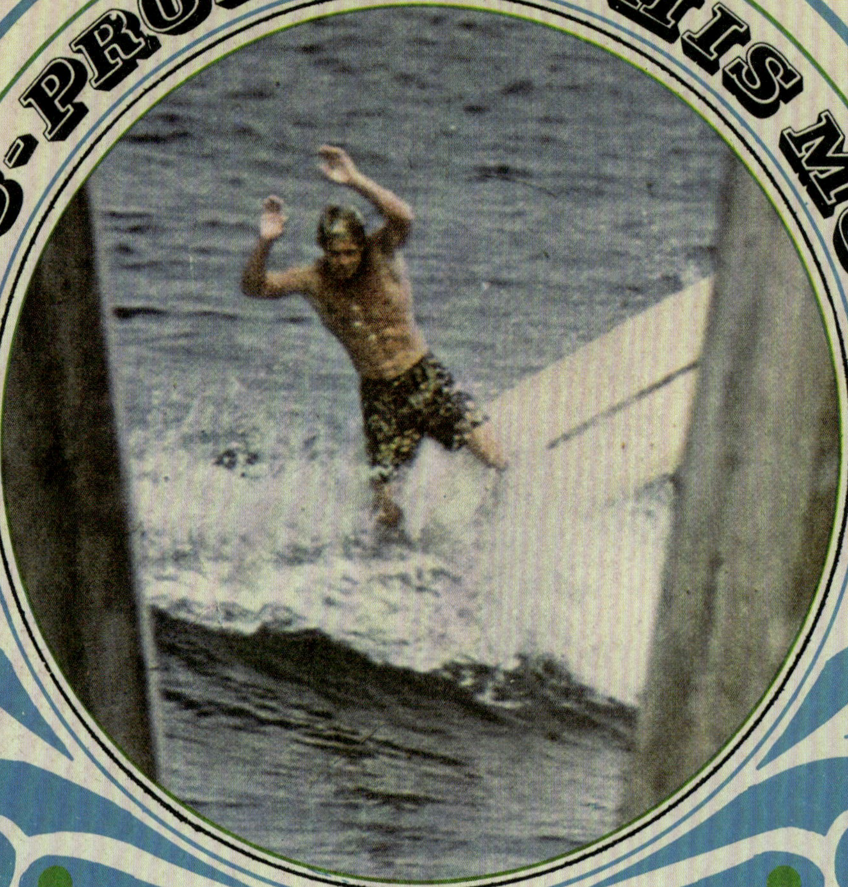

G.P. doing a re-entry at Ormond Beach, Fla. Wilkinson Photo

KNOWLEDGE IS EXPERIENCE.

No one is more qualified to design a surfboard for use on the East Coast than Gary Propper. In these two pictures Gary proves the fact that he is Number One on the East Coast. Look for both his models at these Hobie dealers:

RYE BEACH, NEW HAMPSHIRE — HOBIE SURFBOARDS, Perkins Road

HULL, MASSACHUSETTS — NARRAGANSETT SURF SHOP, 305-A Nantasket Ave., Phone WA 4-7023

WILMINGTON, MASS. — SEACRAFT SPORTING GOODS, 3 Church Street

WORCESTER, MASS. — MACBEND SPORTING GOODS, 530 Main Street, Phone 756-7210

SO. HADLEY FALLS, MASS. — HOLYOKE UNDERWATER SUPPLY CO., 50 N. Main Street

NEWPORT, RHODE ISLAND — SPICER'S SURF SHOP, 36 Aquidneck Ave.

NARRAGANSETT, RHODE ISLAND — SPICER'S SURF SHOP, 56 Beach St.

FOREST HILLS, NEW YORK — EMILIO'S SKI SHOP, 112-32 Queens Blvd., Phone LI 4-0404

LEVITTOWN, L.I., NEW YORK — EMILIO'S SKI SHOP, 2726 Hempstead Turnpike, Phone 796-1565

PHILADELPHIA, PA. — WILBURGER'S SURF SHOP, 1352 Wagner Ave., Phone DA 4-4700

BELMAR, NEW JERSEY — MANATEE SEA CENTER, 12th & Ocean Ave., Phone 681-3947

BEACH HAVEN, NEW JERSEY — A SUMMER PLACE, 23rd & Blvd.

HARVEY CEDERS, NEW JERSEY — A SUMMER PAST, on the Blvd.

OCEAN CITY, NEW JERSEY — MANATEE SEA CENTER, 14th & Asbury Ave., Phone 399-4555

OCEAN CITY, MARYLAND — EASTERN SURFER, 16th & Philadelphia Ave., Phone 289-6520

VIRGINIA BEACH, VIRGINIA — SMITH & HOLLAND SURF SHOP, 300 & 28th & Pacific, Phone 428-8513

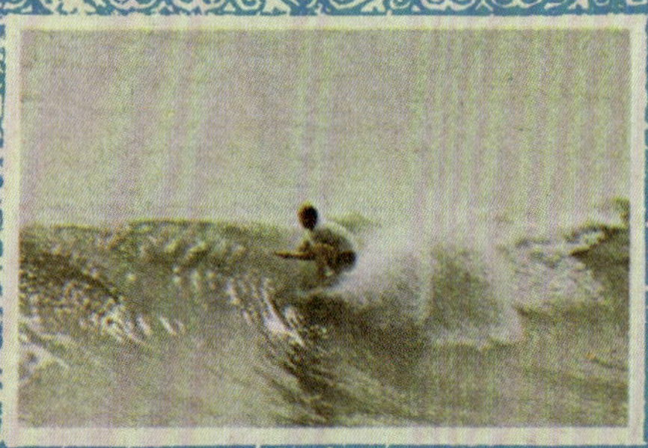

KILL DEVIL HILLS (NAGS HEAD), NORTH CAROLINA — SMITH AND HOLLAND SURF SHOP

WRIGHTSVILLE BEACH, N. C. — OCEAN SURF SHOP, 22 Luminia Ave., Phone 256-9368

MYRTLE BEACH, S. C. — 2ND AVE. PIER SURF SHOP, 204 No. Ocean Blvd., Phone 448-8881

FOLLY BEACH, SO. CAROLINA — MCKEVLIN'S SURF SHOP, Phone 588-9103

GEORGETOWN, SOUTH CAROLINA — FOGEL'S DEPT. STORE, 811-823 Front St., Phone 546-7800

JACKSONVILLE, FLORIDA — UNDERWATER DESIGNERS, 4591 St. John Ave., Phone 384-3655

JACKSONVILLE BEACH, FLORIDA — SKIN DIVING & SURFING CENTER, 13637 Beach Blvd., Phone 246-7305

FORT PIERCE, FLORIDA — THE SURF SHOP, 832 So. Federal Hwy., Phone 461-9752

DAYTONA BEACH, FLORIDA — HOBIE SURFBOARDS, 807 Main Street, • Phone 255-6121

INDIALANTIC, FLORIDA — SHAGG'S SURF SHOP, 4 Wave Crest, Phone 723-0002

NO. MIAMI, FLORIDA — CHALLENGER MARINE, 13301 Biscayne Blvd., Phone 947-4472

SARASOTA, FLORIDA — ECONOMY FISHING TACKLE, 6018 S. Tamaimi Trail, Phone 924-2785

MOBILE, ALABAMA — SOUTHERN WATER SPORTS, 737 Holcombe Ave., Phone 473-9219

HOUSTON, TEXAS — RICH'S VILLAGE SPORTING GOODS, 2412 Times Blvd., Phone JA 9-8767

CORPUS CHRISTI, TEXAS — HOBIE SURFBOARDS, 3329 Padre Island Dr., Phone UL 3-4342

Hobie Surfboards/34195 Coast Highway, Dana Point, Calif./Ph. (714) 496-1251

SURFER

JULY 1983
VOL. 24, No. 7
$2.95
14246

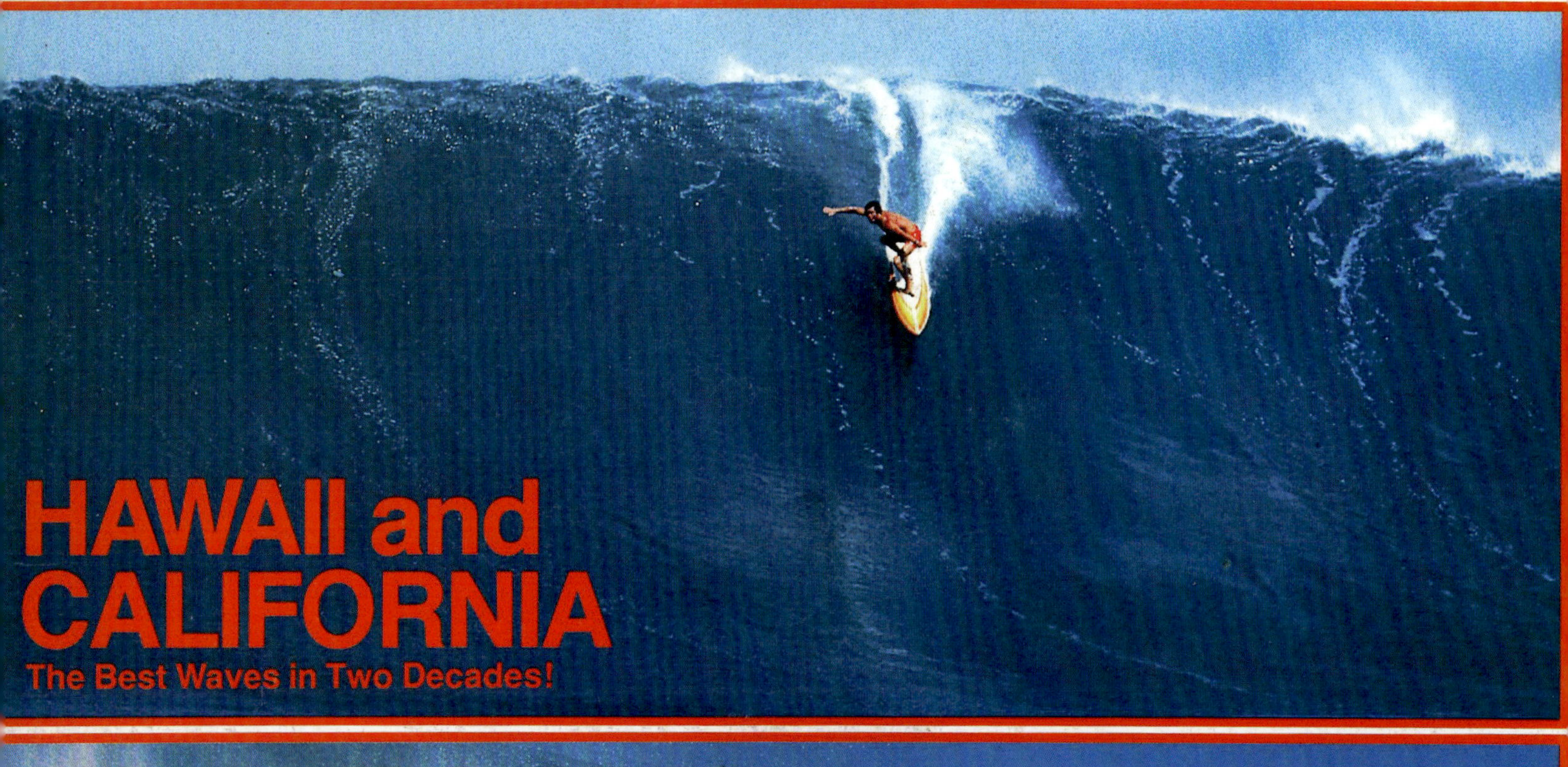

HAWAII and CALIFORNIA

The Best Waves in Two Decades!

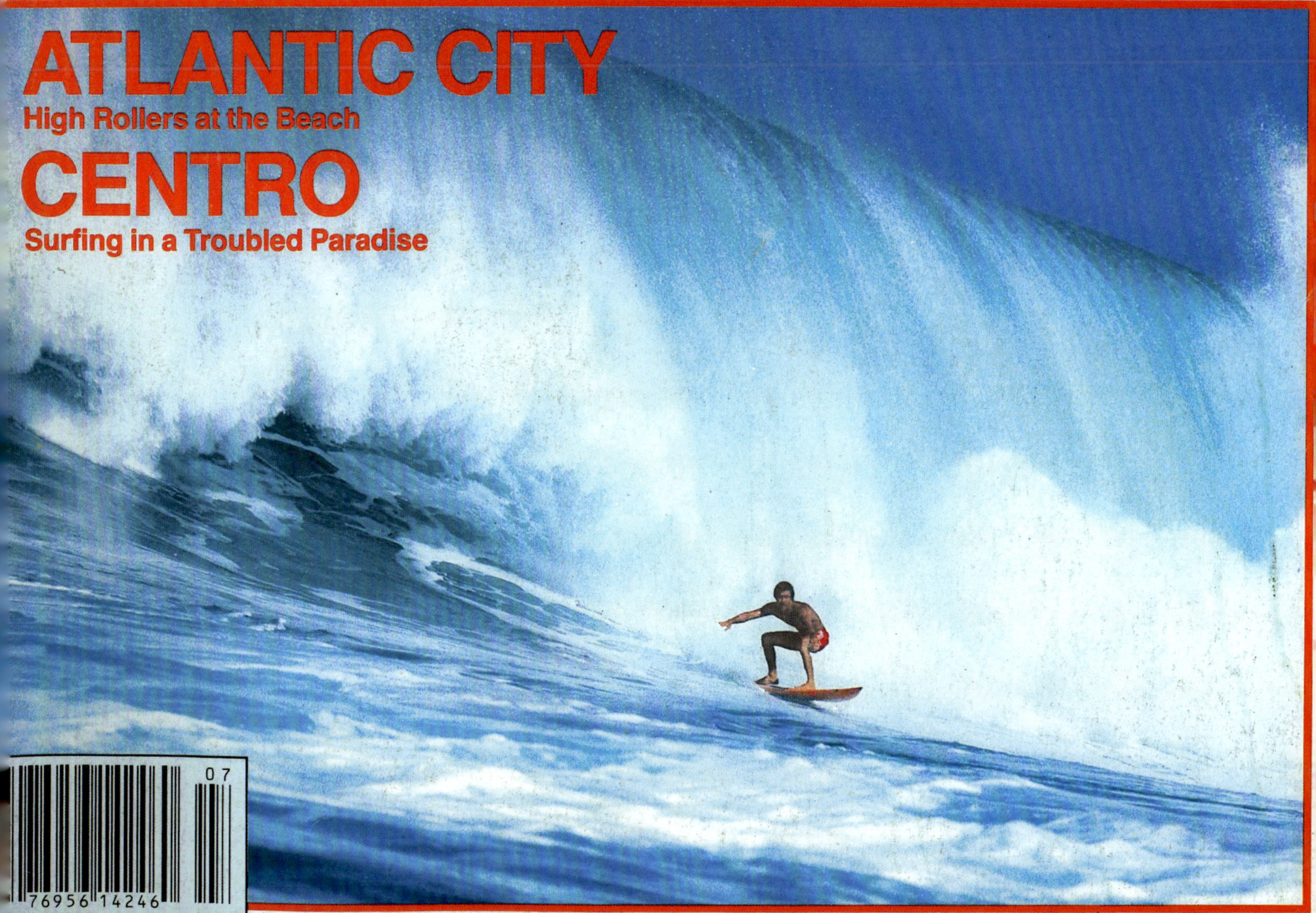

ATLANTIC CITY

High Rollers at the Beach

CENTRO

Surfing in a Troubled Paradise

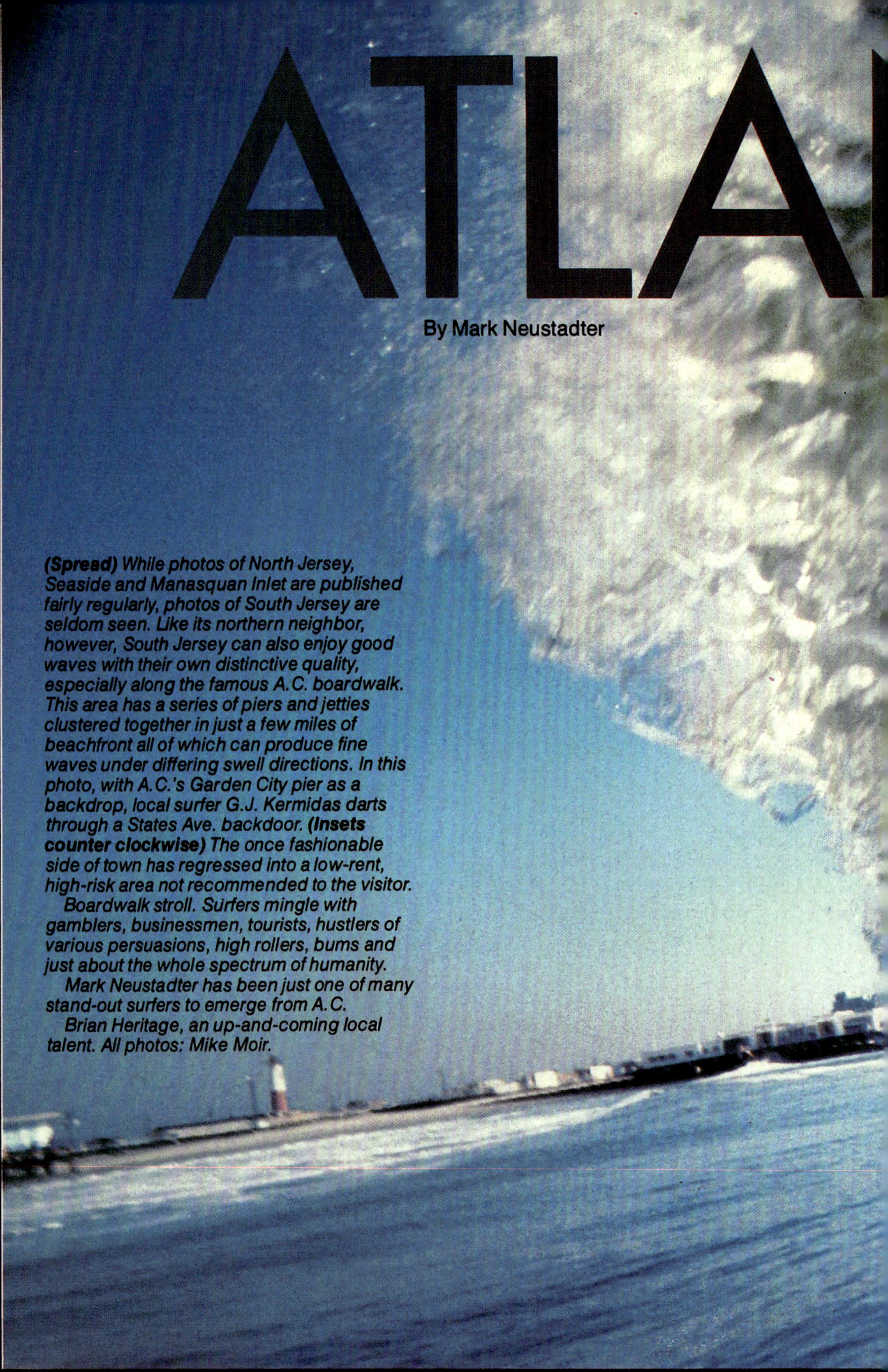

ATLA

By Mark Neustadter

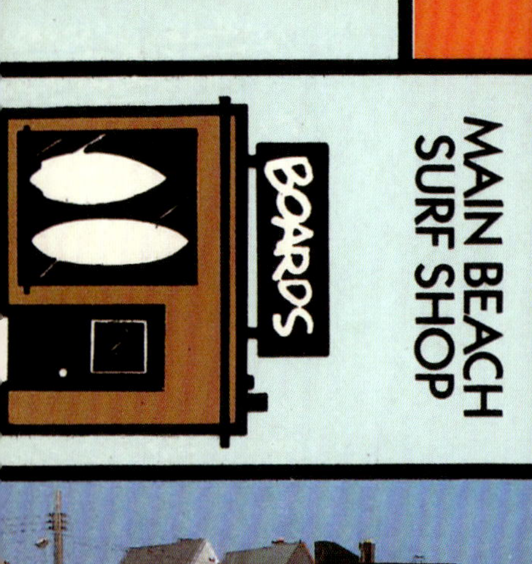

MAIN BEACH SURF SHOP

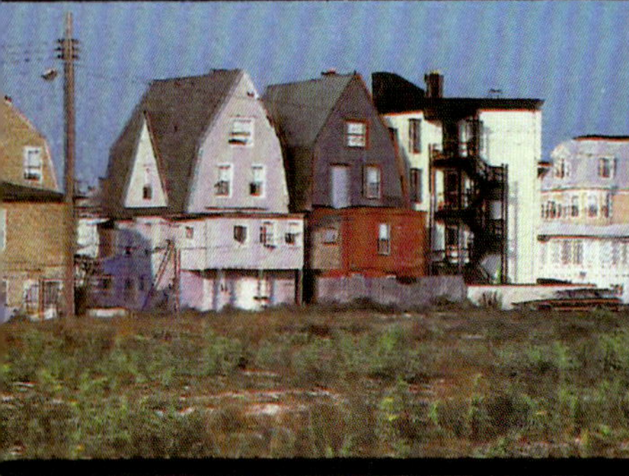

WAVE STREET

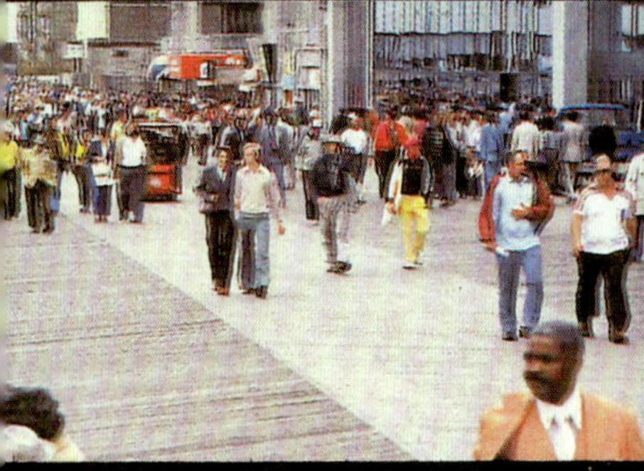

TUBULAR AVENUE

***(Spread)** While photos of North Jersey, Seaside and Manasquan Inlet are published fairly regularly, photos of South Jersey are seldom seen. Like its northern neighbor, however, South Jersey can also enjoy good waves with their own distinctive quality, especially along the famous A.C. boardwalk. This area has a series of piers and jetties clustered together in just a few miles of beachfront all of which can produce fine waves under differing swell directions. In this photo, with A.C.'s Garden City pier as a backdrop, local surfer G.J. Kermidas darts through a States Ave. backdoor. **(Insets counter clockwise)** The once fashionable side of town has regressed into a low-rent, high-risk area not recommended to the visitor.*

Boardwalk stroll. Surfers mingle with gamblers, businessmen, tourists, hustlers of various persuasions, high rollers, bums and just about the whole spectrum of humanity.

Mark Neustadter has been just one of many stand-out surfers to emerge from A.C.

Brian Heritage, an up-and-coming local talent. All photos: Mike Moir.

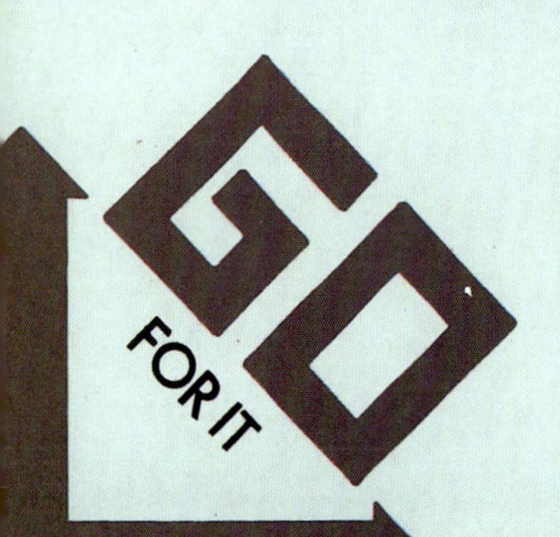

REEF ROAD

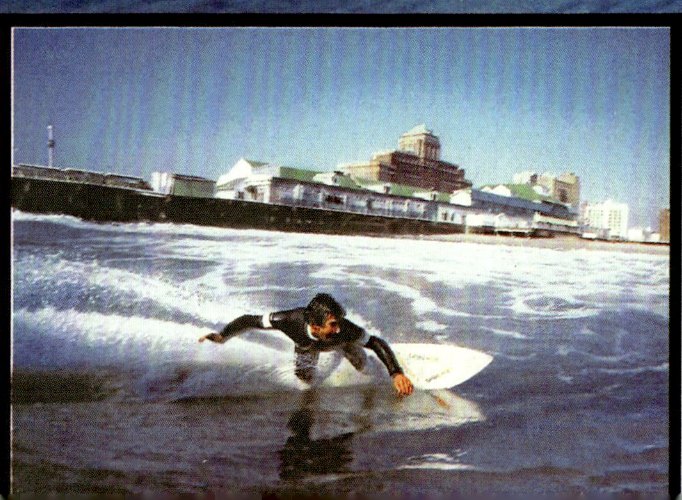

L
TAK

NTIC CITY

It's about 6 a.m. and you've already done the surf check — it's offshore and 3-6 feet. Not many surfers actually live in Atlantic City proper so you have to get in your car and boogie up to one of the many hot surf spots in the city.

This is where the adventure begins: it's a dash through the intercity lighting system that's supposed to be in a sequence so you can make all the lights without stopping. Well, it's like doing the Malibu Grand Prix only A.C. style. Speeds up to 60 mph, running red lights, and watching old people, tourists and hookers jump back off the curbs like Mexican jumping beans.

Atlantic City is one of the most radical surfing towns on the entire East Coast if not the world. The city itself is on a barrier island with three other towns called Ventnor, Margate and Longport; Longport being at the opposite end of the island. Somehow A.C. was gifted with having the best surf in all of the Southern New Jersey coast. Some of the other places get real good and I've surfed them plenty good. However good ole A.C. packs the power and delivers the punch and there is a variety of groins and piers that work on any swell.

This Grand Old Lady, Atlantic City, was once the resort capital of the world, and has had more ups and downs that any city you can imagine, just ask anybody who's lived here. Through all the good and bad times Atlantic City is still famous for the Miss America Pageant, the Monopoly Game, the Steel Pier (which just burned down this winter) and most recently casino gambling. While out surfing and looking back towards the beach, the skyline is changing rapidly. The addition of 10 new casino-hotels, some upward of 30 stories high, somewhat resemble Surfers Paradise in Australia. At dusk the 20 x 30 foot color T.V. screen in front of Caesars Palace located at Chicken Bone Beach on

WAX FACTORY

BOARDS

WIPEOUT ROW

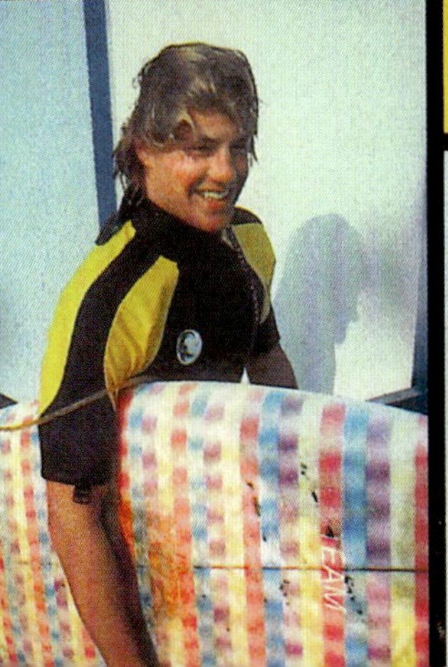

CUTBACK BOULEVARD

THRUST CIRCL

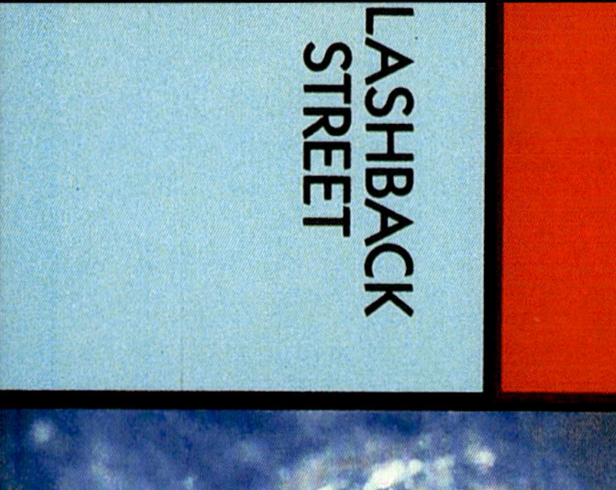

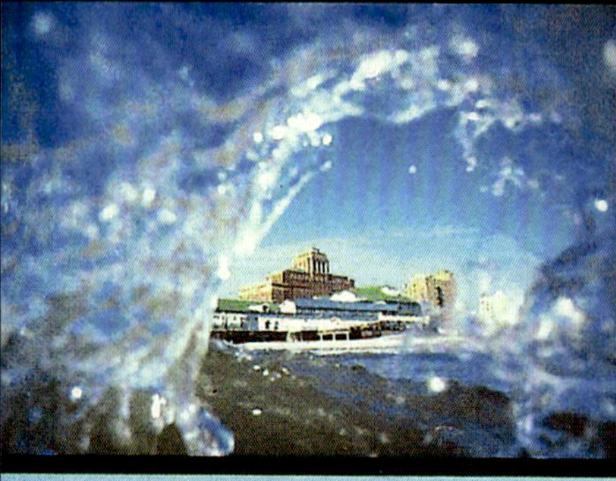

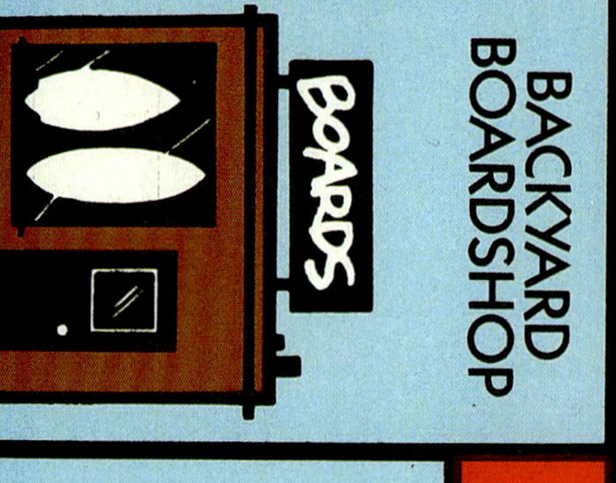

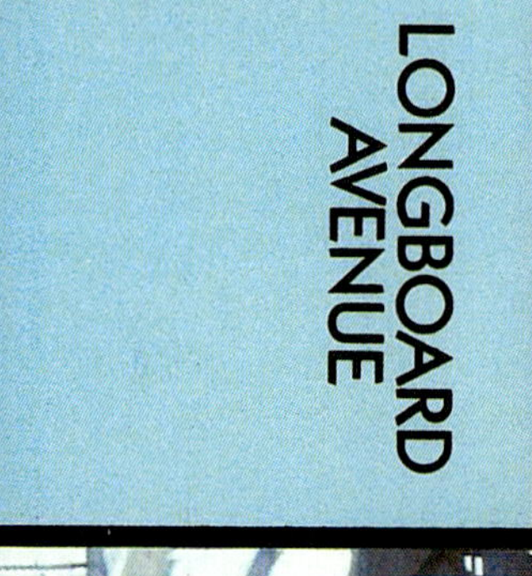

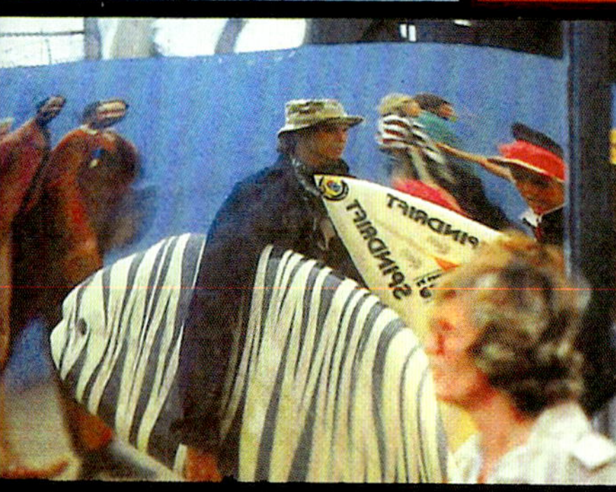

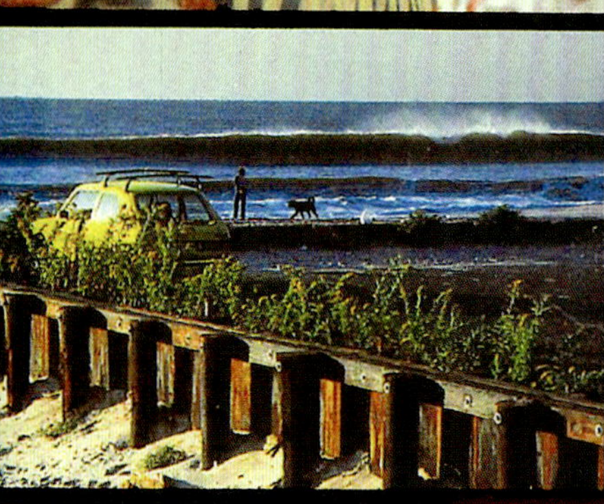

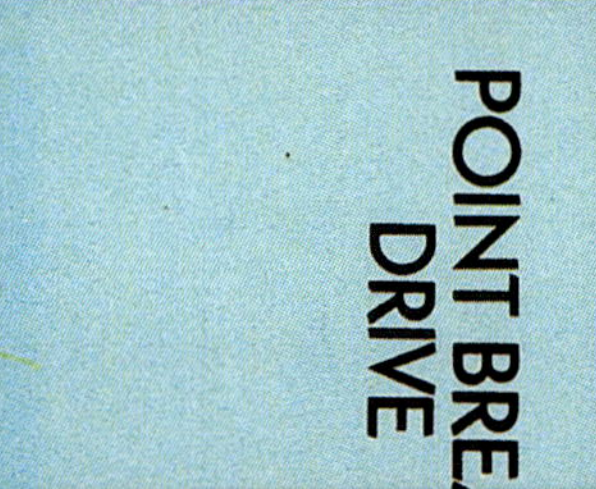

people like you've never imagined.

Last and certainly not least, before you leave town make sure you have one of Atlantic City's famous Italian Submarine sandwiches. Everybody from The Beatles to Frank Sinatra down to Rodney "can't get no respect" Dangerfield has had them. All the local surfers will tell you after a long session there's nothing like a "Sub." Everybody has their favorite sub and sub shop.

All in all the Atlantic City area has produced some of the most incredible watermen to be found anywhere. From surfers to sailors and swimmers to rowers, A.C. has turned out its fair share and will go on to do so in the years ahead.

So to all the tourists, blacks, whites, yellows, greens, hookers, bookers, freaks, geeks, pigeons, seagulls, coppers, boppers, wheelers and dealers, Atlantic City will welcome you with open arms. You just might experience some of the best surf that the East Coast has to offer and certainly some unforgettable night life.

Mark Neustadter was born and raised in Margate, N.J. He has been surfing for 17 years, was East Coast Champ in '72 and has traveled from Bells Beach, Australia to Biarritz, France and lots of places in between. He is currently employed with Rip Curl Wetsuits as East Coast Sales Manager. He grew up on Marvin Gardens Beach and is presumably the King of Marvin Gardens.

BEST BETS for HIGH ROLLERS

by Steve Dwyer

The best season is autumn.

The first signs of the change from summer to fall show up in late August. There is the ever-present possibility of a hurricane to head up the coast. If there isn't any hurricane action going on you can pretty much count on a good low pressure to hit. The winds will be onshore while the storm approaches and the waves are building. Behind this system will be a frontal system bringing clear skies and offshore winds. The intensity of these low pressure systems can vary between a 1-to-2 ft. piddler to an 8-to-10 ft. "nor'easter" as they are so affectionately nicknamed. These storms will produce waves that'll rival any in the world after the wind goes offshore.

The best time to catch this type of action is between September and March.

The surf in the winter can get absolutely perfect, but the temperature can make all but the most hardcore surfers forget about surfing for these few months. Perfect conditions in the water can and will often be

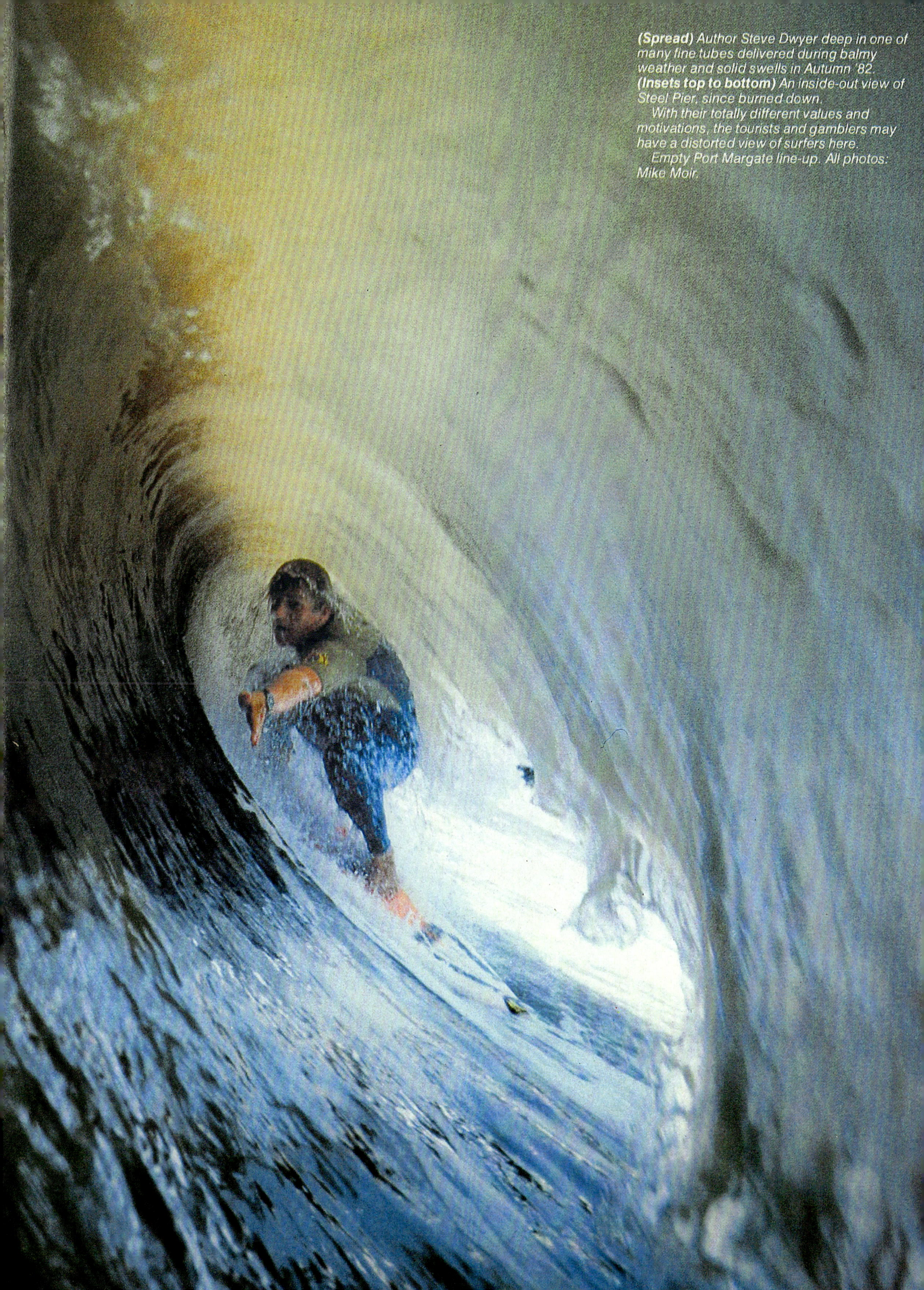

(Spread) *Author Steve Dwyer deep in one of many fine tubes delivered during balmy weather and solid swells in Autumn '82.*
(Insets top to bottom) *An inside-out view of Steel Pier, since burned down.*
With their totally different values and motivations, the tourists and gamblers may have a distorted view of surfers here.
Empty Port Margate line-up. All photos: Mike Moir.

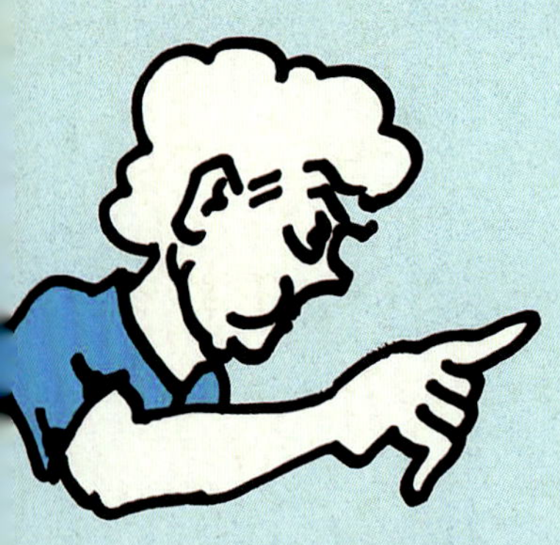

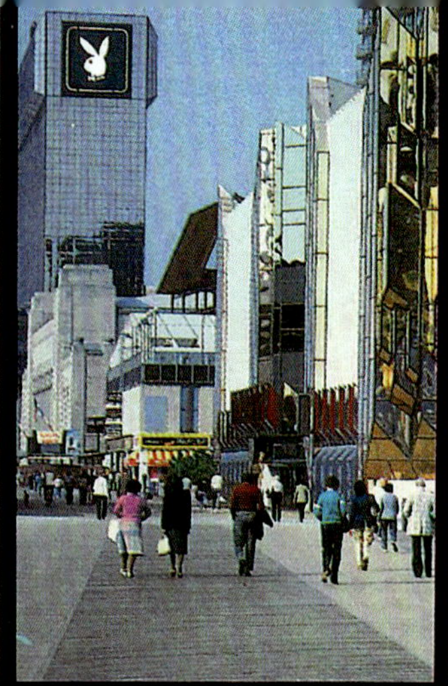

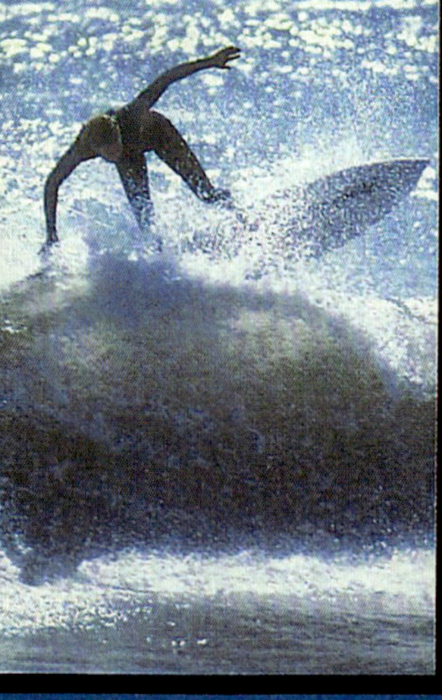

TSUNAMI DRIVE

SURF

the Boardwalk is a trip to watch from the water. The lights of the casinos illuminate the beach and water no end.

Most people would agree that Atlantic City itself has some of the weirdest sleaze-ball vibes to be found in any city east of Vegas. Just imagine Reno, Newark or St. Louis on the beach. As a matter of fact it's that sleazy weirdness of the city that makes it so hilarious. You can't help but laugh when you see the various tourists and jive people looking at you walking down the boardwalk with a wetsuit and board while they're eating cotton candy and you're going surfing.

Absecon Island is really a special kind of place to me and to a lot of the surfers and lifeguards who were born and raised there. My father and uncles and their friends were always down in the surf in the summer, boogieboarding with their mom's ironing board or anything else they could ride waves on. It seemed from my grandparents time some 60-70 years ago up until the time when I was a grem, all the families had a unique kind of closeness. It's all changed a bit since then, but it's all the people and places in and around the city that have made it a great place to grow up and learn how to surf.

When summer comes to the Jersey coast so does every Shoobie and their grandmother. It's packed to the gills. Everybody from Philadelphia bombs down to the shore and goes nuts for the sun, beach and lots of partying. With the recent addition of casinos it's absolutely torture on the dawn patrol. I've heard

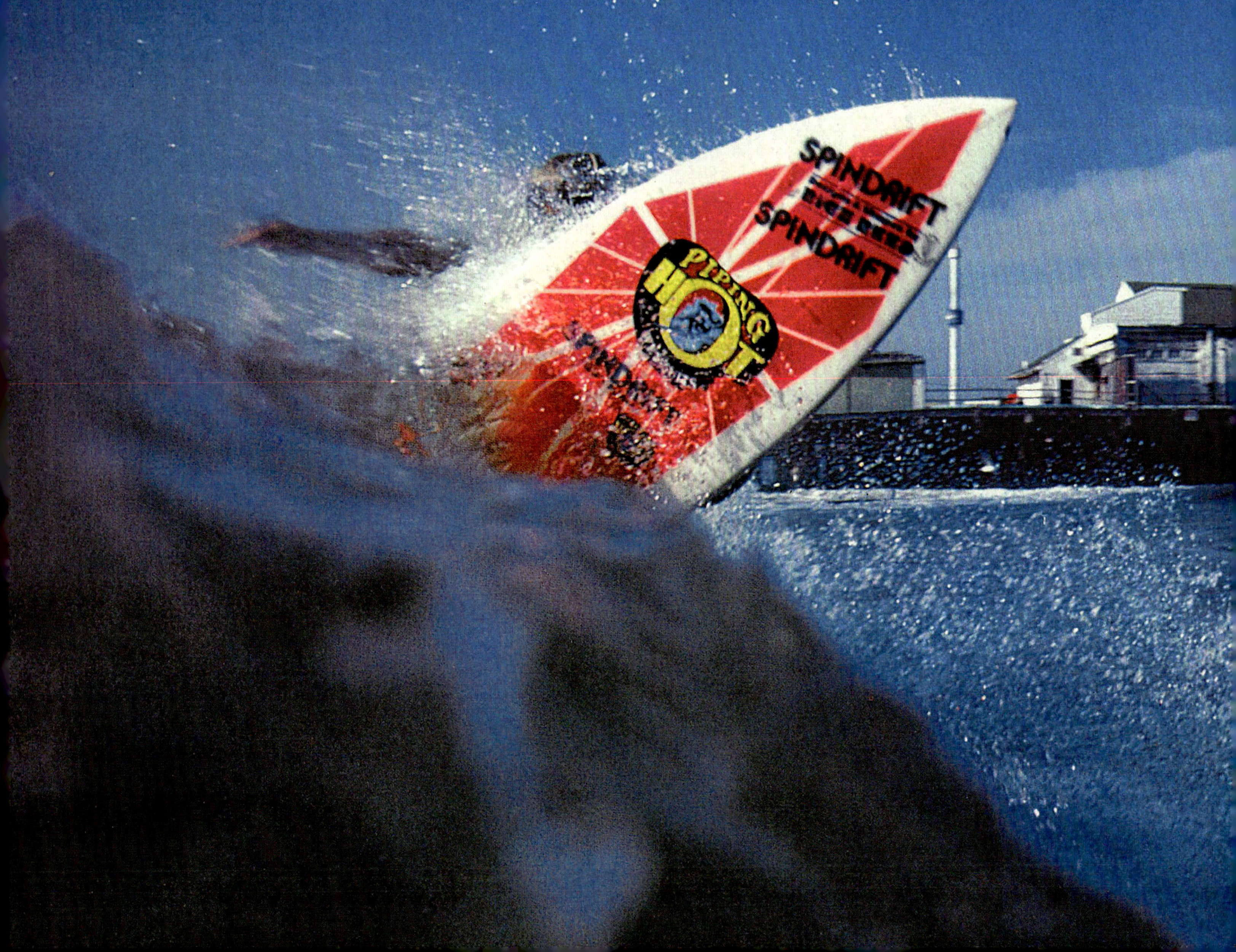

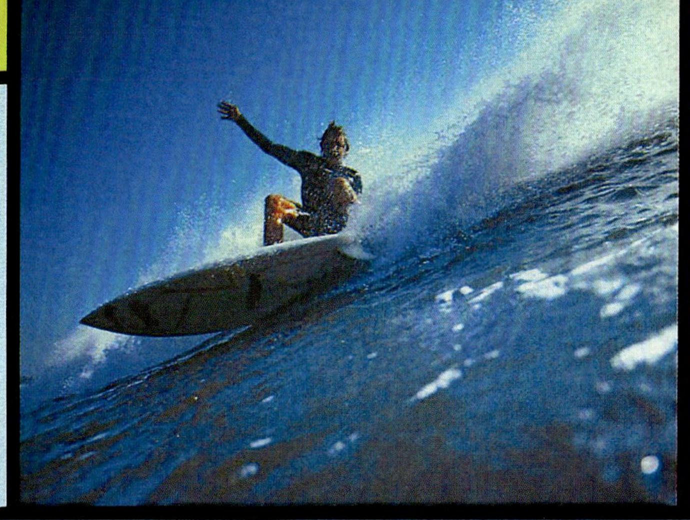

TOADS AVENUE

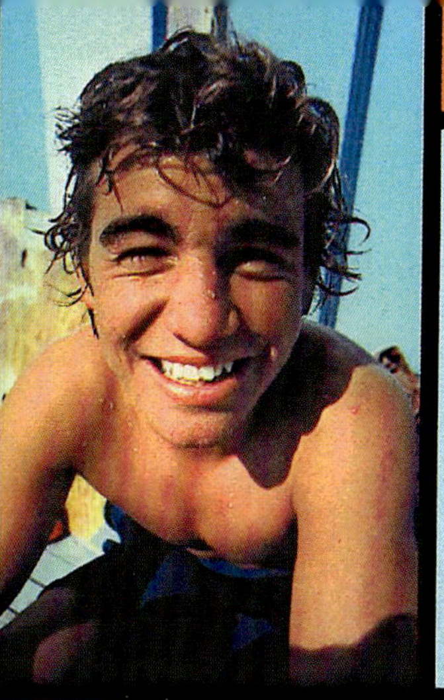

THREE-SIX STREET

some of the dealer/surfers who work the graveyard shift go surfing after work at 6 a.m. They get a couple hours of surfing in and then go home and sleep all day only to do it again the next day.

Compared to the masses, surfers are really unaffected by all the raz ma taz of summer. Spring and fall surfing offers excellent waves with few crowds. It's quite obvious from surfing here this fall for the first time in four years that the state of surfing is very healthy. The hot young guys are out slashing on twins and tris every day it's good.

Surfers like Corky Carroll, Terry Fitz, Kieth Paull, Mike Tomson, Greg Loehr, Mike Purpus and many other top pros have stopped through to surf the famous "Gas Chambers," leaving behind huge amounts of enthusiasm and guidance to surfers like myself and others who went on to pursue competitive surfing careers.

Most notable was Linda Davoli from neighboring Brigantine Beach who is a former U.S. Womens Champion. She consistently has finished in the top five world standings for years. Linda still rips better than ever and is extremely well traveled.

If you're going surfing in Casino City, leave your valuables home or watch them like a hawk. As for your money, if you're the surfer type who loves late takeoffs you'll probably like to make a couple of bets in one of your favorite casinos. Whether you make lots of late takeoffs or not there are no sure bets once you pass through the doors of the casino madness. They suck money out of

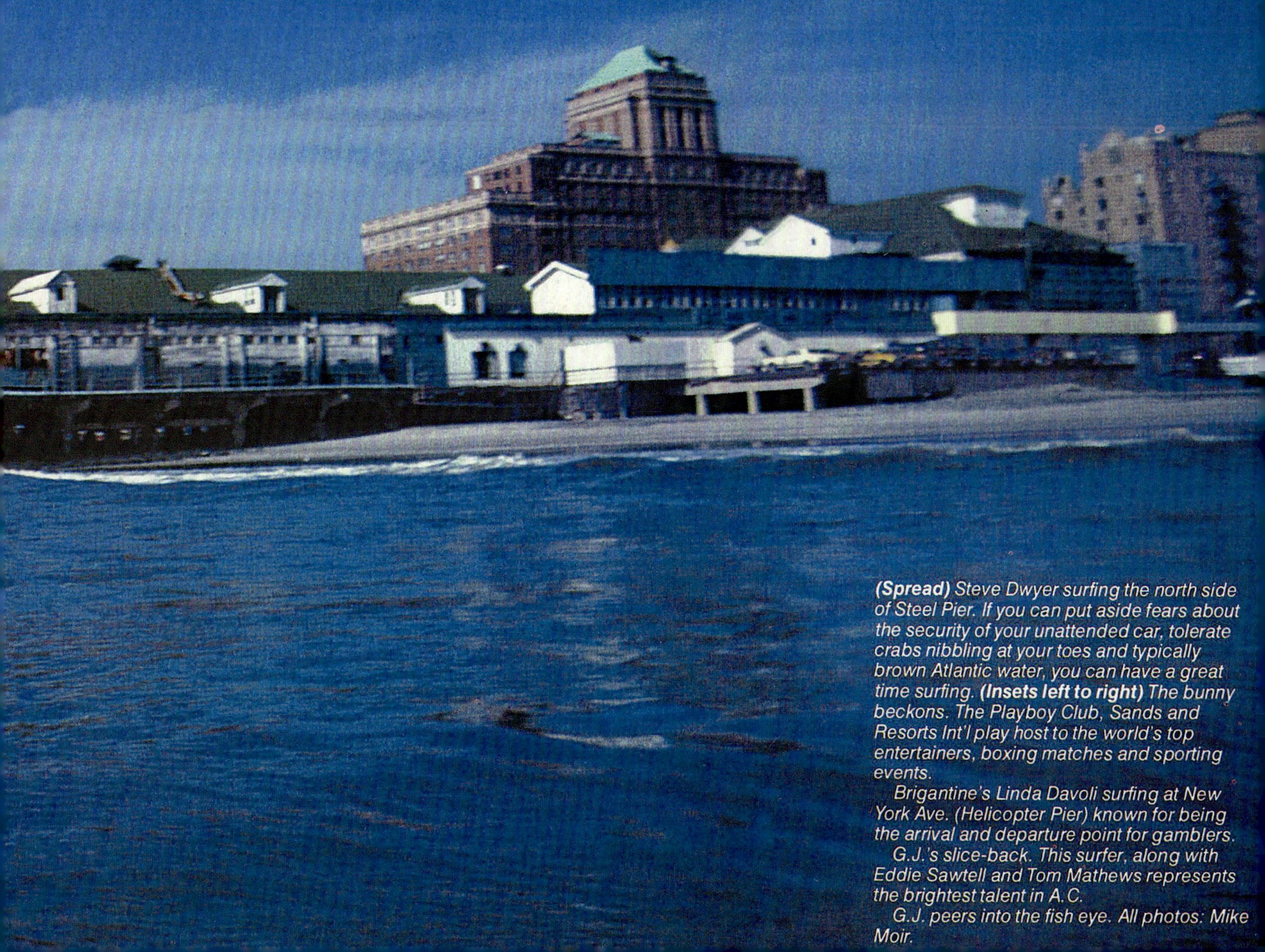

(Spread) *Steve Dwyer surfing the north side of Steel Pier. If you can put aside fears about the security of your unattended car, tolerate crabs nibbling at your toes and typically brown Atlantic water, you can have a great time surfing.* ***(Insets left to right)*** *The bunny beckons. The Playboy Club, Sands and Resorts Int'l play host to the world's top entertainers, boxing matches and sporting events.*

Brigantine's Linda Davoli surfing at New York Ave. (Helicopter Pier) known for being the arrival and departure point for gamblers.

G.J.'s slice-back. This surfer, along with Eddie Sawtell and Tom Mathews represents the brightest talent in A.C.

G.J. peers into the fish eye. All photos: Mike Moir.

BEACHBREAK ROAD

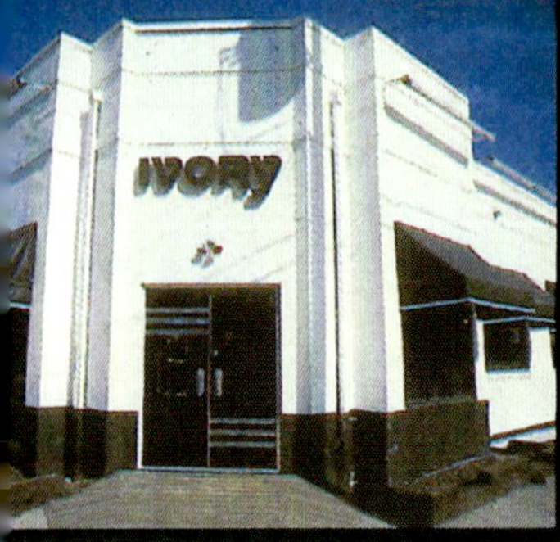

LATE TAKE-OFF

BOARDSHORTS AVENUE

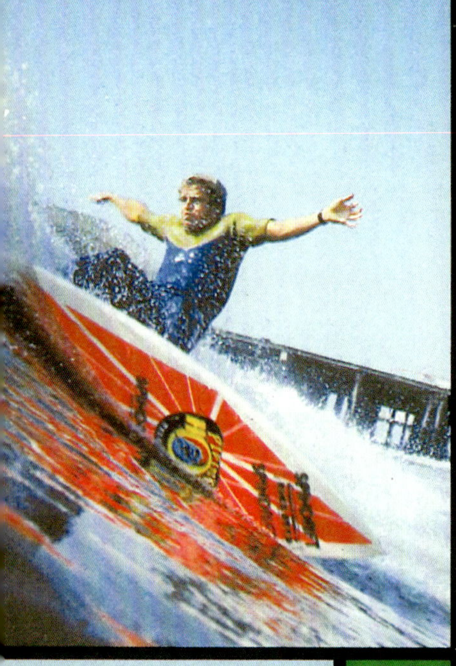

SNAPBA CIRCL

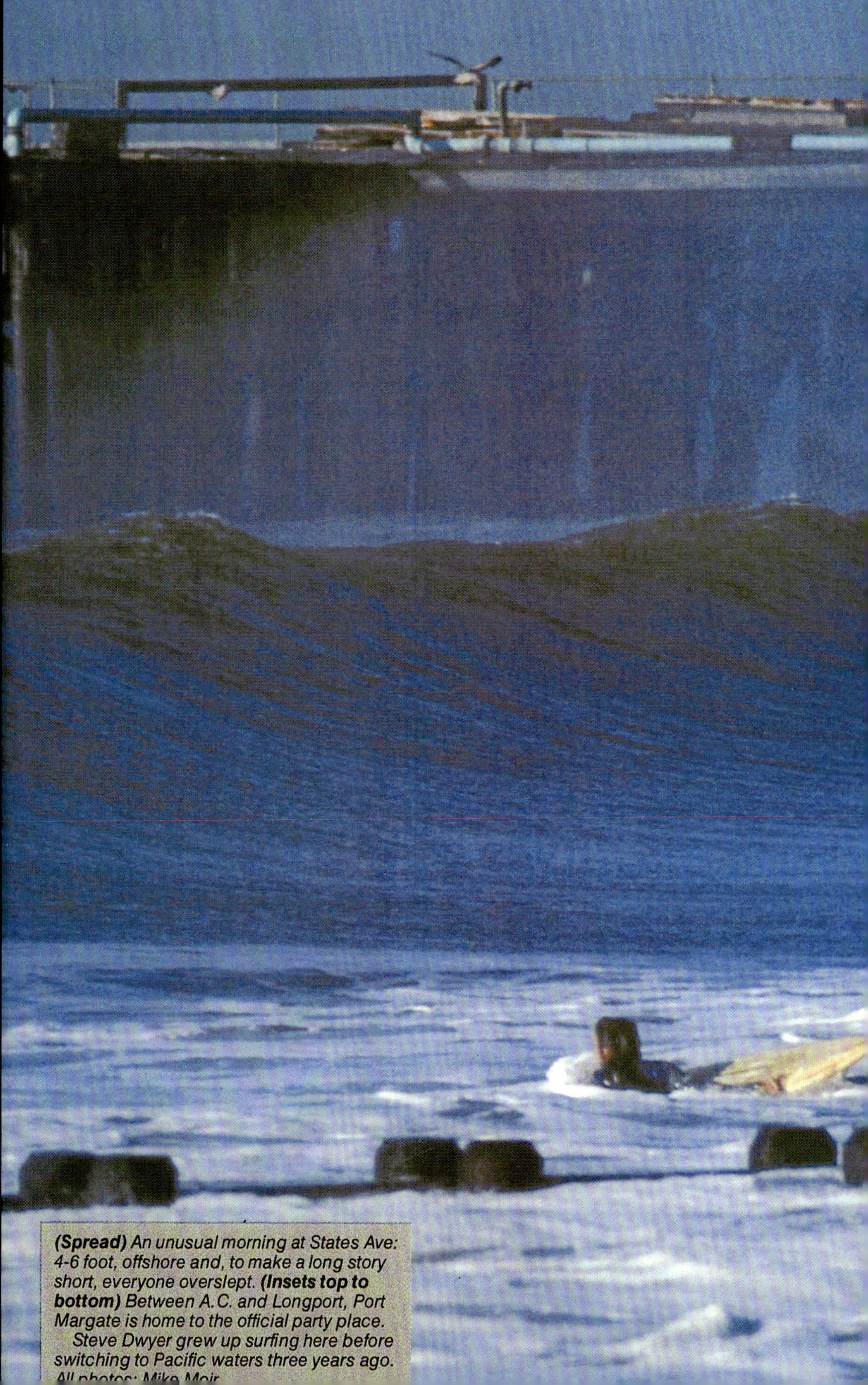

accompanied by as cold as 29° water and 20° air temperature. Not to mention the 15-to-25 mph offshore wind.

The combined damage between the hurricanes that have hit the area along and with the nor'easters (that can be just as nasty) have done a real number on the island. Since the turn of the century these storms have been accountable for the loss of ten streets and half of the boardwalk, both of which used to be part of the island.

The house my parents own was built with a twin on 9th Street. When that end of the island started to go underwater, the owners moved the house to 13th Street where it stands today. Needless to say, its twin is no longer with us along with those 10 streets. The island now begins on 11th Street.

Spring can put out classic surf as well with less wind and more sunshine.

(Spread) *An unusual morning at States Ave: 4-6 foot, offshore and, to make a long story short, everyone overslept.* ***(Insets top to bottom)*** *Between A.C. and Longport, Port Margate is home to the official party place. Steve Dwyer grew up surfing here before switching to Pacific waters three years ago. All photos: Mike Moir.*

Glassy conditions are not uncommon and neither are decent-sized swells between 2 and 6 ft. By April the water starts warming up. Now you can take off your hood, but maybe wait a month or so before the glove and booties come off.

You must appreciate the waves of spring, however, because once June brings in summer the chances of good surf are slim.

Sometimes you'll get a really good summer, but quite normally you won't. So you can now focus on diversion tactics. Hatteras road trips, water skiing on the back bays, fishing, and lots of hanging out on the beach looking at the wind-chopped, close-to-flat ocean. The best diversion, though is dreaming about those perfect fall conditions, and by then you are ready to start all over again.

Steve Dwyer is perhaps the hottest talent from Atlantic City in recent years. Born and raised on Absecon Island, he has moved to Santa Barbara, CA. On a return visit to home grounds he found new enthusiasm and leadership in the young upcomers and the healthy ESA district competition, not to mention two surf shops where before there were none. He gives us a quick rundown on the local conditions.

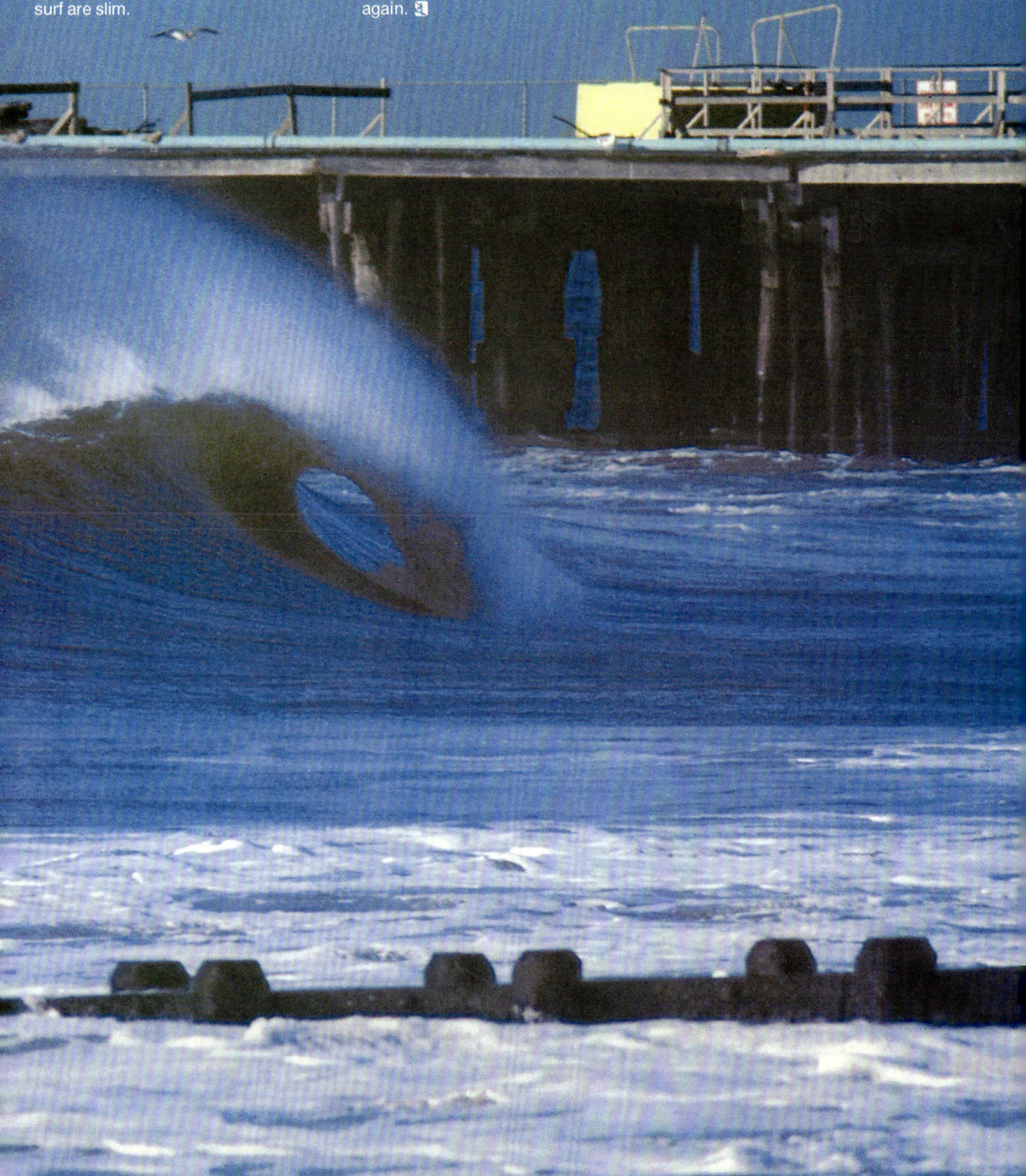

A DAY IN OCTOBER

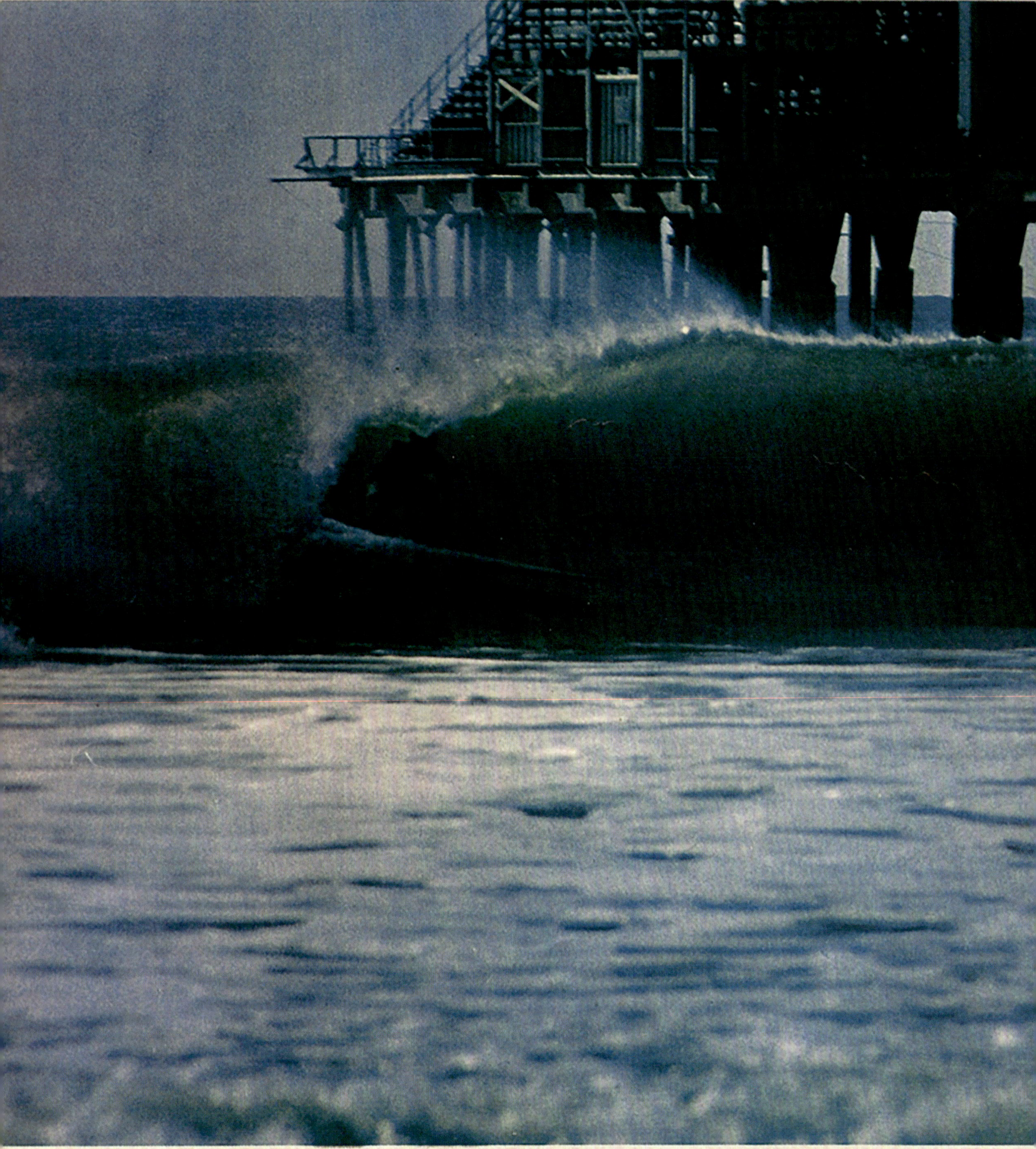

Bob Leeds screams across an Atlantic City tubing wall. The Steel Pier at States Street has many waves like this during the month of October.

The Steel Pier at Atlantic City offers a hollow tube with tremendous speed ... impressing the unbeliever; the East does have waves.

PHOTOS BY DANNY MITTELMAN

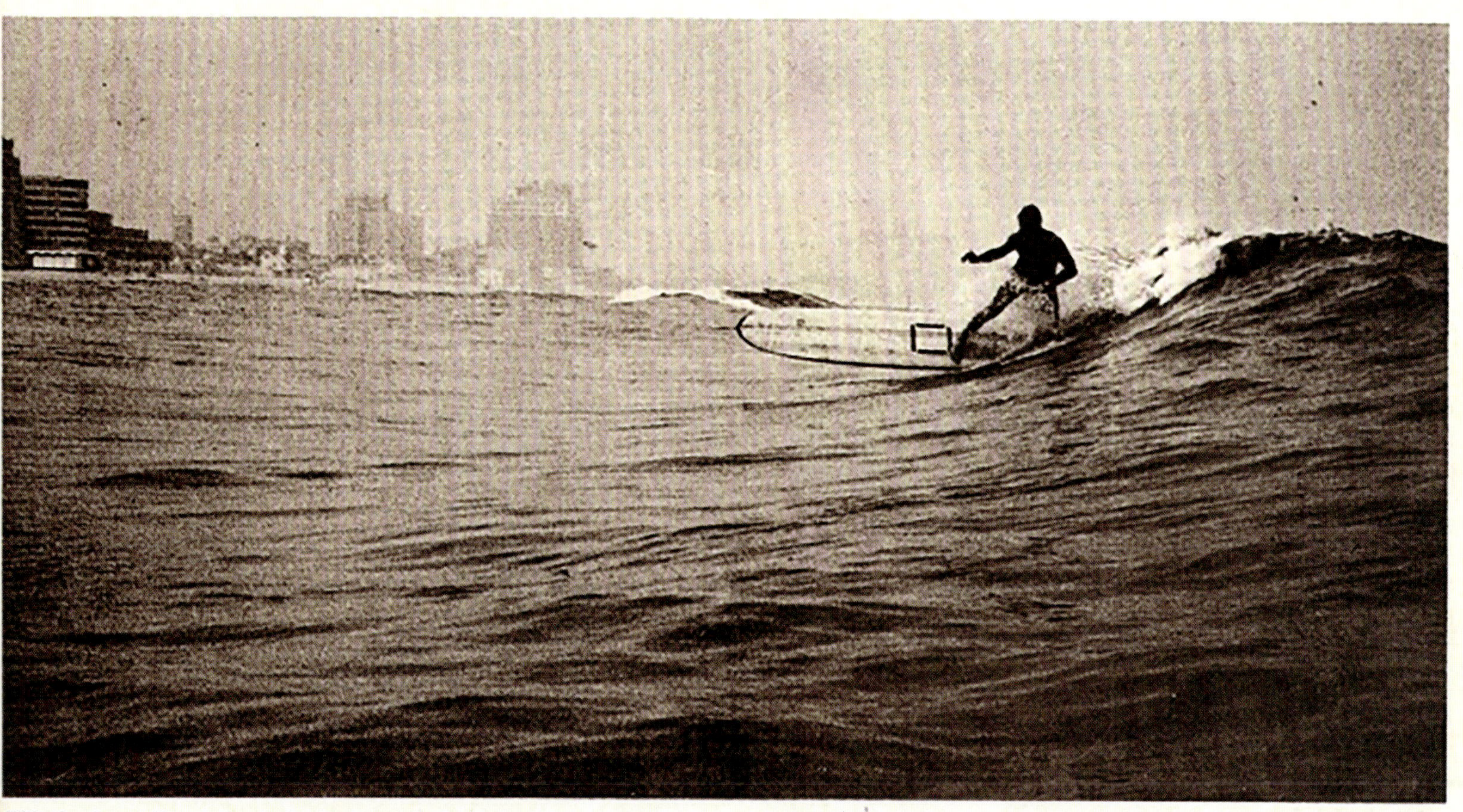

With the Ocean City skyline in the background, Jim Earle makes a sweeping turn at Jackson Street. The water temperature stays around 65 degrees in the summer.

When the long hot summer is coming to a close, and the students are back on campus, the East Coast surfing season is nearing a close. To most,this might seem like a dismal time of year, but that is not the case. Just when the monotonous adjustment of a new semester is about all the surfer can take, the month of October arrives. Everyone in the know is sitting on the edge of his chair waiting for the weather report.This is the hurricane season, and the surfing year will go out in grand style. This is especially the case around Atlantic City.

This Absecan Island area has much to offer on a big storm swell, and there are many locations to ride. Some of the most popular are Seaside Avenue, States Avenue, Arkansas Avenue, and Chelsea Avenue in Atlantic City, Ventnor Pier in Ventor, and Brunswick Avenue in Margate. During the fall hurricane season the off shore winds prevail, making the area one of the best surfing locations on the East Coast, and the locals feel it can rival almost any spot in the United States. Located here are the biggest piers in the world, (Steel and Million Dollar Piers), and through summer wind conditions and shifting bottoms a large amount of sand builds up around the piling forming almost perfect bottom conditions. This, plus the fact that the beaches slope gradually rather than drop off rapidly, gives surf that approximate coral or rock-bottom surf. The surf on this coast is generally

(Continued on next page)

A DAY IN OCTOBER

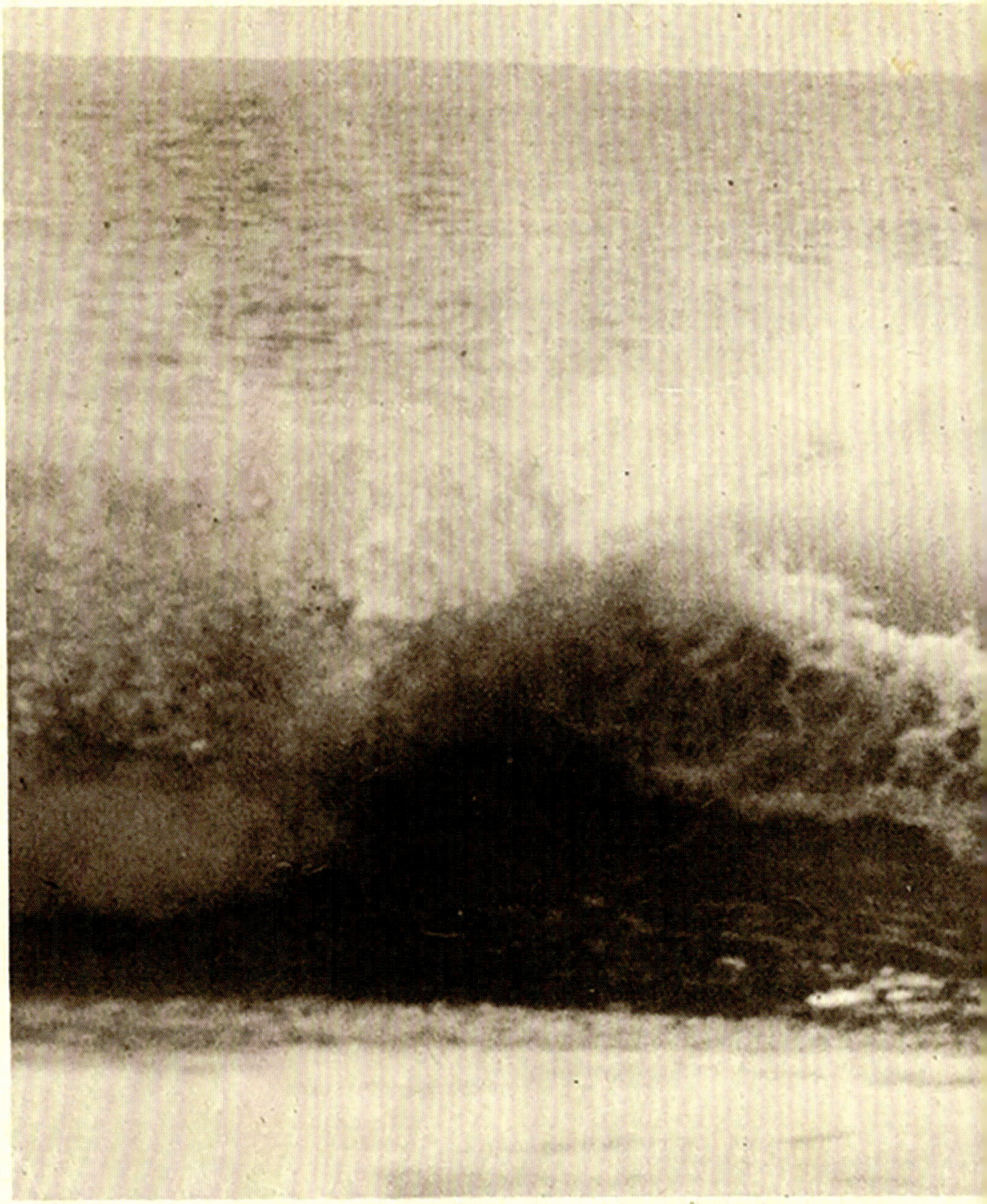

Right — Bruce Dougherty to left of Steel pier

Below — Wet suit for Joey Sykes at Steel pier.

Below Right — Dougherty in his favorite position.

a better shaped break than any other spot in New Jersey, Gilgo Beach, or in Virginia Beach, Virginia.

Judging from the photos sent in by Jim Earle and Danny Mittleman, getting locked-in one of the Steel Pier walls would really be something to "hoot" about. However getting a good ride at the pier is nothing new. It seems that between 1912 and 1915, Duke Kahanamoku was on a tour of the East, and stopped off to give an exhibition of body and board surfing. The event made front page news, and the fabulous Duke did it again. We think we are the first ones to publish an article on a spot, and he was there making news fifty years ahead of us.

(Continued on page 35)

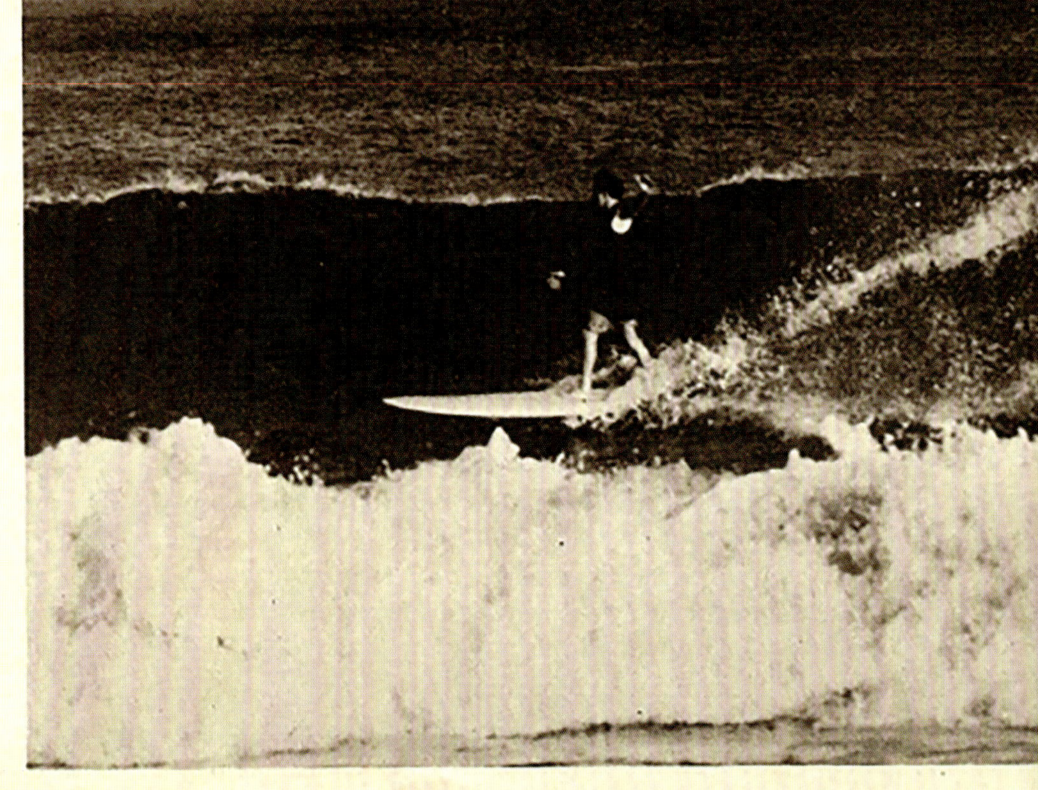

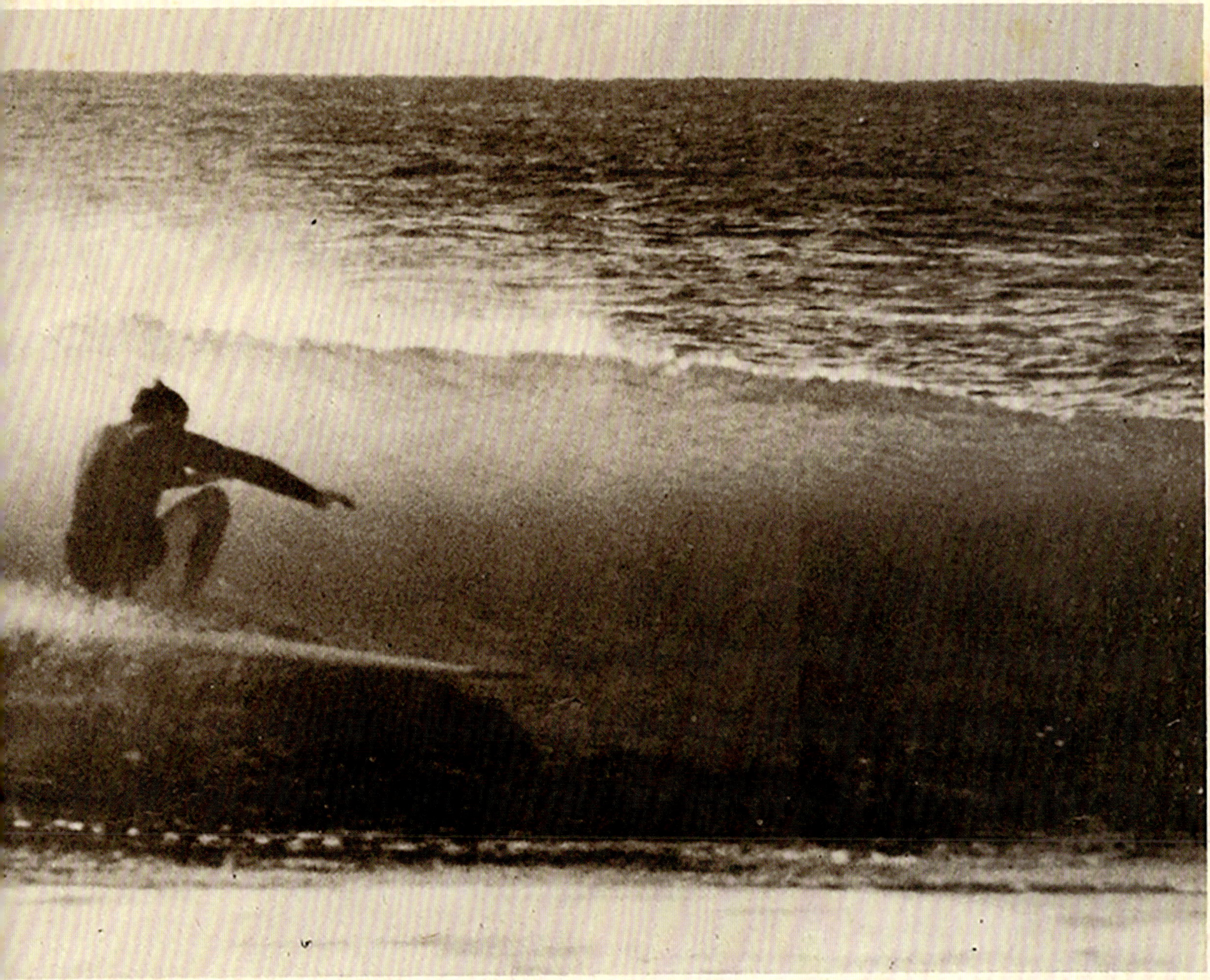

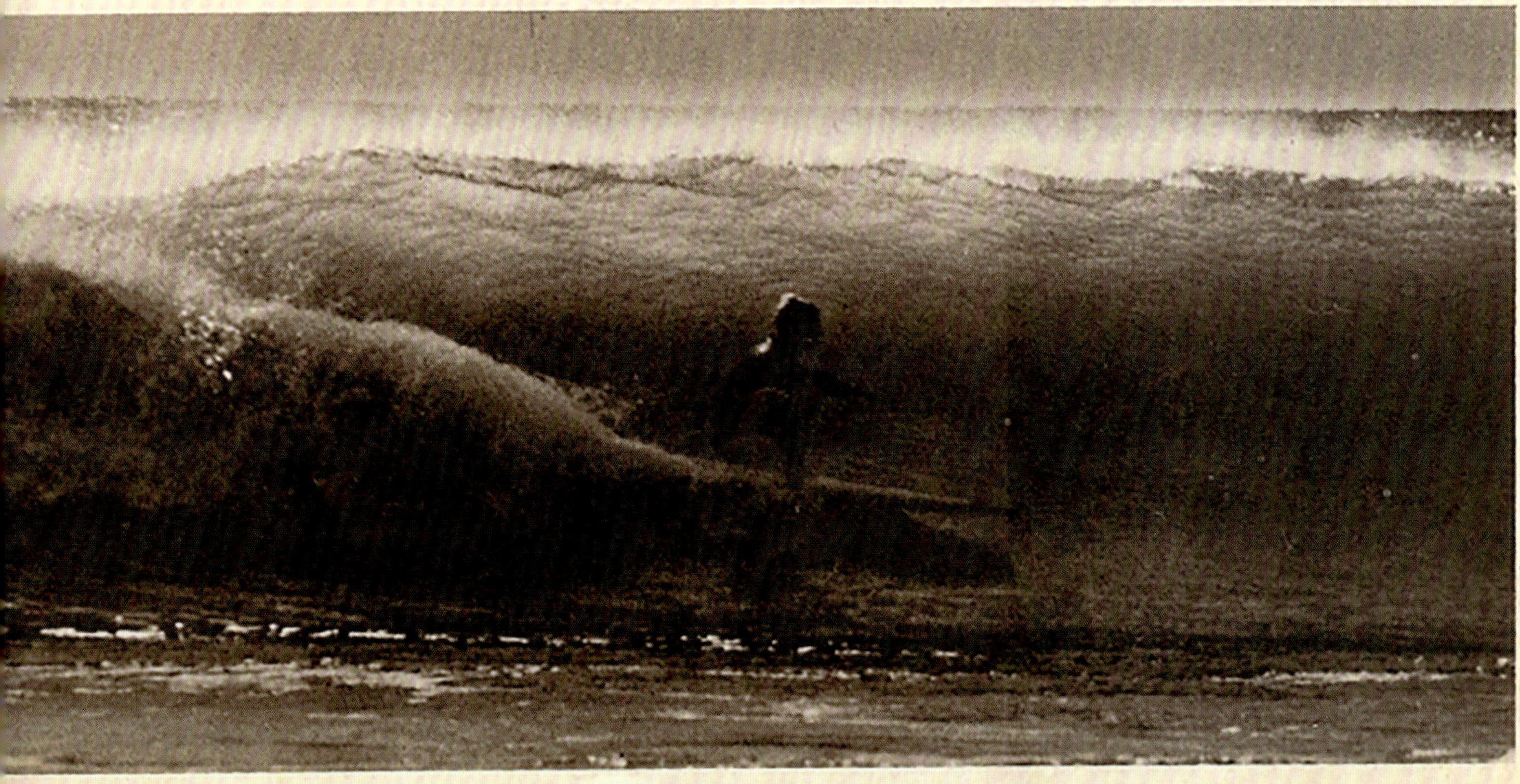

POINT PLEASANT...
...ICE BREAKERS

SURFERS FROM THREE STATES COMPETE IN 36 DEGREE WATER AS NORTH-EASTERN SURFING SEASON GETS AN EARLY START.

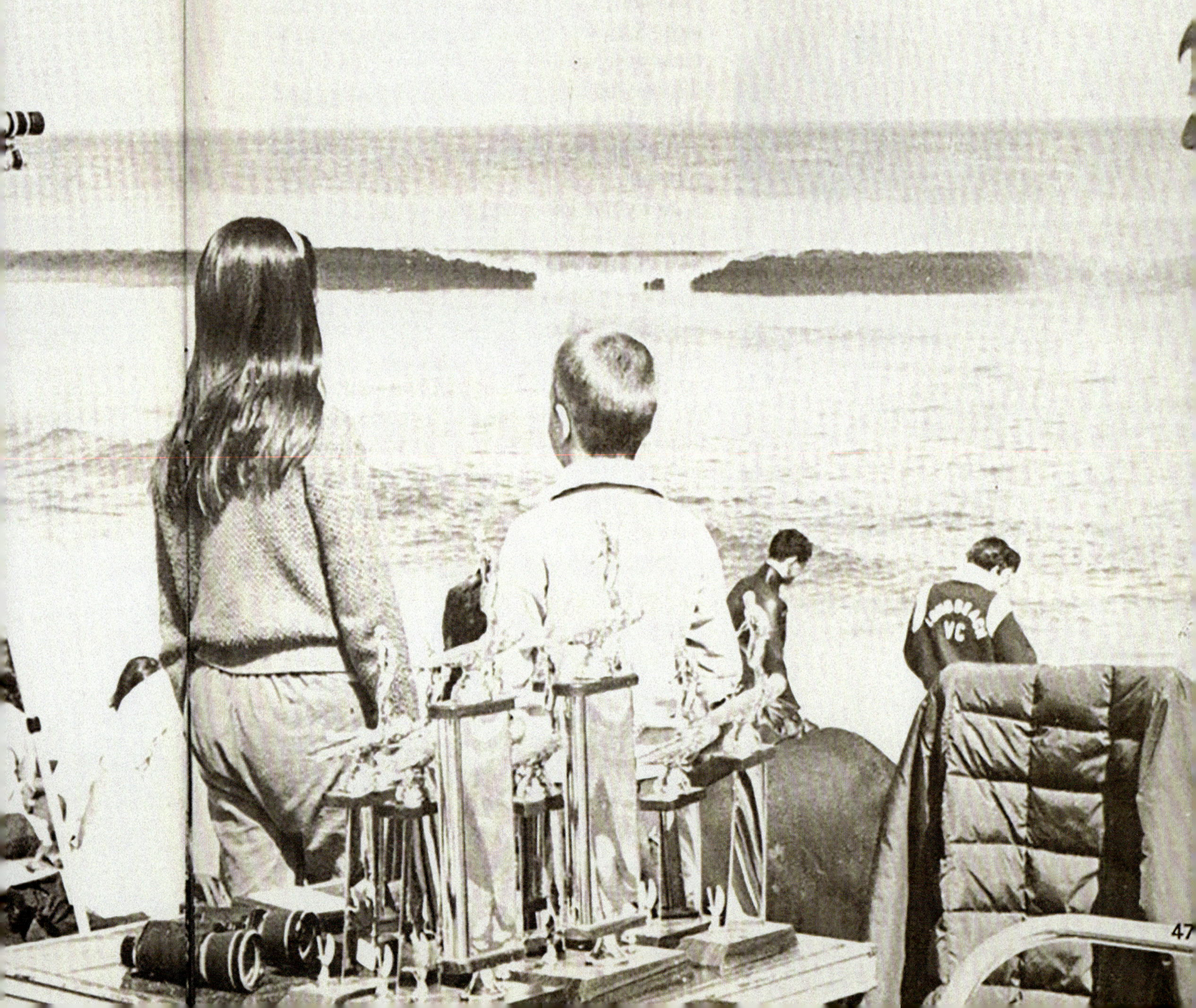

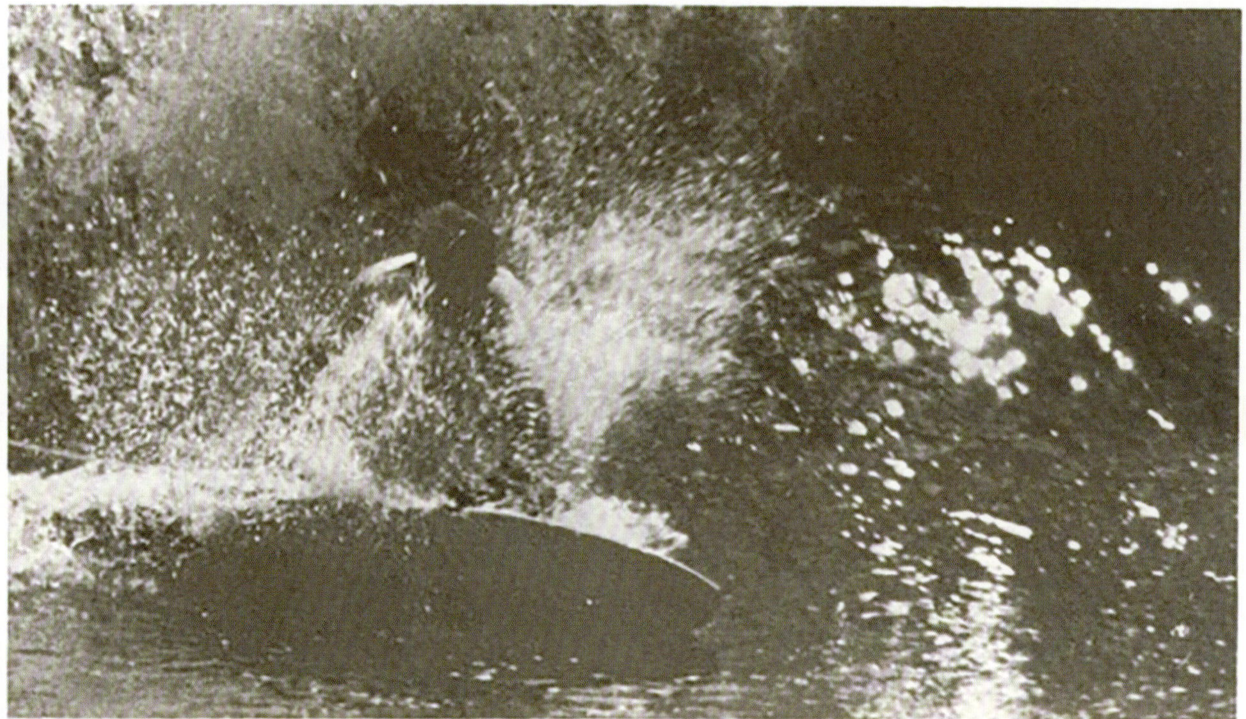

Men's Finals

Final Place	*Name*	*Final Points*
1	John Sullivan, Belmar, N. J.	109
2	Chester Feldman, Oceanside, N. Y.	106
3	Deane Yamone, Philadelphia, Penn.	103
4	David Nelson, Long Beach, N. Y.	99
5	Ron Caragias, Point Pleasant, N. J.	98
6	Paul Lucier, Point Pleasant, N. J.	94
7	Hank Leonard, Neptune, N. J.	86
8	Thomas Ackers, Ship Bottom, N. J.	84
9	John Gibbs, Wanamessa, N. J.	83
10	Vic Plumbo, Ventnor, N. J.	78

Junior Men's Finals

Final Place	*Name*	*Final Points*
1	Phil Cusano, Long Island, N. Y.	99
2	Terry Conroy, Long Island, N. Y.	93
3	Glenn Klotz, Margate, N. J.	92
4	Frank DeLisa, Long Branch, N. J.	90
5	Bruce Dougherty, Margate, N. J.	89
6	Dennis Doyle, Lavallette, N. J.	87
7	Ray Mitchell, Long Beach, N. Y.	81
8	Michael Weisberg, New York, N. Y.	80
9	Ed Lister, Belmar, N. J.	79
10	Gil White, West Belmar, N. J.	70

Open Paddle Board Race

Final Place	*Name*
1	Doug Hausman, Lido Beach, Long Island, N. Y.
2	Bob Sullivan, Belmar, N. J.
3	Jim Walzer, Point Pleasant, N. J.

SU

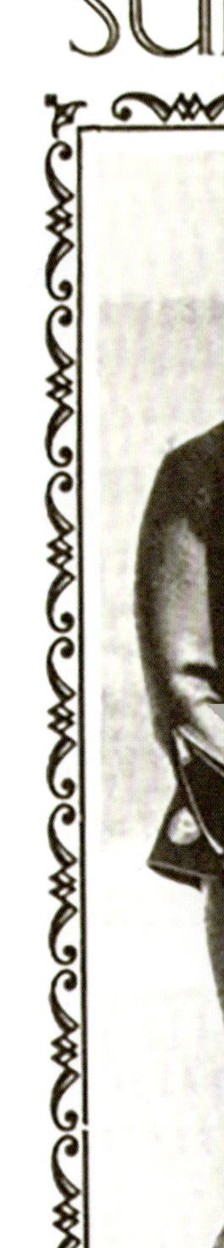

Left to
Vickie A

The
Pleasant
unexpect
agement
creased
the wise
were the
experien
of their
There
the five
and all
another
friendshi
test whe
another
sure I hit
from me
after twe
and battl
Becau
girls wor
becomin
and boar
Gowan, a
Wall, Ne
board a
guarding

a complete line of atlantic surfing products

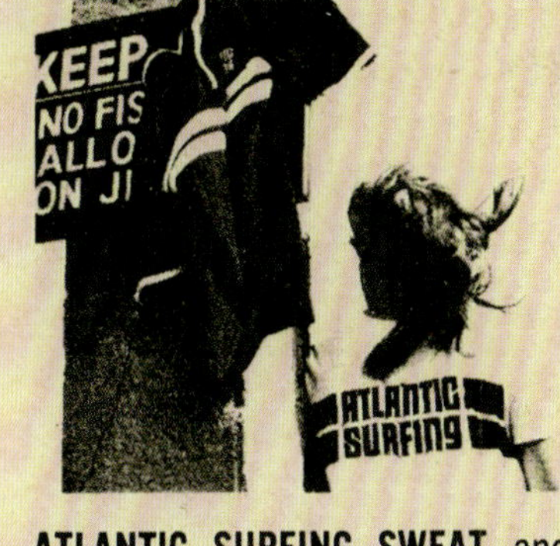

ATLANTIC SURFING SWEAT and **TEE SHIRT** with double competition stripes: These high quality shirts are white with black stripes.

Sweat shirts $3.50
Tee shirts $2.25

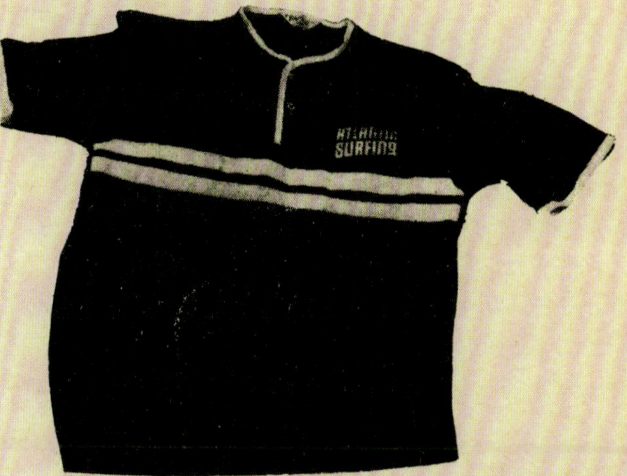

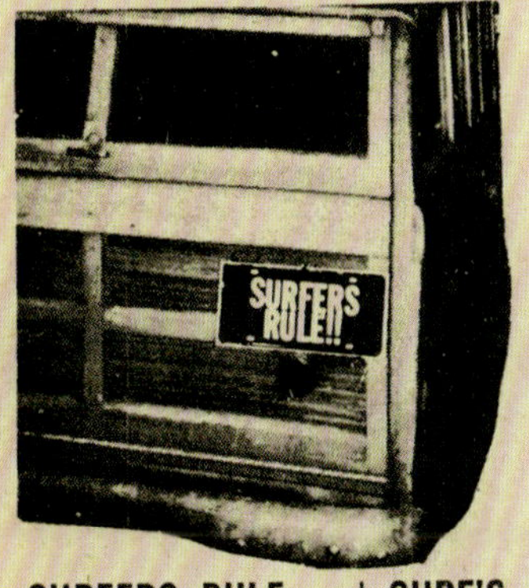

SURFERS RULE and **SURF'S UP CAR PLATES** are very similar to regular license plates and can be attached to any automobile. These blue, high glossed enamel plates, with yellow lettering, are a must for every surfer's car. Available for only $2.00.

SURF SHIRTS! These popular shirts with double competition stripes are made of 100% cotton and can be worn to the beach or after surfing as regular sportswear. **SURF SHIRTS** are available in the following color combinations:

Navy blue, Powder blue and Maroon, all with white stripes.

White with Navy blue stripes.

SURF SHIRTS are only $4.00

The **SURF SHIRT** is also available in a short sleeved sweat shirt without stripes for $3.75.

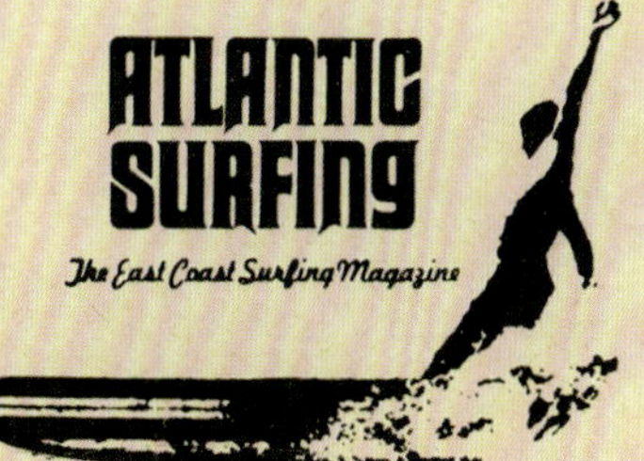

ATLANTIC SURFING DECALS in three bright colors: white, red and blue, are available for the first time. These King Sized decals measure 6 x 5 inches and look great on any car window. Only 50 cents.

Giant sized **BEACH TOWEL** with competition stripes and ATLANTIC SURFING lettering! Towels are white with black stripes and black lettering. Only $5.00.

---

order form

SWEAT SHIRTS $3.50
Indicate color choice________
Size: ☐ XL ☐ L ☐ M ☐ S

TEE SHIRTS $2.25
Indicate color choice________
Size: ☐ XL ☐ L ☐ M ☐ S

SURF SHIRTS $4.00
Indicate color choice________
Size: ☐ XL ☐ L ☐ M ☐ S

SURF SWEAT SHIRT $3.75.
White only
Size: ☐ XL ☐ L ☐ M ☐ S

CAR PLATES $2.00
Surfers Rule ☐
Surf's Up ☐

DECALS $.50

BEACH TOWELS $5.0C

Name__________

Address__________

City__________

State________ Zip________

All prices include tax and postage. Send check or money order to:

SURFING PRODUCTS • P.O. Box 96 • Dyker Heights Station • Brooklyn, N. Y. 11228

A HISTORY OF SURFING IN NEW JERSEY

TIMELINE BY BILL SIMON

1888

August 1888, Asbury Park, New Jersey, the Sandwich Island Girl takes to the waves, *National Police Gazette.*

1910

Alvin D. Keech giving surfing exhibitions in Atlantic City.

1912

August 1912, Atlantic City, New Jersey, Hawaiian Olympic Waterman Duke P. Kahanamoku performs surfing exhibitions at the Million Dollar Pier on a solid redwood board shipped to the East Coast by his brother, David.

1930

Hawaiian Hula Huts were set up on the boardwalk to showcase music, life, and watersports, including the famed high diving that took place at Steel Pier.

1932–1934

Duke Kahanamoku, Tom Blake, and William Mulihea demonstrate Blake's hollow paddle boards for lifesaving and surfing, and the boards spreads along the entire East Coast. They had solid redwood boards with them as well.

1936

Henry "Stretch" Pohl was building and surfing Tom Blake's boards on Long Beach Island. Simultaneously, John "The Bull" Carey in Ocean City and Mike House in Northern New Jersey also constructed Blake Boards.

1956

The Balsa Malibu Chip Surfboard shaped by Matt Kivlin is brought to the Cape May Coast Guard Station from Hawaii. Also around this time a Californian brought 10 balsa boards to Atlantic City, demonstrated them, and sold them all. The balsa era was still pretty isolated.

1958–1960

George Gerlach, Charlie Keller, and Jimmy Grecca begin to make Styrofoam and epoxy resin surfboards in Ocean City, New Jersey.

1961–1962

Surf shops begin to pop up all over the New Jersey coastline.

1914

Duke Kahanamoku returns to New Jersey and surfs in Atlantic City and Ocean City, New Jersey, hosted by John Kelly Sr., Princess Grace's father. He introduced much of Hawaii to the people of the Jersey Shore.

1916

Sam Reid, at 11 years old, shapes his own board made out of pine after riding his mother's ironing board for four years after seeing Duke Kahanamoku in Atlantic City in 1912.

1917

Small wooden belly boards were being made by visiting Hawaiians for the beach hotels in Atlantic City.

1939

Henry "Stretch" Pohl brings in several redwood balsa planks from California as attempts to make their own boards begin.

1940S

Rich Lieswski makes and surfs paddleboards.

1950S

Many lifeguards in New Jersey are still surfing hollow paddleboards and using them for rescues.

1968

Cecil Lear starts the Eastern Surfing Association across the entire eastern seaboard.

1970S

An increase in professional surfing contests coming to New Jersey, like the Seaside Pro, Belmar Pro, and Atlantic City Pro.

1980S

The OP Pro in Atlantic City.

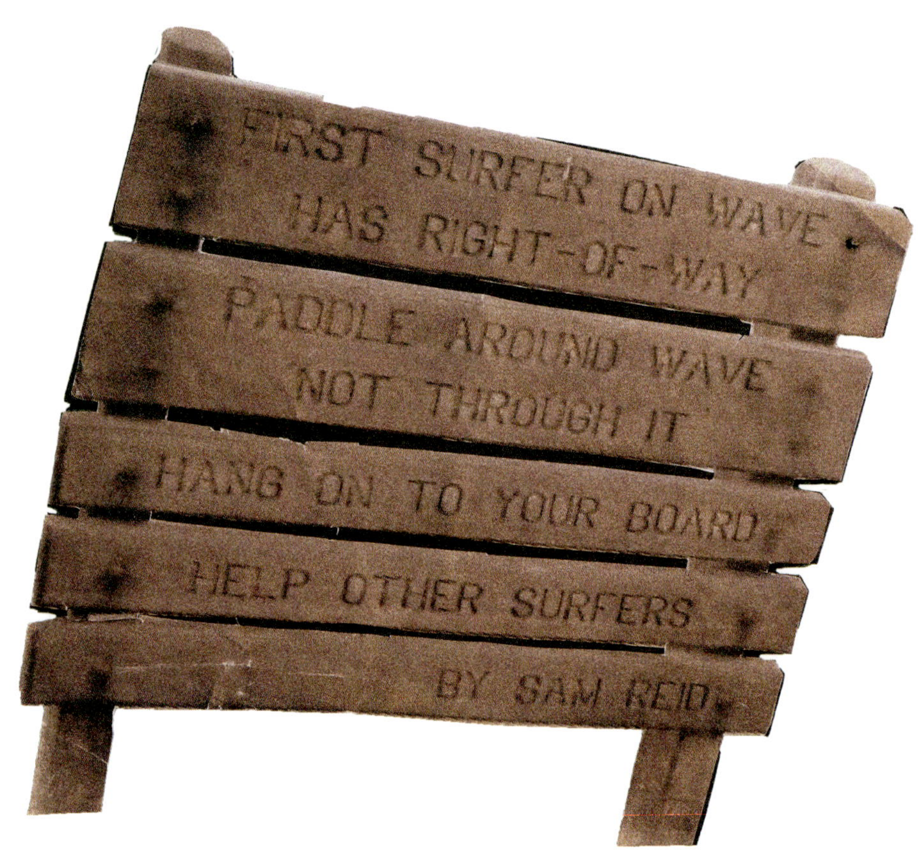

When Sam Reid was seven years old in 1912, Duke Kahanamoku gave a surfing demonstration in Atlantic City, New Jersey, close to Sam Reid's home. Sam Reid began riding waves the next day using his mother's ironing board. In September of 1926, Sam Reid, alongside Tom Blake, paddled out at First Point in Malibu.

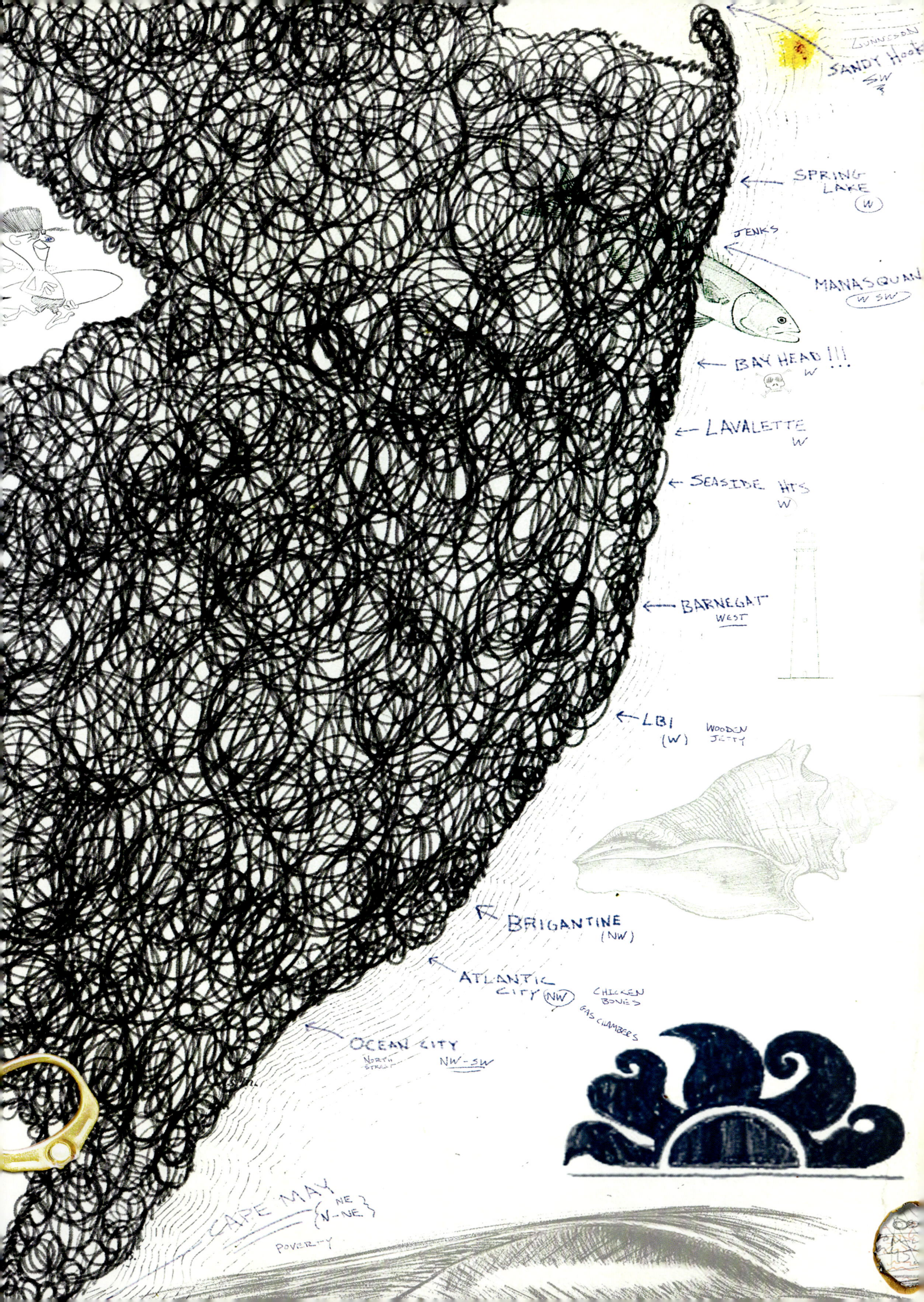
GUNNISON
SANDY Hook
SW
SPRING LAKE
(W)
JENKS
MANASQUAN
(W SW)
BAY HEAD !!!
W
LAVALETTE
W
SEASIDE HTS
W
BARNEGAT
WEST
LBI
(W)
WOODEN JETTY
BRIGANTINE
(NW)
ATLANTIC CITY
(NW)
CHICKEN BONES
GAS CHAMBERS
OCEAN CITY
NORTH STREET
NW-SW
CAPE MAY
NE
N-NE
POVERTY

FIRST PUBLISHED IN THE UNITED STATES OF AMERICA IN 2024 BY
RIZZOLI INTERNATIONAL PUBLICATIONS, INC.
49 WEST 27TH STREET, NEW YORK, NY 10001
WWW.RIZZOLIUSA.COM

PHOTOGRAPHY BY
DAN MITTELMAN AND MARK NEUSTADTER

EPHEMERA COURTESY OF
NEW JERSEY SURFING HALL OF FAME AND NEW JERSEY SURF MUSEUM

FOR RIZZOLI

PUBLISHER
CHARLES MIERS

EDITOR
JACOB LEHMAN

PRODUCTION MANAGER
REBECCA AMBROSE

PRODUCTION ASSISTANT
OLIVIA RUSSIN

MANAGING EDITOR
LYNN SCRABIS

COPY EDITOR
SARAH STUMP

FOR THE AUTHORS

CONSULTING NEW JERSEY SURF HISTORIAN AND TIMELINE CURATOR
BILL SIMON

CONSULTING NEW JERSEY SURF HISTORIAN
MIKE MAY

MAP BY
ADAM GREEN

ADDITIONAL EPHEMERA AND PHOTOGRAPHY FROM
GREG MESANKO

DESIGN BY
TALLEY CARLSTON

SPECIAL THANKS
JOEL TUDOR
SATURDAYS NEW YORK CITY

PRINTED IN CHINA

2025 2026 2027 2028 / 10 9 8 7 6 5 4 3 2
ISBN: 978-0-8478-9973-9
LIBRARY OF CONGRESS CONTROL NUMBER: 2023921239

INSTAGRAM.COM/RIZZOLIBOOKS
FACEBOOK.COM/RIZZOLINEWYORK
YOUTUBE.COM/USER/RIZZOLINY

THE AUTHORIZED REPRESENTATIVE IN THE EU FOR PRODUCT SAFETY AND COMPLIANCE IS MONDADORI LIBRI S.P.A., VIA GIAN BATTISTA VICO 42, MILAN, ITALY, 20123
WWW.MONDADORI.IT

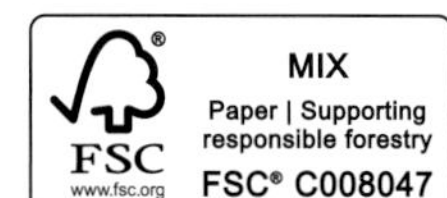

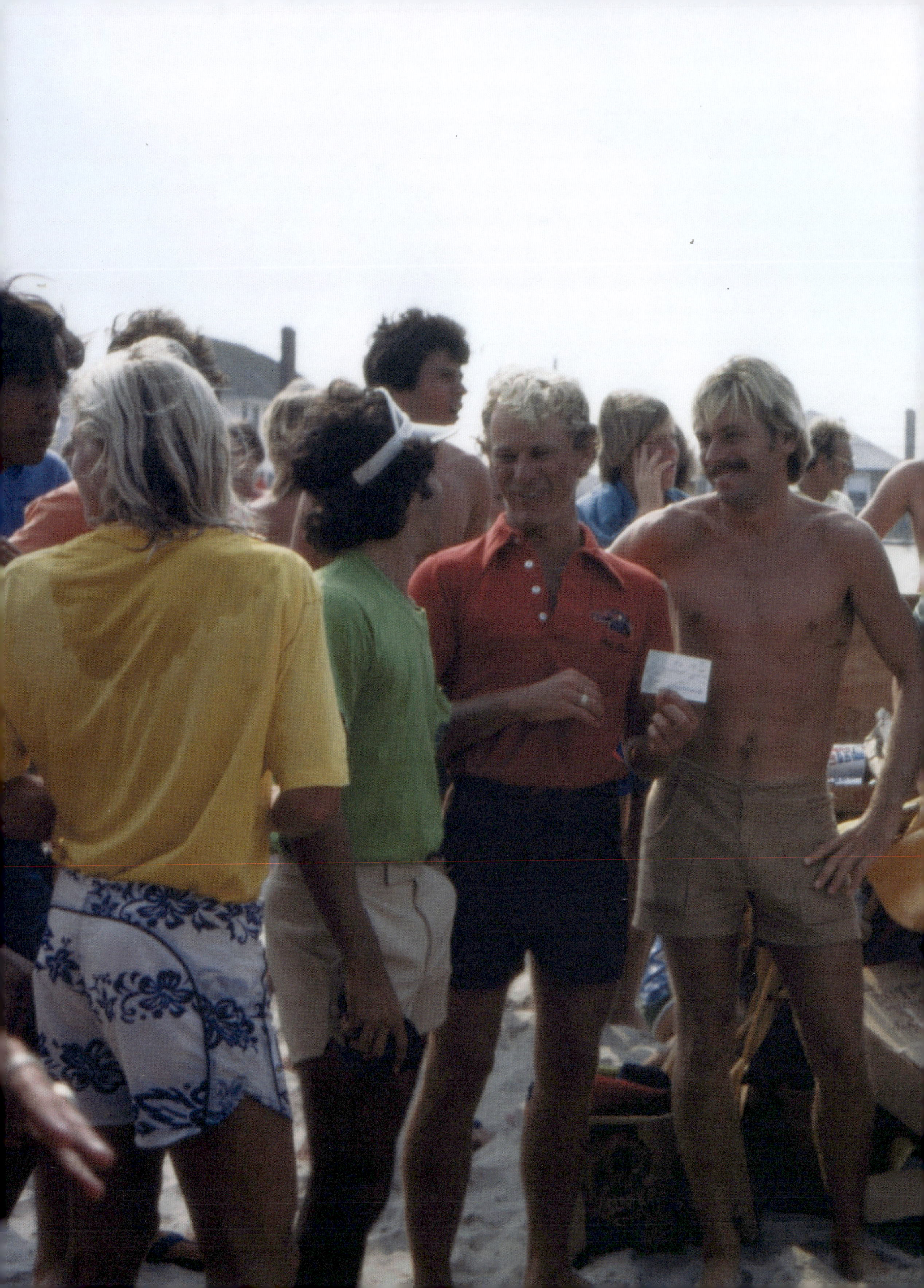